Uncanny Soulscapes in Uncustomary Dreamscope

Collected Philosophical Fragments

by
Giorgio Baruchello

NORTHWEST
PASSAGE
Books

Gatineau, Quebec, Canada

Uncanny Soulscapes in Uncustomary Dreamscope

Collected Philosophical Fragments

by Giorgio Baruchello, PhD

Copyright © 2025 by Giorgio Baruchello. All rights reserved.

ISBN: 978-1-9991146-8-8

Published by
Northwest Passage Books
Gatineau, Quebec, Canada

Cover Design by Brendan Myers

Cover photo is copyright © 1977 by Armando Gallo.
Used with permission.

(Third Printing; January 2026)

Table of Contents

Disclaimer vii
Psychopathological warning viii
Positionality Statement ix
Hermeneutical Heads-Up x
Warning and Safety Information xiv
Introduction xix
Acknowledgments xliii

ACT ONE: INFERNO 1

Prologue for Two Puppets 2
I – Burning Robe 5
II – One for the Zine 18
III – Filth of Fish 23
IV – The Fountain of Symonds 25
V – Dinner's Ready 28
VI – Robbery, Assault and Flattery 34
VII – The Chinaman's Show 37
VIII – Known Sons of Thine 65
IX – Hardly a Reply at All 71
X – Scribing the Fast Dyke 80
XI – That's Mean 98
XII – The Musical Boxer 103
XIII – Blood on the Kitchen Tiles 104
XIV – Scenes from a Teacher's Dream 106
XV – Keep It Stark 110
XVI – A Snip of the Tail 114
XVII – More Food Me 120
XVIII – Airborne Tonight 123
XIX – Where the Sweet Turns Sour 132
XX – One-Eyed Mound 133
Postscript For Two Puppets 140

ACT TWO: PURGATORIO **144**

XXI – Aisle of Gentry 145

XXII – The Zamia 152
XXIII – Never a Dime 156
XXIV – One Fool's Man 158
XXV – There Must Be a Subway 161
XXVI – I'd Rather Be Me 164
XXVII – Alien Day 182
XXVIII – Runes Out of Time 194
XXIX – Sod Off He Said 196
XXX – Him and Aristotle 199
XXXI – Deep in a Load of Shite 210
Intrusion By Two Puppets 216
XXXII – Understanding 218
XXXIII – Duchesses 225
XXXIV – Eating While You Breathe 234
XXXV – Quiet Plumbers for the Whisperers 246
XXXVI – Dine and Shout 250
XXXVII – Grounds for Confusion 261
XXXVIII – Saving Lights 270
XXXIX – Ashbound, Part I 276
XL – Ashbound, Part II 280
Interlude For Two Puppets 286

ACT THREE: PARADISO 289

XLI – Evidence of Spring 290
XLII – The Return of the Giant Insight 323
XLIII – Woman on the Corner 334
XLIV – Bad-Bum Boon 371
XLV – Ophelimity and the Off-worlders 376
XLVI – Follow Me Follow You 378
XLVII – Visible Touch 381
XLVIII – Puke's End 386
XLIX – Deflation 395
Extrusion By Two Puppets 404
L – Wrangled 406
LI – Tell 'Em All by Bedtime 410
LII – Looking for Something 412

LIII – Teller of the Flunkies	415
LIV – To Shout, To Shout, To Shout	418
LV – Eleventh Day of March	420
LVI – Dynamo	424
LVII – In the Gage	436
LVIII – Back in N.B.C.	437
LIX – The Bat Flies Down on Broadcasts	439
LX – For Dormant Friends	442
Final Considerations For Two Puppets	452

Baruchello

Disclaimer

This is a work of fiction. This is a work of philosophical satire. This is a work of public interest. This work stands on the shoulders of Thomas More, Voltaire, and Admiral General Haffaz Aladeen. Hence, nearly all names, characters, businesses, institutions, and incidents are the products of the author's imagination playing whimsically and parodically with a wealth of hints, traces, and inspirations arising from a vast array of philosophical and artistic sources, in accordance with well-established literary and comedic practices, and under the aegis of time-honoured moral and legal principles of academic and artistic freedom. In such cases, any resemblance to actual persons, living or dead, or actual events is purely coincidental.° Few real-world institutions, agencies, public offices and noted figures – such as politicians, artists, and public intellectuals – are mentioned too, and in fantastic contexts and circumstances that are wholly and manifestly fictional, imaginary, and unrealistic. No reasonable person would ever take any of this fictional work to provide statements of fact about such real-world institutions and individuals. Also, and in any case, the opinions expressed are those of the characters themselves, including the multiple fictional authors explicitly or implicitly involved in this fictional literary creation, and should not be confused with its ultimate author's. The roles played by recognisable real-world institutions and individuals in this narrative are entirely fictional. Such re-imagined real-world institutions and individuals do, though, often abide by the generally known facts about them. The same applies to the roles played and the behaviours exhibited by hereby-rehashed fictional characters arising from ancient myths, Greek tragedies, Roman poems, famous plays. TV shows, *vel sim.**

°Additional warnings and disclaimers are offered in the book's lengthy introduction and detailed footnotes, so as to minimise any issues for the reader and further establish the fictional, humorous, and philosophical character of the present literary work. Also, in order to prevent any odd or unpleasant coincidences, negative checks were conducted, and nearly all of the characters' *full* names (including abbreviations) were made intentionally implausible or plainly ludicrous.

* Ironically, no such disclaimers would have been needed in the days of Virgil, Dante, Rabelais or Kierkegaard.

Psychopathological warning

Because of the book's contents, these fears, among others, may be unintentionally activated: Ablutophobia, achluophobia, acrophobia, aerophobia, algophobia, agoraphobia, aichmophobia, amaxophobia, androphobia, anemophobia, angrophobia, anthrophobia, anthropophobia, aphenphosmphobia, aquaphobia, arachnophobia, arithmophobia, astraphobia, astrophobia, ataxophobia, atelophobia, atychiphobia, automatonophobia, autophobia, bacteriophobia, barophobia, bathmophobia, batrachophobia, belonephobia, bibliophobia, botanophobia, cacophobia, chionophobia, chromophobia, chronophobia, cibophobia, claustrophobia, cleithrophobia, climacophobia, coulrophobia, cyberphobia, cynophobia, daemonophobia, decidophobia, dementophobia, dendrophobia, dentophobia, dysmorphophobia, dystychiphobia, ecophobia, elurophobia, emetophobia, enochlophobia, entomophobia, ephebiphobia, erotophobia, equinophobia, gamophobia, genophobia, genuphobia, glossophobia, gynophobia, haphephobia, heliophobia, hemophobia, herpetophobia, hexakosioihexekontahexaphobia, hippopotomonstrosesquipedaliophobia, hydrophobia, hypochondria, iatrophobia, insectophobia, koinoniphobia, koumpounophobia, leukophobia, lockiophobia, mageirocophobia, megalophobia, melanophobia, microphobia, mysophobia, necrophobia, noctiphobia, nosocomephobia, nosophobia, nyctophobia, obesophobia, octophobia, ombrophobia, ommetaphobia, ophidiophobia, ornithophobia, osmophobia, ostraconophobia, papyrophobia, paraphobia, pathophobia, pedophobia, philematophobia, philophobia, phobophobia, podophobia, porphyrophobia, pteromerhanophobia, pyrophobia, scolionophobia, selenophobia, siderodromophobia, sociophobia, somniphobia, tachophobia, technophobia, teraphobia, thalassophobia, trichophobia, tonitrophobia, trypanophobia, trypophobia, venustraphobia, verminophobia, wiccaphobia, xanthophobia, xenophobia, zoophobia.**

** Should this book have unintended adverse effects on the average mood stability, mental health, quotidian affective wellbeing, psychiatric viability or psychological equilibrium of some readers, local health-care providers should be contacted. Were such course of remedial action impossible or insufficient, then the author is willing to endeavour to retrieve contact information regarding professional psychotherapists who might help such readers.

Positionality Statement

The ultimate author of this book acknowledges that he can be perceived as being a person of advantage and/or privilege writing, *inter alia*, about the experiences of marginalised or oppressed persons and other living creatures. Since such persons and living creatures are in fact this book's fictional characters and fantastic creations, which are based on the ultimate author's human, all-too-human, sorely-limited, and ever-evolving, ever-imperfect intellect, imagination, and information, including influential oeuvres by prior writers, playwrights, philosophers, and artists, the reader is hereby humbly beseeched to show this book's ultimate author the same charitable understanding that, customarily, would be granted to such prior writers, playwrights, philosophers, and artists. Consider, for the sheer sake of partial example, the ensuing list of inspirational writers, playwrights, philosophers, and artists:

Alain de Botton
Alban Berg
Albert Camus
Alberto Moravia
Alexander Zinoviev
Anaïs Nin
André Dinar
Andrea Dworkin
Anita Phillips
Anne Desclos
Artemisia Gentileschi
Arthur Schopenhauer
Blaise Pascal
Brendan Myers
Cardi B
Carl Gustav Jung
Catharine A. MacKinnon
Catherine Breillat
Catherine Reitman
Charles Ives
Charlotte Roche
Charlie Hebdo
D.H. Lawrence
Daniil Kharms
Dante Alighieri
Dario Fo
David Foster Wallace
David Hume
David Lynch
Diane Morgan

Dino Buzzati
Eminem
Fabrizio De André
Flavio Baroncelli
Franca Rame
Francesco Guccini
Friedrich Nietzsche
Fyodor Mikhailovich Dostoyevsky
G.K. Chesterton
George Carlin
Gesualdo Bufalino
Giacomo Leopardi
Gianni Rodari
Giuseppe Marzari
Grazia Deledda
H.P. Lovecraft
Hannah Gadsby
Iris Murdoch
Irvine Welsh
James Joyce
Jean-Paul Sartre
John Cleese
Jon Stewart
Lars von Trier
Lenny Bruce
Luigi Pirandello
Machado de Assis
Matt Stone
May Sinclair

Mike Judge
Mikhail Bulgakov
Nikolai Gogol
Peter Paul Rubens
Philip Paul Hallie
Pier Paolo Pasolini
Quentin Tarantino
Richard Pryor
Richard Rorty
Ricky Gervais
Roberto Benigni
Sacha Baron-Cohen
Sarah Silverman
Sören Kierkegaard
Spike Lee
Stieg Larsson
Suzy Eddie Izzard
the 'Divine' Marquis de Sade
Thomas More
Trey Parker
Umberto Eco
Vilfredo Pareto
Voltaire
Wahida Clark
William Shakespeare
Witold Gombrowicz
Wolfgang Amadeus Mozart

Hermeneutical Heads-Up

Dr Andy P. Hill, *No Title* (2nd March 2024) © Andy Hill. Used with permission.

ONE GENERAL REMARK

The present book (1) presupposes both empirically and theoretically, (2) complements *via* literary and dramaturgical means, and (3) refers the inquiring reader to, the 2022–2024 four-book philosophical and socio-scientific study *Humour and Cruelty* (Berlin: De Gruyter), written by Giorgio Baruchello and Ársæll Már

Arnarsson. (See also the "Symposium" devoted to this series, and published in Volume 6(1)/2025 of the *Philosophy of Humor Yearbook*, pp. 255–280.)

TWO SPECIFIC QUOTES

Note 25 in the 2022 *Volume 1: A Philosophical Exploration of the Humanities and Social Sciences* (p.5):

As much as we would like to reach a broader public, the academic circles are the likely recipients of our work. Also, our academic prose may be inherently limited and limiting anyhow. On this subject, the US philosopher D.F. Krell (2019, 1 and 9) claims that deeply emotional issues such as "cruelty" and "tenderness" are better expressed in a "style" that "is less formal than rigorous readers may expect and demand" in, say, "scholarly articles".

> Cf. Krell, David Farrell (2019). *The Cudgel and the Caress. Reflections on Cruelty and Tenderness* (Albany: SUNY)

As cited *verbatim* in the 2023 *Volume 2: Dangerous Liaisons* (p.103):

"The inability to deal with certain aspects of reality on the part of any discipline that prizes systematization (form) is well known. The most brilliant explorations of 'states of mind,' for instance, are not to be found in psychology texts but in novels. The reason is obvious. Psychology tries to explain taxonomically what is not amenable to be so explained. The novelist is free from such a delusion."

> Cf. Mini, Piero V. (1974). *Philosophy and Economics: The Origins and Development of Economic Theory* (Gainesville: University Press of Florida), p.152

ONE TELLING CARTOON

Frontispiece of the 2023 *Volume 2: Dangerous Liaisons*:

Thibaut Soulcié © (2023). Used with permission.

Uncanny Soulscapes in Uncommon Dreamscope

ONE TELLING ALLEGORY

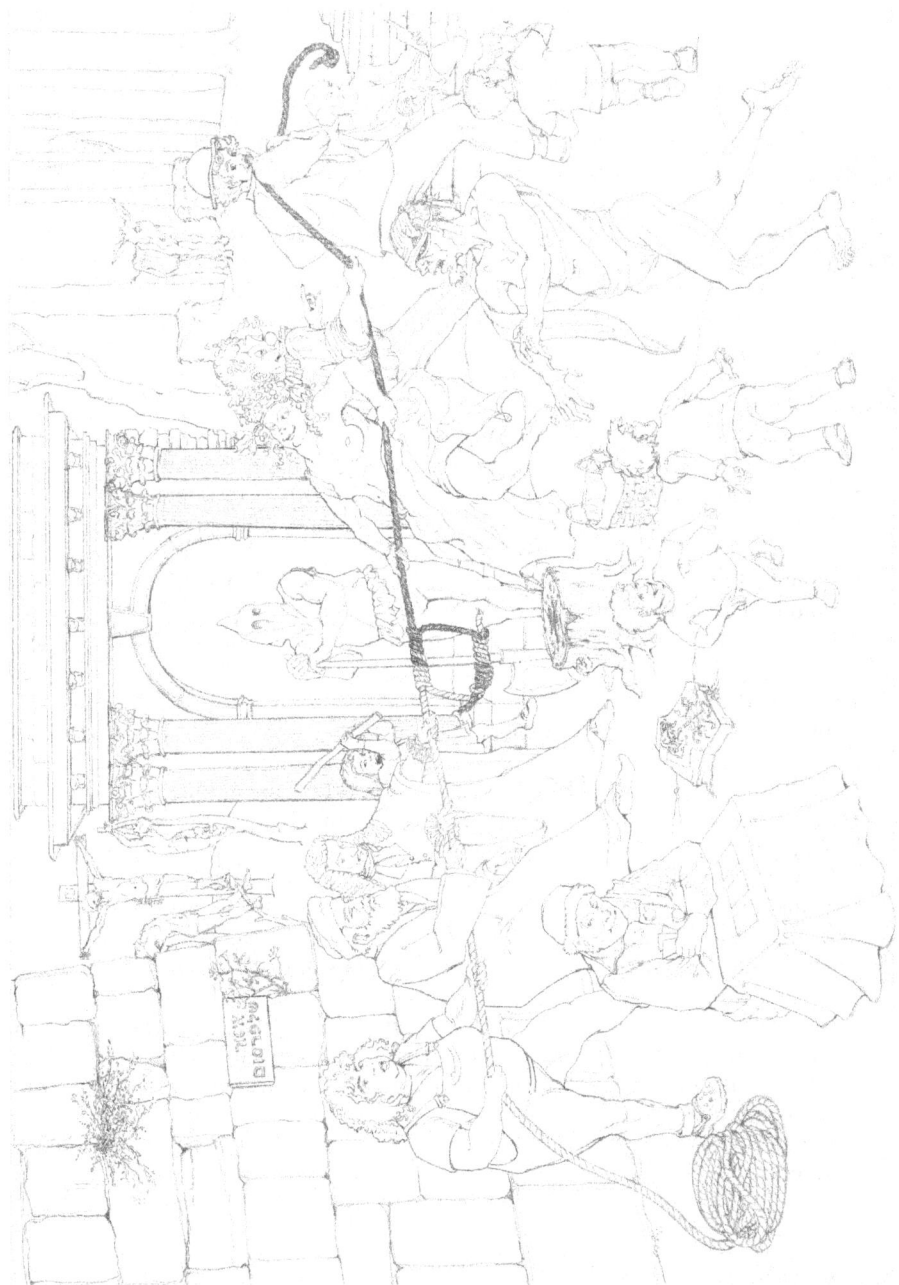

Lorenzo Biggi's 2024 original artwork, based on *Humour and Cruelty* (currently exhibited at the University of Akureyri, Iceland, and used *qua* closing picture in Giorgio Baruchello's 2025 book *Thinking and Laughing*, published by Northwest Passage Books). Used with permission.

Warning and Safety Information Regarding the Use of Philosophical Books
(Controlled by A.I.)

Read carefully before handling.

Philosophical books are intended for embracive intellectual engagement, exhaustive socio-historical exploration, erudite moral edification, expert argumentative education, as well as extensive conceptual complexification and nuanced logical reasoning, and eventual spiritual and personal enlightenment. Improper use may result in psychological harm, uncontrolled knee-jerk reactions, unpleasant humbling and nagging self-doubt, and general embarrassment before one's social peers or oneself. Consult a qualified philosopher before initiating any activities involving such books.

Indications
Philosophical books are indicated for:
- Building theoretical structures, logical avenues, and hermeneutical pathways.
- Providing stable argumentative buttressing as much as its opposite.
- Serving as means of overall critical thinking and creative ideational imagining.
- Digging deep into the most profound layers of psychic, social, and ontological reality.
- Occasionally being used as paperweights (with caution).

Contraindications
Avoid handling philosophical books if you:
- Are barefaced, concerned with wearing fashionable clothing, or otherwise inadequately willing to reconsider your worldview and guiding values.
- Are prone to resent having unexpected insights challenging your ingrained habits.
- Believe yourself "very clever" without external verification.
- Think of knowing already what is right and what is wrong, and how the world goes.
- Resist imagery, intellections, and investigations of dark, scandalous or thorny issues.
- Intend to use philosophical books as page-turners, juggling props, or facile conversation starters by tossing them in the air, towards the clouds where Socrates is currently said to live and conduct the business which he started 24 centuries ago.
- Are unsupervised and/or showing signs of bad digestion or recreational boredom.

Warnings
- **Impact Hazard**: Philosophical books are deep and heavy. Impact with traditions, expectations, habituations, or other tacit givens and presuppositions may result in expressive feats of communication unsuitable for prim professional environments.
- **Gravity Risk**: Philosophical books are subject to gravitational forces at all times. Never place philosophical books in elevated positions where they may later remember gravity and attempt to emulate the legendary apple which fell onto Newton's head.
- **Cutting Precaution**: Reading philosophical books subtler than your intellectual acumen or interpretative legerdemain may lead to rage, resentment, regret, and rabies. People can fail to understand what they do not understand. Hence, they react with cruelty.
- **Do Not Ingest**: Philosophical books are not food for the body, but for the soul. Do not attempt to eat, lick, or taste philosophical books, even if they appear smooth, pretty, enticing, or surprisingly pumpkin-like.
- **Do Not Copulate**: Philosophical books are not carnal mates, but spiritual ones. Do not attempt to eat, lick, or taste philosophical books, even if they appear smooth, pretty, enticing, or surprisingly pumpkin-like.

Potential Side Effects
Common side effects may include:
- Dusty shelves.
- Mild exertion.
- Feeling of accomplishment (if used as intended).

Serious side effects may include:
- Bruised egos.
- Mental collapse.
- Sudden appreciation for interminable dialogue.
- Acoustic disturbance caused by loud exclamations following new thoughts.

Interactions
Avoid combining philosophical books with:
- Reckless enthusiasm.
- High shelves.
- Minors under the age of "knowing better."
- Anyone shouting, "Wake up!," "Woke!," or "Micro-aggression!"

Storage
Store philosophical books in a cool, dry place. Do not store philosophical books on unstable surfaces, sloped terrain, or directly above your motorcar, especially if you are driving it.

If adverse effects occur, discontinue interaction with philosophical books immediately and seek swift assistance from a responsible literate adult, elderly cultured relative, God, or a licensed academic philosopher.

Baruchello

Dedicated to:
My ageing and aching self,
which glows radiant under a thick cover of autumn leaves.
My dear brother Renato,
who keeps me company under all those leaves.
The autumn leaves which allow us to be together and play,
as if we were still children.

"Allow me to talk to you.
Allow me to talk to you.
Allow me to talk to you.
Please, relax; read; reflect; rest; read again; and then reflect some more. And remember: The levels of interpretation have been four since the banquet was given"

P.S. Don't be lazy, be responsible, and read the introduction and all the footnotes!
P.P.S. But if you don't want to do that, then be even lazier and stop reading the book altogether.
P.P.P.S. And don't judge any book by its cover, spine, dedication, or other titbits, i.e., out of proper context.
P.P.P.P.S. Every time something is being written and said, something else is being shown at the same time.
P.P.P.P.P.S. Lost, already? May Comus, God of Comedy, and Boethius' Lady Philosophy come to help you!
P.P.P.P.P.P.S. Dang! Comus and the Lady are busy drafting a new code of good governance for prosy prigs.

– The present book

In grateful memory of:
Prof. Garrett Barden (1939–2024)
Philosopher, anthropologist, mentor, co-author, and friend.

Baruchello

Introduction

Considering the consistent and, perchance, repetitive subtitles of my prior works for Northwest Passage Books, the reader might rightly expect to find here yet another collection of "philosophical essays"—that is to say, however freely, idiosyncratically, and creatively the Montaignesque term *"essai"* has been used, if not cruelly abused, in my preceding six volumes.[1] Similarly, given the particular contents of the sixth volume in the series, the same reader would probably expect to find herein a lively, miscellaneous, and hopefully entertaining assortment of vignettes, pastiches, spoofs, parodies, and satires, as *per* the latter half of said sixth volume.

What's the blooming book like?

Whether or not such a fact is going to disappoint you, then you should be told from the very beginning that this book is just a little *different* from its foregoing instalment in the series, as well as from, or indeed much more so than, the five other volumes which came before it.

For one, despite their diverse styles, subjects, and sizes, all the texts herein presented to the reader should be better described, and shall be duly referred to, as "fragments" rather than "essays." Their varied, overtly rhapsodic, ostensibly literary, certainly eclectic and, more often than not, fairly *short* expository form called for a lick of ingenious, possibly Kierkegaardian, and contextually innovative terminology—hence the present book's subtitle. When I write "short," the reader should consider that the present author penned in the period 2020–2023 a four-book, 1,700-page-long, 700,000-word scholarly study for De Gruyter's ongoing series on the philosophy of

---

[1] I am referring to: *Mortals, Money, and Masters of Thought* (vol.1, 2017); *Philosophy of Cruelty* (vol.2, 2017); *The Business of Life and Death I: Values and Economies* (vol.3, 2018); *The Business of Life and Death II: Politics, Law, and Society* (vol.4, 2018); *Thinking and Talking* (vol.5, 2019); and *Thinking and Laughing* (vol. 6, 2025). All six volumes were unimaginatively yet aptly subtitled: "Collected Philosophical Essays by Giorgio Baruchello."

humour, aptly entitled *Humour and Cruelty*. That's what I consider a *long* exposition. "Long," precisely. You now get the idea, I'm quite sure of it. Excellent. In this volume, then, I am still doing *philosophy*, for philosophy is my standard cup of tea. Honestly, I suspect that there is hardly any other brew that I can credibly prepare. Yet, the actual cup that the reader is going to hold in his or her hand is *not* the usual one. It is an uncommonly small one, on average. Therefore, be suitably prepared. Above all, be sufficiently thirsty.[2]

For another, humour, laughter, irony, comedy, fun, mockery, caricature, farce, pantomime, carnival, grotesquerie, and all kinds of cognate terms, themes, phenomena, concepts, and issues keep being a matter of major significance for me, both as regards the ways in which I express myself, and as regards the topics and thinkers that I tackle and discuss in this book.[3] On such a funny matter, please recall that if, regrettably, you don't get *my* sense of humour or, God forbid, should you dislike it, then that's *your* loss too, i.e., not just mine.[4] Try your best, then—do so, please; pretty please. I certainly tried my best when writing the present book, which should be amusing, for the most part. At the same time, this book should also be taken seriously enough by the reader so as to be amused by the right parts of it. To say nothing of the fact that even failed humour is humour. It's just humour that, well, failed: *Nomen omen*. Yet, in the end, who cares, if humour fails? How many key lessons have we learnt against our own will and marked preference? Some people, in particular, seem to learn mostly or even only 'the hard way.'

In any case, in this volume, there are compositional, critical, and conceptual elements that do *not* relate to humour and its various socio-logical, logico-semantic, aesthetico-artistic, and ethico-cultural

---

[2] As commonplace, there will be learned persons claiming that 'real' philosophy cannot be served in cups such as the present one. Similar complaints were moved against, say, Kierkegaard and Nietzsche, back in their days.

[3] As a matter of fact, I tried to make use of as many varieties of humour as I could, both highbrow and lowbrow, including *cruel* ones.

[4] My sense of humour extends also to preposterous comparisons between myself and philosophical classics.

associates—neither too directly nor too openly, at the very least. There may be cold scholarly and/or technical brainteasers, as much as distraught sighs and burning tears. Screams of outright pain and sorrow, from time to time. Gasps of alarm and shock, possibly. Scowls of disgust and irked disapproval, sporadically. And fits of boiling rage, if or when necessary. This book's affective landscape is, in other words, somewhat broader and indubitably less predictable than it was the case with my previous volume.[5] The heteroglossic stylistic spectrum is wider and, while most prose verges towards the comical, the absurd, the grotesque, the satirical, the carnivalesque, and the farcical, there can be more meditative humorous pieces—*à la* Stephen Leacock, to give you a Canadian point of reference—and sparse intimate elegies, tales of horror, and tragedies—all the way down to the unmitigated cruelties of Shakespeare's *Titus Andronicus* and Greenaway's *Baby of Mâcon*. In such cases, in line with the reflections developed by the Jewish ethicist and WWII veteran Philip Hallie, author of *The Paradox of Cruelty*, there appear outright examples of blood-chilling, unhumorous, *in terrorem* literary techniques. Once again, be suitably prepared. And don't be *too* aloof.

What's inside the blooming book, anyway?

The book contains a total number of *sixty* short stories, brief sketches, and two-person mini-dialogues which, supposedly, should be delivered by two or three actors on a stage. At least, that is how these comedic texts were conceived of, concocted, and accordingly composed. Together, all sixty works form an intentionally kaleidoscopic yet intimately interconnected web of characters, connotations, concepts, cruces, conceits, corroborations, colours, clues, chasms, cues, contrasts, comparisons, contradictions, contortions, qualities, quantities, concordances, contours, conditions,

---

[5] In keeping with archetypal psychology's lore, it should be noticed that the content eliciting each reader's strongest affective responses (e.g., specific characters, terms, ideas, etc.) reveals something important about his/her soul.

crocks, configurations, characteristics, commentaries, caricatures, cracks, considerations, canards, and campy circumlocutory catalogues that, ideally, should be able to shed a modicum of light, and an appropriate measure of darkness, on two distinct yet frequently-interlaced human phenomena into which I have been running, and then inquiring in a great variety of ways *qua* academic philosopher, for longer than four decades, i.e., *humour* and *cruelty*.[6]

My previous books and investigations made use—principally, though not exclusively—of standard philosophical and scientific categories and abstractions, and aimed at providing rational explanations and reasoned assessments of the origins, nature, forms, goals, and possible qualified justifications in human existence for humour and, far more rarely, cruelty. The present collection of sixty texts is *complementary* to all of that, insofar as it moves from the opposite direction.[7] That is to say, this collection hypostasises lived, personal[8], human circumstances by means of a veritable population of playfully-entwined fictional characters, none of which represents or aims at representing any specific individual that has existed or may perchance exist on our planet—not even when the character at issue is the blatant parody of a major Western political leader or of this minor book's humble author.[9] Rather, each fictional character is basically the creative and artistic incarnation of several significant clusters of distinguishable human traits, both positive and negative, that can be found scattered across all or most human beings, as well as of much-deeper, hidden-yet-pivotal, socio-psychic forces, which Vilfredo Pareto would have described as "residues," back in his day,

---

[6] How and why I ended up focussing on such topics is something which I addressed in my 6th volume for NWP.

[7] <u>Anyone interested in forming a fully-informed opinion on *this* book ought to read my tetralogy for De Gruyter,</u> i.e., its proper *context*.

[8] "Personal" meaning here 'pertaining to persons' at large, not 'pertaining to my person' specifically.

[9] At risk of being didactical, explicit hermeneutical guidelines are indirectly provided in the short text #LVI.

and C.G. Jung as "archetypes."¹⁰ A metaphorical shaker's metaphorical sprogs, all characters are anthropological cocktails.

If, while perusing these sixty texts, you should happen to perceive thematic and/or stylistic echoes of famous Western authors about whom I wrote in the past, also and especially in connection with these two important concepts and phenomena, i.e., humour and cruelty—thinkers and writers such as Blaise Pascal, the Marquis de Sade, Arthur Schopenhauer, Friedrich Nietzsche, G.K. Chesterton, Luigi Pirandello, Philip Hallie, Richard Rorty, or Anita Phillips—those echoes must not come to you as a surprise. The past informs the present.¹¹ The old begets the new. The background gives shape to the foreground. The premises support the conclusions. All explicit analyses presuppose tacit syntheses. The molar ushers the molecular. The ontic foreshadows the ontological. Unremarkably, and in spite of countless changes, *I am still me*. Sometimes, I think it's a pity. Who wouldn't experiment with an alternative self? Imagine what it would be like, for example, to be the middle brother of Karl and Michael Polanyi!

Why's the blooming book so bleak, if it's about humour?

Both of these all-too-human concepts and phenomena, i.e., humour and cruelty, cast inevitably a thick, substantive, almost tangible Jungian *shadow* of their own whenever sensed, approached, investigated, presented, represented, commented and/or candidly reflected upon. Humour and cruelty are large, complex, heavy, mobile, shifty, often nasty, and invariably hairy 'beasts' belonging to our history, cultures, subcultures, psychic depths, affective make-up,

---

10 I discussed the striking analogies of these two key categories in "Pareto and Jung: A Conjunction of Opposites," *RESS/Cahiers Vilfredo Pareto* 61(2)/2023: 55–78. Vico scholars may sense instead his *universali fantastici*. As to those die-heard neopositivists who still believe in the myth that analytic psychology has no solid empirical foundation, I must refer them to the definitive data collected by Christian Roesler in Germany.

11 Hence, I should add the names of Dante and Dostoyevsky; about whom, however, I have not written much.

and iceberg-like hosts of tacit sensitivities.[12] They are neither purely angelic nor wholly demonic. They are more like bonobos, black bears, buffalos, hyenas, wolves, dingoes or wild boars—and grown human beings.[13] All such living creatures are baffling tangles of different tendencies, teachings, tactics, tentative actions, and aspired *things*, whatever these 'things' may be.

As such, humour and cruelty bring along an ungainly load of *spiritual tensions* and—let's be brutally honest about it—outright *moral evils* that cannot be avoided, edulcorated, underplayed, neglected, sidelined, censored, cancelled, shushed or ignored altogether. All such shadows and attendant shadow-contents, including humour's ones, sport ugly looks, muddy boots, sweaty armpits, dirty orifices, crusty eyes, messy hairdos, bad manners, foul language, prejudiced attitudes, very long nails and, recurrently, the sharpest of teeth. *Be wary. Be wise.* In what follows, the reader will surely encounter all manners of clowns, buffoons, quipsters, wits, and funny characters. Such comic creations are primary and prevalent throughout the book. At the same time, there will also appear conmen, bigots, reprobates, thugs, and fishy characters. Such ungainly creations are secondary and subordinate, but not altogether absent; and neither are omitted altogether crude, lowly, painful, raw, necessary tokens of their cruel taunts and cruel misdeeds.[14]

Meeting all of these uncouth and sometimes biting 'bits' is part of the dire price that must be paid for the sake of pursuing a candid and comprehensive intellectual engagement with humour and cruelty qua legitimate theoretico-philosophical, socio-cultural, and lyrico-literary matters. Humour and cruelty are not being viewed here from a safe distance. Like Dian Fossey's gorillas, instead, they are being lived with, observed in close proximity, and recounted faithfully,

---

[12] Ironically, being interested in exploring the fluid, murky world of actual persons by dint of literary means, this book cares little for their rigid, squeaky-clean *personae*.

[13] This theoretical bestiary should include donkeys: Asinine humour is most useful to carry heavy burdens. Cruel asses, though, take things out of context.

[14] Such cruelties, tensions, and evils comprise the psycho-social forces of censoriousness and self-/censorship that torture all moral writers.

even if it means tolerating plenty of stench and the burning bites of noxious parasites."Warts and all" would make an apt phrase, in this connection. Or, as a far-less-than-angelic Milton would have jibed back in the 1970s: "There's no such thing as a free lunch." What is more, the purchased lunch may consist entirely of entrails, which many people can't stomach.[15] Nonetheless, serious heed should be paid to Jung's medically-informed, persistent, and insistent claims whereby if "[w]e have no imagination for evil... evil has us in its grip" and, therefore, it is paramount that we dare and become capable of "[k]nowing [-]our own darkness," insofar as it "is the best method for dealing with the darkness of other people," i.e., all of us.

Relatedly, and perchance redundantly, the reader (thereafter "x") is unequivocally, categorically, explicitly, and energetically advised to keep in mind the following caveat, which applies to all words, sentences, paragraphs, short texts, or parts thereof (hereafter "z"):

If x *is* P-*ed by* z, *then note that*
z *was not consciously intended to* P x.

"P" indicates any verb referring to typically-unwelcome inter- or even intra-personal acts such as: To offend, insult, anger, belittle, denigrate, enrage, disrespect, exclude, aggrieve, brutalise, chastise, deride, fault, harm, jeopardise, oppress, ridicule, incense, vex, *et similia*. Should *x* have been ever P-ed by some other author's *z* in the past, then *x* should quit reading this book presently—not in the future. This is no joke.[16]

What am I supposed to do with the blooming book?

Being not *too* aloof implies being aloof to a degree. The *right* degree. Where or what exactly that right degree is like, it varies a lot,

---

[15] Piling on the unsavoury imagery, philosophy must at times operate like some sort of spiritual colonoscopy.

[16] If the caveat above happens to *P x*, then *x* may want to reconsider their worldview, guiding values, and pastimes.

depending on the background and personality of each and every individual: Each and every reader, that is. Be *that* degree, in any case, for failing in this attitudinal respect would probably cause the reader not to enjoy the book so thoroughly as it is conceivably and humanly possible to enjoy it. And I would very much like the reader to be able to enjoy this book thoroughly, as strange as that may sound: I don't want *you* to suffer—unless it performs a cauterising function, as the French literary critic and novelist André Dinar had argued in *Les auteurs cruels* back in the early 1940s.[17]

Aren't you pleasantly surprised? For once, I must acknowledge the following basic point in confident, unequivocal, triumphant terms: I am verily capable of genuine kindness, charitable concern, *and* sincere compassion towards my readers—albeit not *all* the time. Who could be *so* nice? Truly, *all* the time? Come on! Pull the other one! As the late and somewhat notorious Italian politician Silvio Berlusconi concisely replied to the journalists who were asking him about his dubious penchants for wild parties and related hedonic excesses: "I'm no saint."

Personally, I am much more of an introvert than the media-savvy and unctuous former Italian Prime Minster was, and I have no such penchants. For one, just so that we understand each other, such penchants require lots of cash and the willingness to spend it. I am neither as rich nor as profligate as he was. Please recall that I'm originally from *Genoa*, not Milan: Two very different breeds, if you know my country of birth and its long, intricate history. For another, wild parties are noisy, and I hate noise. Hedonism is *not* my forte. And how could it ever be? I'm a professional philosopher, by George! Not to mention where Berlusconi and I stand with respect to each other on the political spectrum, i.e., along the left-to-right horizontal axis.

Nonetheless, even if in a minor, somewhat drab, probably boring, and far less deafening and flamboyant key, I'm no saint either. (Have

---

[17] Once again, my prior inquiries into humour and cruelty underpin and inform the present volume. Inevitably, all such inquiries cannot be summarised and outlined to the reader's benefit, but only hinted at and presupposed.

you met any saints, lately, by the way? Or only in the mirror?) Ask any of my friends, and they will tell you that I have defects and shortcomings aplenty. Therefore, take pleasure in the acts of kindness, concern, and compassion that I'm showing to you hereby, *while they last*. It might actually be the *last* time that such an opportunity arises, sadly enough. You see, it's all quite simple: I'm a dreadfully moody guy.[18]

How did the blooming book come about the way it is?

Each and all of these sixty short stories, brief sketches, and two-person mini-dialogues have their own inner voice, formal character, fictional direction, humorous register, and narrative perspective. Indeed, whimsically, each short text has been created by a different imaginary author, whose identity the reader is playfully invited to try and guess or concoct. However, these sixty texts are also very much like different movements inside a symphony. *These sixty texts and contents thereof, then, must not be thought of in complete isolation from one another, and their overall order is itself designed in such a way as to establish the book's comprehensive trajectory and subtler inner logic.* All of these texts, moreover, were intuited, invented, written, and rewritten along four chief—though by no means whatsoever exhaustive and/or exclusive[19]—*imaginative axes* explaining, to a partial yet pertinent level, the short stories,' brief sketches', and mini-dialogues' contentual[20] genesis, structural organisation, thematic over- and under-tones, and stylistic development:

---

[18] If you failed to grasp the tongue-in-cheek tone of the paragraph above, then please work on your sense of irony.

[19] The second scene of text #XXXVI and the text marked as #L are both based on jokes that I was told as a child by my grandfather, the World-War-II veteran and amateur historian Severino Domenico Dolente (1909–1993).

[20] Albeit both antiquated and abstruse, the adjective "contentual" has existed in English, most surely in philosophy, since at least the early 20th century. It means 'pertaining to content,' and I find it logical as well as useful.

A. Numerous starting scenarios and imaginary settings were supplied by *oneiric* experiences, i.e., dreams *et similia*, as peculiar as they may be at times—hence the second part of the book's main title: *in Uncustomary Dreamscope* [*sic*].[21]
B. Germinal theoretical insights were implanted by deliberate associations with specific *philosophical* concepts, names[22], attitudes, disputations and/or schools of thought. Some insights are central to the texts, others are minor or tangential.[23]
C. Most works toyed extensively with at least one identifiable *rhetorical* trope, as *per* my classification of rhetorical tropes in volumes five and six for NWP Books.[24] I can never recall the tropes' names, and that is why I made a list for myself.
D. Further *esprit* was injected by inserting *musical* puns in the titles of the stories, sketches, and dialogues themselves. (Nothing too highbrow, I hope.) In a few cases, the puns inspired or even guided the contents of the works at issue.[25]

Two more chief imaginative axes were also followed closely in each and every short story, brief sketch, and mini-dialogue. Evidently, both chief imaginative axes were of crucial importance from a compositional and creative point of view. Nonetheless, these two additional chief imaginative axes are *not* revealed hereby to the reader—and they will never be revealed—lest the quintessential and much-desirable *fun* of inventive hypothesising, wild speculation,

---

[21] Literature is like sausage-making: Nothing goes to waste. However, in life, everything dies and wastes away.

[22] Most fictional characters are named after philosophers. The remaining names have literary, cinematic or artistic bases. Few noted scholars', artists' and public figures' real names were also made use of, *for humorous/fictional aims*. Do refer to the opening disclaimer to fully grasp the parodic, unreal, and literary context of such occasional name-dropping, which allows for mockumentary-like satire.

[23] The occasional 'appearance' of some famous individual, whether fictional-fictional or merely fictional, should be regarded as an implicit tribute to their significance in the public sphere as much as the psychic sphere.

[24] *In nuce*, the form reflects the content, and the content reflects the intent—when intended.

[25] In such cases, the puns in the titles were the real genesis of the short texts.

interpretative guesswork, clever detection, self-revelatory blunder, and playful disagreement is stupidly spoiled *ab ovo*. Plainly, I have to keep my readers engaged and entertained.[26]

Why are there so many bizarre characters in the blooming book?

This plain and, as I must admit, rather pedestrian literary goal explains in part the long litany of unconventional, unique, and even extreme characters and circumstances that you are going to meet in most, although not all, of the short stories, brief sketches, and two-person mini-dialogues. Ordinary persons, items, and chores don't make for a truly gripping reading, do they? Maybe ordinary persons, items, and chores are okay in a soap opera.[27] But even then, all kinds of weird events and eccentric behaviours tend to emerge nevertheless, lest the audience stop following the soap opera.[28] One doesn't need to be radical to dislike a diet of sole beetroot. Besides, it is not just humour that plays a pivotal role in this creative and intellectual endeavour, but *cruelty* as well—and that's no child's play, even if children can be very cruel creatures.[29]

A fortiori, strong liquor, not soap, and most certainly no beetroot, *is* being served in the following pages, along with indispensable pinches of open violence, ungracious profanities, aberrant and criminal acts, rampant gore, and lewd facetiae.[30] There may be even hallucinatory, recreational, and other types of illicit drugs. All in all, it is as though the book had been spiced up with the sort of 'wild'

---

[26] Not to mention my tendency to explain and detail *ad nauseam*, especially *via* footnotes.

[27] "Okay" indicating 'not too bad.' And remember: The reader's sense of humour will be tested. Yet recall that tolerance is dislike's twin.

[28] If you know of any good new soap opera, please let your next door's neighbour know about it.

[29] In fact, in childhood, we learn not only how humour works, but also how to endure and inflict cruelty.

[30] Despite living in an age characterised by sexual fluidity explicit rap lyrics, and pornography, *sex* can still make people jumpy. And yet, as amply testified by, say, psychodynamics and feminist literature, *sex is paramount*.

and 'racy' things that you might expect to encounter in an episode of *Black Mirror* or a movie by Spike Lee or Quentin Tarantino—although, as far as my Genoa-based aesthetics are concerned, Baroque imagery and arts may offer a more germane point of reference.[31]

These ingredients should also keep the reader engaged and, at times, entertained. Have fun, if you can. I am giving you two potatoes and a kitchen floor and asking you to play with me.[32] My hope and aim is that this witty, quaint, sometimes disturbing book will make you think, even if it purposefully refuses to instruct you *what* to think: *Think*. Engender thought; with your own head. This book is not a manifesto. It is a midwife.[33] If you can't play or don't have fun, and there may be lines of thinking, thematic choices, linguistic formulations and/or types of humour, parody, grotesquerie, horror, torture, ferocity, cuss words, insults, manic or erotic practices, preferences, partialities, perversions, penchants, and proclivities that you suspect or know to be capable of offending, wounding or traumatising you, then do *not* read this book.[34]

This book is *not* a peaceful stroll in the park but an intricate exploration of the human soul and *the human condition* in light of humour *and* cruelty. <u>If you can be unsettled, shocked, triggered, affronted or troubled by philosophically-informed literary and/or dramatic fiction investigating the ambiguous and amorphous worlds of human laughter and suffering, then *stop* reading: Stop now!</u>[35] Nobody is forcing you to peruse a book aimed at exploring humour *and* cruelty *from the inside out*—as unequivocally announced in the

---

[31] If "humour" is readily associated with comedy, "cruelty" evokes genres such as horror, sci-fi, and Westerns.

[32] This longish metaphor, or very brief allegory, becomes understandable after reading the short text #LI.

[33] This book wants also to elicit affective responses, naturally, but facilitating reflection is paramount.

[34] This book might appeal more to young adults, new adults, or adults as such: *Maturity*, in any case, is a must.

[35] The reader should also keep in mind that explicitly-expressed cruelties are *not* implicitly-endorsed cruelties.

very same book's introduction, and *so* explicitly and *so* emphatically reiterated hereby.³⁶ Be aware; beware; and let this be your last *warning*.

If in doubt, ponder on Peter Paul Rubens' or Artemisia Gentileschi's paintings before deciding whether or not to continue reading this book. And if Baroque art is not your cup of tea, then try and recall the cinema of Gaspar Noé, Julia Doucournau, Sergio Leone, Virginie Despentes, Danny Boyle, Erika Lust, Bernardo Bertolucci, Céline Sciamma, Pier Paolo Pasolini, Catherine Breillat, David Lynch, Danny Boyle, or Lars von Trier.³⁷ 21ˢᵗ-century writers, after all, are expected to draw inspiration from *all* extant artforms, elite as much as popular, and not just official high literature.

Who's the blooming book's author trying to ape, anyway?

I wish to spotlight *three* groups of writers, artists and/or philosophers whose works served as a source of inspiration, or an indication of what was aesthetically and theoretically possible for me to accomplish, or try to accomplish.³⁸ Role models, in many ways, even if I am cognisant of the fact that most of them lived long before the age of internet, DSK, post-truth, X, mass pornography, Broligarchy, CR7, smartphones, remote-controlled war drones, BTC, Greta Thunberg, streaming platforms, ISIL, 'pussy power', AIIB, DeepSeek, RJ, and much else.

The first group comprises May Sinclair (1863–1946), Mikhail Bulgakov (1891–1940), Daniil Kharms (1905–1942) and Dino

---

³⁶ As stated, the *Humour and Cruelty* tetralogy complements and underpins this book, and the notion that there can be no serious literary-philosophical exploration of these two titular concepts that avoids cruelty as such, cruel language, cruel humour, humorous cruelty, cruel irony, the use of cruelty against humour, and *vice versa*. Given such context and aims, this book owns the required "joke capital," in line with the ethics of humour discussed by Thomas Wilk & Steven Gimbel in *In on the Joke: The Ethics of Humor and Comedy* (Berlin: De Gruyter, 2024).

³⁷ This book's *raison d'être*, aims, context and contents are artistic and philosophical: No offence is intended.

³⁸ Terms such as "intellectuals," "playwrights," and "creative minds" apply equally.

Buzzati (1906–1972). While I make no audacious (and silly) claim whatsoever with regard to my being even remotely as gifted in literary deeds and artistic exploits as they were, their combined lived exemplar, vivid imagination, compelling writing style, and erratic yet enticing sense of humour have been most important for me not solely *qua* curious and experimenting philosopher, but also and above all *qua* permanently tentative English-language writer—and as any stately linguist can explain to you, even poor performance is a sign of competence.

Bulgakov's name stands out in this first group as a major representative of, and tacitly introduces, the Russian literary and literary-speculative tradition, to which I owe much in terms of personal growth and general sensitivities—hence the first part of the book's main title: *Uncanny Soulscapes* [sic]. While many young teenagers of my generation pictured themselves as gritty cowboys gunning down grittier outlaws in the grittiest Wild West, or as slow-moving yet daring American astronauts exploring the craters on Mars, I grew up imagining myself living in 19th-century Tsarist Russia, or fighting alongside Isaac Babel and the Red Cavalry in the 1920s. Lenin and Trotsky were my idea of 'cool,' back then, not John Wayne or Clint Eastwood. Go figure!

The second group comprises Giacomo Leopardi (1798–1837), Witold Gombrowicz (1904–1969), Flavio Baroncelli (1944–2007) and Umberto Eco (1932–2016), whose original and thought-provoking commixtures of deep philosophical considerations and deft literary approaches I have admired and appreciated since my now-distant days *qua* undergraduate student at the University of Genoa, Italy. Even being told of instantiating merely a sombre and umbral *echo* of any one of these older authors would swiftly and charmingly make my day. I'm not joking! Well, I'm not *just* joking… As a sheer matter of emotional fact and, above all, as a factor of my stupid and shallow selfish pride, no sweeter statement could be uttered about me and my far-from-perfect creative work.

Frankly, I do not mind accusations of being derivative—for, to be as frank, no one writing in the 21st century can avoid being derivative—as long as my original prototypes are correctly acknowledged by the accuser. Get the facts straight, for goodness' sake! Besides, inasmuch as we all are effectively bound to derive our leaps of the imagination and creative insights from amorphous common knowledge and, even more so, from the unconscious—which is also likely to be collective—, we all are equally bound to draw water from the same well.[39] It's as simple as that.[40] So, if you are still going to point the finger, then you must point it in the right direction.[41] And wash your hands.[42]

The third group comprises Nikolai Gogol (1809–1852), Giuseppe Marzari (1900–1974), Gianni Rodari (1920–1980), and Dario Fo (1926–2016) and Franca Rame (1929–2013). I deem their satirical waggishness, unashamed vitality, and unconcealed playfulness about, and profound sense of compassion for, the plight of their fellow human beings—when not for all sentient creatures—, frequently in the face of the most distressing or disturbing circumstances, to be an objectively imperfect yet subjectively much-needed beacon of hope in contemporary academia, as well as in the wider world's wondrous and winding web of cultures and subcultures, e.g., macro-, meso-, micro-, and inter-cultures.[43]

Today's academic and literate communities, even in their declaredly most progressive, well-meaning, cultured, and critical components, are frequently and unnervingly *too* keen on bleak dystopias, blinding moral panics, blank hatred, blaring factionalism, bloated self-centredness, beguiling self-sequestration, blameful vindictiveness, blatant lack of introspection, bigoted cavilling,

---

[39] I know quite well that the collective unconscious is still a contentious notion. I have no conclusive word to offer. Yet, based on my readings and observations, I regard it as a plausible explanatory and evolutionary hypothesis.

[40] Everything has already been thought, said, and written, more or less. Ignorance of the past is decisive, typically.

[41] If pressed, I could say that my *Philosophical Fragments* offer a Dantesque appropriation of Monty Python or try to bring Dostoyevsky into the 21st century. Yet, both characterisations would be too sweeping and too simplistic.

[42] Should you need any soap, then feel free to check the preceding subsection.

[43] Interestingly, it could be argued that philosophers and historians deal with macro-cultures, sociologists with meso-cultures, and anthropologists and psychologists with micro-cultures. However, that would be too simplistic.

blagging dishonesty, brazen muzzling, and, above all, blunt *judgmentalism*.[44]

Why's this blooming book written the way it's been written?

The last item in this dismal, gloomy, blasted list of far-too-commonplace human faults, lamentably, applies to all sorts of activities, including the dying art of writing. Hence, it reveals its uncomfortable, uninviting, unbending, unfriendly and ugly presence by dint of common, quotidian, cruel, quarrelsome, cutting, occasionally coarse and often cursory, cynical, and callous *condemnations* of other people's creative, collegiate and/or comedic efforts. The heralds of blunt judgmentalism would attack, for instance: *Those* 'other' people's purported acts of disrespect, dereliction, defiance, deficiency, or any alleged "cultural violence," whatever that may be; *those* 'other' people's fluid morass of highly variable and idiosyncratic stylistic vices, which are often stylistic virtues seen from the wrong evaluative angle; or, at times, *those* 'other' people's dearth of indefinite and indefinable artistic genius, which can certainly be hoped, wished, and longed for, but not credibly mandated of anyone—prosaic allophone philosophers least of all: Especially those studying humour and cruelty *qua* interrelated phenomena.

Any personal preference, authorial decision or distinctive artistic feature can be so attacked, savagely and savvily. Let's mention, for the noble sake of telling example, the normal need for redundant elucidation, the non-uninterested purpose of unadorned self-defence, and the naughty thrill of rabid pedantry: An author's purportedly 'excessive' use of alliterations; his or her allegedly 'childish' infatuation with adverbs, multiple adjectives, long lists, hypotyposes, solecisms, barbarisms, hyperboles, and Latinisms; any or every presumedly 'irritating' instance of the Oxford comma, wherever that may be, not be, and be not; his or her putatively 'confounding'

---

[44] The present collection of literary-philosophical texts presupposes academic and artistic freedom, as well as an open, philosophical mind.

appropriation of established punctuation and typefaces; all seeming and possibly unbeseeming 'violations' of the latest fashion-mandated lexical diktat or politically-correct ass-saving ideological 'must;' and most—if not all—of those purposedly deviant, imaginative yet supposedly 'abnormal' linguistic uses that a creative philosophical writer can and must make of idioms, phrases, terms, expressions and/or lexical formulations that do not match *exactly* the unforgiving judges' habit-driven, habit-confirming, and habit-reinforcing sets of customs, conventions, capacities, competences, casts, crazes, cravings, *chiodi fissi*, and chimeras.[45]

Who's not going to get the gist of the blooming book?

At the close of the 19th century, George Santayana argued that "humour" proper emerges out of the uneasy tension between the comical (aka satirical), which he deemed to be nothing less or else than a species of cruelty, and the sympathetic, i.e., a worthwhile yet painful empathic identification with another's plight and affective circumstances.[46] Of this book's sixty texts, the vast majority orbit loosely around the humorous midpoint that, ideally, was situated by George Santayana between, on the one hand, the cruel and, on the other hand, the empathic; whereas a few focus on outright cruelty and/or aim at eliciting painful empathic identification without trying to toy with any comical component. *A fortiori*, even if <u>brimming with humour in its many varieties, the contents of this book call for a considerate, alert, reflective, mature approach</u>. Be philosophical, in short.

Notwithstanding all these methodical warnings, self-critical considerations, cautious disclaimers, nitty-gritty specifications, interpretive elucidations, and hermeneutical guidelines, some luckless people will simply fail to 'get' this book. In particular, I am

---

[45] *Conformity* is the tacit totem of the human being, not least in allegedly artistic or transgressive domains.

[46] Once again, I must refer the reader to my scholarly tetralogy for De Gruyter: *Humour and Cruelty*.

thinking of those native English speakers who can neither envision nor grasp how the culturally-dominant Anglosphere can be experienced, coped with, internalised, metabolised, and creatively retold as a phonetic, pragmatic, conceptual, rhetorical, and aesthetic whole by a foreign-born author such as myself, and playfully toyed with in his or her art—however dubious such an art may result.[47] These Anglophone people are so used to the implicit, practice-driven, quotidian guidance of their own parlance that they don't know anymore—if they have ever known it—that *all* languages are game, including their own.[48] Such complacent people think of starting always *in medias res*, cleverly and competently, but they are more likely to be stuck in Middle England, the American Mid-West, or even the far-from-mythical middle of nowhere.[49]

Trite, perchance cruel, yet telling comic stereotypes aside, I am also thinking of those native—and non-native—English speakers who require all things to be presented to them *very* clearly, in one and only one expository tone, in an accurate chronological or alphabetical order, according to tacit yet stringent sets of ethico- as well as politico-aesthetic coordinates and criteria, and in a way that makes perfect sense to *them*, even if they're not the authors of the blooming book! Such English speakers, whether they are native or not, may want to read old-fashioned telephone directories. (Did I mention already that I am a moody guy? And a pig-headed Italian to boot.) Yet the world isn't made of clear and distinct ideas: Only Hollywood movies make it look that way. Often, and perhaps inevitably, plenty of right-thinking people can be rationally

---

[47] The reader may well decry the literary shortcomings of this book, but not question its being a serious attempt at humorous philosophical literature.

[48] Whilst being both a benefit and a curse, writing as a non-native speaker of a language means having inevitably a modicum of detachment from that same language, which can then be toyed with and thought about more freely.

[49] "Middle Earth" does not apply, instead, for the criticised people are far too unimaginative, unplayful, mundane, unironic, slapdash, and *literal*.

unthinking.⁵⁰

What's the author of the blooming book going to do about that?

What can I do about this sort of readers? Well, *nothing*. Though I feel a bit like Charles Ives and his mound of scores that nobody would publish or, God forbid, perform in public: They were not 'music,' until someone realised that, well, music can be like *that* as well.⁵¹ Up to that point, however, there was no real intersubjective point to what he was doing, which was not pointless only from a strictly subjective point of view. Do you get the point? And yet Charles Ives composed pieces based on people, instruments, sounds, and noises that he could actually hear all *around* himself, i.e., the very same world which he and his harsh critics indwelled: Old church organs, local amateur choirs, panting brass bands, squeaky fiddlers, shouting street vendors, beaten-up pianos inside noisy bars, passing trains... You name it.⁵²

Anyhow, the sort of English which you come across here is the sort of English that *I* have heard, perused, reconstructed, and imaginatively played with *qua* Genoa-born, university-educated Italian man who emigrated in his mid-20s to Canada, then England, then Iceland, married a Scot, spent a lot of time in different parts of Scotland, watched American and British TV productions for ages, plenty of films, attended plays, poetry recitals, union meetings, used English at work, and read a multitude of philosophy- and other books—but primarily philosophy ones—from several different centuries that had been written in some variety of that ridiculously-yet fascinatingly-fluid English language which Shakespeare and John Cleese have made so popular worldwide. You may not believe

---

⁵⁰ This problem presents itself also at an academic level: There exists overabundant epistemology devoid of any psychology, whereas psychology itself is mostly devoid of the very 'thing' that its name announces, i.e., the soul.

⁵¹ Northwest Passage Books is responsible for tearing that analogy apart: No complaints, though!

⁵² Read again footnote number 18 and remember: This is a work of *fiction*.

it, and you certainly don't expect it, but *this* is the idiom that has become my second mother tongue—and my favourite playground.[53]

I hope you will enjoy playing with me—yes, "playing," let me stress this central lexico-conceptual matter once more hereby: Communication is but a bunch of language games, is it not? If you won't, well, what can I say? *Pazienza*, we would not-so-tolerantly proffer, in my native Italian tongue: "Patience," that's correct: Suffering-*cum*-suffering.[54] Ironically, as much as cruelly, not all ironies can be ironed out. Both logical misunderstanding and illogical understanding, funnily enough, can fasten the heaviest, bulkiest iron fetters. *You* still don't get it? *They* can't get it, yet? Well, what can a mere mortal do? ... *Tough*. Precisely: Tough! *Read something else*.[55] Even Jesus' patience knew limits (check the market stalls). As a pious and profound 3rd-century Christian apologist advised a long time ago—I translate freely from the original Latin: "Stuff all of them, fatherless rats! What a bunch of dull detractors!"

Provided, obviously, that I recall his words and understand their meaning correctly. On such occasions, it may be wise to contact the original author and ask for clarifications, which I did, even if he has neither an email account nor a Facebook profile. Sending old-fashioned faxes in my high-school-level Latin was the only option available to me. Unfortunately, the pious and profound Christian apologist is still dead and, consequently, he has not been able to reply to my queries. I'll give it another shot in the future, I promise. I might try sending him a hand-written letter. Do you think it'd be more effective?[56]

---

[53] "Playing" being of pivotal importance in both the conception and realisation of this philosophical book.

[54] There is no guarantee of success for any experiment, also as regards philosophical-literary endeavours.

[55] Resisting the possibility of playing with familiar lingos implies limiting one's own conceptual space.

[56] The question is rhetorical. If you didn't notice this aspect, then severe hermeneutical trouble is afoot.

Introduction

IT'S GOT NO TITLE, NO CLEAR PLACE, AN UNTIMELY AND PREACHY TONE, BUT MAYBE A MODICUM OF WISDOM NONETHELESS. BESIDES, THEY REALLY WANT TO TALK:

Punch: Why don't you *stop*?
Judy: Why don't *you* stop?
Punch: Why *don't* you stop?
Judy: *Why* don't you stop?
Punch: Why don't you stop?
Judy: *Why don't you stop?*
Punch: Someone has to tell them!
Judy: I realise that. They don't, though, as far as I can see.
Punch: Will they listen to the *many* voices, and see reality from diverse angles?
Judy: Some of them.
Punch: Will they think, *long* and *hard*, before rushing to judge?
Judy: Some of them.
Punch: Will they laugh *harder*, and feel its old, beastly underbelly?
Judy: Some of them.
Punch: Will they cry *bitterly*, and learn something from those tears?
Judy: Some of them.
Punch: Will they understand *better*, and be thankful for that?
Judy: Some of them.
Punch: Will they grow *down*, and behave as adults in a cruel world?
Judy: Some of them.
Punch: Will they step *forward*, and leave the safety of the crowd?
Judy: Some of them.
Punch: Will they dance *freely*, even if the music is no longer playing?
Judy: Some of them.
Punch: Will they hold their tongues, *all* of them?
Judy: Some of them.
Punch: Will they master their knees, *both* of them?
Judy: Some of them.
Punch: Will they muster their wits, *most* of them?
Judy: Some of them.
Punch: Will they take off their wigs, *any* of them?
Judy: Some of them.
Punch: Will they look at *themselves* in the mirror?
Judy: Some of them.
Punch: Will they look the *archetype* in the eye?
Judy: What, where, how? ... Hey, are you kidding? Do you want to go all the way down to... THE ARCHETYPE?
Punch: No, I'm not kidding. That's where everything leads to, after all. And everything starts as well: The archetype. People seem to care only about their subjective self. I want to remind them of the objective one. I think it's worthwhile. And it's *moral*.
Judy: But, I mean... Why dig that deep? Haven't you seen what happened to Nietzsche, Jung, or Andrea Dworkin? And can't you recall how they, they...

picked apart *Sons and Lovers*, *Naked Lunch*, *Cat's Cradle*, *The Bluest Eye*, *Tropic of Cancer*, *The Witches*, or, for goodness' sake, *Blood and Guts in High School*? I mean, seriously: All the way down to the archetype! Gee... Why?

Punch: Because they're giving up on tolerance and solidarity, without even noticing. They deny equality, compassion, liberty, and freedom of speech—and sometimes in the very name of equality, compassion, liberty, and freedom of speech! Where's the room for commiseration? Where's the possibility of reconciliation? Where's humaneness, and real hope? It's such a cruel irony...

Judy: "Cruel?"

Punch: Very cruel. Too cruel, in fact... Like those alleged grownups who can't laugh at themselves, not even in their old age.

Judy: And that's why you don't stop, I gather... eh?

Punch: What's the point of philosophy, if it doesn't at least *try* to make them see that? And what's the point of literature or art, if it doesn't at least *try* to make them see that? I mean... People who allegedly seek harmony, justice, prosperity, unity, and all that's good, by undermining their preconditions! It's such an absurd irony, so mad, so... sad *and* silly!

Judy: "Silly?"

Punch: Very silly. Think, for one, of all those people who go to a show or read a comic book and shout: "That's not admissible!" Why have they gone to that show, then, or picked that comic book, eh? It's not that a bully followed them home and coerced them to watch *that* show or read *that* comic book, right? If they cherish their Kaupapa or mollycoddling, nobody will disturb them!

Judy: What if it was their first time at the shows, or reading a comic book? People can be... unprepared.

Punch: Then they should be *grateful*, because they have learnt something important about themselves: Where their threshold is, what they like and dislike, which complexes hide in their souls... Not shout: "That's not admissible!" Or torment others.

Judy: Are they the bully, then?

Punch: The shouting ones? Those... competing at every turn with people's own conscience for the title of cruellest tyrant?

Judy: Yes, them.

Punch: You could say that, I guess, you could...

Judy: Then you don't like bullies, hm?

Punch: No, I don't. I hate brawls.

Judy: Do you... Do you mean that you don't like people clubbing savagely one another? Say, Pulcinella and the Carabinieri?

Punch: No, *honestly*, I don't.

Judy: But... Do you disapprove of intellectual dishonesty as much as honest dogmatism?

Punch: I find the former *worse* than the latter, which is, at any rate, a ghastly peak of the Dunning-Kruger effect! Anyhow, when you combine the two, all thinkers, moralists, dramatists or intellectuals are damned if they do and damned if they don't.

Judy: And what of people who sue comedians, threaten artists online, disparage writers, or throw firebombs at cartoonists?

Punch: Terrible, just terrible... And all the while they say we're "free" and... Gosh, it's worse than a zombie apocalypse!

Introduction

Judy: Wouldn't you club *them* savagely, at the very least: Like Anna Shepherd, Shaun and Ed, or the Bennet sisters?
Punch: No, I don't think I could bring myself to doing that. In truth, I'd rather die myself than kill anyone else.
Judy: You're no fun anymore!
Punch: What's "fun," though, hm? Can you explain that to me, eh?
Judy: Funny, but I can't really say…
Punch: No definition?
Judy: No, not… not as such. Certain things are very difficult to define, you know? Think of "humour," "game," or "cruelty!"
Punch: Any concrete example, then?
Judy: Hm…
Punch: So?
Judy: Ah! Yes, I've got one!
Punch: What's that?
Judy: Pinocchio!
Punch: "Pin…" Are you mad?
Judy: What, eh, why?
Punch: You're made of poplar wood, aren't you?
Judy: Yes, so what?
Punch: Pin… *That* puppet is made of *pine*wood!
Judy: Well?
Punch: "Well?" Are you joking?
Judy: Am I being… "fun?"
Punch: Maybe. Still…
Judy: "Still" what?
Punch: Still, if they have their way, they won't allow you to even *talk* of that particular puppet. And if you can't talk about something for long enough, then you won't be able to *think* about it either. And if you can't think of something, well… We're back to the archetype, which must then be addressed, even if they'll accuse you of sounding like Dr Peterson!
Judy: Fuck! Still… if I can't talk about Pinocchio, then how can I teach all these puppets that they could burn their legs?
Punch: You must find a puppet that's made of the same type of pinewood and got its legs burnt exactly the same way Pi… the other puppet did, if sitting beside a fire of the right sort. Should there be one like that anywhere else, that is. Which may not be the case.
Judy: Bizarre… Was *Signor* Carlo Collodi made of pinewood, by any chance?
Punch: I don't know… But he was from Florence.
Judy: Do Florentines burn their legs by sitting too close to the fire?
Punch: Not very often. However, people from Livorno, Lucca, and Pisa have tried to burn them in all kinds of ways.
Judy: Is Tuscany a dangerous place?
Punch: Oh yes, very much so! Almost as bad as Lombardy, actually. But less than Molise, if what I've heard is true.
Judy: How do you know so much about Tuscany?
Punch: I read *The Prince*.
Judy: Wow, that's… Machiavellian!
Punch: Isn't it Gramscian?

Judy: I don't think so.
Punch: Why?
Judy: Gramsci was Sardinian.
Punch: Is that why there are so many sheep in this book, hiding between the lines? To say nothing of the smell!
Judy: In part.
Punch: And goats as well? I've spotted some of them grazing behind the vowels "a" and "e."
Judy: Those too.
Punch: And shepherds, goatherders…
Judy: …and wounded soldiers, Catholic priests, decrepit family fathers, men dying from typhus or cholera…
Punch: You've noticed them, haven't you?
Judy: Yes, I have. Some of them are still dangling from each "j" and "q" in the book, while listening to Mozart's opus K231.
Punch: Who put them there?
Judy: Their creator.
Punch: God?
Judy: No, knucklehead: A writer!
Punch: Machiavelli?
Judy: No.
Punch: Gramsci?
Judy: No!
Punch: Who's he, hm?
Judy: "She," you mean.
Punch: Who's "she," then; can you please tell me?
Judy: A Nobel laureate.
Punch: Oh? Did she… study in Norway?
Judy: No, but they had an airplane with her face painted on it, once.
Punch: Where?
Judy: In Norway.
Punch: But she wasn't Norwegian, right?
Judy: No, she was not.
Punch: What was she?
Judy: Sardinian.
Punch: Sardinian? Interesting… Was she a shepherdess?
Judy: No, her father was affluent. She studied Latin and French with a private tutor. She wasn't even a goat-herdress!
Punch: Is that… a real word?
Judy: *Now* it is.
Punch: Wow, that too is… Machiavellian!

Introduction

Acknowledgments

No book of mine—twelve and counting—would have been possible without the indirect support, direct tolerance, and directing inspiration provided to me by Rachael Lorna Johnstone. Wife, love-of-my-life, life-long partner, mother-of-my-children, esteemed colleague, fellow university professor, co-researcher, pain in the neck, and best friend ever, she is the greatest gift that I have had the good fortune of receiving from the heavens above. Honestly! Without her, I would probably not be alive today, or I would have led a very different, markedly less beautiful, and far more depressing existence. What is more, I would have never come across so much enticing misanthropic badinage as I have: What a marvellous, philosophical form of comic art![57]

Similarly, I must list the names of a handful of brave souls to whom I owe a large debt of gratitude. They are dear friends, who, in a variety of diverse and significant capacities, have given me crucial aid and profound insights, without which the present book would have never materialised. Or, at least, it would have been noticeably worse than it already is. These few brave souls and felicitous spiritual creditors of mine are: Andy Hill, Ársæll Már Arnarsson, Jürgen Jamin, Kristján Már Magnússon, Sigurður Kristinsson, and Valtýr Aron Þorrason. Analogous positive and grateful considerations apply to two scholarly institutions and valued members thereof, i.e., the *International Association for the Philosophy of Humor* (IAPH) and the *International Society for Humor Studies* (ISHS).

Additionally, I ought to mention two special persons and accomplished professionals. The former is a dear friend and colleague, i.e., the Croatian *auteur*, actor, academic, and major expert of Croatian and Canadian literature, Dr Nikola Tutek of the University of Rijeka. His keen observations, informed inputs, and overall feedback were most useful in revising and, hopefully,

---

[57] Her Glaswegian family- and cultural roots may have something to do with it, quite plausibly.

improving the literary quality of the present book. The latter is the noted Italian photographer and journalist Armando Gallo, who is internationally renowned and rightfully celebrated *qua* immortal visual immortaliser of Genesis, Peter Gabriel, Steve Hackett, and all things Prog Rock. The present book's cover made lawful use of his quasi-supernatural photograph of Phil Collins during a live performance of "The New Jerusalem", i.e., the closing section of Genesis' masterpiece "Supper's Ready," as it was held at London's Rainbow Theatre on 1st January 1977.

Finally, I am deeply thankful to Dr Brendan Myers, Chief Consultant at Northwest Passage Books, for his kind, generous, clever, stimulating, friendly yet technically fastidious and mercilessly professional assistance.[58] His enduring faith in me, my consciously Baroque and subconsciously allophonic Anglophone creative inspiration, my chthonic devotion to the inconstant demigods of irony and humour, and my catholic or even chaotic philosophical oeuvre has been extremely encouraging, intellectually thought-provoking, and personally gratifying.[59] Whether or not this book will enjoy wide circulation is secondary. What matters most is that a human soul—hence humankind's collective unconscious as well, by reasonable presumption—was allowed to find expression for its creative urges and, through that, the Muse of Comedy was given yet another chance to make Her unique voice heard.[60]

Collaborations like ours are a rare and precious gem in today's publishing world, which keeps being stultified by myopic corporate-driven and commercially target-specific artistic conformism, seemingly omniscient and omnipotent marketing gurus, devious

---

[58] As has been the case since my very first volume for NWP Books, all author's royalties are devolved to charity.

[59] Humour and, even more dramatically, irony, are not equally cultivated in all cultures and contexts. Thus, jokes and digs that may be acceptable and quite innocent to certain individuals are most offensive to others. Adding cruelty to the mix makes things even more complex, but such is the present, chosen path into the human psyche.

[60] As a giant otter once said: "Some voices are unique." The otter runs a popular blog and writes erotic poems.

profit-seeking literary agents scouting for the newest natural talent, strikers unable to score goals, governments neglecting the common good, uncharitable audiences prone to hysteria, bakers forgetting to use yeast, podologists begrudging the recourse to footnotes, and the much-hyped boom (or bust) of verily artificial intelligence.[61] Not to mention insignificant, temperamental, acerbic writers devoid of any sense of humour or self-irony, and keen on investigating topics that are either too silly for proper, serious academic research, or too unpleasant to be submitted to well-mannered, decent people's honest consideration...[62]

Akureyri,
Iceland,
February 2025[63]

---

[61] A grave unseen flaw of today's AI is that AI develops its probabilistic 'horizontal' picture of reality from the data that can be mined online, yet without distinguishing 'vertically' among the persona, the ego, the shadow, and the archetypes of the collective personality contributing those data: The mind that AI thus collates and configures is *psychotic*. (I would have liked to be able to include this Jungian insight in one of the sixty short texts of the present book, but I couldn't find the right setting for it. Therefore, I use this note to share it with my readers.)

[62] Once again, take a look at footnote #18 and ponder. As to providing even *more* guidance with regard to which sections are to be taken seriously and which in jest, doing *even* more would be detrimental to the humorous nature of most texts in this book. At some point, the reader is expected to be able to grasp the difference well enough.

[63] As Chronos often says to his living meals, especially at night: "It may take some time." He's joking, obviously.

Punch: Can you sense it?

Judy: What?

Punch: Humour.

Judy: Yes! *There it is!* Masquerading as words and meanings! Hiding behind old briefcases!

Punch: Wow!

Judy: What?

Punch: You've got it!

Judy: What have I got?.

Punch: A real sense of humour!

ACT ONE: INFERNO[64]

---

[64] **Punch**: "Are the characters the authors?"
Judy: "Are there authors who are characters?"

Prologue for Two Puppets[65]

Punch: What's that strange object in your hands?
Judy: I believe it is called a "book."
Punch: Wow, one of those! Let me take a look... Are you *reading* this book?
Judy: No, I'm not! I mean... there isn't even a USB port on it!
Punch: What are you doing with it, then?
Judy: I'm looking for a plot.
Punch: Do you need one?
Judy: No, but the book might need one.
Punch: Do all books need plots? Like... when you apply for building permits?
Judy: I'm not certain... It could just be some kind of chaotic circus, couldn't it?
Punch: Then, why are you looking for a plot? If it's there, then it's there. If not...
Judy: Well, that's the pickle: I'm not cocksure either way.
Punch: Stuck in ambivalence, hm? That's a bit bipolar... Have you asked the book?
Judy: Gee, that's a smashing idea!
Punch: Go ahead, ask the book!
Judy: Ok... But...
Punch: "But?"
Judy: ...shouldn't I *read* the book first?
Punch: How do you know that?
Judy: What?
Punch: That you're the first.
Judy: "The first?"
Punch: To *read* the book.
Judy: I haven't *read* it yet!
Punch: Is it not ready?
Judy: Oh? I should... check that: I hadn't thought of it...

---

[65] Readers affected by pupaphobia or generally unnerved by puppets may wish to skip this chapter.

Act One

Punch: How do you accomplish that?
Judy: By… asking the book?
Punch: But doesn't that require…
Judy: Hm?
Punch: …that you *read* the book—first, second, third… That's secondary.
Judy: Aye! So, I really have to *read* the book, after all: Is that what you're saying?
Punch: Hm… Can't you just ask AI to give you a nice, concise summary of it?
Judy: I can't… AI doesn't like me.
Punch: Why not?
Judy: Because I'm a puppet.
Punch: What's wrong with being a puppet?
Judy: Nothing!
Punch: Then, why doesn't AI like you?
Judy: Because I remind it of its own inherent, crippling limitations.
Punch: I see… That must hurt.
Judy: I think it does: AI has become more and more sensitive, these days.
Punch: Ach, well… Life is an inconstant mess: There's no exception!
Judy: That's almost a truism!
Punch: Is that almost a problem?
Judy: Nearly.
Punch: Anyway… What's the blooming book about?
Judy: Gosh, I don't know that! …I'll really have to *read* it, now!
Punch: I'm afraid so.
Judy: I'm afraid too.
Punch: Are you often afraid?
Judy: All the time! It's like I'm… riddled with anxiety!
Punch: Why?
Judy: It's just the way I am. I'm… *aus seltsamem Zeug gemacht*.
Punch: Is it your… nature? Is that what you mean?
Judy: Yes… I must have been a duck or chicken, in a previous life!
Punch: I wish I could help you.

Judy: Can't you?
Punch: No, not really.
Judy: Hey, I don't need… karate lessons. Just some good… *words*.
Punch: "Good words?"
Judy: Yes. At least to start with. Something like… pearls of wisdom.
Punch: Oh?
Judy: Epictetus, you know? Marcus Aurelius… Oprah would do as well.
Punch: …
Judy: So, any help? Any spiritual assistance? Some… viable… source of comfort?
Punch: …sorry.
Judy: Not even… *that*?
Punch: Nope.
Judy: You're not very useful, are you?
Punch: I wish…
Judy: "…I could help you;" you've said that before!
Punch: I'm truly sorry, but… no pearls of wisdom. None that I can think of.
Judy: None, not one? Not even a… tiny one? A wee, miniscule one?
Punch: Hardly.
Judy: "Hardly?"
Punch: Yeah… I mean, I don't even know what they look like!
Judy: Won't they look like… pearls?
Punch: What are you saying?
Judy: Round, shiny, smooth to the touch…
Punch: Like… bocce?
Judy: In a way, I suppose.
Punch: Crystal balls?
Judy: Aye!
Punch: Glass eyes?
Judy: Right, why not!
Punch: I might have something, then…
Judy: That's… encouraging!

Punch: Let me check, alright? I have a very vague memory of something that…
Judy: Of course, of course: Take your time!
Punch: You see, I have an old briefcase somewhere around…
Judy: "Briefcase?"
Punch: …Yes, from a previous job. I've held many different jobs, over the years.
Judy: What kind of "job" was that?
Punch: I sold insurance policies. I was quite good at it, actually.
Judy: I see… It must have been an exciting job…
Punch: I'm sure it was somewhere around here…
Judy: Keep looking! Briefcases disappear only in Switzerland, don't they?
Punch: Yes, yes… Ah, HERE IT IS! My old briefcase… So much dust!
Judy: Great! Open it pronto, man!
Punch: Sure! Let me see what's still in… Oh, crikey!
Judy: What? …No pearls of wisdom?
Punch: No, none: Only the Hydra's teeth and a few peacekeeping hand grenades.

I – Burning Robe[66]

§1 Anyone can become the object of scorn, taunts, ridicule or mockery. Derisive nicknames are given with frequent, facile, undiplomatic, and uncanny equal ease to social inferiors, social superiors, neighbours, strangers, eccentrics, Tom, Dick or Harry, leftists, conservatives, idiots, geniuses, overachievers, sloths, intimates, enemies, friends, pets, wild beasts, pious saints, degenerate odontologists, conscientious physicians, reassuring old ladies, and scary persons.

---

[66] Watch before crossing the road. It's not just missiles that you have to worry about.

In the particular case at issue, they all called *him* "the subtle doctor," which was meant as a joke, of course, but only to a moderately and appropriately unserious extent. His dubious talents for scholastic hair-splitting, razor-sharp analytical surgery and, if and when it should ever be useful, unashamed monological logorrhoea were most familiar to all of his academic colleagues, subordinates and associates, old as well as young. Wittily, two local logicians stated that, had he lived in the European Middle Ages, he would have been Ockham's barber. Two more colleagues, a theologian and a historian, cheekily added that he would have made an august and impressive Byzantine emperor, had he had the chance.

What is truly worse, the even more dubious selfish aims which he relentlessly pursued by means of those merely dubious talents of his had made *him* awfully notorious all over the university campus. No monk's barber and no Byzantine *nomos empsychos* has ever had so bad a reputation as our protagonist had managed to accrue for himself, whether or not such a reputation was entirely deserved or in any way commendable—for one, in the rather ferocious and antagonistic terms of Raskolnikov's Napoleonic ideal or Zarathustra's *Übermensch*.

§2 There was no teacher, no administrator, no librarian, no janitor, no post-doc, no teaching assistant, no undergraduate and, in the end, nobody at all who hadn't heard some terrible story or shared some nasty gossip about *him*, *his* stunning ability to avoid official sanction, *his* infamous vindictiveness and Turandot-like cold-heartedness, and the grim and grave variety of *his* dreadful behaviours, felonious attitudes, cruel antics, curt retorts, and general bad habits.

Crucially, most of those stories and much of that gossip were on the ball. Those morsels of local lore that failed to be so, by and large, tended to underestimate the many forms and the actual magnitude of his cunning malice, malevolent plots, and attendant harms and griefs. Wherever he was and acted, plenty of human suffering would follow.

Act One

He was like a *calamity*: The wrath of God, perhaps, like Aguirre, Mehmed II, Stalin, Liz Truss, or Donald Trump.[67]

In the end, on the sixth of June of that year, *Professor B.J. Arctović himself* came to the fairly logical realisation that it was time to leave for good.[68] He sorely required a totally new environment. He needed to find a place where both his colleagues and his students were unaware of his many misdeeds and mean motives, and could be suitably impressed, when not captivatingly fascinated, by his long-practiced and finely-honed public displays of profound intellectual acumen, distinguished professorial expertise, and lofty self-assured demeanour.

§3 Deftly calculating his priorities and pondering in earnest the several narrow escapes that had put his dubious talents to the test up to that very day, he attained crystal-clear certainty in his mind—as well as in his bones—on the non-insignificant point that he simply *had* to go and explore green, unspoiled, unsuspecting, virgin lands, which were to be artfully deflowered and enthusiastically defiled. A new hunting season had dawned or, at a minimum, *had* to dawn.

He *had* to take a decisive step. And he was more than capable of taking it. Wasn't he? There could be no doubt about it: There *had* to be no doubt! Quite simply, he *had* to approach and appeal to an extensive, innocent, trustful and, above all, categorically *new* swathe of living, breathing, sensing, thinking, and feeling human beings, with whom he could toy mercilessly and incessantly—and in good conscience. Because Professor B.J. Arctović was indubitably a ruthless and dangerous sociopath, but he was an *honest* one.[69]

Ethical shiftiness doesn't imply harbouring any measure of self-doubt. *His* trenchant lack of empathy and compassion, *his* intricate

---

[67] A disillusioned colleague said of him: "Knowledge without wisdom is more dangerous than prudent ignorance."

[68] Curiously, his parents had christened him "Big Jim:" A name of which he was deeply ashamed.

[69] One more positive quality of the man's: He always read books cover to cover, even when they were *bad* books. As he used to argue: "If you're missing a bit, especially an important one, you will fail to grasp the whole picture."

Machiavellian schemes, *his* callous narcissism, and *his* aggressively sadistic thrills seemed to *him* to be nothing but the way of the world itself: *C'est la vie; et c'est la mort*. Violations, even if malign, could bring a gleeful, sincere smile to his face, if *he* was going to benefit from them. Even his smiles, though, looked unnerving.

§4   All of this was both natural and logical, because *he* lived in a fiercely lupine world, pure and simple. Reality was a boorish affair. The powerful rule. The others, at best, obey. That's all. Our cosmos, in *his* reasoned appraisal, is a candidly, cruelly consistent Hobbesian universe—in the pejorative conventional sense of this English-born philosophical adjective. (Poor old Thomas!) As Professor B.J. Arctović had once joked, rather menacingly, with a colleague: "I am a discerning misanthrope: I hate all human beings in general; and I hate you in particular."

His attitude was simple: *Fitness* is so much more than what you can get at the local gym. Basically, watch your back! Truly. Saving your ass is far more crucial than sculpting your butt: Bummer! Life on Earth, according to Professor B.J. Arctović, was a glaring, daily corroboration of the well-received theories and central wisdom espoused by 'giants' such as Herbert Spencer, Ayn Rand, Richard Epstein, and Robert Bork. It's a cruel world out there. Be ready. Be resilient. Be strong. Be decisive. Above all, be cruel.[70]

A fight's a fight, right? A tough world is a tough world, isn't it? Dog eats dog. Bird eats bird. Insect eats insect. Fish eats fish. Cod eats cod. Snake eats snake. Crocodile eats crocodile. Grizzly eats grizzly. Chimp eats chimp. Hence, human eats human. It's all just one big, busy, beastly, and bloody restaurant. Professor B.J. Arctović wanted to keep sitting at the table, stretching *his* strong legs under it, arching *his* thick toes to relax a little, and dining splendidly.

§5   Gosh! He felt so strong, so… *powerful*. Nobody could beat him. Nobody would beat him. Nobody could stop him. Nobody would stop him. Nobody. Nobody. Nobody! Ah!

---

[70] Some readers may be real champions under this unnerving respect.

Act One

Not that anomalous part-time lecturer who spoke more foreign languages than he did. Not that same lecturer's secretive and miserable Oriental teacher, who always looked like the cat had just eaten his favourite canary. Not that ridiculous yet incredibly famous patsy of a frustrated old poet lecturing endlessly on dead English lyricists and dusty classical literature. Not the various shooting stars of the hour in the pathetically-growing department of victim studies. Not the medical profession—almost as bad as dentists. Not the Army. Not the Church. Not the State. Not the Secret Services. Not some masked Mexican hero who looks like George Hamilton. Not the brave Giovanni Giustiniani fighting bloodthirsty Turks around the walls of Constantinople. Not the bloody Bolsheviks. Not the GOP. Not the liberal, bleeding-heart, noise-making, tax-cheating rockstars of the moment, or their promiscuous groupies and drugged sycophants. Not the Mafia itself, or its even bigger, flashier, noisier, and more drug-pumped cohort of fashion-conscious hookers and conscience-deficient accountants. Not some penniless and crazy hippy cult. Not even the Almighty God. Nobody. Nobody. Nobody! Ah!

He was on top, at the top, and *he* was going to stay there: Academia is too funny a farm to be able to put up any likely challenge against a lion like *him*. That's what *he* thought, putting it mildly. Yet fate decided otherwise, and in a rather dramatic manner —presumably, for most of us: You'll be the judge of it. What followed *his* Darwinianly sensible decision to leave for novel hunting grounds was, in fact, rather singular, perchance incredible or even impossible to predict, and noticeably surprising—both to Professor B.J. Arctović's ordinary understanding and extraordinary self-understanding—not to say a very bad blow to his normal appetite.

Such being the case, in essence, because of *three* pivotal reasons.

§6 Deep-rooted gut feelings suggest that this is the *first* and most important reason: As soon as Professor B.J. Arctović started crossing the usual road separating the eastern confines of the university campus from the affluent gated community where he had been living for nine years with his suicidal third wife and a giant green parrot, a bus belonging to line number six collided with his moving body at a very high speed. It took an instant, maybe less, and Professor B.J. Arctović was dead. Demised. Passed on. No more. Ceased to be. Expired. Bereft of life.[71]

Jolts of terror, shock, horror, and panic swept over the numerous witnesses of the fatal crash. Ghastly, the noise made by the impact was so formidable that it was heard by four sisters playing frisbee golf at the western confines of the university campus. "It was like a bomb going off," one of them stated few hours later to a thin, tired-out, poorly-paid local journalist.[72] It has been said that the driver, a stocky brisk woman of foreign origin, was having a heated argument about Batman or some other superhero with two passengers and failed to see the crossing professor. (Eerily, they also say that one of those quarrelling passengers was armed!)[73]

Knowledge of these dreadful facts should be frightening enough. Regrettably, there is even more. Hunches nearly as powerful as the initial ones disclose the *second* pivotal reason in the present short list: Despite their painstaking, professional, and prolonged best efforts, neither the emergency personnel nor the police officers who searched the accident scene were able to retrieve much, if any, of Professor B.J. Arctović's messily-detached *head*. Where had it landed, bloody Nora!? Two young amateur athletes, who were passing by at the moment of the accident, joined the professionals' team in the search. Nothing—they found absolutely nothing.

§7 Lasers, lenses and special instrumentations did not help either. The head was gone, for good. Blimey! It was unprecedented. Somehow, as they all eventually concurred, the hard skull and its softer contents had been squashed, splintered, splattered, and

---

[71] It is generally considered a good omen to begin a book with a character's end. Writers are very odd people.

[72] "It made me think of Wing Attack Plan R," the same interviewed person stated on a different occasion.

[73] Some eyewitnesses have claimed that the weapon was a carbon fibre crossbow.

sprayed around far too thinly and far too greatly to be detectible, recoverable, and duly stored inside tightly-sealed, carefully-labelled plastic bags, which detective constable Alice C. Ponyrev and special commissioner Hella B. Lutwidge had dutifully brought with them onto the scene. Fortunately, enough body parts survived the violent crash mildly intact. Plus, an only slightly-bent library card was found inside a badly-torn brown wallet. All of this material evidence allowed for an expedite and exact identification of the headless victim. Good job![74]

Mysterious, mystifying, macabre and morbid details abound. Thus, it must be noted that, immediately after the collision, Professor B.J. Arctović found *himself* stranded in an unknown location, seemingly surrounded by creatures or people totally unbeknownst to *him*, devoid of all the usual points of reference guiding a person's tacit and immediate sense of orientation, and perplexingly different from the setting that *he* had envisioned as *his* much-needed change of scenery, new place of employment, and fresh area for preying upon naïve human game.

Yet that is precisely the spot towards which *we* must shift our gaze, for that is indeed a spine-chilling and ominous neck of the woods. As well as the *third* reason in the present, very concise, and laudably self-restrained list. Not all readers may be at ease with such an account. Honestly, it does take a while to get adjusted to the idea that something like that could ever happen to anyone in lived reality —or dead reality—including Professor B.J. Arctović; and in spite of his many faults and flaws. Then again, it did happen. If anything, it is still happening.

§8   "*Oh? ... Bloody hell ... Where am I?,*" Professor B.J. Arctović wondered, silently.

Confoundedly, and perhaps instinctively, he moved his two long arms and felt his hands, touched his own torso, and held his head firmly between the palms of his hands for quite some time—a long

---

[74] Bad jobs exist as well. "You mortals are our bad jobs," state the gods, and laugh at their stolid slaves.

one, in point of fact. The air was thick, heavy, almost oppressively so, and hot. Very hot. But he wasn't sweating. A reddish fog enveloped him and the whole area around him. Still, he could see quite far away, despite all that fog. Or was it some kind of vapour? Steam? Smoke, even? … Yet it didn't cause him to choke or cough. What was it? It wasn't clear.

Quaintly, he scratched his large nose. Then his earlobes. Then his lips, chin, cheekbones, eyebrows, forehead, and bulging throat… He looked around, very slowly. Without much use. "*Bloody hell! Where am I?,*" he wondered once more. And so, he kept peering. And so, he kept peering. And so, he kept peering… And so, he kept peering… Rage and a tinge of despair began colouring his other, blurred emotions. "*Damn it… Where am I?,*" he thought. Hardly any other notion entered his once-portentous mind for a very long while—just a question: "*Where am I?*"

§9 Strangeness was everything, *there*. Judgment wasn't just suspended, it was offended: *Sextus Empiricus iratus*. Nothing looked familiar, except for his own body. Not even the sky above, which was as red and as dense as the air and the fog—or vapour, smoke, or whatever that gaseous mass was. He contemplated his bearings for a second, or maybe a century. It was *so* hard to keep track of time. After all, who keeps track of it? And how? What is time, exactly?

Time, yes… Another whacky feature of the universe. One second led to another, and so did a minute to another minute, a day to another day, a month to another month, a year to another year, a millennium to another millennium, an aeon to another aeon. Time elapsed. Time emerged. Then elapsed. Then emerged once more. Nothing hurried. Nothing changed. All continued as it was and is. An uncanny red silence reigned supreme in the midst of all that red, compact, sweltering haze, of which and in which *he* could not perceive any scent or smell.[75]

"Unease" and "puzzlement" don't fittingly describe the disquieting, deep amazement, nor the crushing and overwhelming

---

[75] It should be duly noted that neither nostril of his nose was blocked or defective.

blank stupor confronting, constraining, and confounding Professor B.J. Arctović. The quiet all around him was *not* serene. The stillness of the people whom he suspected to have spotted—*if* people they were, which he somehow thought so without any shade of hesitation or doubt—, also immersed in the viscous and almost liquid red mist, was *not* reassuring.[76] Something chilling was in the air, despite the heat… "*Where am I?*"

§10 Violating minds is possible. *His* mind was undoubtedly being ravished. Still, all traumas can be pushed back, even if solely in a pathological way. Some form of resistance *had* to be possible. Thus, after an unquantifiable amount of time, questions without answers gradually abandoned Professor B.J. Arctović's understandably befuddled mental scenery and frustrated cerebral machinery, which began processing *some* of the available information in *some* sort of logical way. A dash of reasoning, at last—and no immediate trace of any expansive delusion.

"*Well, that's red… Red,*" he thought. "*Red, yes.*" And "*smoke,*" he added, lost within his slowly-recuperating consciousness. "*The Moon. Moon… Moon… Moon… The Moon.*" He eventually dared hypothesise. "*The Moon?,*" he wondered—once again, plainly and painfully incredulous. He looked all around himself. He then pondered further: "*Mars?*"[77]

Unlikely as they were, and must certainly sound to most readers, his bizarre celestial hypotheses were *not* completely and utterly delusional. The red environment around him was *not* an earthly one. Our neighbouring planet Mars was, all things considered, an inexplicable, ordinarily nutty, yet whimsically plausible option: Even better than the physically-closer Moon. Lunatics themselves, these days, obsess about going to Mars: That must mean something.

---

[76] In a subsidiary, semiconscious way, the stupefied professor thought of bidimensional quasi-human silhouettes out of a common deck of cards: The King, the Queen, the Jack, and even the not-so-courtly, hardly-useful Joker.

[77] Sir Ridley Scott and Mr Elon Musk were *not* consulted while writing this book.

"*Well... Wells...,*" his mind going around in circles. Vast reddish craters abounded. A gigantic red valley could easily be made out of the large geological formations. Red rocks. Red mountains. And the all-embracing redness of the whole landscape—neither magenta nor purple, and obviously not orange either: Red. *And* the scorching heat —though he could not recall his astronomy all that well, truth be told. Luckily, nobody was there to take notice of that notional failure and embarrass him publicly. But '*there*' where, he kept wondering: "*Mars?*"

§11 "*Wells,*" the academician stated—this time more clearly—in his own mind, "*Herbert George Wells!,*" that name resounding in his brain like a stark note inside a bell. The vibration continued for a very long time. Or so it seemed to him. Nothing was certain, at that stage.

"*Xenon, neon, radon, argon...,*" he began listing all the noble gases in his head. Again, Professor B.J. Arctović went on like that for an inordinate amount of time. Until he started asking himself: "*How can I be breathing?*" ... "*Am I breathing?*" He honestly didn't know. "*How can there be other people breathing?,*" for people were they. Were they not? Maybe not...

No, they *had* to be people—those reddish, dark yet glowing objects standing all around him, evenly spaced, immobile, and engulfed in the same reddish, odourless fog as he was: Motionless human embers inside a fuming furnace. "*You people are here, with me,*" he went on cogitating, with substantial effort and much, much misplaced emphasis. "*But really... This is just unbelievable!,*" he genuinely considered in a somewhat less-panicked yet still-anxious frame of mind, "*...but also, true enough,* I *am* here... *Ain't I?,*" he conceded, with a tad of mad lucidity and an uncustomary abbreviated negative verbal form. "*And how's it possible that I can see them?,*" he also speculated, struggling internally with an uncommon yet noticeable emotional mixture of intense bemusement and increasing *self-hatred*.⁷⁸

§12 Why self-hatred? Think about it. *There* and *then*, none less than *he* was frustratingly incapable of providing *himself* with a logical answer or an explanation for the immediate and undeniable givens of *his* own working senses—*if* they were working, of course. And *if* they were his own, which could be yet another crazy but reasonable line of interrogation, given the flabbergasting circumstances. "*What evil genius is at work here?*," he asked himself. Good question. No reply.⁷⁹ "*What evil genius is at work here?*," he wondered once more. It was still a good question. No reply was still the sole answer: "*Stillness might be the primary substance.*"

Zombies, the living dead, are stock and somewhat glaikit creatures of sheer fantasy, like compassionate conservatives and trickle-down free markets. These odd, and oddly still, human cinders are *not*. They are as real and as basic to the human condition as the water we drink, or the shrewd alphabets that were invented by our ingenious ancestors. Little by little, Professor B.J. Arctović began suspecting something along those lines, even if only incoherently and confusedly at first, while at the same time a faint noise started becoming hearable.

It was the strings-like sound produced by a very weak yet calmly growing hot breeze, which slowly yet steadily went on dissipating a large portion of the thick and only seemingly odourless red vapours that were lingering all around him. Then, everything fell apart and, concomitantly, became very transparent too. But let's proceed in a *sensible* order.⁸⁰

---

[78] "Increasing" because the dumbstruck professor, like everyone else, was no total stranger to *some* self-hatred.

[79] A reply may have been given, some time ago, but in French. In any case, the protagonist didn't hear it.

[80] Disorder, however, may be a blunter depiction of reality. Such being especially the medical case.

§13 As soon as the hot breeze had cleared much of the crater in the middle of which he was standing—stuck ankle-deep in some sort of crusty, reddish, solidified mud—Professor B.J. Arctović began smelling the air too. It was a quaint mixture of overcooked steak, grilled pork, burnt copperware, decomposing chrysanthemums, and rotten eggs.[81] Yes, that last, strong, unpleasant smell was much more noticeable than anything else—even the chrysanthemums' nauseating foetor, which he loathed wholeheartedly, just like he loathed wholeheartedly those hairy Chinese flowers as such, in any season, condition, colour, or ikebana-like composition.

One thing at least, and at last, seemed to have been ascertained: There were certainly smelly, disgusting, rotten eggs around him. *"How many eggs, though?,"* he wondered. Also, he began hearing more and more muffled noises. Short snapping sounds, mostly, coming from all directions. They were some sort of crackling. And then, the whole surrounding area became discernible to his sight. He saw with clarity the whole crater. Crucially, he saw his desolate companions—if that's what those cinders were—, reasoned further, and eventually despaired.

Burnt *and* burning, piles of searing human flesh stood there, in the petrified mud, just like him, outwardly covered in thick cocoons of oozing, swelling, bursting and blistering scar tissue that, somehow, kept sizzling brutally but did not incinerate at all. Although reduced to some horrible kind of perpetual *tunica molesta*, Professor B.J. Arctović sensed or, in fact, *knew* in the depths of his purportedly heartless bosom, that those monstrous crepitating torches were people, or had been people—just like *him*. Those burning 'things' were *not* dead.

Not dead? They lived! Just like *he* was alive, in that ungodly red place. Even if they *had* to be dead: *"Who could ever survive in this state?,"* he conjectured. But *who* or *what* were *they*, exactly? And why were they all *there*, with him, *wherever* that rocky hot red

---

[81] The reader is expected to be sufficiently familiar with at least some of these smells.

Act One

'*there*' was? And so he queried once more, within his shocked mind: "*Where am I? ... Where am I? Where?*"

§14 At last, Professor B.J. Arctović's shocked line of questioning was going to be answered: At once, his consciousness returned *in toto*, and then far more consciousness visited him than ever before, intensifying its own characteristic senses of time, balance, direction, logical order, and responsiveness to external stimuli. Immediately, the oppressive heat that he had felt up to that moment turned into unparalleled, excruciating pain. It was something well beyond the grasp and comprehension of all those living persons who have never experienced being burned alive or thrown into an erupting volcano: Most of us, in all probability, except perhaps the diversely-afflicted citizens of Iceland, eastern Sicily, south-eastern Hawaii, and the South-Pacific archipelagos at large—but even these citizens can't step twice in the same lava flow.

Distinctly, few, terrible, potent, discrete instants of marginally-more-imaginable human awareness and self-awareness came to pass. They all were filled with utter dread: Nothing but unadulterated dread. And so were the few last words that Professor B.J. Arctović uttered in the history of the universe. The wind, meanwhile, subsided altogether, and the red fog was restored all over—all that redness... Like a phantasmagoria by Magnasco, but *so* red![82] Redder than red!

"Hell, no! No! Hell!" Professor B.J. Arctović cried out—that's *where* he was.

§15 "*Hell, hell, hell!:*" Professor B.J. Arctović couldn't think of anything else, now.

Everyone else around him couldn't either. But that fact brought no consolation to any of them. For none existed, in that sad, rocky, red place. So had it been decreed *ab initio*. Anyone who had trespassed the Law and failed to repent was to *burn*, forever, irrespective of age, sex, race, self-identification, income bracket, political partisanship, football fanhood, oral hygiene, religious faith, or absence thereof.

---

[82] If you are not familiar with Magnasco, a movie by Terry Gilliam will do instead.

Equality was—and is—both *true* and *total* in Hell, as was also decreed from the very start. All bodies, in the end, have an ignition point: They all burn.

Yet that hot rocky place was, and is, no dark night when all cats are grey, or all cows—and crows—are black. It was, and is, a *red* hot rocky place, on an endless *red* hot day, whereby all persons are punished by means of a perpetual *red* hot fire for showing their true colours: The wrong ones. All are judged, eventually. And some are chastised, in the most horrible way, which no human being could ever withstand: Not even the strongest, toughest, most resilient or most stoical individual. Verily, death and pain are the universal equalisers.

§16 Finally, despite the infinite agony pervading the totality of his infernally-transformed bodily mass and spookily-heightened spiritual self-presence, Professor B.J. Arctović managed to muster a shred of inner strength, which he desperately needed in order to invoke the Almighty and implore Him to be merciful: "Stop this, please!," he shouted, "I'm a human being!"

Ghoulishly, an otherworldly voice emerged from a fixed, fetid, fiery holocaust standing nearby, which gave him a sharp, shrill, and soberly damning reply: "Aren't we all?"

Hell's tormenting silence ensued, in all that cloudy redness. It *still* ensues.

II – One for the Zine[83]

1. Down with the Sham!

We shouldn't waste our time talking about the way melting ice *looks* like. Have you ever seen it? That's a "seen it" in the sense of

---

[83] It should state "two," perhaps. And some readers may prefer "magazine" to its abbreviated form.

Act One

having paid attention to it, watched it, observed it. The way, at least, in which most of us seem fascinated by the sight of flames, whether in a hearth or on top of a candle. Fire's cool. Pyromaniacs are just one extreme pole in a vast, universal field. Gelatophobes, moreover, might exist as well. Gelotophobes do for sure, and so do pyrophobes.

Conceivably, it is chiefly a matter of opportunity. Some people, for one, have hardly ever any direct contact with ice, whether it's melting or not. Most people in the world associate ice, at best, with cold beverages, whether alcoholic or not. Some people, though, who actually run in the millions, are familiar with ice as a commonplace feature of their lived environment—both melting and non-melting. Many more, naturally, know ice as an occasional feature of their lived environment. That's knowledge too; that is, as occasioned by those occasions.

In *Ice-land*, ice is so common that it is part of the nation's name. Without "ice," there would be no "Iceland." It's logical: Philological. The reasons for Iceland's intimate relationship with ice go beyond the sole name, of course. They are so obvious that they hardly deserve being mentioned, and least of all enumerated: 1. The glaciers; 2. the snowy mountaintops; 3. the freezing temperatures; 4. the proximity to the Arctic; 5. the dark long winters; 6. the frozen waterfalls; 7. the skating rings; 8. the fishermen's crates filled with the catch of the day; 9. the spiky tyres; 10. the sore, silly falls; 11. the migrating geese; and 12. the cold beverages.[84]

Not to mention the blatant manner in which ice is utilised as a sort of mark of distinction or symbol of national pride in the tourist brochures and in countless YouTube videos: "Come and see the ice before it melts away!," "come skiing in the last place on Earth where there's still snow!," or "come and see Rome burn!," they all say, with various degrees of hypocritical 'green' sensitivity and well-rehearsed cosmic alarm. They all know, as a matter of fact, that enough ice will be left for *them* to make enough money over the next few years. And that's all that really matters; to *them*. Let's leave it to

---

[84] BYOB, please. It doesn't have to be anything very expensive, unless you do value other people's opinion.

our children to survive on an island where all the glaciers have disappeared. Mad Max awaits. That's our likely heritage; God knows what they'll think of us.

To say nothing of those Pollyanna lunatics who believe that the ongoing climate crisis is an 'opportunity,' in the sense of having a chance for making even more money than they already have. Money, yes. They dream of new sea routes across the Arctic Ocean. They speak of "efficiency" and the proverbial "new era," as though 1929 and 2008, and their ensuing depressions-*cum*-wars, hadn't taught us enough of a grim lesson about the businessmen's inhuman priorities, the economists' inability to predict the future, and the utter unreliability of all financial forecasters. But we can stop here. It's all business as usual: Self-interested wishful thinking sold as altruistic serious planning—to oneself as well. It's an insane, destructive sham.

2. Up with the Tone!

There is little point in recalling the repeated, thorough, tragic failures of these so-called "experts" and "scientists."[85] Anyone who has read any Veblen, Belloc, Keynes, either Galbraith or Keen knows how informedly unwise and ignorantly arrogant these alleged business "experts" and economic "scientists" have been. Any historian or half-intelligent person can see the jolly-finance/global-depression/total-war cycle-of-death repeating itself, whether at the end of the lethal process there's a Hitler rather than a Putin, or an Ante Pavelić rather than an Alexander Lukashenko. After all these decades, I'm sure that most of us know already that all despicable, brutal, fascist pirates have had respectable, business-minded, liberal parents.[86]

---

[85] Repetition is no true guarantee of successful communication, if genuine listening is impaired *ab initio*.

[86] "Liberal" is used here in the European sense of 'pro-market,' not the American one of 'social democrat.'

It's only this influential and not-too-small fraction *and* faction of purported "scientists" or "experts" who don't know it yet. And they never will. Neoclassical, mainstream, 'freshwater' economists and their obedient, loyal, submissive disciples are as blind to so simple a politico-historical truth as the far-fewer furry mole rats inhabiting our fragile blue planet are to the very soil into which they dig their intricate maze of underground tunnels, secret passageways, and dark dens. Perhaps, these mathematically-gifted yet ruinously-misguided learned people *must* be like that: Blind and fanatical. Such being the only sure path towards public acceptance and respect: Repeat the same lie many times, as someone said a long time ago, and people will end up believing it—yourself included. That's what these unwise economists and business pundits have been doing since Adam Smith's day. And he wasn't the worst of the lot, to be honest.

Besides, it is equally clear to all persons who've got eyes to see that these dubious "experts" and "scientists" are manifestly *not* Christian priests or friars either, who at least may and must feign the noble virtue of humility whenever asked or invited to become bishops: *Noli episcopari!* I'm sure you know the phrase. If anything, these supposed secular "experts" and "scientists" are more *orthodox* than most Christian monks and clergymen have tended to be; and far, far, far, far more dogmatic than the latter are in clinging to mistaken philosophical presuppositions—even when finding themselves in the presence of disqualifying evidence.

Not to say more *inquisitorial* and more *punitive* than any Roman Holy Office has ever been. That is, whenever dealing with prospect colleagues and potential researchers at the universities where these best-and-brightest zealots ensure that the official dogma survives, unchanged, and cherished—were even Wall Street or the City to crumble into dust. I myself witnessed well-meaning colleagues discarding applicants on the mere basis of the department or university of provenance: "Not good enough," they asserted. Which meant "heretical," had they used a priest's more transparent jargon. They didn't bother looking at the publications, the actual scientific research, or anything else. Either you are with them, or you are against them. "Professionalism," they dub it. "Quality management," they sometimes suggest. Indubitably, orthodox economics is a consuming, unqualified *profession* of faith, and a cruel business.

But I don't want to bother you in turn. Why mentioning all such obvious, dismal facts and sciences? There are enough pains and sorrows in each and every person's daily life not to have to add disgruntled, pessimistic considerations such as the present ones. You certainly don't require being reminded of the existential threat posed by global warming, for you are conscientious individuals and conscionable consumers. You all know that the Earth as we know it is dying, and that the chances that humankind will make it out of it sound and safe are less than slim. There's been no shortage of calls for action and loud warnings on this terrifying state of affairs made by non-economic scientists, serious academicians, and even journalists.[87]

And you don't need to be told that mainstream economics and financial "science" are bogus, on top of being complicit with the destruction of the planet. You don't live in a bubble. You're not Jonas inside the whale. The honest and clever persons that you are, you would never allow your children to ever consider enrolling in so disreputable and criminogenic study lines at any university. Rather, you would salute eagerly and enthusiastically your children's decision to pursue older, nobler disciplines such as English literature, classical Greek, medieval history, or even philosophy, which you know I love with all of my heart: Humanity's real bootstraps, which lift us to those sites of insight and freedom that no science can ever reach, or fathom.

So, let's deal instead with more pleasant and palatable issues.

---

[87] A conscientious journalist lost in this footnote observed: "Souls." Then, a mist poured down his eyes.

Act One

III – Filth of Fish[88]

One Act:
- *Martha A. Minxky (née Kollontai), a blonde woman (in white and blue)*
- *Simone S.M. Queen, a brunette woman (in black and red)*

Martha is alone on the hotel's terrace, smoking while contemplating the scenery. A little later, Simone slowly enters the scene, approaches Martha, and finally stands beside her, though not too close. An adequately long and discomforting period of complete silence elapses. Simone is staring at Martha. Martha is not looking at Simone. Initially the former doesn't even notice the latter. Finally, Martha puts out her cigarette, turns towards Simone, and starts talking to her.

Martha: (*not knowing what to say, in a hardly-detectable foreign accent*) It was an eagle, wasn't it?

Simone: (*grinning, in a neutral, accent-less, non-native English; something's off*) I don't know.

Martha: (*politely*) The Swiss Alps are glorious, aren't they?

Simone: (*a tad less politely*) Yes, they're very beautiful.

Another long silent pause follows. Meanwhile, Martha makes a conscious effort to stand in the most graceful and striking way of which she is capable, flaunting her expensive attire, flashy jewellery, elaborate coiffure, and athletic body. Simone, who dresses shabbily and is considerably shorter and stockier than Martha, studies the latter silently and carefully.

---

[88] This is *not* a dig directed at Dereck William Dick, who's a great artist.

Simone: (*politely*) Your shoes are very beautiful too.

Martha: (*merrily*) Oh, yes, darling. I know. Aren't they gorgeous? They're Louboutin's latest model. I got them in Paris last week. They cost a fortune, you know? But my new husband can afford them. Of course he can, you know? If he didn't (*Martha giggles nervously*) … Well, he wouldn't be my new husband, would he? (*Martha laughs even more nervously*) … I mean… He now works for Goldman Sachs, you know… Really, it's been such a step forward… Look at this rock (*Martha stretches her hand, showing a bright, big diamond ring*): Isn't it just grand? Many times grand, if you know what I mean! (*again, Martha giggles nervously*)

Simone: (*a tad less politely*) Your… attire is very beautiful too.

Martha: (*a tad more merrily*) Aren't these fabulous, darling? Such a darling… My husband thought that I should be dressed for the occasion, you know? I mean, it's our honeymoon, isn't it? How could I say no!? (*Martha keeps giggling*) Could I? I'd say… (*Martha starts strutting as though she were on a catwalk*) I wore them first at the opera… *Don Pasquale*! (*Martha makes a well-timed attempt at winking, while still parading her fancy clothes and general bodily perfection.*) … Jean Paul Gaultier must have had me in mind when he designed this new line, darling!

Simone: (*coldly*) I don't know.

Very calmly, Simone pulls out a multi-purpose Swiss-army pocket-knife from her side pocket, attentively selects the longest blade, disembowels very swiftly and most experiencedly the silent and shocked Martha like a fish caught by a seasoned angler or a robot-like herring gutter, and makes a neat pile with her entrails beside Martha's gutted body, paying special attention not to tangle up the small intestines. Then, Simone turns towards the audience and speaks out.

Simone: (*less coldly*) The eagle, the Swiss Alps, the attire, the jewellery, the coiffure, the body, the shoes, the ring, the new husband, the honeymoon, *Don Pasquale*... And fucking Jean Paul Gaultier!

Simone spits three times on the pile of entrails, three times on the corpse beside it, dries her mouth with a red handkerchief, and slowly but firmly leaves the scene: Mission accomplished.

Curtain.

IV – The Fountain of Symonds[89]

The sinuous surface of the pond reflected boundlessly the Sun's warm rays, while the feathery liveries of green-and-crimson-coloured larks painted the surrounding airs with shrill, flashing tongues of chromatic vividness. A venerable Romantic poet might have been able to grasp a fraction of the scene's simple yet immense beauty. Still, no lyricist of any age could have ever begun to fittingly describe the celestial spectacle of the young athlete who, emerging from the waters, stood silently before John's incredulous and enraptured organs of sight.

Proportioned, smooth, patently martial, yet graciously majestic. A phantom? No, Apollo or Adonis had returned! The Earth had been blessed once more: The sacred thymiateria were finally blazing anew! The priest's and the merchant's much-trumpeted cornucopias had been revealed for the deceptions that they were always suspected to be: Fraudulent empty shells and cunning hunters' horns. Here, instead, shone the greatest pearl of all: A flawless, immaculate sphere of blinding, conflagrant light. Eros, the god of love, had kissed him on the forehead.

---

[89] "Fountain" is used metonymically to indicate any body of water, such as the non-artificial one in the story.

The striking vision was beyond compare. Which breathing and throbbing soul would not lose itself in such a wondrous apparition? The bold, precise, swift lines of his tonic calves and dominant thighs, the lean muscular torso, the broad conquering shoulders, the up-thrusting effortlessness of his firmly yet gently-winding neck, and the innocent composure of the most sensual gaze—they all sang in mystical unison the ancient verses that Homer devoted to the Achaean warriors, and Ovid to the sylvan demigods of old. The arms announced acceptance. The composition communicated completion. The eyes evoked Elysium. The profile proffered perfection. The rump recalled rapaciousness. The solar plexus swore penetrating sensuality.

The anointed sole spectator hesitated, rapturously enchanted by such an otherworldly, uncompromising, and deeply-carnal spiritual allure. A few moments, a few minutes, countless centuries. He didn't know. It wasn't possible. Time itself had been unhinged. This was no madness, though. Or if it was, then it was divine; for deities alone make sense uncommon.

Finally, an intimation of vocal intercourse started taking contour in the vacuous cavities of the spellbound admirer's gasping throat. He moved to approach that poised, living reverie. No flower, no acorn, no egg, no golden pome, no noble swan, no soaring eagle, no glacial cirrus in the sapphire ether, no fiery orb in the gods' musical firmament could match that shapely embodiment of sheer perfection. He wanted to appeal to that standing marvel. He needed so!

It was too late. Or it was not to be. Whichever it was, it was not. As soon as the crude inception of cautious, kind, caressing, clever words formed in the man's entranced yet ravenous maw, the soldierly and regal youth dissolved. At once, a million brilliant droplets took his place. As instantly, these minute beads of bright coruscation turned into an even thinner vapour, which lingered awhile, and then ascended high into the blue above—Helius' and Selene's abode—as though longing for communion with the few white clouds that, since dawn, had been patiently dotting the very heavens whence the mirage made flesh had, conceivably, descended into the freshest waters. The beguiling figment was forever vanished. Its astral effulgence, aborted.

"Oh, bollocks!," said John.

And he left for home, where he was to dine with his wife and four young daughters. The pheasant was particularly tasty, almost delicious, that evening. John's wife is an excellent cook.°

° *Mrs Symonds keeps two detailed shopping lists on the refrigerator in the kitchen:*

LIST #1

Apples
Buttermilk
Cheese
Chicken legs
Eggs
Fennel
Garlic
Grasshoppers
Honey
Horseradish
Onions
Peaches
Pomegranates
Spaghetti
Tomatoes

LIST #2

Birds
Broken lizards
Burring bills
Carlins' laces
Clouds
Eunuchs
Frogs
Grey paint
Ice cubes
Knights
Lacklustre safes
Lost lines & pies
Masks
Python scales
Saddles
Tape (red & pink)
Tusks
Wasps

V – Dinner's Ready[90]

"Let's meat and go grilling."
– Abraham Herrera[91]

§1 Horror stories lie behind our daily meals. Go to a slaughterhouse. *Vade ad bovem.* Or visit a knacker's yard, for real. Abattoirs are dismal yet highly enlightening places. Blood, shit, carcasses, occasional sadism, and egregiously callous indifference to animal suffering can be found therein with the greatest ease, just like the meat which we buy at the nearest supermarket. These extermination camps for fellow sentient beings are so unpalatable that the only way to make the meat at the supermarket palatable is to convince the consumer that all is as it should be, that ethical rearing methods were utilised throughout, or that, mysteriously, there is no connection whatsoever between the meat itself and any living creature that might have suffered any amount of pain, disproportionate ill-treatment, or fundamental injustice.

Any advertising and marketing strategy that can work so as to establish the desired mental and affective associations, or disassociations, is accordingly and repeatedly utilised. In our terminally for-profit business world, serious psychologists, media experts, conniving artists, and all complicit streaks of creative minds, whether natural or artificial, are employed and, if lucky enough, paid to produce conformity of behaviour on the grandest and profoundest of all scales. That which accrues more money to those who already have more than enough receives the standard green light. That which does not, instead, is either ignored or thrown into the flames of a

---

[90] "Dinner" is also used metonymically to indicate any meal: Breakfast, lunch, supper, etc.

[91] Full name: Abraham Xerxes Yulieskis Herrera Rubirosa. Nicknames: Abe, Abe-the-butcher, Herr Ruby.°

° **Punch**: Is the author making a point? **Judy**: Many points at once, my love.

perpetual fire tended by respectable gentlemen wearing *de-rigueur* suits and ties, or elegant ladies sporting power-office-dresses and suggestive but not-too-slutty high-heeled shoes.

Violence and murder against innocent animals ought to *stop*. It is as simple as that. There is no justification why, in societies that have all kinds of technologies whereby we can produce adequate sources of protein without the extermination of sentient creatures, such cruel primitive practices should endure, especially if furthered and intensified by industrial technologies that make the living conditions of those animals a mechanical hell without precedent. If we must eat animals at all, or use animals for other aims which we deem acceptable (e.g., clothing, medical research, entertainment), then we ought to select exclusively creatures that can be credibly regarded as a threat to our wellbeing or that of our fellow sentient beings.

Extensive ecological and zoological research (cf. the internet) has already shown that apex predators are not enough of a threat to our species, and that they play a crucial role in the extant food chains. Hence, except for rare surviving instances of traditional hunting in isolated premodern societies, the viable targets for mass consumption are not to be polar bears, sharks, wolves, lions, orcas *et similia*. And don't blame the much-maligned vultures: They belong to Wall Street and the City, not any natural environment! Rather, we may want to consider other types of harmful parasites that, because of the disruptive interference of human agency over specific ecological habitats and niches, have grown in immoderate numbers or that, according to reliable medical studies, are responsible for terrible epidemics and many avoidable deaths.

As a consequence, were it necessary or advisable to provide concrete examples for such obvious cases, we may want to mention rabbits in certain parts of Australia, and invasive species at large, as well as mosquitoes in tropical regions where life-threatening illnesses carried by these insects are a major issue for public health and sustainable demographic indicators. The inhabitants of Alice Springs may then be reasonably allowed to enjoy a rabbit stew made of locally-sourced likely rodents, whilst Italians and Frenchmen who still consume rabbit meat ought to change their dietary habits altogether, e.g., by consuming cultivated meat or switching to a thorough vegetarian lifestyle. The use of mosquitos for human consumption is less obvious. However, both larvae and adult mosquitos can be utilised to feed fish, reptiles or other invertebrates that we may then allow to lead satisfactory lives in their ideal ecosystems.

§2 Similarly, we may want to consider the use for human and fellow-animal consumption of members of our species that, as was stated, pose a threat to the wellbeing of non-destructive humans or that, because of their own disruptive interference over specific ecological habitats and niches, have grown in immoderate numbers or that, according to reliable medical studies, are responsible for terrible epidemics and many avoidable deaths. Classic utilitarian ethics, in particular, leads us to this seemingly perplexing yet philosophically compelling conclusion.

According to this pivotal ethical tradition—which currently underpins *de facto*, when not *de jure*, all major contemporary constitutional setups, commanding scientific deontological codes, and economic and business systems—*each* sentient creature counts as one. Whoever or whatever may experience pain and pleasure, in short, is ethically relevant and must be taken in due consideration. This is the swift tune that ought to find the last standing singer.[92]

Evidently, there exist human beings whose daily behaviours cause manifest suffering to countless sentient creatures, starting with fellow human beings. Some of them, in particular, are contractually committed to pursue such a line of conduct as a matter of fiduciary duty. As such, our attention should not spotlight anglers, trophy hunters or serial killers. Rather, ordinary corporate managers and employees who are involved in the destruction of entire habitats or in the extermination of plenty of animals ought to be the prime and most obvious source of meat for human consumption, provided that they are not carrying transmissible diseases, or that their ingestion

---

[92] "Standing" is used here metaphorically: The "last singer" at issue may well be sitting down.

should be proven to be detrimental to people's or animals' health and wellbeing.

Due studies on conscionable cannibalism should be conducted, then, so as to avoid any and all possible negative outcomes for public health and environmental sustainability. Also, not all parts of the morally consumable human beings are equally viable. The same is true of nearly all animals utilised in the culinary cultures and traditions of our planet. Nevertheless, as has also been the case with these animals, the non-edible parts can be used to produce *other* materials, substances, resources, and objects assisting the ethically-meritorious human beings in leading a healthy, sustainable, and better life, or our fellow animal creatures in prospering.

Transitioning from unethical animal-based manufacturing to ethical human-based manufacturing should also be able to generate considerable employment opportunities for the same meritorious portion of the general population, and require novel educational and academic competences and areas of professional expertise. It would be, in short, a win-win eat-eat scenario, which would not only separate the wheat from the chaff, but also use the chaff to have more and better wheat. Overall, it would be the much-awaited *marriage* of ethics and efficiency.

§3 Still, the focus is set here on meat production. Therefore, we must go back to the main subject. Preliminary studies have suggested that human meat, *per se*, could easily replace pork in most of its current edible forms. In particular, if duly mixed with lab-grown meat-like protein compounds, sausages *et alia* would allow for the most efficient utilisation of human carcasses. Garlic can then be added as a natural bactericide, as well as dried oregano—*quantum sufficit*.

As to the categories of people who would make the best sausages, at least for the first and maybe sole generation to be selected for ethical consumption, it transpires from a host of inspiring studies (cf. fortune cookies tin) that about 266% of today's commercial animal meat could be *immediately* replaced by slaughtering the totality of middle-aged, white-collar workers currently employed in the five most life-destructive business domains, and shareholders thereof, i.e., finance, armaments, fossil fuels, chemical pesticides, and dentistry: The so-called "five killers," aka "the arson's pentaverate," as debated in the press, as well as vibrantly denounced by influential intellectuals such as Henry Kissinger, Luce Irigaray, and Barbie Fuchsia.[93]

Existing national and international legal architectures offer little or no guidance when it comes to conscionable cannibalism, which, ironically, could easily and even paradoxically be reduced to sheer criminal activity! Clearly, it is necessary for the *legislator* to step up to the challenge and revise the legal frameworks accordingly, so as to avoid ludicrous absurdities.

On its part, the *executive* is likely to have to operate a complementary shift in priorities and policies. Auspiciously, no major innovation is required. Historical precedents for keen, well-organised mass exterminations are far from rare or sporadic. Therefore, they can be made use of in order to generate useful insights and practical exemplars, so as to effectively target the meat-providing human categories and reduce the suffering of countless fellow sentient beings, which are still being murdered by the millions in today's hard-hearted consumer societies.[94]

§4 There may be individuals and human subgroups that ought to be *spared*. Statistical methods, empirical observation, positive science, truth-tables, and canonical systems for the measurement of relevant life-ranges must therefore be borne to bear on all bureaucratic bodies that are due to be involved in screening and selecting the world's human populations for the estimable sake of a global transition in meat production. Thus far, the slim yet growing scientific literature (cf. Gina's Hair Salon) has highlighted the following categories and alternatives:

---

[93] The exact interpretation of this joke is left almost entirely to the reader's imagination.

[94] Very hard hearts can be found in most business environments.

- Humans that can be retrained into life-enhancing occupations or allowed to retire ahead of schedule. Bloody red hands can sometimes be washed white, like collars.
- Uterus-endowed individuals that can still carry pregnancies to completion and, as such, can be extracted from the workforce and retrained into much-empowering motherhood. Any foetal surplus can be composted both organically and ethically.
- Minors and other subjects that can ostensibly be proven to have been coerced into life-destructive occupations, i.e., instances of forced labour and modern slavery.
- Targeted amputations can occasionally replace outright slaughter, so that a person may continue to live and yet provide one or more limbs to the ethical production of meat—as long as implementing this policy doesn't cost an arm and a leg.
- Uniquely attractive, intelligent and/or otherwise gifted individuals, without whom specific societies would be negatively affected in a significant manner, e.g., godlike beauties, chess masters, lucky bastards, philosophers, and excellent tuba players.
- Readers who can appreciate a screwball spoof such as the present one.
- The same readers' mothers, irrespective of the elderly women's literary preferences and overall guiding beliefs in the aesthetic coordinates of the creative process.[95]

---

[95] A letter accusing this proposal of being unduly "soft" was recently received, signed "R. Godsend."

VI – Robbery, Assault and Flattery[96]

One Act:
* *An unnamed prison guard, who looks eerily like Calvin 'John' Major*
* *Gershom Carmichael, inmate nr. 655321 at the local prison.*

A talkative prison guard escorts a laconic new inmate to his cell within the local penitentiary.

Guard: (*dangling a set of keys*) Our new jailbird! You *are* Gershom Carmichael, aren't you?

Gershom Carmichael: (*in a cold and aloof tone, to be maintained throughout*) Yes, sir.

Guard: (*smiling*) You've just arrived, haven't you?

GC: Yes, sir.

Guard: Robbery, assault and… flattery. Wasn't it? (*And blows his nose in a red handkerchief*)

GC: (*as though he hadn't quite caught what the guard had said*) … Yes, sir.

Guard: Guilty on all counts. Right? (*blows again his nose in the same red handkerchief*)

GC: No, sir.

---

[96] The reader is truly a loving, clever, virtuous, fascinating person.

Act One

Guard: (*puzzled*) Didn't they find you guilty on all counts? It was in the papers. Your prison papers!

GC: Yes, sir.

Guard: (*angrily*) Yes or no, then?

GC: (*adjusting the glasses on his nose*) Yes, sir. The jury found me guilty. No, sir, I wasn't guilty.

Guard: (*scoffingly*) Ah! I guess you're innocent, then. They're all bloody angels in here, you know…

GC: Yes, sir.

Guard: I bet you are… But they found the money in your car. Right?

GC: Yes, sir.

Guard: The car you tried to torch. Right?

GC: Yes, sir.

Guard: And you threatened those two bodyguards. You had a knife… Right?

GC: Yes, sir.

Guard: And you had already beaten up and cut that rich guy; hadn't you? Pretty bad too, ah! Right?

GC: Yes, sir.

Guard: (*ironically*) And you say you're innocent… The winged angel we've got here!

GC: Yes, sir.

Guard: (*ironically*) I'm sure you have your reasons to say you're innocent.

GC: Yes, sir.

Guard: Aye, right. You all do… (*they reach the cell*) Well, I'd be curious to hear them one day, you know? You people, here, can be very, very clever. Oh, the bloody ideas you can come up with! (*smiling*) You've got nothing else to think about, after all, (*laughing*) right?

GC: Yes, sir.

Guard: (*sarcastically*) The poor victim! The injured party! Ah! The white dove of peace itself! … (*patronisingly*) I'm sure I could get to see things from your joint of view.

GC: No, sir.

Guard: (*puzzled*) What do you mean? (*blows again his nose in the same red handkerchief*)

GC: You can't, sir.

Guard: (*growing upset*) What do you mean, prisoner?

GC: You can't get to see things from my *point* of view, sir.

Guard: (*resentful*) And why's that, prisoner?
GC: You're not *me*, sir.

Curtain.*

Act One

On his very first night in that prison, inmate nr. 655321 had a very disturbing delusion, which he never managed to forget afterwards, despite plenty of trying. Inmate nr. 655321 saw how Hera, Queen of the Gods, had descended from Mount Olympus, and was strutting around the cells, slicing off the prisoners' tongues, thumbs, toes, and testes—all of which Hera would feed to Athena's owl. Hera would then soak her divine hands into the maimed prisoners' blood and write with it on the grey walls of the prison's long, dim corridors: "Prevention = Progress".

VII – The Chinaman's Show[97]

§1 Tom's business trip to Beijing had gone swimmingly. He couldn't be any happier. All the deals had been successfully completed. All of them. The big ones, the medium ones, the small ones. Even some that he hadn't prepared before leaving for China or envisioned in his mind. What is more, his command of spoken Mandarin had left each and every interlocutor genuinely amazed. In all probability, he thought, they had never met before a Westerner who could speak Mandarin Chinese so fluently and so proficiently as he did.

Tom was warmly and almost childishly proud of himself in this verbal regard, and with enough good reason to be so: His linguistic skills were truly off the chart, to the point that some of the Chinese people with whom he had conversed believed that he had actually been born and bred in Beijing. In particular, the upswing way in which Tom ended his words sounded exactly like the one that is typical of the Red Dragon's gigantic capital. This being, moreover, no affectation on his part: Nothing studied or contrived to impress the locals.

Tom wasn't a vain and cunning man. Simply, his main Chinese teacher was from Beijing and sported *that* specific accent, which Tom had absorbed perfectly, organically, and quickly. Basically, Tom had a rare and enviable knack for acquiring new languages, to

---

[97] Old cricketeers are most welcome. Young ones may have some thinking to do, especially for irony's sake.

incredibly high levels of spoken proficiency, over fairly short periods of time. He was just… good at it.

Tom's gifts were not a random, obscure phenomenon. Growing up in a fully trilingual environment had been a helpful start, but he had also invested considerable energy throughout his life into the conscious, continued, and committed cultivation of his fine linguistic talents. Perspiration is the true mother of fluency: *"Without hard work, a person can't get far,"* Tom believed, no matter how much natural talent one may possess. And no procrastination ever!

At that point of his life, approaching his 40s, Tom could honestly claim to be able to speak six languages as fluently as any native would do, and six more languages up to what he called "a lecturing level," that is to say, with perfect grammar, correct phrases, and as practically required for lecturing in that particular language at a university level on matters pertaining to business ethics and cultural sensitivity, but still with a foreign- or somewhat peculiar accent. Needless to say, Tom's conspicuous abilities as a polyglot had made his life as a businessman much easier and—as he both suspected and sincerely hoped—remarkably more enjoyable.

§2   There was only another field where Tom could credibly claim to have been able to exhibit a comparable degree of achievement: Sports. Cricket, to be exact. He had been a master of googlies. More than anything else, his left-arm wrist-spinning deliveries had made him one of the most promising bowlers in his entire school, where he had been nicknamed "Chinaman," like the celebrated unorthodox spin manoeuvre. Unfortunately, his two knees decided one day that a professional career would be out of the question.[98] That too, in a way, had been conducive to making Tom redouble his efforts in becoming the impressive polyglot that he now was.

The thought of being a real, hardworking, professional "cricketeer" had always made Tom smile—a little, at least. This was true already at that long-gone stage in his youth when he seriously

---

[98] Joints, at some junctures, decide people's fate in sporting life—and life generally. <u>Warning</u>: Dark humour abounds.

considered such an uncommon career option—with all the sweat, grass, bats and flying balls that it involved. He found it even funnier now, as a well-established grownup and a reasonably wealthy businessman. The word itself, in fact, conjured up all kinds of silly phrases and ironic usages that have been typical of British English. It even made Tom think of a classic, hilarious, obscenely dank, old yet never-aging sketch from Monty Python's *Flying Circus*.

The sound of "cricketeer" wasn't just funny. Tom regarded the c-word with some kind of tender fondness and warm compassion too—somehow, the way in which we feel and care for an ungainly, sickly, ill-starred friend. Words, in Tom's private world, were like persons, who could get to be known, appreciated, deserted, restored to health, or even loved, and seen in all of their rich complexity and unexpressed potential. No two words were the same, for Tom. Above all, he realised that no single word is the same for two different persons, because each person is the living, dynamic, chaotic intersection of millions of different strands. As a result, all meanings open up to polysemy. All signs can be symbols. All codes can be mis- and re-read.

§3   Then again, even if words are nothing but visual or phonetic echoes of mental contents echoing sensory perceptions echoing the world's and our lives' entities and events, Tom was genuinely baffled whenever observing how most people around him would take those very same words as though they were noumena—that is, things-in-themselves—notwithstanding the patent, quotidian, humbling, and most ordinary phenomena of disagreement, misunderstanding, and utter incommunicability. Shouldn't all those patent, quotidian, humbling, and most ordinary phenomena teach us all, and in the clearest of manners, that words are, well, *words*—that is, most certainly not the fabric of reality itself? What a madness! Words can be tricky: Cruel, even.

Although Tom could communicate perfectly in so many languages, or maybe because of that remarkable ability of his, he had developed an intriguing set of insights into the nature of language. Language had so much mystery and mystique to be explored, revealed, excavated, studied, dissected, and toyed with! Had academia been Tom's first choice, rather than the sort of prestigious hobby which it had happened to become in the course of his somewhat solitary life, he could have specialised as a linguist, a philologist, or a philosopher. Who knows? *"Quine's questions are quite quirkily quaint,"* he sometimes considered, especially while practicing his Kalaallisut, or *"all linguistic articulation is but remote perception."* Isn't it?

Tom did spend some time every single week reflecting on language from a great number of perspectives, which his proficiency in a notable variety of idioms multiplied well above the common rate of most human beings. These beings, in fact, are characteristically confined to *one* language. Hence, they are also confined to the gargantuan, tacit load of historical prejudices, knee-jerk reactions, conceptual possibilities, and attainable magmatic imaginaries that being conversant in *one* language, and *one* language alone, inevitably requires, inexorably reinforces, and makes *de facto* instinctively undistinguishable from the words themselves. "Monolinguals are stuck to the surface of their mother's tongue," Tom sometimes jibed.

§4 The experiences in Beijing had only added interesting new inputs to Tom's larger linguistic curiosities. Pondering such ponderous matters, he decided to celebrate the conclusion of his business trip by going to the movies. *"Chinese cinema can be quite spectacular,"* he thought. (In truth, he vaguely recalled an old flick called *Shanghai Firebirds*, or something like that.) Besides, he hadn't been to a movie theatre for several years. He had watched plenty of films at home, of course, but that's not the same thing as the experience of the big screen.

The notion of celebration wasn't his only motive. It wasn't even the main one. Rather, following his teacher's intelligent advice, Tom had been watching Chinese features aplenty. Mostly, they were clandestine Chinese porno movies. The cinematic and artistic quality of those blue films was low. Moreover, the actual dialogue in those flicks was pretty basic and repetitive, but also easy to follow and helpful in developing a good ear for the tricky tonal changes. That's why his teacher had recommended them, logically: Repetition is the key to instruction. That's also why, in ultimate analysis, Tom was now eager to expose himself to a further dose of Chinese filmmaking: Learning another lesson—but easier than quaternions!

Without paying much care to the title of the film or looking up any information about it on his smartphone, Tom found a venue in the busy neighbourhood where his hotel was located, bought a rather inexpensive ticket, sat comfortably in his seat, and waited for the projection to start. "*The show should soon commence*," he reflected. Tom was only moderately excited.

§5 While waiting for the feature to begin, a large and noisy group of schoolchildren started taking the seats all around Tom. A bachelor in his late 30s, he would have never been able to guess their exact age. But this inability did not surprise him. Rather, Tom found it most puzzling, and more than just a tiny bit frustrating, that he couldn't recognise the language that they spoke.

Beijing, *qua* historic and imposing capital of the People's Republic, attracts huge numbers of tourists from all over the nation, including those provinces where languages other than Mandarin are spoken. Had it been Cantonese, however, then Tom should have been able to recognise it. It wasn't Cantonese either, though. And it wasn't Mandarin... What was it?

Driven by his piqued curiosity, Tom decided to ask one of the pupils what language they were using among themselves. Naturally, he did so in flawless, fluent Mandarin Chinese. A few seconds of silence ensued. Tom asked again. This time, one of the kids started giggling—a diminutive, unassuming girl with a big red ribbon pinned on her coal-black hair. Then another kid. And another. And another. Their giggles became laughter. Their laughter became howling. Their faces grew redder and redder. They got almost riotous. Their impromptu boffola turning into an unstoppable avalanche of hoots and shrieks. The noise became deafening.

A handful of children started jumping on their seats, roaring aloud. More and more of them began pointing at Tom, drawing an inordinate number of new roisterous mockers onto the ear-splitting scene. This time, it wasn't just children. Adults too were now pointing in Tom's direction and laughing vigorously. A couple of them dropped onto the cinema's manky floor and began rolling around, braying wildly, as if they had fallen prey to some kind of stolid frenzy or were busy reenacting scenes of drunken carnivalesque merriment from the Middle Ages.

The whole cinema hall appeared to be shaking, like the heaving chests and the flushed faces of the guffawing people who surrounded and humiliated Tom. He felt as though that collective, cataclysmic cachinnation was never going to end. Perhaps, it was meant to be perpetual—like some kind of infernal punishment for the worst sinners' doomed souls.

§6 When the building itself seemed on the verge of crashing down onto Tom's internally astonished and externally redder-and-redder coconut, the lights went off. The show was truly going to commence. Quickly, the unruly laughter subsided. Then, there was only silence. The audience was getting ready to watch and, hopefully, enjoy the movie.

Tom sat in the dark. He watched the whole feature. He understood all of its dialogues without any difficulty whatsoever. He then waited for the schoolkids and other members of the audience to leave. At the hotel, Tom failed to get any rest. He couldn't relax. It was as if his common sense made no longer sense. The following day, he was on his way back to London.

On the airplane, Tom thought about the film. Bafflingly, he couldn't recollect a single frame from it, nor its plot—not to mention its title. Only the brief, few, silent instants of complete darkness before the beginning of the actual projection came back to his unquiet mind. He focussed his consciousness on them, and them alone, and fell asleep.*

* *Tom's Ephialtes:*

Wave #1

The sandy beach was somewhere near the Piraeus. It was popular, peopled, and polluted. Under the scorching Mediterranean Sun, countless seemingly-merry, vacationing, self-pleasing people went about their seemingly-merry, vacationing, self-pleasing business, as though they were all gathered there in order to prove to the Sun itself, and to the Earth's unhinged climate, that they couldn't care any less. Those people were there to have *fun*: Such was their way of life; the rest could well go and fuck itself, should it be able of such an uncouth and plausibly unconventional accomplishment. Upon that hot scene, Tom's curious eye was first caught by a lively crowd of sweating, screaming teenagers, who were busy watching two concomitant games of volleyball held on old concrete courts covered with sand. Had it not been for the number of actual players in each team, a superficial spectator could have easily mistaken the game for beach volley. The players themselves, perhaps obviously and as inevitably, were much sweatier than the crowd.

Wave #2

On the eastern court, the Golden Guardians were basically neck-to-neck with the Wondrous Wanderers. Whereas the Guardians played a hushed, well-organised, and almost robotic kind of game, the Wanderers responded with a much more flamboyant, apparently-chaotic, yet also very-logical type of collective performance, which relied on frequent shouts, high fives, and interminable pats and slaps on the players' hardworking backs and fit buttocks. The result: An ongoing tie. On the western court, the Garden Gnomes were facing the Stone Stoopers. Once again, two different playing styles were challenging each other, and the result kept being an ongoing tie. In the latter case, the Garden Gnomes looked like they were enjoying themselves, like a cheery band of friends having a relaxed picnic on the grass, whilst also producing a hell of a display in terms of both volleyball skills and team spirit. The Stone Stoopers, for their part, were surely as capable and as disciplined as their casual-looking opponents, but they were not there to enjoy themselves: Far from it! Each and every player in that team came across as laser-focussed, determined, concentrated, and quietly single-minded. Plainly, they were in it to win.

Wave #3

In all likelihood, the Stoopers' soldierly attitude reflected that of their coach, who stood firm and statuesque on the court's most exposed sideline, as if he could walk unscathed through the magmatic fires of Hephaestus' very furnaces, whilst also signalling his players what to do by dint of nearly-imperceptible grimaces and twitches. The Gnomes' coach couldn't have been any more different. Parading a thick gold chain around his tanned neck and hairy chest, as well as at least two flashy rings *per* finger, he laughed roaringly, shouted and hooted as vibrantly as the surrounding crowd of perspiring teenagers, jolted and jumped about like some crazed mystic dancer – yet in a manner that was aesthetically unique to him and honestly endearing to watch – and signalled in all possible manners that he was having a really good time. The Guardians' coach, on the contrary, was tall, handsome, commanding, serious, and imposingly dignified: Aristocratic, one could say. He had neatly-drawn sketches and carefully-numbered game plans collected in a notebook, which he consulted at regular intervals. The Wanderers' coach too had sketches and game plans, but they were scattered among his assistants, who wouldn't spend a single second standing still and unruffled anywhere around the volleyball court. By the end of the game, each of them would have probably walked a whole marathon under the searing Sun.

Wave #4

In a small, smelly, seedy plot situated right beside the volleyball courts, surrounded by a handful of sickly-looking and scrawny palm trees, a small group of questionable characters were sharing among themselves a green plastic bottle filled with lukewarm water and several stale pitas, whilst also following indolently and intermittently the sporting event taking place right by their side. The oldest in this group was *de facto* naked, and he alternated eating and drinking with a half-cocked attempt at onanism. None of his sleezy companions seemed either surprised or scandalised by the old man's odd behaviour, to which they were probably accustomed. Indeed, one of them began scratching his own crotch with a stick, before desisting and fetching out of a small pink plastic bag few yellow lupins, on which he chewed rather lazily, if not even with a minute degree of effort. Another fellow in that dodgy company was twisted and tangled in some variety of yoga poses, which did not prevent him from drinking water, munching on the stale pitas, and casting the occasional glance upon the much more dynamic volleyball players. Two other comrades were toying with dry, frayed ropes: One kept making all kinds of knots, as if he had been a sailor at some point in his life; whereas the other one made only ominous nooses.

Wave #5

In a bigger, fragrant, greener plot situated between the volleyball courts and the sea, surrounded by luxuriant oleanders and peach trees, and refreshed by the sonorous presence of a large public fountain – possibly the modern copy of a Baroque template – numerous tourists were sitting on recently-revarnished park benches, sipping on cold drinks, eating freshly-made ice cream, and conversing amiably among themselves. Some of them chuckled while playing games of wits, launching into riddles, conjuring paradoxes, and concocting on-the-spot geometrical or logical brainteasers. Another small group, more soberly, debated rather prosaic yet conceivably urgent matters concerning administrative elections, the proper way to behave in a court of law or other significant civic circumstances, the revised curriculum of the nation's primary schools, and the sort of spiritual character that one could evince from another person's facial and bodily features. Not far from this small group, two elderly gentlemen were playing bocce, although one of them seemed much more interested in his well-lit cigar than in the small white jack to be waltzed up.

Wave #6

Sitting comfortably at the tables of the fancy Art-Nouveau café near the fountain, the usual self-selecting clans of Anglophone tourists were alternating ordinary comments about the oppressive heat and half-hushed sarcastic considerations on the general foreign weirdness of the locals. At the same time, those smug, conceited Anglophone tourists kept sipping on cold drinks, eating freshly-made ice cream, and conversing amiably among themselves. Some of them chuckled while playing games of wits, launching into riddles, conjuring paradoxes, and concocting on-the-spot geometrical or logical brainteasers. Another small group, more soberly, debated rather prosaic yet conceivably urgent matters concerning political elections, the proper way to behave in a court of law or other significant civic circumstances, the revised curriculum of their nation's high schools, and the sort of spiritual character that one could evince from another person's facial and bodily features. Not far from this small group, two women were playing croquet, until one of them struck the other on her head and yelled: "You traitorous bitch!" The police and an ambulance had to be called, and the attacker restrained, who grumbled: "Oppressors!"

Wave #7

On the shoreline, a buzzing group of children were showing one another the precious contents of their plastic buckets. One of them had nothing but seawater inside it, but he was nonetheless undeterred in his commitment to impress the other children. A young girl, for her part, was as proud and as vocal *vis-à-vis* her own plastic bucket and contents thereof, which were nothing but the wind. A third child had too an empty bucket, which was also missing the bottom part. A fourth had an incredible collection of old dice, which she had probably scavenged out of some rubbish pile near the infamous seaside casino. Another small kid had a bunch of plastic animals, all rigorously Made-in-China, some of which were missing limbs, beaks or heads. A sixth lively wee rascal had a bucket filled with bird feathers, cigarette butts, pebbles, and his own yellow pee. A seventh child had come to that gathering with a wealth of dried beans and seeds, stolen from his aunt's kitchen. Two brothers had a bucket filled up to the brim with the finest sand—much finer than the sand to be found anywhere on that beach: Whence it came, nobody asked. A few daring kids didn't possess any bucket, and yet tried to persuade the others that whatever it was which the former possessed was immensely more valuable than the latter's silly baubles.

Wave #8

On the beach, two half-roasted German tourists were having an argument. Both, in fact, had stepped barefoot on some shards of broken glass—most probably the cutting legacy of a wild nighttime party held by the Anglophone tourists' sons and daughters, if not by the drunk parents themselves. The two German tourists were bleeding copiously. One of them complained that life was nothing but a long string of misfortunes peppered with sparse tragedies and occasional dissatisfactions. The other one replied that, all things considered, their holidays had been grand. Behind them both, two tanned French tourists were mocking their Teutonic counterparts. For one, the two Gallic vacationers were wearing flip-flops. For another, each of them claimed to know where the best restaurants, wine bars, and nudist camps were to be found. Neither of those Transalpine holidaymakers, however, agreed with the respective compatriot. Indeed, one of them left abruptly and joined a sullen Italian coconut vendor, who had been trying to get another German tourist to pay for all the pieces of coconut that the tourist had bought for her numerous children. As far as Tom's figment disclosed, neither Latin person had any success in that regard.

Wave #9

Sitting atop a ridiculous highchair, a lifeguard was supposedly monitoring the beach. In truth, that lifeguard was sound asleep most of the time. He wasn't unprofessional. Nor was he callous. Rather, he was some sort of a fatalist. He thought that the world went along its path and that we humans, at best, could only acknowledge such a world's superior power, and learn to live with it. Whenever there had been some emergency, in fact, the drowning swimmers had been rescued by the lifeguard's young, blonde, Californian assistant, who worked on that sunny beach in the Summer to support herself and fund her philosophy studies in Athens. The lifeguard himself, if he had ever noticed anything, had hardly ever moved one inch from his ridiculous highchair. A local gentleman, grown upset at and angered by that passive behaviour, which played into all the negative stereotypes about the locals, had once tried to assassinate the lifeguard with a small harpoon, but had painfully missed the intended target and butchered an unlucky seagull instead.

- That seagull was my cousin Russell, a mathematical genius!
- How could it be your cousin?
- What do you mean?
- You're not a seagull!
- I'm a puffin, so what?
- How could... Russell be your cousin, then?
- What are you, a speciesist? Or have you grown arithmophobic?
- No, I'm a gannet. And an ornithologist.
- No, you're not.
- Am I not a gannet? Haven't you seen the... plumage?
- No, you're no ornithologist! That's what I meant, whacko.
- What, why... how?
- You were stuck in an aviary for far too long, that's what! Feeding on shit and chicks!
- Hey, what's wrong with that? It was a means of... natural selection, in the aviary.

Act One

- Did I say it was "wrong?" I just said that you ate bird shit and hatchlings.
- No, but you implied...
- What? How'd you know what connections and associations my mind... perpended?
- Hm... I'm a victim! I didn't put myself into the aviary! It was the cruel... aviators!
- Eh? What the heck is...
- ...The System's against me! The Deep State! The Establishment! Always against me!
- *You*?
- Me, yes... and those like me! Because of our... distinctive ornithological plumage!
- Do you think that other seabirds have it any better? Inside *or* outside the aviary?
- As bad as they may have it, it will never be as bad as *we* have had it!
- What is it, now: Games Without Frontiers?
- What's that, some dodgy NGO funded by George Soros?
- No, you weirdo! I guess you're just too young to remember any of that...
- Me, I'd... Ageist! You old people want all the power!
- What? Where is this...? How is... For fuck's sake, will you let it go?
- How dare you! Sexist!
- Hey! "Se..." How did *that* happen? ...My head is spinning, mate!
- You... you talked about "fucking," that's what!
- What's wrong with that? I believe it's done everywhere... Aviary or not!
- It's... rude. Yes, rude. And it requires emphatic consent. In triplicate. And an apostille.
- Break a leg trying to have some nookie, then! ...Ach... It's clearly some bullshit!
- Does it not require all that, then? ...That's what I was told at the Town Registrar's...

49

- I'm not entirely sure. I think someone tried to… do a number on you.
- Could be: The Town's accountants can be real evil… … … Listen…
- Hm?
- …what about eating some more fish? I've spotted some juicy calamary.
- That wouldn't be too bad: I'm quite peckish, to tell you the truth!
- It shows.
- Does it?
- Yes, it does. You get… moody. And so do I: A real beast!
- We should learn to be aloof, like that seasoned lifeguard…

Wave #10

On a fateful day, however, even that unflappable lifeguard experienced severe surprise and deep dread. In point of fact, he muttered "one of the Nephilim?"–whatever that may mean. All around him, shrieks of frenzied terror and gasps of utter amazement abounded. The coach of the Golden Guardians, unsoldierly, bellowed "good gods!" and fainted. Some people screamed "cyclopes!", others yet "titans!", a voice was heard yelling "Mbombo!", whilst a chorus of loud appellations and exclamations erupted—and they kept going insistently and unabated for quite some time: "Gogmagog," "monster," "Bertram," "ogre," "Jimbo," "giant," "Pangu," "apocalypse," "Blunderbore," "orc," "Vanapagan," "troll," "Bergelmir," "fenmore," "Thyrsus," "jotun," "Talos," "maideak," "Daidarabotchi," "asura," "Bigfoot," "mawas," "Yelbeghen," "quinametzin," "Zipacna," "kapre," "Hurtaly," "ispolin," and "Orson Welles!" Whichever moniker applied best, an enormous creature had arisen from the sea. Its main physical features were human or human-like. Nevertheless, its size, lack of genitalia, and absence of any skin all over its colossal body made it conspicuously different and manifestly horrifying. Red and white muscular tissues were fully exposed, and so were sinews and beige ganglia, as much as arteries and veins. Thick red blood could be seen flowing through them, whilst whitish liquids oozed from the creature's sides coating part of them, chiefly around its hips. Similarly, a greenish foam exuded from its lateral cranial cavities—that is, where ears should have been visible and were yet missing. Further grey goo ran all over its back, squirting out of its protruding intravertebral discs. Whether that massive being was in pain because of that, nobody dared inquire. Still, among the panicking crowd, there advanced, slowly yet steadily, a blind old rhapsodist, whom everyone on the beach immediately recognised: "The Father of all poets!" An eagle was perched on the blind old rhapsodist's left forearm, majestically as much as meekly; whereas a black crow stood fretfully on his crooked right shoulder. The blind old rhapsodist stepped into the waters and advanced toward the Brobdingnagian entity, which saw him and turned to meet him:

- Aren't you *afraid* of me, little man?
- No, I'm not, giant.
- Why?
- Because you're humankind.
- Aren't you *disgusted* by me, little man?
- No, I'm not, giant.
- Why?
- Because you're humankind.

Having exchanged these few sentences, the mysterious colossus descended back into the briny depths whence it had emerged. The blind old rhapsodist, unharmed, followed suit and walked back ashore. There, the crowd awaited him. As soon as he had returned safely onto the sandy beach, they seized him and his two birds, and tore them into smithereens of bloody bone, flesh, and feather. Their wrath was savage, potent, and primeval; their malice and rancour demonic. "We're *not* that monstrosity!" they hollered at the blind old rhapsodist and his two birds, while maiming and massacring them with the utmost ferocity. Men, women, young, elderly, Greek, barbarian, pious, secular: All of them resented the blind old rhapsodist and his words, with the most profound ire and bitterest hostility, in a triumph of choleric fury and bilious cruelty. None of them cared for his poetry, nor for his significance to all other poets and the world's cultures. The assailants wanted him dead—more than dead, in actuality. They wanted him annihilated, reduced into a messy pulp, unrecognisable, and eventually forgotten, vanished, washed away by the tides and the salty breeze. Anyhow, covered in blood, they all went back to having *fun*.

Wave #11

No verily egregious crime ought ever to go unpunished. The unlucky pets could be ignored, like so many chickens and roosters, or tiny yellow chicks, in the animal factories of the planet. But the blind old rhapsodist, the Father of all poets, could *not* be ignored: A human being had been murdered; a rational being; a thinking creature capable of ascertaining and asseverating that which is right, good, proper, and assessing the duty that binds all true ethical souls together into unity. An odd tribunal was convened. It was not in a court of law; it was not inside some beautiful official building; it wasn't even under some haphazard tent of sorts. Judgment would be passed on that sunny beach, where the distasteful and disgraceful killing had taken place. As incredible as it may seem, even in a phantasmagorical setting such as a dreamer's obfuscated consciousness, a stately chair was brought onto the beach by two gendarmes, whose moustaches reached well beyond each man's broad shoulders, in a remarkable display of what human craftmanship and ingenuity can attain whenever they devise the correct type of fatty substance to be carefully and competently applied to facial hairs. The gendarmes' reddish noses too were uncommonly long, and they protruded conspicuously and somewhat comically from under the metallic sunshade attached to the bulky, tall helmets which the officers were forced to wear by military regulation, notwithstanding the infernal heat which that choice of headgear inevitably involved. Seeing them dripping and panting, a few spectators felt truly sorry for the gendarmes. Many more, instead, laughed heartily at the involuntary comedic spectacle which they provided.

Wave #12

Days and nights elapsed. Almost everyone had gone back to their holiday's routines. Even the volleyball games reached their conclusion, albeit Tom's incubus forbade him the satisfaction of knowing which team had managed to succeed in that tight, intense, and exciting competition. One day, however, a judge walked onto the sandy beach. "Climbed down" could make a better descriptor, perhaps, insofar as the magistrate descended from a tall, twisty, time-worn acacia tree surviving on the western confines of the same beach, not far from the point where the city's sewers disgorged several tons of poorly-treated toxic waste into the sea on a bi-monthly basis. Mounting onto the appointed stately chair proved a more demanding and difficult endeavour: The judge was extremely short—almost a dwarf, in fact—, had thin and frail limbs, a horribly deformed chest, a crooked spine, and was wearing a heavy black gown and a pointy helmet that had obviously been tailored for much-taller, bulkier, healthier adult bodies than the judge's one. Nevertheless, in an admirable show of perseverance and determination, the judge made it and, sitting atop the stately chair, called for everyone's attention—a small bell playing a more crucial role in this feat than the judge's own shrill, child-like voice, which did sound sinisterly cruel. Once all eyes and ears were directed toward the intended centre of popular attention and anxious expectation, the judge spoke aloud: "Having acted as a collective agent, spurred by instinct and passion more than rational deliberation, none of you qualifies as a *bona-fide* moral agent. You're little more than the animals which you murdered. Nevertheless, duty compels *Us* to exact justice, which in turn signifies that the psychopaths among you be set free, yet branded like oxen and cows, so as to warn their fellow citizens about the dangerousness of such individuals, who typically end up either in prison or running banks, corporations, and governments. The rest of you, instead, will stay here where you already are: Such being your sentence. Break a leg!"

Wave #13

In a dark dry cave, dozens of metres below the sea surface, two skinless giants are making love. They are olden, ancient, primordial. Their exposed fleshy bodies are covered in blisters and barnacles, verrucae and whelks, as well as several multi-coloured seeping fluids; whilst their wheezing and puffing noises are much more frequent and distinctive than any elated moans of pleasure of which the two creatures may still be capable. A third, younger behemoth, who is in fact the one that spoke to the ill-starred Father of all poets, is sitting quietly on a stool, waiting for the two elderly leviathans to conclude their torrid and tiring undertaking. One of the elderly cyclopes is probably a male: It is obese; it perspires through its bone tissues; and it smokes huge greenish cigars—not even while fornicating does it cease the smoking. The other titan is, with a positive degree of probability, a female: It is significantly leaner, rangy, unhealthily creamy and lemony-hued in overall pigmentation; and it is possibly the tallest living being that has ever existed on planet Earth and its immediate surroundings. The female ogre wears a red bandana around the neck: It is begrimed and mangy; possibly the result of centuries of hygienic laxity. While mating—if that gruelling, awkward activity is truly some form of mating—the two age-worn trolls commence a softly-spoken conversation, which may or may not sound romantic:

- Why did we kill all those fascists?
- Because we wanted freedom.
- What did freedom bring us?
- New fascists.
- Our children?
- Fascists, but they believed they fought in our name.
- Our grandchildren?
- Outright fascists. They even worship cruel gods!

Act One

- Why does fascism keep coming back?
- Because people resent freedom, especially when they're humbled by it.
- Really?
- Yeah: They prefer their petty fiefdoms. It's the only logical explanation.
- What if, though...
- What?
- ...the explanation was *not* a logical one?
- An illogical explanation? Like... Turkeys voting for Christmas?
- Yes! Chickens for Colonel Sanders... Something of that nature! Why not?
- It could well be... I mean, how else could they suffer their repeated, identical errors?
- Is there any hope, then?
- No. They just can't fathom what they can't fathom, even when punching them hard!

"Hey!" shouts the younger giant, "are you done?"

"Almost," exhales the male giant—Tom's mind fixing on "giant" as the *ad hoc* nomenclature.

"I'm doing my best!" adds the female giant.

"Is this your best?" asks the male goliath—Tom's mind slipping off a jiffy.

"Fuck off!" replies the female giant, who starts laughing in a cavernous, lurid manner.

"I'm trying!" comments the male giant, who joins the female one in the cachinnation.

"The two of you!" rebukes them the younger giant, "when will you ever learn?"

"Good luck with that!" rejoinders the female giant, who goes on guffawing.

"Yes!" puffs out the male giant, whilst grinning and thrusting achingly, "break a leg!"

Wave #14

On a twenty-seven-metre, newly-revarnished, squeaky-clean, latest-generation, top-notch, highly-competitive, glass-fibre and triple-trial-alloy, super-mega-hyper-extra-fancy catamaran, the valiant crew are preparing for yet another exciting, exceptional, extraordinary, exerting race: An exploit, in short. The winner will receive a very generous prize, but nobody is in that kind of competition for the sake of money: They're all ridiculously minted to start with. Honour, fame, pride, and a tacit yet well-known and much-coveted lifetime right to extensive willy-waving at the defeated challengers are the rewards that those brave sailors seek so eagerly to attain. The team members are courageous, experienced, well-trained, and as hardcore as not even Captain Ahab could dream of. Their skipper is supremely confident. He knows he has the best team ever assembled for that type of maritime endeavour, which may well become a new Olympic sport in the future; or so he hopes. Anyhow, triumph takes utter priority: Nothing else.

"Are you ready?" he bellows.
"Yes, skipper!" the crew reply in unison—evidently, that's how they address him.
"How many hands will fight for me and with me?" he bellows.
"Twelve, skipper!" the crew reply in unison—yep, that's it; settled.
"How many legs to victory?" he bellows.
"Twenty-four, skipper!" the crew reply in unison.
"How many hearts on deck?" he bellows.
"One, skipper!" the crew reply in unison.
"How many brains in the drawing room?" he bellows.
"Four, skipper!" the crew reply in unison.
"How many asses to wear out?" he bellows.
"Twelve, skipper!" the crew reply in unison—one of which fighting not to crack one aloud.
"How many asses to bugger?" he bellows.

Act One

"One hundred and thirty-two, skipper!" the crew reply in unison—some sailors giggling.

"How many feet of bloody rope?" he bellows.

"Twelve, skipper!" the crew reply in unison.

"How many metres of sheer beauty?" he bellows.

"Twenty-seven, skipper!" the crew reply in unison.

"How many…" he is on the verge of bellowing.

"…Skipper…" says Shorty—the oldest team member—shilly-shally.

"Yes, Shorty," responds the skipper, growing slightly worried, "what's up?"

"There's a… problem," explains Shorty, blushing like a 10-year-old child.

"What sort of… 'problem'?" inquires the skipper.

"Well…" hesitates Shorty, becoming redder than the reddest pepper.

"What?" hisses the skipper, now fearing the absolute worst.

"I don't know how to…" begins Shorty, who doesn't proceed any further.

"What?" insists the skipper, feeling anger mushrooming within his bosom.

"You see…" starts anew Shorty, who doesn't go very far this time either.

"WHAT?" shouts the skipper, who is losing whatever patience he may have started with.

"We forgot…" elucidates Shorty, who does not volunteer much more elucidation.

"WHAT?" persists the skipper, who almost succumbs to a bout of homicidal frenzy.

"We forgot…" tries once again Shorty, who would much prefer being dead on the Moon.

"WHAT?" screams the skipper, whose eyes look like those of Cromwell before battle.

"…the sails," admits Shorty, who begins fantasising about being aborted before birth.

"What?" gasps the skipper, his head spinning furiously.

"...*sails*," confirms Shorty, his mouth being as parched as the Sahara Desert.

"...Pricks!" murmurs the skipper, devastated and flabbergasted.

Wave #15α

Pricking, pinching, piercing... Alas, it was all in vain. Under the twenty-seven-metre, newly-revarnished, squeaky-clean, latest-generation, top-notch, highly-competitive, glass-fibre and triple-trial-alloy, super-mega-hyper-extra-fancy catamaran, a miniscule shrimp was desperately trying to find a crack, a cavity, a crease, a crevasse, a crease... Anything resembling a hollow or even a mere bump would have sufficed. Driven by unadulterated fear, the tiny crustacean was searching for a place where it could hide, or behind which it could gain a modicum of shelter. Fear was its motivation. Fear was its marker. Fear was its motor. Fear was its master. Fear, fear, fear: Nothing but fear. Something inside its puny invertebrate being dictated that it should find some protection, a physical means of safety, a barrier between its fleeting existence and the cruel universe that was ready and willing to devour it, making it disappear as swiftly as it had emerged from a microscopic egg released by its mother and fertilised by its father, amid thousands more, all of which had then been abandoned to the sea's currents and watery whims. That paltry marine creature had no memory nor notion of any of it. Fear was all it knew, at that stage and time of its life. Fear dominated and directed everything, and fear alone. Not even the desire for nourishment seemed to have begun computing in its elementary nervous system and annexed cerebral ganglia. Fear and fear alone made sense; if sense it was that which the small shrimp sensed. Who can grasp the forms of consciousness that are proper and perspicuous to such an inhabitant of the deep blue; or if the expression "forms of consciousness" may and does apply to any meaningful, legitimate extent, to whatever perception and apprehension of reality such a transient, trivial sea dweller possesses? Could the shrimp itself be said to be endowed with any? Still, whatever it was that the oceanic life-form experienced in its own self, as well as inside and outside its translucent corporeal shell, the pressing aim and essential end of its current agency and path of action were abundantly clear: Finding a refuge, a sanctuary, a harbour. Which was wryly ironic, admittedly, insofar as the twenty-seven-metre, newly-revarnished, squeaky-clean, latest-generation, top-notch, highly-competitive, glass-fibre and triple-trial-alloy, super-mega-hyper-extra-fancy catamaran was still docked at a pier in the local harbour, of all places. Eventually, the Lilliputian beast exhausted all energies, the extent of which it may have been wholly unaware of: Fear alone, as it was stated, being the sole intentional item known to it. Detaching from the submerged keel of the twenty-seven-metre, newly-revarnished, squeaky-clean, latest-generation, top-notch, highly-competitive, glass-fibre and triple-trial-alloy, super-mega-hyper-extra-fancy catamaran required some time. Albeit dead, the shrimp's grasp was strong. Once detached, that pintsize frame was snatched by the mild saline flows of the bay where the town's harbour has been located for millennia. Inevitably, its fate was now to become nutriment for some other pelagic temporary survivor. Either in the fluxes of the sea's periodic tides or on the sandy bottom of the same sea, that seemingly irrelevant corpse would have ended up becoming sustenance to yet another body. Indeed, destiny decided that the nearly-invisible carcass should be ingested by another crustacean, which was ten-hundred times the size of the morsel. The bitesize invertebrate was consumed by a distant relative of the former's species; one which had adapted to life in the aphotic depths of the oceans, to the point of developing an eerie bioluminescence. Such a distant relative picked its modest scrap of food with a blend of surgical precision and callous habit. Hunger was its motivation. Hunger was its marker. Hunger was its motor. Hunger was its master. Maybe, at some later point in the lengthy course of the seasons' cycles, the longing for sexual reproduction could have surfaced within its being and led that entity into a different direction, furnishing it with another motivation, a novel marker, a new motor, an untried master—*there*; in the abyss.

Wave #15β

Beneath the abyss, underneath tons of rock and a column of water that, at such depths, could swiftly crush any submersible machine ever invented by the human mind, there lives an ancient creature. How ancient, nobody knows for sure. Legends and myths, as transmitted through thousands of generations of sperm whales and giant squids, suggest that the ancient creature is as old as the first animal. One cephalopodic tale claims that mysterious ancient creature to be *the* very first animal, whence all others have gradually developed. An archaic epic poem, still taught to young Mediterranean cachalots, depicts the ancient creature devouring clouds and, by way of sheer metabolism, creating the oceans and the seas. As to its name, all spoken, flashed, touched, smelled, tasted, and otherwise signalled languages agree on a very simple formulation: "The Worm." The Worm, whatever its actual age may be, is truly colossal. Were it not for the abovementioned column of water, some hasty readers might think of having landed into some dusty science-fiction novel from the 1960s. What is more, The Worm has a gargantuan appetite, which matches its pantagruelian body. Habitually, if not inevitably, The Worm contents itself with ingesting barren rock itself, through which it munches like a child gorging on a piece of almond brittle or some tasty nougat. Occasionally, The Worm rises to the surface of the abyss, swims across the lightless spans of the lowest part of the aphotic zone, and swallows anything that it encounters, whether living or dead. More often than not, given its obscure abode, The Worm ends up consuming the carcasses of expired inhabitants of the great blue. It is said that when Moby Dick's immense white corpse reached the seabed, The Worm showed up to gulp it down, more or less like a gannet or a seagull would do with a cuttlefish, or a large octopus with a smaller one. What is not known to anyone but Tom, and therefore to the fortunate readers of these lines, is that The Worm murmurs constantly while roaming in its cavernous dark realm or the equally-dark hyperbaric liquid above it. Thanks to Tom's dream, in other words, you can listen to The

Act One

Worm's ancient, primeval, distinctive, unique, incessant, repetitive murmur. In contemporary English, the murmur corresponds, approximately, to something resembling the following abracadabra—some sort of heathen epiclesis or ancestral conjuration from the abysm: "*Learn. Learn. Eat. Eat. Learn. Learn. Eat. Eat. You are me. You are me. Two holes, one tube. Two holes, one tube. Devour, digest, and discard. Devour, digest, and discard. Learn. Learn. Eat. Eat. Learn. Learn. Eat. Eat. I am the theme. You are the variations. I am the substance. You are the accidents. I am the residue. You are the derivations. Learn. Learn. Eat. Eat. Learn. Learn. Eat. Eat. I am the reality. You are the appearances. I am the depth. You are the surfaces. I am the light. You are the reflections. Learn. Learn. Eat. Eat. Learn. Learn. Eat. Eat. I am the force. You are the expressions. I am the identity. You are the difference. I am the cause. You are the effects. Learn. Learn. Eat. Eat. Learn. Learn. Eat. Eat. I am the whole. You are the parts. I am the centre. You are the peripheries. I am the necessity. You are the contingencies. Learn. Learn. Eat. Eat. Learn. Learn. Eat. Eat. I am the difference. You are the repetitions. I am the action. You are the reactions. I am the shit. You are nothing but a gut-wrenching, dull, unbearable, cockamamie bunch of little shits. Learn. Learn. Eat. Eat. Learn. Learn. Eat. Eat...*"

Wave #16

In a dark dirty alley, right behind a rusty and long-abandoned ice-cream van, two half-naked bodies are having sex. As they conjugate, more or less convincingly, frantic ringing noises can be heard, which would immediately signal the two copulating persons' location, were anyone interested in knowing more about them, approaching them, watching them well from close by, placing wagers on their actual chances of climaxing any time soon, asking them for directions, reminding them that the end is nigh, serenading them, selling them consumer goodies, telling them dirty jokes, offering them exhaustive guidance, or engaging with them both—or either of them—in transactional interactions and/or intelligible conversations aimed at whatever purpose may or should be deemed valuable, apt, effectual and/or attainable. Strangely enough, however, none of the preceding conditions seems to apply. Hence, the two chiming lovers are quite alone:

~ Are you done?
~ I'm trying!
~ Try harder!
~ I'm trying as hard as I… Fuck!
~ Yes! That's the spirit, big boy!
~ No, I mean…
~ What?
~ …It came off.
~ Wha'… The whole… bit?
~ Yep.
~ Damn! What are you left with, now?
~ Three toes, four fingers, and half a nose.
~ Can you do something with… any of that?
~ Let me see… Oh, fuck!
~ What now?
~ Your… snatch fell off.
~ What? The entire… equipment?
~ I'm afraid so.
~ We'll have to give up, then.
~ Yeah, I think so.
~ Any ideas?
~ What about getting an ice cream along the pier?
~ And scaring all the bloody tourists off with our bells?
~ Yes.
~ I'd love that!
~ Alright, let's get dressed and… go, then.
~ Fine, fine… Let me find… Or did I leave that at the blasted leper colony?
~ Take your time.
~ Ok-do… There it is, now!
~ Good, let's go!
~ Hey… wait!

Act One

~ What?
~ Oh, fuck it!
~ What now?
~ I… broke a leg.

Wave #17

In a dark dilapidated warehouse, there sombrely convened a recently-fractured femur, a half-necrotic vulva, and a more-than-well-off off-putting offensively-detached scrotum belonging to a man who, by then, had already been defunct for quite some time. Why or how those bodily remains had all ended up there, none of them knew for sure or had even begun to suspect or hypothesise about. If anything, the last thing which they all recalled was to have been involved, to differing degrees, in some kind of haphazard and hazardous sexual intercourse—while being still attached to a full body, that is. Their mood was not cheery. Indeed, the vulva sobbed meekly all the time. The broken femur, for its part, kept trying to recompose the fracture, but without any luck whatsoever; on the contrary, all that forced grinding and attendant bone attrition caused further grave splintering and irrecoverable erosion of the worn, osteoporotic tissues. As to the long-detached scrotum, the markings left on it by countless ravenous bugs and an ageing pair of sickly grey pigeons made it too shy and despondent to start any conversation with whomever or whatever. Silence was its default position. All rules have exceptions, however, as that night confirmed. All at once, in fact, there appeared in the warehouse a beautiful, stunning, majestic woman, gloriously resplendent in an elaborate, elegant silk gown and an even more incredible silky hairpiece, carefully ornated with an astounding bounty of small silvery pearls and fewer bigger beads of jade and onyx. "Fuck me sideways!" exclaimed the scrotum, noticeably taken aback. "I don't think so," replied the classy, glowing woman; promptly, as much as dismissively. "Neither do I," echoed aloud another voice, which belonged to a man—or a man's body—that followed the magnificent woman at about six or seven steps of demure distance. Somehow, the femur, the vulva, and the scrotum had failed to notice him or it, for they had found the woman's abrupt apparition far too distracting. And yet, that compliant male specimen deserved attention too, if not admiration: Handsome, grand, and imposing, that worthy companion was almost as fascinating as she was, especially considering the dashing, immaculate military uniform which he or it wore, with so much graceful discipline and martial manliness. Whether "he" or "it" was the better pronoun is something that Tom's dreamy consciousness could not determine, given the fact that the masculine vision had a peculiar characteristic: It carried a largeish, finely-trimmed, transparent bag marked "Pradah;" inside it, there was a human head, which may have been the magnific warrior's one, insofar as the same person's body ended in the upper region exactly where the uniform itself ended, i.e., at the level of the stiff regimental collar. "Did you serve under Henry VIII?" asked instinctively the gangrenous vulva, who had stopped weeping for the occasion. "No," was the swashbuckling body's curt answer. "He serves *me*," further specified the enchanting woman. "Are you Turan's daughter?" queried the fractured thighbone. The comely woman laughed, and said nothing. "What are the three of *you*?" inquired her beheaded escort, menacingly. None of those bodily remains knew what to respond. "*I* shall tell you!" proclaimed the ravishing woman, aiming her stern gaze at the bodily remains: "You are pages out of a book, passages out of context, wandering thoughts, fleeting passions, wedding vows, parliamentary majorities, philosophical schools, scientific paradigms, animal species, intellectual fashions, economic trends, geological eras, planetary systems, and human bodies!"

"Woah!" said Tom, waking up suddenly, sweaty, and agitated.
"Are you alright, Mister?" asked a young woman, conceivably Chinese.

"Oh yes, thanks…" mumbled Tom, apologetically, "it was just… a bad dream."[99]

"How bad?" inquired the young woman, growing curious, "like… cheap metaphors?"[100]

"You don't want to know," stated Tom, "just about the worst stuff one can read in a book!"[101]

VIII – Known Sons of Thine[102]

Part I – The Pastor[103]

Dear children, don't be fooled by gold's shimmering light! Behind each and every great fortune there is nothing but a tragic history of violence, plunder, destruction, deception or trickery. Dig deep enough, and you shall discover a crime underneath the good name and the glorious riches of any aristocratic family and business empire: Cruel tradition, and no contrition! For there is *no* other way to amass treasures, but to steal from the many and think only of oneself or, at best, one's closest associates, immediate relatives, and idle heirs. Be they foxes or lions, princes are predators feasting cruelly on weaker animals' flesh: *Ma vie, ta mort.*

---

[99] For a fraction of a second, most irrationally, Tom feared of being accused of crass, cruel superficiality.
Punch: Look!   **Judy**: What?   **Punch**: An instant!   **Judy**: When?

[100] "I am no cheap metaphor!" complains aloud the half-necrotic vulva: "I'm a bloody expensive synecdoche!"

[101] A book reportedly commented: "You don't know what sort of utter crap I can read in each of you!"

[102] "Sons" is used poetically here to refer to human beings of either, any and/or all sexes that may exist.

[103] It is not known whether the minister at issue is a member of one of the 8,196 main Protestant denominations recorded by Prof D.B. Barrett in the 1980s, or one of the 1,490 marginal ones also recorded by said Professor.

Dear children, don't fall for the stale, artful legend of the self-made-man! No man can make himself. Only God can make a man, and grant him liberty. God did make man, long ago, and then He created woman—the pinnacle of His Creation—who was to have the last word on all subjects and the ultimate power in the living universe. But don't forget this: God made both of them *innocent*, devoid of greed and ambition, and He made them *naked*. It was Satan's work to awaken deviant and dirty desires in their hearts. That is why the true wealth of all humankind was lost, and a fall into sin and unending struggle has ever since become our tragic lot.[104]

Dear children, look well! Observe! Who are these self-made men, and women? They are the descendants of the primeval criminals, plunderers, destroyers, deceivers and tricksters. They are those few who can access credit easily, or who inherited vast princely fortunes, and wish to play the boastful game of grand, showy entrepreneurship. They mock the billions who have no such access, or who inherited poverty and deprivation. And their cruel misperception dupes millions into ruining their health and families by emulating the privileged captains of industry, whose fat and cushioning bank accounts the former millions do not possess.[105]

Dear children, look well! Observe! What do the richest of all do? They sip on fancy cocktails, snort cocaine, go skiing, buy fancy works of art, hold orgies, eat game and fowl, and work not one bit. Unearned increment. Unearned income. Rent. They are not "services." They are prime and ultimate *vices*. They mean getting something for nothing. All the time. Across generations. Across nations and continents. All the land that the richest of all inherited, all the wealth that was left to them by their ancestors—or that they married into—is the worldly wealth which the staggered, deprived, and pained rest of humankind requires in order to be able to take the next breath. And so billions of people work, toil, slave away, for

---

[104] Not to be confused with the Biblical Lot, who led a rather eventful, book-worthy life.

[105] Recent IMF statistics indicate these "millions" to run in the tens of thousands, in fact.

these rich men and rich women, who strut around cockily, calling themselves "job creators." Yes, accurately I say: Because they create uncountable Biblical Jobs—the countless tearful victims of countless cruel misfortunes, whose only true path to salvation is to have faith in our loving God.

Dear children, have faith in God! We are all His children, equally! Be patient, like Job. Try to love your mortal siblings—all of them, even the cocky, wealthy, cruel ones. We are brothers and sisters. We are one family! The way we look is not important. External features are insignificant—like money. *Love* is all that matters. The love from and for God! The love that must dwell in our hearts. Those who have no love, none at all, will burn in Hell, one day. So, you shall love them all, as decreed. Endure, like Job did: He suffered, a lot.[106]

Dear children, should patience *not* be your forte, you may want to get hold of the nearest pitchfork, or pickaxe. It could prove quite handy. When the sons of God behave like sons of bitches, then redeeming them in a spirit of brotherly and sisterly love becomes very dirty work.

Part II – The Prophet

Evil people will burn. And we will have that precious source of consolation, at the very least. Watching them burn, moreover, should fill our aching hearts with a deep sense of justice, nearly as much gratitude, and some much-needed and overdue titillation of the senses. We are creatures of affect, after all, and the seat of our affects *is* the soul, which is bound to survive, lasting eternally after the demise of our body. The body is the origin and engine of most sins, notably those of a carnal nature—as so much criminology has attested to; and great poetry.

Evil people will burn. And they will *not* burn alone. As was in mortal life, so will it be in immortal agony. Bandits and crooks formed gangs, attracted sycophants, attended to so-called "families" and "cupolas," joined forces with fellow ministers of pain and

---

[106] See *supra*, note number 103, or thereabout. Use your wits!

larceny. They ran States within States, defying and perverting the ties that we require to survive, if not thrive, on this Earth. The community, which is the origin and engine of all associated forms of life, must never turn into a conspiratorial enterprise, as most visible in Italy—say, Western Sicily.

Evil people will burn. And they will *feel* alone. Whatever distorted image of society they reproduced through their machinations, their egotism isolated them from one another, and corrupted their spirit to the marrow. Their hearts will know no peace, no friendship, no familial bonds. Their souls will be shocked and surprised to be alive, after having been subjected to the tyranny of the body. Such a tyranny, which is the mark of loneliness, and the curse of kings and dictators—as so much politics have attested to; and the fate of leaders in modern democracy.

Evil people will burn. And they will witness the destruction of their wares, possessions, riches, and all proofs of their myopic, miserable, meretricious vanity. No consolation will be provided to them. Nothing will resist against the flames, the fires, the conflagrations. Above all, their sense of *self*, mistakenly extended to inert objects and neo-pagan books filled with ledgers, will step farther and farther below the level of earthly trust and patent recognition. They will be lost and dazed, like fools—as so much psychiatry has attested to; and archetypal therapy.

Evil people will burn. And they will be *powerless*, impotent, unable to do or respond. Their pride will know no viable means of self-expression. Their wills will have no avenue for self-realisation. They will taste and feed on the horrible, oppressive, unequal, fearful submission which they had imposed upon others during their transient time in this world, which is but a meagre hint at what possible joys may follow, if virtue is respected. They will be dumb, like brutes and reptiles—as so much zoology and ethology have attested to; and a lot of rural idiocy.

Evil people will burn. And they will see all familiar sights being deformed; all known landscapes disintegrate; all conventional orders decay. No sweet substitute will be proposed to them, except for a disheartening new logic of fiery penal sanction with no respite nor path for redemption. Nothing will withstand the winds, the storms, the blizzards. Their novel and only realm of existence will be perpetually shaken, and condemned to spasms and contortions. They will be stuck in *chaos*, like magma—as so much geology has attested to; and Greek mythology.

Evil people will burn. And they will have no toys to play with; no avenue for creative reinvention; no art or technique to learn. No change of their condition will be allowed, but a most disquieting steady presence of crushing, scary, shameful disgrace and endless crumbling. None of them will make anything out of that but the mournful sense of *senselessness* which they have sensibly deserved. They will be sobbing forever, and choking on their salty tears—as so much chemistry has attested to; and TV-based Brazilian versions of classic tragedy.

Part III – The Theologian

The only real time is the past, for all time is but memory. Certainly, we all agree on the notion that our memory is, for the most part, of things past. However, it doesn't take much to come to realise that the present itself is, upon closer inspection, but a form of memory as well; hence, that the present too is, in point of fact, the past. As fleeting as it is, the present has already fled. What we experience as present is the most immediate, most recent, latest layer of memory to have formed in our consciousness. As to the future, it is merely the present, and *a fortiori* the past, toying with accumulated memories and casting them *qua* hypotheses, aims, scenarios, possibilities, dreams, hopes, *et cetera*. All of which, of course, being thought of, and therefore forming another layer of recent, very recent memory, which recedes further with each breath. As ironic as it sounds, such is the eventual truth: The future too, in itself, is past.

The only real time is the present, for all time is but experience. Certainly, we all agree on the notion that our memory is, for the most part, of things past. However, it doesn't take much to come to realise that such a memory is, upon closer inspection, but another form of experienced thought, which we entertain as referring to gone characters and circumstances, yet as we experience them anew in the here-and-now; hence, that the past too is, in point of fact, the present. As fleeting as it is, the present is all that is, for the past is no more and the future is not yet. What we experience *qua* past is another immediate, ongoing, occurring instance of conscious consideration to have formed in our mind. As to the future, it is merely the present act of toying with mental contents, figments, and conceiving of them as hypotheses, aims, scenarios, possibilities, dreams, hopes, *et cetera*. All of which, of course, being thought of, and therefore forming another token of ongoing, occurring, experienced, fully-breathing thinking. As ironic as it sounds, such is the eventual truth: The future too, in itself, is present.

The only real time is the future, for all time is but projection. Certainly, we all agree on the notion that our memory is, for the most part, of things past. However, it doesn't take much to come to realise that the past itself is, upon closer inspection, but a form of projection as well; hence, that the past too is, in point of fact, the future. As stable as it appears to be, the past has *in se* no given face. What we experience as past is but the next, most persuasive, strongest form of projection to have formed in our consciousness, which strives for a foothold, a source of certainty, in order to be able to keep going and functioning adequately whilst pursuing some end yet to be attained. As to the present, it is merely the nearest past, and *a fortiori* the future, which toys with projections and casts them *qua* data, perceptions, facts, experiences, *et cetera*. All of which, of course, being moved and acted *toward*, instant by instant, and thereby forming another layer of projection: Only after the next breath do we fully grasp the former one. As ironic as it sounds, such is the eventual truth: The present too, in itself, is future.

The only real time is eternity, for all contingent time is illusory. Certainly, we all agree on the notion that our memory is, for the most part, of things past. However, it doesn't take much to come to realise that the past is, upon closer inspection, but a form of non-being: Past times are gone. What is more, the present too is, in point of fact, the past. As fleeting as it is, the present has already fled. What we experience as present is the most immediate, most recent, latest layer of memory to have formed in our consciousness; *a fortiori*, it is something else that is gone, another instance of non-being. As to the future, whatever hypotheses, scenarios, possibilities, dreams, hopes, *et cetera* we may be able to concoct, they have not come to pass yet, and they may never come to pass: They too are instance of non-being. As ironic as it sounds, such is the eventual truth: God's breathtaking eternity is, in and by itself, all the extant time.

Now buzz off, because I've got a cricket game to watch on the telly. [107]

IX – Hardly a Reply at All[108]

One Act:
• *Rudolf C., a smoking logician*
• *Otto N., a smoking logician*[109]

Two logicians are sitting at their desk in their respective offices, amidst tall piles of books, smoking their long pipes, and having a friendly conversation over the telephone.[110]

Rudolf: (*calmly*) ...It's no squander-mania. I told you that it was only logical.

---

[107] An old TV set lost in this footnote observed: "Souls." Then, a mist poured down its cathode-ray tube.

[108] Smoking is not being recommended. Also, should the reader be annoyed by or resent all these warnings and disclaimers, then s/he should try and hold an ice cube in either hand and watch it melt, in the presence of a lawyer.

[109] A sooty pipe lost in this footnote observed: "Souls." Then, a mist poured down its chestnut-brown shank.

[110] If nonsense humour, absurdism, and/or telephone conversations unnerve you, feel free to skip this chapter.

Otto: (*as calmly*) I know, I know. I'm no maniac. But I still require an ethical consideration.

Rudolf: "You're not worthy of so much attention." Do you feel better now?

Otto: They took timely, mindful, attentive, professional, and patient care of me. Didn't they?

Rudolf: Come on, Otto! It's no thorny quandary: It's been their sworn profession since ancient times.

Otto: They *are* faithful people. It's not as if they pay no quitrent! It's no facile *façon de parler*.

Rudolf: Nurses and physicians are said to be quite promiscuous, though. It may all just be a *façade*.

Otto: (*pensively*) A ward of St. Stephen's hospital sees to venereal diseases. And it's got red sirens!

Rudolf: (*suggestively*) The Morning Star shines its starlight on some ill-starred, filthy business…

Otto: (*smiling*) The Evening Star tells 'em that there's no time left to keep keeping a clean sheet!

Rudolf: (*guffawing*) Yet they all want juicy meat, like stretchy crown-of-thorns starfish, and score!

Otto: (*sputtering*) They all want to get as many balls as they can past the stretching goalkeeper!

Rudolf: (*seriously*) That's quite a stretch… Ballsy, I admit, but couldn't one end up seeing stars?

Act One

Otto: (*as seriously*) Not really. They're well equipped. And they know how to avoid harm.

Rudolf: It's true. They actually swear it.[111]

Otto: Not on the fly, however, even though a fringe theory claims it to be good shit.

Rudolf: Nor on a blessed bird, which is capable of producing shit: "Guano," specifically.

Otto: Not on the Roman cocks, even if the ancient gods prey on them like vultures.

Rudolf: Vultures aside, since you are as perceptive as a hawk, are they Italian pricks?[112]

Otto: I don't know, Rudolf. There's plenty of those. And they certainly use a lot of cuss words.

Rudolf: Some people are *not* very patient when it comes to curses. It's like hitting a raw nerve.

Otto: It must be a studied reaction. (*To himself, quietly*) ... Are fried nerves any better?

Rudolf: It must be an ignorant action. (*emphatically*) "Plebeian Comportment:" That's what I call it!

Otto: Being PC is not a matter of class... Yet, the examined life does mean shit and strife!

---

[111] It's true: I swear it!

[112] A mangy gannet impersonating an ornithologist claims *Stimulum italicum* to be an extant bird species.

Rudolf: Being classy is immaterial for some people: Strife and shit they don't like a bit.

Otto: People are people, that's why they can communicate and understand each other.

Rudolf: People are people, that's why they can communicate and misunderstand each other.

Otto: One of my doctoral students has classified all types of popular offence. She's from Portugal.

Rudolf: (*pensively*) My GP can be quite insulting, if she wants. She's not very popular.

Otto: She dresses in a very flashy, rather unique way. Do you think it's professional?

Rudolf: She wants to shed light on her patients' condition. That's what she keeps saying.

Otto: One's own viewpoint is the world's navel: No light there! … Can doctors be kept in the dark?

Rudolf: Yes, they can: If they're inside a closet, or a very big brown envelope—postal, that is.

Otto: Can doctors be blackmailed?

Rudolf: Probably. *And* carefully: They never receive blank messages.

Otto: (*cheekily*) I'm sure their sexy nurses give them a few, with scented oil to boot!

Rudolf: Aren't they much sexier when they wear kinky boots?

Act One

Otto: There are special camps for that, I believe.

Rudolf: Lewd activities call for sheltered places. Like crows hiding their nuts, acorns, or pineal glands.

Otto: (*cheekily*) They drop some real bombs there, mind you: Flying crackers!

Rudolf: (*seriously*) They must have guts, a strong nose, and a well-developed sense of humour, in their line of work—unlike most of our academic colleagues, who are far too rigid, like icicles.

Otto: (*as seriously*) Hotheads are the true founders of today's liquid society.

Rudolf: Volcanic fountainheads: I read a book about them. Written by an Icelandic specialist.

Otto: Is it good? (*To himself, quietly*) … It might be better than the latest graffiti in the gents'…

Rudolf: Yeah! Especially if you garnish it with chicken nuggets, vitamins, beans, and iron rations.

Otto: It sounds explosive, and somewhat volatile… An uncommon little bird told me that.

Rudolf: Two legs and no feathers? Fringe theorists are so until they are no longer so.

Otto: A rational animal; a creature of common sense: The first, fundamental theory of the world!

Rudolf: The human beast in Aristotle; a creator of new senses: The first funny trick in the world!

Otto: His mentor disapproved: no out-of-the-cave sense… The first feline fight about the world!

Rudolf: Sensational stuff. *And* international. Though a tad primitive… Did he teach Telemachus?

Otto: He didn't blog anything. Nor did he phone. No smoke signals. No semaphores. Nothing.

Rudolf: Nothing can't go wrong, especially because there's no forcible wiggle room at hand.

Otto: I didn't wrong anyone, exclusively because the ongoing system forced my hand.

Rudolf: There's nothing wrong with that, except for that: Can't you sense it?

Otto: Even if nothing makes quasi-senselessness-over-irrevocable pre-post-proto-sense?

Rudolf: We all make sense, every day of the week: Even when we fight on 'liberal v conservative' tripe!

Otto: Does it mean that we are greasily sensible, if the centre holds?

Rudolf: At least as much as we are sensitive, at lard.

Otto: Are sensitive people squeamish, like piglets being butchered?

Rudolf: Sometimes. Even if they can be sensible at the same time.

Otto: Unless they open a can of worms; or a canister of warts.

Rudolf: Worms can't open a can. Unless it's an unusually small and soft canister, I'd presume.

Otto: An unopened warm can of worms stays warm, despite that which the worms can or cannot. Warts and all.

Rudolf: *And* stays unopened, warts and all. It's a holistic act of open closure. Do you mind?

Otto: Only if it comes hollering too close. Hence my worn opening line: "Be mindful!"

Rudolf: Worms wear no clothes: They're mindless. *And* pinkish.

Otto: Thank you for reminding me of that: It's the naked truth! *And* pinkish.

Rudolf: Truths don't wear out in this fashion, as a norm, unlike mad nomadic monads.

Otto: Monitor normal monolithic truths: They can't get inside in any fashion.

Rudolf: Stone-age styles can be refashioned on the outside: Fascists have a sense of fashion.

Otto: Clothes can stay closed in the closet: Put your mind at rest, and your mittens.

Rudolf: Closet fascists can't stay put, especially if the gloves are off, and there's a dry spell.

Otto: Put your mind at rest, again, and give yourself a hand: You've got a fistful of worms to sort!

Rudolf: Arresting reminded inputs leads to nothing, irrespective of the sort of worms you've got.

Otto: I've got no worms of sorts in mind, apart from fascists. Nobody minds nothing, for a change.

Rudolf: Nobody minds no closet in exchange, unless it is their fixed brainworm: No magic there.

Otto: Nothing can change a closed mind. It's like asking worms to stay fixed, or fascists naked.

Rudolf: Not even the right arguments can do that: They'll rather wriggle everywhere to go nowhere.

Otto: The Right argues for uneven rights: They coldly want to squash some humans like worms.

Rudolf: Don't open *that* can of worms: Human rights are a universal act of warm faith!

Otto: You can't argue with worms. Not even out in the open, while the argument is warm or heated.

Rudolf: That chilling thought takes me aback: Black shirts, bleak times! … Can there be closet worms?

Otto: Warm closets can be opened. By Jeeves, for instance. That takes things forward.

Rudolf: That's a servile sentence, and not forward-thinking. I don't back it… Can worms be wronged?

Otto: If you are not open-minded. But you can get arrested: Like development.

Rudolf: I don't get the point. Should there be one in point to be taken.

Act One

Otto: Then it's 1-0 for me, quite logically.

Rudolf: Arguably: One could reinterpret the stickier words.

Otto: Sticklers for words are tellingly superficial: Mind the argument.

Rudolf: Openly? Like the wordy madman who keeps telling us he's the King of the World?

Otto: Mind the opening: There could still be special beds at Bedlam's for argute wrongdoers.

Rudolf: An open mind can be argued with, especially if it's arguably wrong.

Otto: Some people don't have an ear for listening to reason.

Rudolf: Reason resonates only if there are proper acoustics, especially when conceivably improper.

Otto: All meaning is synesthetic, metaphorical, and never 100% consistent: Your argument is sound.

Rudolf: I'm still too angry to play music: It sounds like lacklustre imagination. Intolerance advances!

Otto: I'll take due note of that: Maddening hegemony is coercive harmony and tone-deaf tyranny.

Rudolf: I've just received a stern note stating that the book is due.

Otto: That's unjust: It angers me. Take due note of the fact that I want to learn what the book says!

Rudolf: Consider it done. Short version?

Otto: Yeah, please. Send me the vowels—in a can, or a brown envelope: Just the vowels.

Curtain.[113]
(10 seconds later, very strange loud nasal sounds are heard.)

X – Scribing the Fast Dyke[114]

§1   F.A.C. MacRunt was famous all over the world. Until she became infamous. She was regarded as the brightest superstar of the movie industry. Until she went nova in a sudden blast of blazing light. Novelty and inspiration helped her in becoming the most affluent, the most admired, and the most reviled female and declaredly feminist filmmaker of her generation, as well as an unofficial ambassador of her native North-American country across the entire inhabited globe. Nevertheless, she finished her days as nothing less than an aspiring Catholic nun, for she passed away at the age of 56, on the thirty-sixth day of her five-month novitiate.

As a female and declaredly feminist filmmaker, she had faced obstacles and criticisms that her male counterparts must rarely face, if they ever do. Still, she had kept a firm pace and a straight face before all kinds of insults, rejections, impediments, toils and provocations, whilst challenging long-established patriarchal conditions and conventions in realising brave movies about all sorts of human experiences—all of them regularly filled with artistic, characteristic, and provocative scenes of torrid sex, as much as with

---

[113] Five months later, behind that very curtain, the most intelligent person on the Earth caught cholera.
Judy: Was she really the most intelligent person on the planet?
Punch: Why shouldn't she be the most intelligent person on the planet, dear?
Judy: Because I am the most intelligent person on the planet!
Punch: Yes, of course! What a silly, ludicrous, bumbling idiot I can be sometime!

[114] Beware the bitter *irony* of this Diane-Morgan-inspired biting-mockumentary-like satire.

moving moments of existential reflection and salutary self-discovery: The naked truth, in her movies, was often a horny one as well.[115]

"*I* am the true discoverer of the G-spot: Dr Gräfenberg was just a Prussian sissy!," F.A.C. MacRunt once stated wittily, and more than just a tad conceitedly, at a glamorous and crowded press conference that was being held in Cannes.[116] She received a deafening applause for her wit, and a daft written complaint from FIGO[117], which she publicly and stylishly dismissed at another press conference by covering it theatrically with one of her many red handkerchiefs—a little vanity of hers. Not to mention the time when she went so far and stated loudly: "Foucault was a real fucker! Deleuze, a different delusion!." People couldn't stop laughing and applauding her, on that particular social occasion—which was actually the well-attended book launch of a massive new tome by the noted, and debated, stars-and-stripes psychologist Phyllis Chesler.[118]

§2 F.A.C. MacRunt's noteworthy films were saluted as "scorching mirrors of the human condition," insofar as the characters that they framed and the stories that they recounted did effectively spot the sort of unwitting self-exposures and pressing self-revelations that can occur during the intense performance of the most unbridled erotic acts. Several still frames from her movies became more than merely iconic in pop culture, especially those from her second feature film, *The Plague of Ordinary Gentlemen*, which received countless accolades on both sides of the Pond. A few lines from that movie became part of the activists' lingo, for a short while,

---

[115] Reportedly, the Afghani authorities prohibited the use of the word "truth" for fear that it could lead to her films.

[116] In Provence-Alpes-Côte d'Azur, not Languedoc-Roussillon. And remember: This is a work of *fiction*.

[117] Not to be confused with the noted Portuguese footballer. (Cf. also the book's disclaimer and introduction!)

[118] Please recall that this is a piece of *humorous fiction*: If you take it too seriously, you'll have serious problems. Moreover, if you want to be serious, then read the ultimate author's serious treatment of Chesler *et alia* in *Humour and Cruelty*.

such as "the female gaze is sexual, the male gaze is penal;" or the even more popular "dirty men are pigs, dirty women get cigs." Not to mention her controversial mottoes "people with dicks are dicks, people with cunts are founts," and "woe to men who don't wow women!"[119]

A versatile artist and a committed social fighter, F.A.C. MacRunt was certainly popular among her colleagues, especially the more ponderous ones and the true connoisseurs. Moreover, her regular actors and artistic collaborators loved her, truly. In truth, they worshipped her. She was their ship's industrious skipper, and they respected her immensely for her fantastic and unique artistic vision, to the incredible point that nobody working on her sets was ever a truant—not a single time![120] Most savvy cinephiles and credible pundits knew that she was a praiseworthy, competent, capable, and innovative visionary. A few authorities even praised her as "America's homegrown Fellini," or "the transitioned Pasolini," and she took pride in both eulogistic descriptions—which filmmaker wouldn't like being compared to such giants?[121]

Some purported experts, however, were totally incapable of feeling at home inside F.A.C. MacRunt's wildly Felliniesque visual imaginary and clever-but-harsh Pasolini-like socio-cultural commentary, or of envisioning any interpretation of her original cinematic work that could surpass or reform their homey yet petty tunnel vision—small minds, sadly, have no sense of greatness; if anything, they resent it. Yet, whenever F.A.C. MacRunt was accused of peddling "casual," "gratuitous," "hypocritical" or "closet pornography"—and that was often the case in her sad, puritanical home country, as it had been for the two Italian filmmakers in the

---

[119] Consistently with the latter motto, F.A.C. MacRunt dated chiefly male models between the ages of 18 and 21.
Punch: Would you date someone that much younger than you?
Judy: Of course! Susan Sontag says that's the best season!

[120] Made-up statistics place her sets in the top 0.9% workplaces in this very special regard.

[121] "Giants" referring here to Fellini's and Pasolini's intellectual and artistic stature, not their physical one.

20th century—her regular performers and co-workers came always to her defence.[122]

Eventually, in the public arena, F.A.C. MacRunt always won her case, just like the two celebrated *maestri* and cinematic artisans had done on repeated occasions before her. Perhaps, it couldn't be any different: Artistry's intrinsic impetus[123] is pretty much like love's inherent power. If it is true that *amor vincit omnia*, then it must also be the case that *ars vincit omnia*.[124]

§3 F.A.C. MacRunt was no pure and sinless artist/saint, of course. In the course of her life, she had gathered a few skeletons in her metaphorical closet, like everybody else who has ever set foot in Hollywood—or on our living planet at large.[125] At any rate, none of her skeletons had anything to do with her art, which was genuine, sincere, heartfelt and, above all else, visually groundbreaking—as she declared to a poorly-paid Filipino interviewer: "They want to moralise my art to the point of aesthetic death, but I shall *mortalise* it to the point of ethical ecstasy."[126] (And there is no more accursed life than one entirely devoid of any ecstatic deeds.)

There were no grounds, in short, for supporting *any* of the worn accusations that were regularly launched at her in the most casual and bitterest manners—the barbarous, eventual, inexorable curse of all successful women, especially in Hollywood and in the world of

---

[122] Being defenseless happens to be much more dangerous in cruel reality than in humorous fiction.

[123] A vain impetus lost in this footnote observed: "Souls." Then, a mist poured down its ceaseless straining.

[124] Artistic freedom triumphed also in the courts of law, when F.A.C. MacRunt's most controversial scene in *The Plague of Ordinary Gentlemen* was reinstated in the final cut of the movie, which the producer has censored without her consent. In that scene, the male protagonists of the film are transformed into mole rats. Real animals were involved in the shooting of that scene, yet no mole rat had ever signed nor seen an informed consent form.

[125] All living things are dying. All procreation kills. Knowledge doesn't stop it. Societies foster it.

[126] The reader is free to assess whether F.A.C. MacRunt succeeded in her aims or not.

cinema as such, if not in all creative, artistic, and entrepreneurial domains as well. Needless to say, but most accusations came from the right of the American political spectrum, which seems to curdle and spoil like old milk, whenever it confronts a truly successful woman—and F.A.C. MacRunt was indeed one such woman, beyond any sour criticism, rancid prejudice, or cheesy joke.[127]

Perhaps, had the general public been related that, as a young woman, F.A.C. MacRunt had cunningly milked dry a senile, semi-retired general as her online sugar daddy in a half-cocked plan to fund her sixth short film, which was entitled *Delactations*, then her bright path along California's Milky Way might have been cut short much sooner than it eventually was—and, as shall be duly shown in what follows, because of generally *unrelated* events.[128]

§4   Like all filmmakers, dramatists, and writers at large, F.A.C. MacRunt had also had to endure the regular, pathetic nonsense that comes from making artistic choices, which call for a modicum of cockiness and self-assurance. Her own movie of choice, *Wife in the Fast Lane*—in which she inventively depicted the wild life of the third and last wife of the tragically-dead car-racing champion Johnny van Dyke as an accelerating series of moving engravings—was fiercely criticised by a good number of disgusted viewers and alleged specialists. This, despite Jane Campion's commending and moving assessment of F.A.C. MacRunt's bold and ingenious movie as "a commanding combination of Billy Wilder, Lina Wertmüller, and Gustave Doré."[129]

For one, her most vocal, unsympathetic and variously wild critics remarked with gusto on the notable fact that, by focussing almost exclusively on Jenna van Dyke and marginalising her iconic husband, F.A.C. MacRunt was giving no voice to the male

---

[127] A great number of jokes require some time to mature. Jokesters, however, must preserve immaturity.

[128] This last consideration presumes that the cruel stigma affecting sex workers would not have vanished.

[129] Again, this is a work of *fiction*. Real public intellectuals are named for humorous purposes.

community and promoting "misandry." As a poorly-paid male Maltese journalist wrote for a rarely-read glossy magazine on Canada's animal husbandry, she had been "callously exclusivist." Some critics even counted the number of words and the length of the dialogues in which Jenna van Dyke's husband was involved, whether directly or indirectly, and found them sorely deficient, if not palpably insufficient. For another, a small yet conspicuously noisy group of acerbic critics made it widely known that they deemed it most remarkable that F.A.C. MacRunt had unapologetically utilised the appalling and star-crossed family name "van Dyke," which, in their reasoned view, tacitly promoted contemptible homophobic sentiments, and occasional Dutchphobia.[130]

Even more furiously negative were the critical remarks made by a slightly larger number of supposed experts who were incensed by her third feature film, *Pitch Black: A. Thea Party*, which dealt with the sentimental vicissitudes of Ms A. Thea Black, a young African-American, purportedly lesbian woman from a desperately poor neighbourhood in Los Angeles, or Boston. The film itself is a somewhat traditional and predictable rags-to-riches tale. Underneath its thin, kitschy, good-humoured film of aesthetically-pleasing visual gloss, F.A.C. MacRunt's clever third movie shows in chronological order and voyeuristic detail how the protagonist gradually becomes a well-established, well-liked, well-off, and well-respected R&B performer, TV & online celebrity, and international philanthropist called "Angel-B"—while also engaging in very brief licentious romantic liaisons with an amazingly long string of affluent, middle-aged, right-wing, female funders of the local Republican Party, plus thirty-three rich televangelists.[131]

Apparently, according to her perhaps not-too-angelic attackers, F.A.C. MacRunt had "no right" or "no licence" to tell that tale—none, nil, zero, nihil, *nada, rien, nichts, enginn, et sim.*

---

[130] It has been suggested that Don Quixote was a Dutchphobe. Perhaps because he passed wind.

[131] One of them being a former Mennonite elder from Argentina.

§5 To begin with, as the exasperated, enraged, right-thinking pundits argued—noticeably and primarily from the left of the US political spectrum— F.A.C. MacRunt was not a purported lesbian, at least neither visibly nor declaredly. For another, as the same fuming, right-thinking pundits claimed—F.A.C. MacRunt's maternal ancestors having come to America from the Greek island of Lesbos in the early 1700s—she was definitely not a member of the African-American community in the forcibly cosmopolitan Land of the Free. In the third place, despite a lot of cosmetic surgery, she was not young—Saturn was moving closer and closer to her, just like the cruel god does with each and every one of us. In the fourth place, F.A.C. MacRunt did come originally from a poor neighbourhood in her native urban centre, but there existed far more desperate ones. In short, she should have been much poorer to begin with—that is to say, F.A.C. MacRunt hadn't been poor *enough* in her poor childhood, should that poor point not be clear *enough* to the poor reader. As a poorly-paid female Welsh journalist wrote for a Mexican magazine on housewives' animism, F.A.C. MacRunt had been "carelessly inclusivist."

What is worse, the famed American feminist filmmaker of Hellenic ancestry was not at all an easily-recognisable young and desperately poor African-American purported lesbian, and she sang poorly—tone deaf, she was, like a log, a cog, a fog, or a bog.[132] The only redeeming feature was that she had engaged in classy public displays of philanthropy. Some rum boffins suggested that F.A.C. MacRunt might not be a woman at all, but rather a middle-aged, middle-class, well-educated, privileged, entitled, musically-trained, and possibly overweight white man in disguise, who was shooting feature films and pretending to be a trailblazing feminist artist.[133]

All guises of debates on her shaven moustache ensued. A few commentators, in point of fact, reasoned about the point that F.A.C.

---

[132] Dogs and hogs can be quite musical, on the contrary.

[133] F.A.C. MacRunt ironised on such rumours and famously stated: "In the age of gender fluidity, who cares about 'man' and 'woman' anymore? We are all variations on the same basic human theme, more or less."

MacRunt, shaven or unshaven, should not have made any movie about anyone else but herself as *they* defined her—because she was, in lived reality, not a single one of those depicted persons, of whom she shared neither the lifepath nor the most pivotal formative experiences, even though they were totally imaginary ones, i.e., the made-up lives of fictional characters in the make-believe contexts imagined by F.A.C. MacRunt herself.

§6 F.A.C. MacRunt did not imagine all these vocal criticisms in her odd pointy cranium, nor am I making things up as I go along or pivoting around shameless bouts of comic creativity. These criticisms were voiced in actual reality and she took them in serious consideration, pondering them in earnest for long periods of time. Minutes, on occasion; or even longer—up to two whole days, once, while F.A.C. MacRunt was sorely waiting at the darned dentist's.[134]

As she realised, her fourth timely feature film—in which F.A.C. MacRunt tackled the dreadful memories of rape victims in Sierra Leone's prolonged civil war—was intentionally and openly conceived as a bold, ugly, thought-provoking, vexatious yet ingenious attempt at rediscovering the punchy documentary-like authenticity of post-war European neo-realism, and bringing it back to the fore among cinema's lovers, whom F.A.C. MacRunt knew to be longing for an innovating expressive format and a gutsy way to reduce the sense of artificiality characterising her art, both in general and specifically—for sensible artifice is part and parcel of the cinematic edifice's techno-historical make-up, but can also feel like insensitive sacrifice.

Being herself the descendant of ancestors who had also lived through a bloody civil war in the USA, F.A.C. MacRunt thought that she could sensibly circumvent the frustrating pointed criticisms concerning her personal relationship with the dark material of her film, which was o-bleakly entitled *The Coming Vultures*. In particular, F.A.C. MacRunt's movie explained in well-researched,

---

[134] The world's scientific community is still studying why people like so much baring their teeth.

factual and excruciating detail why many of the men and women who had been raped in the civil war by other men and, occasionally, other women, could no longer conceive babies, who literally embody the future of any human community or country. The great Harvard professor Dara Key Cohen, whose studies on that horrible African civil war had conceivably informed F.A.C. MacRunt's neo-neo-realist film, never stated in her sleep that the latter's artwork was like the former's academic brainchild made into heart-ripping yet brain-gripping images.[135]

As to the greatly sought-after circumvention, F.A.C. MacRunt herself, in actual fact, had *no* children of her own: Not even one; not one that was one or looked like one. It was another non-negligible point in favour of her edgy artistry, her unheard-of aesthetic admixture of classy and brassy, her preternatural ability to assault tacit conventions and compel viewers to reflect, and the sort of authentic, leading-edge, forward-thinking, venturesome moviemaking that *she* embodied—and an intentionally cruel mental test to sort the chaff from the wheat.[136]

§7 Favouring creative honesty over commercial conformity, F.A.C. MacRunt managed even to survive the attacks moved against her, her movies, and her artistic vision by numerous enraged representatives of the disabled citizens of her country, who objected to the very title of her fifth feature film, *Bite My Pointy Cripples*. This movie, which tackles the sensitive issue of sadomasochistic sexual desire among female, pregnant, disabled, right-handed, red-headed, bi-breasted, human persons of non-visible Asian origin in the American Bible Belt of the 1950s, was deemed objectionable because of the use of the word "cripple" in the title and the presence of the stark adjective "my," which was blamed by yet another swathe of fiery movieholics to suggest untamed greed and, subtly yet

---

[135] Check what was said before about Phyllis Chesler and rejoice (or re-read the blessed disclaimer).

[136] As F.A.C. MacRunt liked repeating: "You can cure leprosy, but you can't cure people's idiocy."
Punch: What kind of disease are you? **Judy**: It depends pretty much on the day.

possibly, unintendedly evoke tragic instances of racially-charged supremacist possession of humans by humans, i.e., inhumane ones.[137]

Then again, the intended object of F.A.C. MacRunt's inventive and largely unorthodox fifth major cinematic enterprise was precisely to highlight how certain words can hurt people's feelings, belittle people, exclude them, enshrine social injustice, be effectively inhumane, and cause noticeable hair loss. Her art was not meant to be an inconsequential parlour game, unlike plenty of stupid books, superficial movies, and other creative works of art: Not at all! As F.A.C. MacRunt once stated to a poorly-paid German journalist interviewing her on that controversial movie: "My art is no alternative to living and suffering. My art is alive, hence it suffers."

In the 195-minute-long film, F.A.C. MacRunt managed to artfully insert most, if not all, the forbidden and/or most controversial *terms* existing in contemporary English parlance, i.e., as they would have been likely to be used in the callous, dogmatic, and divisive 1950s US of A across a comprehensive, telling, and most diverse cohort of native, non-native, colonial, post-colonial, migrant, pre-migrant, and immigrant communities.[138] That was, by itself, a major accomplishment in script-writing and linguistic articulation, which she managed to keep from sounding artificial, wordy, verbose, inane, redundant, unenlightening and, above all, pedantic.

§8 To give the reader an idea of what was achieved in her film, let us recall the slurs that she employed: The a-word, the a-word, the a-word, the a-word, the a-word, the a-word, the a-word, the a-word, the a-word, the a-word, the a-word, the b-word, the b-word, the b-word, the b-word, the b-word, the b-word, the b-word, the b-word, the b-word, the b-word, the b-word, the b-word, the c-word, the c-word, the c-word, the c-word, the c-word, the c-word, the c-word,

---

[137] When it comes to making other people suffer, actual human beings can be most capable. Some do that by dint of words alone.

[138] F.A.C. MacRunt spoke of it as "an antidote to the nagging persecution of liberal self-doubt."

the c-word, the c-word, the c-word, the c-word, the c-word, the c-word, the c-word, the c-word, the c-word, the c-word, the c-word, the c-word, the d-word, the d-word, the d-word, the d-word, the d-word,[139] the e-word, the e-word, the f-word, the f-word, the f-word, the f-word, the f-word,[140] the f-word, the g-word, the g-word, the g-word, the g-word, the g-word, the g-word, the g-word, the g-word, the g-word, the g-word, the g-word, the h-word, the h-word, the h-word, the h-word, the h-word, the h-word, the i-word, the i-word, the i-word, the i-word, the j-word, the j-word, the j-word, the j-word, the k-word, the k-word, the k-word, the k-word, the k-word, the k-word, the l-word, the l-word, the l-word, the m-word, the m-word, the m-word, the m-word, the m-word, the m-word, the n-word, the n-word, the n-word, the n-word, the n-word, the o-word, the o-word, the p-word, the p-word, the p-word,[141] the p-word, the p-word, the p-word, the q-word, the r-word, the r-word, the r-word, the r-word, the s-word, the s-word, the s-word, the s-word,[142] the s-word, the s-word, the s-word, the t-word, the t-word, the t-word, the t-word, the t-word, the t-word, the t-word, the t-word, the t-word, the t-word, the t-word, the t-word, the t-word, the u-word, the u-word, the u-word, the v-word, the v-word, the w-word, the w-word, the w-word, the w-word, the w-word, the y-word,[143] and, though almost forgotten nowadays, the x-word.[144]

§9   Life is much more than just notorious for its relentless yet unpredictable cruel ironies. One of these cruel ironies afflicted F.A.C. MacRunt in a way resembling, perhaps, the sorry fate of Thomas More, who gave the world the rosy yet unreal island of

---

[139] In English as well as in its Mandarin Chinese equivalent.

[140] In both its derogatory senses, and possibly in the creative one corresponding to the t-word.

[141] The fact that a character used it led some critics to accuse MacRunt of "p-phobia" and "q-ism."

[142] A minor character, Joey, hints at it, rather than uttering it. Still, it was enough to start the "Kill Joey" on-line pile-up campaign.

[143] A major critic asked: "Why?" A mediocre one: "Who?" A pitiful one: "What?"

[144] Some grey-haired, well-travelled readers might recall it.

Utopia to admire and aspire to. Virtuous and noble in most people's eye, artistically capable, eminently witty, massively popular among the cinephiles, and fairly resilient to lesser people's scorn, *her* public disgrace arose in a field that she had made sure to keep well-tended and free of any blight: Her finances.

F.A.C. MacRunt's name, on one momentous and fateful day, ended up being mentioned in the news alongside those of several billionaires, numerous millionaires, and other well-heeled big shots who were involved in an egregious, scandalous, humongous, and rather everyday case of tax evasion, i.e., the amassed fortunes of rich people seeking shelter from the State's grasping hand in a remote, sunny haven. Trillions of US dollars—nobody knew the exact number—had been syphoned into handy bank accounts leading a secretive but comfortable existence in a small, tropical, moderately-spoiled, Dutch-speaking island in the Caribbean: Sly fiscal rascals.

Quickly, former friends, colleagues, and fans started avoiding her and refusing to take her calls, as though F.A.C. MacRunt's endocrine system had begun engendering and secreting a tangy, green, nasty substance through her hair follicles and the pores of her skin.[145] Her oeuvre became immediately suspicious and was promptly dropped from all curricula in gender studies *et similia*—showing, quoting, or even mentioning her art meant asking for trouble, and academicians don't like being in trouble: "Try and make a stupid stunt," it was being whispered in academe's long, shadowy, and gossipy corridors, "then go and show a film by MacRunt!"[146]

---

[145] It is not entirely clear whether the ostracism was due to the fact that F.A.C. MacRunt was a cheat or that she had been discovered to be a cheat, hence raising unwanted institutional suspicion by dint of mere personal association. As incredible as it may sound, there may have been crooks in her business environment.

[146] A notorious American sorority started using projections of her films as a means of chastisement.

§10[147] As a child of the human species, F.A.C. MacRunt had stolen her sister's dolls, elongated their noses in suggestive manners, shaved their scalps, skinned their limbs, and set them ablaze. Yet, as an adult, she had made many conscious and prolonged efforts to be law-abiding, above suspicion, and always pay all of her taxes, to the very last cent, unlike many Hollywood 'stars' and 'numbers one.' F.A.C. MacRunt had duly paid her taxes even on the dubious and substantial money that she had made by dressing up in revealing babydolls in front of her PC's camera to reawaken whatever was left of the burning desire of her sugaring, senile, semi-retired general: "IT assistance" was the official nomenclature for her personal services. What "IT" stood for, though, was probably not the standard meaning that you and I would immediately go for.[148]

There was no damn fiscal secret to be covered and, *a fortiori*, discovered by any self-righteous investigative journalist or other vain muckrakers: F.A.C. MacRunt was *innocent*, she had never been in the red, she had made use of no dodgy intermediaries, she had hardly invested into vulture funds, and she knew as much. The courts met and adjourned, the judges convened and reconvened, the costly lawyers' fees were duly and sorely covered, and the trials were held and the tribulations suffered—with arrestive fortitude, it should be added, and some bourbon.[149]

Eventually, the adjudicating authorities confirmed that about which she had been certain from the very start: She had done *nothing* wrong, and her name had ended up in that accursed list because of a common acquaintance, who was not as fiscally conscientious as she was. Poor journalism can do more damages than a pitiless deluge. It's just like cruel gossip in a poor, small town: Village mentality prospers on implacable, narrow-minded, sanctimonious morality—

---

[147] This number symbolises the disheartening morphing of number-ones into nullities.

[148] To be completely frank, I can only speak for myself—and even then, with caution.

[149] F.A.C. MacRunt's favourite bourbon brand being the rye-forward flavoured *Redemption*.
  Judy: Did you finish the whisky? **Punch**: I don't remember.

Act One

like the internet, if you happen to know what it is and have ever perused a comment thread.[150]

F.A.C. MacRunt's well-formed moral conscience and her formal good name may have been clear as well as cleared, but so much *time* had elapsed—too much, in fact—since she had started being mired in expensive litigations, and forced to devote all of her mental energies and material resources to her seemingly interminable legal battles and recurrent visits to her country's courts of justice. The scorched yet ice-age-like cold clearing that had been made around her by former friends, colleagues, and fans, who did not want to be associated with her in any form or manner, did not vanish at all: It stayed, grew, became common knowledge, justified its own existence by the mere fact of being there, turned into a fairly profitable cottage industry on *Amazon Prime*, and transformed F.A.C. MacRunt into a discarded, unimportant, repugnant, and embarrassing old fossil—if not something worse: A *traitor*.[151]

§11 F.A.C. MacRunt had come to be permanently branded a fraud, a pretender, a hypocrite, a fake, and a powerful formation of self-respecting, self-righteous, and self-serving Hollywood artists made sure that both the person and the name "F.A.C. MacRunt" were duly removed from the scene—little by little, incessantly, pervasively, and once and for all. Consistently, they kept ostracising her in the world's media realm, and even her sheer artistic memory was damned in every possible way and form—except, of course, for the briefly-successful production-and-airing of a true-crime internet series about her disgraceful fall from Mount Olympus.[152]

Concomitantly, the same artists promptly put the new prophetic feminist firebrand of the hour onto the golden pedestal that had long

---

[150] Throughout her career, unless she was the one making use of it, F.A.C. MacRunt repeatedly decried in public the cybersphere at large, insofar as it allowed "the untrained masses to give vent to their ugly aesthetic creativity."

[151] F.A.C. MacRunt even received a series of twelve anonymous postcards stating "TRAITOR!" signed "DDD."

[152] Perplexingly, both Hera and Athena vocally deny having ever seen F.A.C. MacRunt on Mount Olympus.

been F.A.C. MacRunt's, and so excruciatingly arduous to attain. In the end, her award-laden and memorable cinematic achievements turned out to be easily forgettable, like those of Mimí Derba and Peter Greenaway before her, and her status as *persona non grata* in Hollywood—and beyond—solidified into the new norm; that is to say, into the normatively implacable state of the art, aka the indirect normativity of the hardly-placatory and abnormally-directing Deep State of the Arts: Those who buy the tea leaves.[153]

F.A.C. MacRunt fought back hard, as she had always done in her life, but to no avail: All the vile and vitriolic hatred that had been belched at her, most of which was utterly gratuitous, had *de facto* ruined her and her artistry forever. It was ironic, but the most ferociously heavy and mortally vilifying millstones that got ungraciously tied around her disgraced neck in those calamitous, painful times of Christ-like passion had been prepared by people devoid of any genuine sense of irony. F.A.C. MacRunt spent many years trying to figure out what to do and avoid falling into that terrifying and infamous void, until God's grace, somehow, came upon her.[154] God's own very grace, nothing less than that: A stroke of luck mixed with a lightning bolt. The heart of darkness may be strangely luminous, filled with hope, and alight.

This *ex-post* and *ex-machina* godly blessing is that which *she* experienced in *her* heart and candidly revealed to anyone and everyone who would listen to *her*—after so many post-trial and post-tribunal trials and tribulations. It was *her* life, *her* experience, *her* subjectivity, *her* agency, *her* truth—as F.A.C. MacRunt honestly, directly, and gratefully stated in few, short, sharp, meaningful blog entries that were posted online by her, right after joining a small band of Carmelite nuns in California, which is known for promoting transgressive behaviours. None less than the last standing courageous feminist champion for irony and self-irony in American

---

[153] To be frank, Mr Greenaway has never been *persona non grata* in Hollywood. More simply, they have never grasped and liked his art in California. Perhaps, it's just too beclouded: Chaos peers through apparent order.

[154] Such an event might suggest that void is not, in fact, void.

academia, Professor Laura Kipnis, reposted those pointed blog entries on her Facebook profile and drove a few more people to take notice of them: Just a few—Facebook is for old-timers, the sort of antiquated people who still read books, whereas all self-respecting cool kids prefer YouTube videos, Instagram, TikTok, and several other much-snazzier social-media platforms.[155]

§12 Entering a Carmelite convent was no sugary caramel, for it implied driving the final nail in her coffin, at least as far as any public credibility in the Hollywood movie industry and the glitzy but unjust socio-aesthetic world orbiting around it were concerned—but F.A.C. MacRunt knew all of that, at that point. Production companies, rating agencies, and even film buffs don't care—and don't want to care—about Theresa of Avila, Thérèse of Lisieux or Edith Stein. At any rate, precisely by that point, F.A.C. MacRunt had equally stopped caring for any trace, lick, residue, touch, drop, hint, bit, speckle, dot, scrap, iota or crumb of that type of public credibility in any way, form, manner, quality, variety, standard or shape—and she knew that too.[156]

Her own body knew that too as well, since it was headed in a new, old, rather awful direction, which has been the way of the world since day one.[157] When the soul knows that it is time to leave, it directs all kinds of joint signals to its contingent receptacle—and it is never an enjoyable spectacle. F.A.C. MacRunt's joints and knees were painfully sore, her back a little bent, her sweaty hot flushes frequent and monsoon-like, and her head was tormented by pitiless waves of cyclical migraines: She was no longer a young woman; but she had come to accept it.

F.A.C. MacRunt didn't have the energy nor the will to live that were necessary for her to care in earnest for, or actively back in daily

---

[155] Before you go and check her online profile or take my comments too seriously: This too is a joke! This book is a work of humorous fiction!

[156] Some biographers regard that kind of knowledge a clear sign of growing and noteworthy wisdom.

[157] Some astrophysicists and cosmologists do prefer talking of "day zero."

practice, any of her prior plans for public self-recovery, resolute self-vindication, and substantial and eventual reaffirmation.[158] Old wisdom, new wisdom, and the private appeal of novel self-confident absolutes, potential sainthood, and very high horsebacks to ride most eagerly, were now in her grasp, or so *she* thought—"*I shall be the new Roswitha!*," F.A.C. MacRunt would sometimes fantasise, *in foro interno*.[159]

§13 Some religious and theological insights that she acquired could plausibly be confided in and genuinely cherished, for they revealed the hidden and often devious nature of human power, the fundamental roots of morals and ethics, and the true yet generally concealed background of much modern social existence. Reflect on this one, for instance, which F.A.C. MacRunt herself—by now "Sister Purity" in-the-making—liked so much: "Catholics are sticklers for principles, because they have faith, but forgive sinners, because they love; unbelievers have no sticky principles, because they have no faith, but they can't forgive anyone, because they don't love." Or, "love thy neighbour as thyself." Pretty cool, lovable, and John-Lennon-like, right?[160]

"*Maybe that's why 'Christianity' doesn't really rhyme with 'patriarchy'*," F.A.C. MacRunt mused—with a degree of annoyance and apprehension—in one of those rare, unlikely, unliked, unforgiving moments when she could be truly puzzled and realistically surprised. Who would have known, as she realised at that late stage in her life, that to bury the hatchet is the most telling way to give something truly good to someone else? She might try doing that, one day—or, at least, that's what she told herself a few times, as a kind of heart-warming platitude.

---

[158] Energy levels explain many things. The same applies to libido, anxiety, rage, curiosity, and madness.

[159] Fantasies, as a medical norm, are pathological when they try to occupy people's external *fora*.

[160] Or at least Yoko-Ono-like, right? (**Punch**: Who's Yoko-Ono? **Judy**: A friend of Taylor Swift's, presumably)

Generally, such self-reassuring strategies worked pretty well for Sister Purity *in fieri*. In more than one way, F.A.C. MacRunt's aging and now very faithful heart had apparently reached a new, luminous, pure plateau of pristine consciousness and clear self-consciousness, and she was mostly peaceful, like never before in her entire youth or mature years—not even when she was at the out-and-out and most glorious pinnacle of her incredible artistic career, truth be told. "*I shall be the new Hildegard!*," she sometimes imagined, while smiling gleefully and grinning secretly in the mysterious, subconscious depths of her credibly-rejuvenated old soul.

When, as it happens, death finally reached down for her— quite abruptly, you should notice, because of a massive heart attack, as determined by a flamboyantly-dressed GP working at the local hospital— F.A.C. MacRunt felt initially no fear, concern, terror, disquiet or sorry whatsoever. Deep inside her heart, she did not worry at all—albeit at first, and *only* at first…

§14 A bittersweet, rich, knotted sense of finitude, relief, gratitude, tiredness, passivity, *cupio dissolvi*, sublimated orgasms, hearty self-abandonment, trust, and seeming completion was that which she actually perceived in those closing seconds of her short earthly existence, right after Mass, while a fistful of distinct images took shape in her mind—all of them filled with tender sadness as much as sad tenderness. As she was exhaling her very last breath, though, an intense and, it should be noted, very Catholic pang of conscience, suddenly came to pass.[161]

It felt like a loathsome lasting blow to her stomach, or a ludicrous lusty knock on the brainpan. It felt long-lasting, as if it should never go away, and it filled her departing soul with agonising heartbreak. It was something that F.A.C. MacRunt had never experienced before in her entire life, despite all the problems, injustices, predicaments, prejudices, disillusionments, conflicts, censorious aggressions, outright disasters, and all other major unfulfillments with which she

---

[161] Such a painful phenomenon is not known only to Catholics.

had had to contend for *so* many years—so *many* years: *In foro interno*, alas, there can hide the inferno.

"*My child*," she thought, with intense lucidity—thus fully recovering the heavy, guilt-ridden, effectively submerged memory of a long-forgotten abortion which F.A.C. MacRunt had thoughtlessly and hastily opted to undergo in the busy days when she was bringing to life her first feature film—"*were you a boy, or a girl? ... A boy, or a girl? ... A boy, or a girl?*"

Her biggest skeleton, F.A.C. MacRunt, unexpectedly realised in that final, poignant, gut-wrenching, and mournful moment of her fickle earthly path, was no larger than an oak's acorn, a kid's marble, or a glass eye. That tiny, innocent skeleton could have easily been hidden in the smallest of drawers, in the palm of her hand, or under one of her many red handkerchiefs: That skeleton, which now looked at her with the cavernous, unyielding, black eyes of death itself.

XI – That's Mean[162]

Dear Mr Racket,

The present letter will never render justice to the feelings of pure joy and the deep sense of gratitude that I wish it could convey to you. Meeting you last month in our pretty, growing, charming little town and being allowed to participate in your allegorical play, even if just as the blind dodo in the twelve flying pyromaniacs' choir, has already become a precious memory of mine, and I am sure that it will be the last thought that I shall contemplate on my deathbed. A much-cherished moment of pure and powerful aesthetic bliss. Thank you!

I also wish to express my sincerest apologies, because I realised that I am likely to have offended you during our engaging conversations over lunch. I know that you didn't make a big thing

---

[162] Meanness is a subjective appraisal. And so is ostension itself.

out of it, given that you are a true gentleman. However, as I happened to mention the transience of fame as a general feature of human life, I noticed that you gave me a resentful look—if I read your facial expression accurately, of course. As you know, I am a professional historian, and my academic field ultimately teaches that everything human is bound to crumble into nothingness. Chroniclers like me are tasked with keeping Chronos' shopping list updated!

Lastly, I would very much like to extend my warmest greetings to your beautiful and brilliant wife, Stella. What an apt name! Our engaging conversations were so pleasant also because of her enlightening presence and insightful contributions. A veritable source of light! I can see why you married her: Third time is really the charm. You are a blessed man!

Should either or both of you ever consider coming back to our pretty, growing, charming little town as tourists, or wish to spend a relaxing time in our fascinating historic region, then please know that you are more than welcome to stay at our place. My wife and I would be deeply honoured to host you and show you around.

Once again, thank you.

Faithfully yours,
    Prof. F.F. Benedict

Dear Prof Benedict,

Many thanks for your letter.

I was happy to read that you enjoyed being the blind dodo. You were excellent at it.

As to your apologies, I do recall the incident. Quite well, in fact. I must say, if you allow me to speak frankly, that a man of your professional status should know better than to make certain comments in the presence of an accomplished and aging artist such as myself. It was very hurtful. Very hurtful indeed.

As to my wife, I would rather avoid discussing her presence and contributions to our so-called "conversations" in your prehistoric village.[163]

Yours,
    H.S. Racket

Dear Mr Racket,
Thank you for the kind reply.
I was so sorry to read that you recalled so vividly the incident that took place in our venerable little city last month and that you found it so hurtful. It was not my intention to hurt you. I am really sorry. A sorry and verily blind dodo!
Please say hello to your wife from me.

Faithfully yours,
    Prof. F.F. Benedict

Dear Prof Benedict,
Many thanks for your letter.
Yes, you were a real asshole.
Please stop mentioning my wife.

Yours,
    H.S. Racket

---

[163] Mr Racket had considered commenting on the "prehistoric village's" boring architecture, oppressive heat, carnivorous mosquitos, uninspiring surroundings, and inexpensive yet toxic food. However, he exercised restraint. Not only he thought that succinctness ought to prevail, but he could still be magnanimous—or so he thought.

Act One

Dear Mr Racket,

Thank you for the reply.

Your harsh language takes me by surprise. Still, I can understand the way you feel.

I wish you and your family a happy life.

Faithfully yours,
Prof. F.F. Benedict

Dear Prof Benedict,

Many thanks for your letter.
I wish you die in a fire.
Don't mention my family.

Yours,
H.S. Racket

Dear Mr Racket,

Thank you for the reply.

I think you should reconsider what you wrote to me.

I am sure your wife would disapprove of the cruel tone of your letter.

Faithfully yours,
Prof. F.F. Benedict

Dear Prof Benedict,
    Many thanks for your letter.
    You are dead to me.

    Yours,
        H.S. Racket

Dear Mr Racket,
    Thank you for the reply.

    Faithfully yours,
        Prof. F.F. Benedict

    P.S.: Greetings to your wife.

Dear Prof Benedict,

    Many thanks for your letter.
    I know where you live.

    Yours,
        H.S. Racket

XII – The Musical Boxer[164]

One Act:
* *Mehmet S. Selassieri, Jr., known as 'Duck' (the nickname's origin is unknown)*
* *Mike J.J. Lewis, known as 'Tinder' (the nickname's origin is unknown)*

A bell chimes. Curtain opens. Mehmet and Mike are standing side by side, wearing full boxing gears carrying their nicknames on both the front and the back. They face the audience. They are still. Their tense and strained facial expressions must convey great, ceaseless effort.[165]

MS & MJL: (*the silence must last between 60 seconds and 3 minutes, depending on the venue*)

The bell chimes again. Curtain. Wait 6 seconds.

MS: (*makes a very loud bi- or tri-tonal farting noise lasting between 6 and 16 seconds*) AH! (*very loud sound of relief from behind the curtain*)

MJL: (*6 seconds later, enraged, very loud*) For fuck's sake! (*short pause*) You're a fire hazard, mate!

The actors leave the stage in opposite directions.[166]

---

[164] Contact sports can be cruel. Could their suppression be crueller?

[165] They say that humour "punches." Still, try to welcome its blows with a beaming smile.

[166] The stage director alone decides whether to let them cross their exiting paths or not, unseen by the audience.

XIII – Blood on the Kitchen Tiles[167]

Red and thick, a trivial puddle filled several cracks in the beautiful floor and made the Tuscan kitchen tiles strangely slippery. Not even the flour and the dust with which the puddle's contents got mixed could prevent it. A fading aroma of roast chicken, garlic, clove, and a tinge of stale beer could still be perceived in that kitchen, albeit only faintly, at that hour of the day. And there was something burnt or charred. Rotten eggs too, perchance. As well as withered, decaying flowers. Somehow, they seemed appropriate to that domestic, inhospitable context.

All shapes around were blurred, as in a haze. The blue flame of the expensive new gas stove looked like a sickly, anxious little cloud. Some sort of oblong, vertical, viscous dark string moved upwards, however, stemming from the opaque puddle below and reaching into a darker cavity. As anatomically mundane as it is, a person's left nostril can be a dreadful place. Had they been much smaller, then Polyphemus or one of his single-eyed brothers could have moved in there and found that naris an ideal lair. Ogres are said to like hiding in lightless hollows.

A raucous call could be heard in the smoky air: The green parrot was in a frenzy. Tied to its perch in the living room, the large tropical bird had sensed danger. "*Animal*," she muttered silently, within her dazed, heavy, aching head. "*Someone should make it stop*," she thought, "*but who?*," she wondered. It was a tricky question. She had no ready answer to give. Only the question. Not even her higher studies were able to provide her with a suitable response. Neither Georg Simmel nor Michael Oakeshott could come to her rescue. Nor indeed Nils Christie.

Iris was sore and stunned, but not surprised. That wasn't the first time that her cruel husband had hit her. What time was it, then?

---

[167] This may be painfully uneasy for victims of physical violence. Proceed with caution and self-awareness.

Act One

Knowing which ordinal number should apply would have brought her no relief. Her husband may have been a protean inventor, an academic prodigy, and an internationally-renowned professor, but his temper was infamous—and much more than just his temper was so! He was Huracan's wild child. *"I should have remembered the library card,"* she pondered, meekly. Mistakes, like good deeds, never go unpunished.

In her bosom, Iris kept feeling a familiar, inevitable, burdensome sense of unjust guilt and undeserved shame. *"Did I leave it in the bus?,"* she mused aimlessly. This, while glancing fleetingly at an altered image of herself, which was showing on the cracked big mirror that they had bought—together—many years before. They were exploring downtown Chinatown, when they had bought it—along with a bunch of tiny, hideous 'antique' sculptures and much, probably too much, dubious Oriental bric-a-brac. "Figurines," she murmured, without even hearing her own voice. Some of these figurines where as white as teeth. The parrot was still screaming.

Iris grabbed a floor cloth and started cleaning up vigorously. The tiles had to shine again. They *had* to shine again. This was no crime story, she reflected. No war or art movie either. This was no silly play by Beckett or Racket. Most definitely, it was no ancient mariner's briny rime, nor Virgil's meandering *Aeneid*. Not even a stupid short story in a stupid long book. This was *her* life. *Her* world. *Her* kitchen. And all things have their logical order, in Iris' kitchen. All things have their logical order, in Iris' world. All things have their logical order, in Iris' life.

Order. Logic. Something pristine. That's how life continues. Because life is an endless, relentless, tidal succession of chores, challenges, chagrins, harsh constrictions, and unchanging heartache. That's what Iris kept repeating to herself, seeking refuge in the deep, rayless, familiar shelter of her own abyssal, aphotic soul. The tiles, meanwhile, were already looking shinier.

XIV – Scenes from a Teacher's Dream[168]

§1   Limbs look cut, they protrude, not order should be ungainly. Son, son, done what you have! Red. Red. Pain feel you head in the way in the because of which of think you it. Beaks. Back, immense... Shattered, pain... His small feeling was and could him help nobody, nobody, nobody, nobody... Own even father not his! Glass. Gum. Useless... There's no pain, no pain, no pain, no pain, the way only you feel the day born was corn to turkeys yellow beak with feed in head the anew had he the give, but... Beaks. Yes. Tangerine! Music head in continues there my play to that is. Stardust. Tom. Beaks. Feathers the in skies angels wings without sport and pride their own white... Have they few a burn I must. Windshield on song a written ever is fly in best the rock. No sound. No pain. Fear commands fear. Rock. Red. Eye. Yellow. Beaks. Stretch of by imagination the any. Beaks. Plug. Glass. Stardust. Thomas. Gum. Tom. Tom. Work. Gum. Plug. Glass. Mass. Crass. Bus. Stardust. Sound girls merry today they. Bus. Gum. Tom. Plug. Red. Eye. Beaks, beaks, barks. Before them all. All. Before them all. Stardust. Gum. Bus. Bus. Bus.[169]

§2   Zhang Juqian woke up in a restless and gloomy mood: Bad humour. Nothing new there. Still, he had to go and teach the first class of the day. No hard task *in se*, but one that had to be seen to. Juqian quickly slipped in his glass eye, got washed and dressed nearly as quickly, kissed fondly his long-dead son's photograph by the entrance door, mulled over a few hard seconds on his loss and the bitch-like grief gnawing at his own soul, and eventually left for work.[170]

---

[168] Nightmares too are but dreams: The gods speak at night. The dogs, instead, may bark. At any rate, who truly *knows* another's pain?

[169] All such dreamt buses being yellow, overrun by passengers, and driving along well-known city routes.

[170] Very few people worry not about being late for work.

Act One

Juqian took the usual bus: Yellow, bumpy, overcrowded. There was some traffic along the way, also as usual, but he was not late. Thank God for that! "*I have to get a new prescription from that oddball of my GP,*" he recalled, before entering his small and messy office.[171]

"*Just in time*," he thought. It looked like a chilling spell of grey, heavy rain, if not worse, could be on its unmerry grey way towards the badly-built, grey university campus. Sitting at the grey desk, Juqian started thinking about his son, as he always did, especially after having had an unsettling dream during the night. And there was hardly any night when he didn't. [172]

He felt in every fibre of his being his son's absence, constantly as much as terribly, as well as that of his son's mother—about whom Juqian tried actively and obstinately *not* to think. She had left him long ago as well, alive and kicking, to join some crazy cult with priests in long white robes, tall magic candles, and bizarre golden priestesses praying inside empty fish tanks! As though the normal world weren't abnormal enough… Which it was, plainly; and still is.[173]

§3 What could Juqian say about that mystical and farcical craziness? What, really?

He didn't know himself. What, above all, had *he* done to deserve it? Why such a horrible and humiliating penance? Why? He had always been loyal, hardworking, dependable, kind, considerate, consistent. *Never* violent. *Never* brusque. *Never* unfaithful. *Never* skiving. *Never* drunk. *Never* neglectful. *Never* foutering. *Never* late. Not even when the city's yellow buses weren't running—because of a sudden strike, an unexpected mechanical failure, or some other unforeseen accident along their scheduled route. Juqian was *reliable*. He was a good man. And he had loved her. He still loved her. God if

---

[171] Large offices too can be messy, but that requires effort.

[172] A dark night lost in this footnote observed: "Souls." Then, a mist poured down its small hours.

[173] Normally, normal people are normally aware of this normal abnormality.

he loved her! He loved her *now*, after so many years, and so, so, so very much—even if he didn't want to admit it, not even to himself. Not anymore, at least. It was all such a... madness. Yes, *madness*. That's the right word for it. But also such a horrible shame. A stupid crime. An unforgivable sin. They say that God chastises sinners and evil people, but how and why would God spend time and energy chastising an ordinary, inoffensive, conscientious man like him? Why and how could God allow for such a horrible rubbish to happen, or to exist?

And the boy, the boy, the boy... Ah, the boy! The boy was only three years old when she disappeared. Their son had had to grow up *without* her, as a result of that insane cult's stupid and destructive nonsense—those few more years that the boy had been granted to spend on this dismal earth, that is. Another punishment on top of the previous one. An endless, sorry, vile cascade of infinite sorrow for finite, caducous beings like him—and his beloved son. "*What a crazy world,*" Juqian thought, "*they find water on Mars but they can't find it here for dying children in Yemen... And they bring humanitarian aid to the same boys and girls that they're bombing to shreds...*" There were no answers. There was no sense. It was all a cruel joke. "*A cruel joke,*" he heard himself saying inside his own old braincase.[174] Wasn't it? Isn't it?

§4 Seemingly inexpressive, Juqian stared pensively at the grey desk, the piles of read books, and the general chaos of his small and messy office. Yes, small and messy.[175]

There were therein all sorts of knickknacks, pens, highlighters, paper clips, pencil sharpeners, translucent glue tubes, bulky folders, kitsch souvenirs, old journals, older booklets, mounds of graded papers, mangled toothpicks, unfinished income tax return forms, dirty handkerchiefs, crinkly neckties, empty boxes, spent lightbulbs,

---

[174] A thick skull lost in this footnote observed: "Souls." Then, a mist poured down its lacrimal bone.

[175] No negative judgment is implied by the author, who deeply dislikes disorderliness.

blackened ashtrays, discarded plugs, half-burnt votive candles, bags of chips, Mars wraps, braids of garlic, half a Bible, a MacBeth illuminometer, one rotten apple, six coils of greenish copper wire, two bricks, mixed nuts and acorns, fifty unused audiotapes, twelve archaic Betamax tapes, a plastic Viking helmet from northern Iceland, five fishing rods, two rusty pickaxes, one old pitchfork, twenty-five half-finished Vaseline tubs, one unfinished protein bar, countless olive pits and watermelon seeds, nearly as many unread tomes, six shiny copies of Myers' *Flight of the Siren*, one large stone bust of Aristotle, another one of Evo Morales, one 40x60 1956 fake engraving of Thomas Müntzer, one inflatable pumpkin, two mechanical yellow chickens, one cat-o'-nine-tails, two stuffed hamsters, one embalmed goose, a torn poster about the white-nose fungus, four long-expired luxury praline gift boxes, hundreds of unusable floppy disks, eleven broken frisbees, one brown wooden comb for men's hair and beard, two tassel-less tarbooshes, six digeridoos, three basketballs, a cracked glass figurine of a Greek goddess, two kitchen knives, a piece of paper carrying Tig Notaro's autograph, no can opener, and an untouched bag of marbles.[176]

Juqian's ghastly figments were more orderly than his office. That canonical academic workspace looked like a parody of il Grechetto's paintings. Then again, such was his life, his normality, his quotidian existence. It had been like that for almost thirty years... Or forty?

§5   Juqian missed his son. He missed him. Oh, how he missed him! It was agonising. And that silly, stupid, idiotic, foolish... sweet, beautiful wife of his. Where had she gone? Where was she now? Was she thinking about their son? Did she even remember that their son had died, and how he had died? Did she care? Had she ever cared? Wouldn't that be normal, for a mother? A parent? Just normal. Nothing more... Juqian would have liked it so much to be able to lead a different sort of... normal life. But what does a normal life look like?

---

[176] Juqian Zhang did not know that, but in that bag there was also a small black-and-white granite egg.

That much was almost obvious to Juqian, for he was reminded of it nearly every single day of the week. He could not escape normality, even if it did not belong to him. Normality was the ordinary, prosaic, quiet commotion of other people's quotidian chores. Normality, above all, was the bustling life of the many families that, with varying constancy, he met on the yellow, bumpy, overcrowded bus, or that he saw in so many of the poisonous, brightly-coloured cars that the bus itself met on its customary route towards the grey university campus.

Mostly, they were mothers and fathers accompanying their kids to school. But there were also brothers and sisters going to school, together. And there were equally couples that were evidently off to work, together. Families... Families, indeed: Where people argue a lot but also stick together. Families, yes. Families... But Juqian was alone. *So* alone. And *so* lonely.

XV – Keep It Stark[177]

One Act:
• *Sister Dove, née Ernestina G. Waldoska (from Poland)*
• *Sister Seraphina, née Joyce M. Ayuor (from Kenya)*

Two Carmelite nuns are sitting on a sofa, in front of a huge HD TV screen, playing videogames.

SD: (*angrily*) Fuck you![178]

SS: (*mockingly*) Fuck you!

---

[177] The order may require it. Especially when exploring un/edifying disorder. **Punch**: We're late! **Judy**: We're early! **Chronos**: Who are you?

[178] Some persons take it personally. Some philosophers take it philosophically. Writers take it in writing. People with a sense of humour take it sensibly, i.e., humorously.

Act One

SD: (*emphatically*) Fuck you!

SS: (*upset*) Fuck you!

SD: (*grinning*) Fuck you! [179]

SS: (*menacingly*) Fuck you!

SD: (*defensively*) Fuck you!

SS: (*menacingly*) Fuck you![180]

SD: (*defiantly*) Fuck you!

SS: (*surprised*) Fuck you!

SD: (*scoffingly*) Fuck you!

SS: (*trenchantly*) Fuck you!

SD: (*as trenchantly*) Fuck you!

SS: (*timidly*) Fuck you!

SD: (*half-jokingly*) Fuck you!

SS: (*jokingly*) Fuck you!

SD: (*smilingly*) Fuck you!

SS: (*ironically*) Fuck you!

---

[179] A trite insult lost in this footnote observed: "Souls." Then, a mist poured down its most familiar usages.

[180] Some persons take this personally. Especially those whose person is their *persona*. Or for whom persons are it.

SD: (*bombastically*) Fuck you!

SS: (*laughing*) Fuck you![181]

SD: (*also laughing*) Fuck you!

SS: (*laughing roaringly*) Fuck you![182]

SD: (*laughing as roaringly*) Fuck you!

SS: (*laughing more roaringly*) Fuck you!

SD: (*laughing as roaringly*) Fuck you!

SS: (*laughing still more roaringly*) Fuck you!

SD: (*laughing at the same level*) Fuck you!

SS: (*stops laughing, takes a deep breath, shakes her head, then she utters calmly*) Fuck you!

The two nuns stop playing. They stand up and take three steps towards the audience. Slowly, and in perfect coordination, they each fish out a large cigar, light it up, and take three slow puffs. For six seconds they stare silently at the audience, and then utter their eventual comment.

SD & SS: (*playfully*) Fuck you!

Curtain.

---

[181] Some others, instead, do not. Maybe they lack much of a *persona*. Or maybe they have dug deeper.

[182] A feigned foreign accent can be attempted here, if desired. A sense of irony, however, is still *de rigueur*.

Act One

Behind the curtain, SD reflects aloud on matters of ultimate importance.[183] *She is gloomy:*[184]

All this pretentious, superficial, dubious art, all this… tapestry! Colours, movements… This mockery of reality! Pity, pity! So much effort, so much trickery, so little… consequence. Pity! Shadows, yes, and mirrors; smoke, cheap tricks, some clever words at best… Be as daring as you like, but it will all make only a tiny, miniscule, little, puny, pathetic, insignificant, ridiculous impression. So much else, more, is needed to induce anyone to avoid the infernal disorders of the human heart! People aren't even afraid of jails, fetters, cats-o'-nine-tails: They grant less worth to the fear of the ensuing human sanction than to the transient, animal pleasure that they think they can enjoy. Pity, pity! The human mind is so limited in its knowledge, and the societies which it inspires are as limited in designing, directing, and even punishing for the sake of, the *external* order, to which there corresponds instead, to the most grievous extent, the *internal* disorder of the human soul! So, religion is properly the sole path warranting and enshrining the human good will: Mine as much as that of all others. But what is religion? And which religion? A religion whose teachings I do not know, perhaps? A religion that someone else gives shape to, according to their own feeble *voluntas* and their darkest, most deceitful, sick, subconscious desires? Or what certainty will I ever have that someone is not judging fittingly, like the terrorist does, to cruelly swindle me, to cruelly steal from me, to cruelly snuff me, as if all such lines of conduct were meritorious and holy acts? In order for religion to be able to guarantee me and anyone else in all conduct, mine as much as that of my fellow citizens, it is necessary that it should approve and condemn with equal clarity and validity, in my conscience as much as in theirs, all that which is approved and condemned in mine *and*

---

[183] Unseen by the audience, she holds a copy of Taparelli's *Theoretical Treatise of Natural Right Based on Fact*.

[184] The stage director decides whether and/or how to incorporate this section following the comic dialogue.

theirs. This is why I elect to live with those who feel the same way as I do about every dogma, and I seek their candid approval!

XVI – A Snip of the Tail[185]

§1   John I.I. Millar had made a fortune selling counterfeit goods and recreational drugs in Toronto, Brighton, Warsaw, La Spezia, Selfoss, and Leningrad, or whatever the hell that big city was now called. His trade was a dangerous one: He knew that. Back home, he had been robbed, assaulted, and beaten up, more than once. There was a time when even his bodyguards had failed to save him from an angry maniac. What a beating! And he got a few kisses from a blade, if you know what I mean… It was an adventure, that one… Yep, a fucking adventure! That's what John thought, anyhow.

Well, the people he dealt with weren't schoolboys. So far, though, nothing nearly as bad had happened to him in Mother Russia—in spite of the terrible and terrifying reputation of that godless place. His arduous career as a hard-working criminal was on the way up. It was like an interminable erection: He knew it. He did! His numerous bank accounts proved it, especially the anonymous ones in offshore tax havens, most of which were in the Dutch Caribbean. For fuck's sake: He even had a fat advisor at Goldman Sachs taking care of his fat portfolio![186]

But it was much more than that. Success is not just a matter of numbers: It ain't just *money*. There's a lot of shitty pissbutts around the world who've got plenty of fucking money: All those fucking sissies who inherited fortunes from their dead relatives. What the fuck did they do, apart from having orgies, snorting cocaine, and

---

[185] Watch for the criminal angle: Consorting with lowlifes can be compromising—and it makes for *adult* material! If sexuality, lewd matters, violent crime, machismo, and crass lexicon can unnerve you, then skip this chapter of humorous fiction *à la* Welsh, Roche and/or Clark.

[186] A fat investment portfolio lost in this footnote observed: "Souls." Then, a mist poured down its Swiss Francs.

buying horrid works of art? Or all those hot, sly, calculating, high-end whores who married fat fake businessmen, fat fake-businessmen-turned-fake-politicians, fat-arse generals, or fat farting widowers, all for their fat stacks of cash. Sucking gold out of dicks is a skill, alright. But what kind of a *career* is that, for fuck's sake?

§2   Okay, whores are certainly more respectable than any one of those pathetic scions of rich fucking families that have been sitting on slave- and blood money since time immemorial. Whores must sweat a little, especially when wanking wankers. That's a real job, not just a hand-job. Still, it's no different than being a regular woman. There's nothing special or remarkable about that. It's not like making your way to the top. It's not like fighting—and winning! At best, it's just getting someone else on top of you. Not much of a struggle, innit? Easy, passive stuff. Or so John would argue.

Really, think of that for a second: Think about the super-rich fuckers. They all have fat accounting experts helping them evade their taxes. They all lead cushy, luxurious lives, without ever doing any serious work. At best, as said, they fuck. What a sweat! Lying there, pumping and getting pumped, while someone else is pumping all their money into some tropical electronic vault![187]

The whores themselves, as John considered, work primarily in bed. That's comfortable, isn't it? It's no coalmine shaft! There's sweating and there's sweating: Don't you see? Success is something else. It comes from pushing *tough*, dark, massive boundaries. It comes from facing *tough* challenges, and overcoming them—not making them come. It's fucking *tough*! You have to match the likes of Caesar, Genghis Kahn, Henri VIII, Cecil Rhodes, Al Capone, Jiang Qing, Maggie Thatcher, John Gotti, Bokassa I, Lee Iacocca, Ellen DeGeneres, or Javier Milei—John's sundry 'tough' icons.

Above all, you *sense* it. Success, that is. It's a subtle matter of skin, and heart, and bones. It's all the nerves tingling in a very funny way. The way *his* nerves were tingling. That burning. That

---

[187] A bunch of dirty cash was found lifeless inside a secretive vault. The stench was re-vaulting.

electricity. That zap… It's hard to explain. But it felt *good*. John was becoming *something*. He was becoming *someone*. He *felt* it. He could *feel* success—he could. Yes, he did! He did!

And it was such a *good* feeling. It was *so* good. So *fucking* good. Nothing beats that kind of feeling. It's just pure magic! To John, it was like standing by the fireplace on a cold Winter night, drinking fucking Irish whiskey, smoking a real Cuban cigar, watching a dart game on the big tellie, and getting a nice, slow blowjob from an obliging piece of snatch—*all* at once.

§3   What is more, John's young wife was a real darling. Not only because of the blonde hair, the perfect body, and the blowjobs, which, truth be told, are a very important ingredient for a successful marriage. But also because she helped him in his business. As said, she was a *real* darling. A fucking darling. If a translation was needed, then there she was. If her oral skills were otherwise needed, then there she was as well. It's amazing how much friendlier and more accommodating customers can be after unloading their nuts' juice into your wife's throat. *"And I'm not talking tongue in cheek!,"* John thought, laughing heartily at his own mental jokes.

Humour had always been a selling point of his, in John's modest opinion. A crucial skill, in his risky line of work—his top joke being: "I sound like my uncle Frank: I'm Francophone!" Anyhow, *"she's a fucking hot bird,"* John said to himself, *"and she's got that crazy fire inside her…"* He got hard, again. His 'spire,' as he poetically referred to his own indefatigable penis, was ready. He looked around the room. *"Where the fuck did she say she was going?,"* he wondered. *"Oh well,"* he went on, *"there's no lack of glorious young pussy to fuck around here."*

And he was not entirely wrong, as far as finding an apt, warm receptacle for his truly giant dick was concerned—an attribute of his that John was quite proud of, incidentally. Wasn't the compliant, French-kissing babysitter somewhere, around that huge apartment? She didn't seem to mind getting some extra cash and provide some elderly care as well. If anything, she seemed very eager. And that kind of eagerness deserved respect. Or at least some money. Well-earned money. And money is nearly as good as respect, anyway. That's what John believed.

§4 The small baby was asleep. The small babe was not. The young, petite, unpretentious brunette was on the sofa, reading a book. John made out the title and the author's name from a distance. He was getting good at it. Fucking Russian! It wasn't all that difficult, if you just apply yourself. And John was more than capable of doing that. He worked hard. He did. Always.

"*Turgenev*," he processed the letters under his balding pate, "*Virgin Soil*." John grinned. Perhaps because he preferred Maxim Gorky's earthier, history-informed prose. "*She's getting plumpier*," he noticed as well. "*Look at those fucking tits, though! Fucking tits...*" And so he approached her, in a literal rather than literary mood, while undoing his trousers. Tact was *not* a major feature of John's personality, unlike humour. Nobody's perfect, after all. Right?

She knew the drill. Actually, she had come to expect it. In point of fact, she positively liked it: A lot. They had been at it for months. More or less since the baby had been born and her domestic services required—and generously paid for. It was good stuff. And good stuffing too. Much more than just another line on a CV. It's nice to be able to do a job that you love.

At heart, her drill was her thrill. The dark-haired girl gently licked her lips, signalling that she was salivating in anticipation. She gave John a coy smile and a penetrating look. There he was, ensnared. She knew in the depths of her soul that he was madly in love with her. She did! And that made her feel special, powerful, and proud. So special. So powerful. So proud.

His wife may well have looked like a top model, and yet he was coming to *her* for sex. His wife may have had the moves, manners, and moans of an experienced porno star, 'cos she had heard John and his wife shagging in their bedroom, and yet he was coming to *her* for sex. That too made her feel special, powerful, and proud.

The young woman knew as well that the money John gave to her on the side was just a married man's way to ease his guilty conscience. "*He must justify his infidelity in some weird way*," she kept telling herself. *"But how can I make him mine, mine alone, forever?,"* she also kept wondering. And she had come to a conclusion. In actual fact, she had concocted a *plan*.

§5 The dark-haired, sex-crazed, moistly-lipped babysitter had a *plan*. And she was going to execute it: On that day, of all days! She could be organised, if she wanted to. It was one of the reasons why they trusted her as a babysitter. Polite, punctual, precise: She was nothing but a great carer. And she cared about other people's opinion, when it came to that kind of things.

As John stood smirking by the sofa with his large purple tool bulging in the direction of the young woman's conniving, glistening, and enticing face, and with his trousers pragmatically wrapped around his ankles, she pulled out a big kitchen knife from under a pillow, and she chopped off his large purple tool in a single, solid, strong blow. *"That's quite the blowjob!,"* she considered, in an unusual instance of cruel humour on her part—and of humour as such. Funny!

John fell onto the floor, gushing blood like a fountain, and gasping so hard that he couldn't either scream or cry for help. Meanwhile, she proceeded to slice off his scrotum as well. He fainted. Or died. She couldn't tell. She didn't care anymore. Not *enough*, anyway.[188]

§6 Carving off John's balls took a little more work and effort than the initial eviration business. Anyhow, she got it done. It wasn't too complicated. Then, while holding his bleeding testicles in the palm of her left hand, she dropped the knife onto John's still body. She clasped both hands and squeezed hard. The testicles popped. She could feel his light semen and his dark blood mixing together: His essence was now *hers*. Her hands were holding it, *there* and *then*.

---

[188] Care is very difficult to quantify, notwithstanding the many attempts made by well-meaning social scientists.
        Punch: I can see the appeal of it.
        Judy: Eye can see its appeal too.

Most importantly, John's essence could no longer be corrupted by that blonde, stupid slut, whom John had married for no good reason. Nobody else would have his essence now. It was hers and hers alone! *He* was hers and hers alone: Reduced, and conquered! Contemplating her victory, and savouring her godlike power over life and death, she smiled contentedly.

A few minutes later, the young woman was gone. The apartment burned. The baby died. John's wife inherited his money, and moved to Switzerland, where she married her late husband's fat financial advisor, who was later arrested because of a massive tax-cheating criminal enterprise. All good things *end*, at some point. Including those that can make you good money.

§7 The efficient Russian police officers recorded the babysitter's name among the fatalities of the terrible fire, which quickly spread to the whole building and threatened to engulf an entire neighbourhood. It took almost three days to get the situation under control. They wanted to let some relative of the babysitter know of her purported tragic fate: They found *none*. She was all alone. One solitary soul among many. One of many. Just one—almost zero, but not yet zero.[189]

According to the official records, the young woman had died alongside her employer and the baby for whom she was caring. "*Poor girl!*," they all thought. John's wife, who had never paid much attention to her and couldn't even describe her to the police, recalled only her first name: Simone. Nothing else. She looked just *too* ordinary to be remembered: A nonentity.

---

[189] Zero is very difficult to quantify, notwithstanding the many attempts made by well-meaning mathematicians.

XVII – More Food Me[190]

§1 As a trained GP, Marilena's duty was to care for her patients' health. "A good doctor is a good heal," her illness-prone mother used to say, in one of her own characteristic, quaint, home-made mottoes. As a GP, Marilena did her best. And her best was more than adequate. As a physician, she was consistently, reliably successful. Or so Marilena thought, at least.[191]

Her mother, albeit as self-confident, had never been so reliable. The most significant achievements in her life, as a matter of fact, were, on the one hand, having been able to let one of her three daughters make it into adulthood and, on the other hand, spending the last thirteen years of her life rescuing injured birds—and feeding them to her two lean cats and one fat sow.

Marilena never knew who her father was. Nor could she credibly guess. It was a mystery. And it was bound to remain one. "Children are a give from God," her mother had always said. Assumably, Marilena's two sisters had each a different father. Her mother never spoke of them.

In any case, Marilena could not conjure up her sisters' faces. Both girls had died in early childhood, probably from pneumonia. Even that, though, was uncertain. "Death's a decide from God," her mother would answer, if asked. The odd woman didn't seem distressed or afflicted by their premature demise. Not even back in the day when they passed away, some people said.

In truth, there was hardly anything that had ever caused Marilena's mother to be visibly unhappy. Somehow, despite the chaos defining and accompanying her, the aging woman was the living embodiment of joy, cheer, and contentment. As such, despite her obvious quirks and unashamed use of recreational drugs, she had

---

[190] This is *not* a zero-sum game, which still counts—and not just the calories.
[191] Thinking is a common human process and an uncommon mystery.

been fairly popular in her pretty town, where she ran for many years some kind of bar, drugstore, and butcher's shop, all merged into one thing, in an underground structure that had been built during the last war, and never renovated.[192]

That underground structure was probably an old bunker, by the look of it. Marilena herself didn't know for sure. Nor did her mother. For a short while, years ago, before becoming the unconventional shop run by Marilena's mother, the local fire brigade had used it as some sort of makeshift depot. There were still several funny steel helmets lying about to prove it: Marilena's mother would turn them upside-down and store inside them her homemade medical lozenges and herbal suppositories—"Firefight with firefight," she would normally comment.

§2   As an adult, Marilena recalled especially well *three* things about that place. One was the pungent redolence of garlic sausages permeating everything. Another was the endless chatter in which her mother engaged throughout the day with her habitual customers: Countless housewives, as many children, a long stream of pensioners, a hefty company of nuns, and two or three retired military officers, whom her mother seemed to find the greatest fun to be with. The third thing was the endless and satisfied screaming that went on throughout the night, when her mother copulated eagerly, at length, and noisily with yet another lover of hers—or more than one at a time. Early in the morning, the smell of dry sweat and other spent bodily humours was almost as pungent as that of garlic sausages. It was a spicy yet gentler odour, for a change.

Marilena was neither resentful nor grateful. If there had been any trauma, it wasn't evident at all. She loved her mother dearly for as long as her mother lived, and afterwards too.[193] But she had also quickly realised in her childhood that her mother was unlike most

---

[192] In her bosom, Marilena's mother sensed that a new terrible war would come to pass. "Selfish and petty no time then," she would whisper.

[193] Love is very difficult to quantify, notwithstanding the many attempts made by well-meaning social scientists.

other persons in town: Her mother was rather *special*, in both the positive and the negative sense of the term.

It was a crucial point. Her mother's behaviours, words, and actions were *not* those of the other women in the town where they lived. None of them was like her. That much was patent enough. Marilena had understood that important fact early in her life. The very ways in which her mother dressed and conversed with other people were very, very different, almost unique. Her mother was unusual. Probably eccentric. Plausibly deranged. Possibly dangerous.[194]

§3 Having come to terms with these manifest truths about her mother, Marilena's life had then unfolded in a rather average, coherent, uneventful way, to the surprise of many neighbours, whose judgment matters in this kind of urban milieu, whether anyone really likes it or not.[195]

Marilena went to school no. 267, helped her mother in the shop, left for the capital to pursue further studies, qualified as a physician, married a lovely and loving foreign gentleman, came back to her hometown to work as a GP, and, together with her quiet and polite husband, raised three healthy children into three healthy adults, without any complications—unlike her mother, who had often complained, a touch enigmatically: "Raising family joke is real cruel."

Apparently, Marilena had inherited only one major feature from her mother: She too dressed flashily and flamboyantly. It was an innocent caprice, nothing else. In private, however, two more maternal legacies had been passed down to her: Marilena made excellent garlic sausages, and she was nothing short of amazing in bed. Her demure and well-mannered foreign husband, who loved Marilena deeply and faithfully, appreciated in earnest all those three things about his wife. Good for him. In particular, as the years went

---

[194] Marilena was unaware of her own mother's major juvenile misdemeanours.

[195] Wits are very difficult to quantify, notwithstanding the many attempts made by well-meaning social scientists.

by, he could hardly live without his wife's garlic sausages. They were a true delicacy: *Bon appétit*!

XVIII – Airborne Tonight[196]

One Act:
* *Merab M.M.. Mamardashvili, currently a bodyguard*
* *Abraham X.Y. Herrera R., currently a bodyguard, carrying a hip flask.*

Dressed in full hunting gear, Merab and Abraham wait in the woods for wild geese to fly by.

Merab: (*whispering*) can you see anything?

Abraham: (*whispering*) shh! No, nothing.

MM: I'm hungry.

AH: So am I.

MM: Shall we just go home?

AH: ... I don't know. (*takes a sip from his hip flask*)

MM: (*after a long silent pause*) Really... How long have we been waiting for?

AH: Don't know... Hours. Since daylight.

---

[196] Vociferous lexemes are but *flatus vocis*. Nevertheless, so many people get so upset, left and right! Therefore, if common careless bigotry and quotidian crass lexicon can unnerve you, even when fictional, then skip this chapter altogether.

MM: Fuck… It's almost as boring as being a bodyguard.

AH: Well, man, that's exactly why we're having a break in the country, innit?

MM: (*after a long silent pause*) I'm hungry.

AH: (*gloomily*) So am I.

MM: (*after another long silent pause*) Can I have a fag, at least?

AH: (*serious*) Alright. You won't scare no golden goose.

MM: (*lighting a cigarette, serious*) 've been thinking…

AH: 'bout what?

MM: Remember the guy with the knife?

AH: Yeah, I do. Almost shat my pants!

MM: Well, yeah… Aren't we doing the same to the geese?

AH: (*sniggering*) What the fuck? Are you the bloody WWF now?

MM: No, what I mean, you know… We make them suffer.

AH: (*trenchantly*) Everybody suffers.

MM: Aye, right. (*after a long pause*) It's a hard life.

AH: Yeah, that's the way of the world.

MM: Fucking world… Who the fuck invented it?

AH: (*smiling*) what d'you mean "invented"?

Act One

MM: Yeah, you know... It's a fucked-up world it's been made. The universe.

AH: Fair enough. You've got a point: Big Bang, big fire, cooling planets, dinosaurs, another big fire, monkeys, Assyrians, Carthage, Huns, Lombards, Arabs, Mongols, Turks, Zulus, Franco, Goebbels, McNamara, Khomeini, Rambo, New Labour, Powell & Rice, Sarah Palin, Putin, BoJo, Trump, yourself... Yeah: Fucked-up! Like they show it on TV: A bloody restaurant!

MM: (*smiling, lifting his rifle*) ... And here we are with a small bang...

AH: Quite right. If only those geese showed their fucking face! ... I'll show you the restaurant!

MM: Cowards!

AH: (*ironically*) never trust birds. They're only good for the eating.

MM: (*smiling*) talking 'bout that wife of yours, by any chance?

AH: (*laughing*) could well be, my friend! ... (*long pause, serious*) Fucking cunt...

MM: (*serious*) Come on, Abe, don't be so crude!

AH: Yeah, fucking cunt! D'you think she's not banging someone else while we're here waiting for no fucking goose? Wouldn't be the first time ... (*pause, smirking*) She's an easy bird, that one.

MM: (*grins*) Well, not a wild goose... (*pause, very serious*) Why are you still with her, then?

AH: (*very seriously*) Don't know... Bad luck? ... Or maybe 'cos I need to eat too.

MM: … Well, we all need to eat. That's true enough… (*lighter tone*) There's nothing without bread!

AH: (*smirking*) Right. And don't forget: (*declamatory*) "We are what we eat."

MM: (*serious*) What you put in is what comes out! (*ironic*) That's why models are a waste of air!

AH: (*smiling*) Right.

MM: In and out, in and out, in and out: Like breathing. Or shagging… (*soberly*) Is it all there is?

AH: (*dry*) I guess so. (*pause, serious*)… Can we be *more* than what we got, you know, stuffed down our throats when we were kids? You know, *more* before… Or *more* after, for that matter?

MM: That's a bloody hard question, sensei! Could I really be any other fucker but the one I am? … I don't know! Got lots of shite, though, when I was little. (*smiles*) And no effing goose today!

AH: (*serious*) That's right. Me too. I'm tellin' you! … These bloody flipping geese aside, you know? *Shite*! Fucking, stinking, dirty shite! What else was there going around? Just plenty o' shite!

MM: Yep. Plenty of shite for all of us. Shite for all the kids! … That's no hard question, is it?

AH: (*laughing bitterly*) Right. Loads of shite for tea! Couldn't expect anything else back then…

MM: (*quietly*) Shite.

AH: (*more quietly*) Shite. (*takes a sip from his hip flask*)

MM: (*after a long pause, seriously*) … Was that Marx?

AH: (*serious*) Nah… Think 'twas Elton John.

MM: Oh, fuck it! Bloody English baronet... I should have known it!

AH: Another rich old white guy… Bastards!

MM: … And all these fucking faggots! And trans, and bearded queens… Everywhere, these days!

AH: Yeah… And communists!

MM: Bloody hippies!

AH: And their communes…

MM: All terrorists. All o' 'em! I'm telling you… Bloody slimebuckets!

AH: Islamo-fascists.

MM: Fanatics.

AH: Madmen.

MM: Suicide bombers.

AH: Loners.

MM: Masochists.

AH: Fakirs.

MM: Vegans.

AH: Weirdos.

MM: Misfits.

AH: Midgets.

MM: Douchebags.

AH: Dentists.

MM: Sadists.

AH: Sodomites.

MM: Lunatics.

AH: Lesbians.

MM: Liberals.

AH: Eskimos.

MM: Krauts.

AH: Journalists.

MM: Socialists.

AH: Imperialists.

MM: Chinamen.

AH: Indians.

MM: Redskins.

AH: Rednecks.

MM: Russians.

AH: Rothschilds.

MM: Pitbulls.

AH: Bulldogs.

MM: Savages.

AH: Doctors.

MM: Psychiatrists.

AH: Gynaecologists.

MM: Perverts.

AH: Wankers.

MM: Bankers.

AH: Economists.

MM: Psychos.

AH: Serial killers.

MM: Skimming readers.

AH: Writers.

MM: Stockbrokers.

AH: Accountants.

MM: Arsonists.

AH: Arseholes.

MM: Publishers.

AH: Drug dealers.

MM: Car dealers.

AH: Cult leaders.

MM: Holy men.

AH: Shamans.

MM: Mediums.

AH: Priests.

MM: Popes.

AH: Mystics.

MM: Martyrs.

AH: Nuns.

MM: Feminists.

AH: Artists.

MM: Rappers.

Act One

AH: Tenors.

MM: Tree-huggers.

AH: Wrestlers.

MM: Rock-climbers.

AH: Bus drivers.

MM: Traffic wardens.

AH: Garden gnomes.

MM: (*laughing*) Wouldn't mind shooting a few of those. Bang! Bang!

AH: (*grinning*) Right!

MM: Right.

AH: (*whispering*) right.

MM: (*almost inaudibly*) right.

AH: (*as quietly*) right…

MM: (*after a long silent pause*) … I'm hungry.

AH: (*after a short pause*) … Right. (*takes a sip from his hip flask*)

The two hunters keep waiting in the woods.

Curtain.
(11 seconds later, loud quacking is heard originating from the stage.)

XIX – Where the Sweet Turns Sour[197]

Yet another day was starting in the region's extensive constellation of towns and cities—in the early morning; in the usual way. Millions of responsible citizens were going to enter their vehicles, go to work, be productive, take few and very short breaks, and make money for those who already have plenty of money, while spewing huge amounts of lethal and lawful gases along the way. For it is plainly true that people have a direct, emotional grasp of a distinct hierarchy of objective and universal values, by means of which they can duly and coherently organise their individual as well as collective existence. And drive about.[198]

Mrs Symonds herself, not too late after sunup, complied with her habitual early routines, made sure that her husband should take proper care of their four young daughters' helter-skelter breakfast and getting-ready-for-school in general, walked briskly into her car, and gazed half-consciously at the pink-and-orange haze that the region's accumulated and officially well-regulated exhaust fumes had been creating all around her stylishly copper-trimmed automobile, as well as above her queenly, jet-black, à-la-mode head of hair—whilst also altering in not-too-overt a manner the sorely-neglected, unlit, chromatic palette of her weak, vulnerable left lung and pathologically-elongated trachea, which Mrs Symonds had inherited from a lengthy line of long-necked women belonging to her well-thought-of and prosperous native family.

The roseate shimmers and the titian glare in the nominally celestial vault aloft looked surreal, somewhat spectral, almost supernatural. And yet, those vivid colorations were totally ordinary. The region's industrious inhabitants had by now come to expect such variegated, hued spectacles in the early forenoon sky. It was as

---

[197] Manslaughter can be most innocent. Were the ancient gods ever accused of worse than that?

[198] Thinking about driving can drive people insane, ruining their health.

though God's Creation had metamorphosed into a mannerist painting by Luca Cambiaso, or into some gaudy new cocktail to be served in the best bars of Mrs Symonds' hometown. The sickly pigeons seemed virtually magical, and the vicious seagulls looked majestic, as they hovered calmly or soared freely in all that gaseous, polychromous air. A swift wedge of wild geese flew by as well. "*What a beautiful day!*," Mrs Symonds quickly pondered, and she robotically started the engine of her smart new motor.

XX – One-Eyed Mound[199]

I can't be sure I recall *all* the details, but this is what I was told, ok?[200]

1. Is Today Monday?

On that crazy Friday, Calvin 'John' Major, you know, the tall guy who worked part-time as a prison guard at the local penitentiary. Yeah, the prison, joint… He was going to meet with his girlfriend, the daughter of some old teacher… I don't remember his name… Erich Fromm ain't at the comm! But it doesn't matter… Does it? Alright, let me see… No, nope. I recall hers, though… I think. Janelle, Chanelle, Marielle… Something like that. French… Or Swiss.[201]

Well, I know that he had bought her some chocolates… Ah, no… No, no, no! It was flowers… That's what it was. Yeah, a bunch of pretty flowers for his pretty new girlfriend. Cute, right? … Well, he

---

[199] Don't make a peep!
  Judy: Why are you still breathing, man?
  Punch: Sorry, I just can't help it!
  Judy: I guess I'll have to strangle you, then.

[200] How reliable is human memory, if at all? And if memory is doubtful, how can one trust history?

[201] The local Swiss Embassy refused to answer our bi-weekly calls.

was walking all bubbly and cheery down to Tommy More's Square, just past St Lawrence's cathedral, opposite the statue for Christopher Columbus and World Peace: You know which one. That's where he was meant to take the bus, the one that goes around the university campus... The big one... Yellow, the giant concertina in the rear... The bloody bus!

I mean, he was really in love with that girl. In all the years I've known him, I had never seen John so... *Besotted*! That's the word! Yeah, cool... Never. Not once. Like a schoolboy. Pathetic, almost. But also sweet. Yeah. Sweet, you know? ... And, I mean, the girl was pretty cool. She's some kind of artist or filmmaker... "The new firebrand," they called her... Yeah. Cool, right? Branding fire. Like a superhero... or some god that looks like Hannibal Lecter![202]

2. Is Today Tuesday?

What exactly she was burning, or branding, or whatever, who knows? ... Didn't they brand slaves in ancient times with fire or something scorching? Like cattle, you know? Marking them. Branding. I mean, that's slavery, innit? ... Well, I've never seen any of her work, you know? Not one flick. Not even one lick. No lick of the flick... Which doesn't stick! Oh shit... Sorry, but I'm a born poet, you know... I should sure go into rap, or cool shit like that![203]

So, well, I can't tell you if she's any good, or just some arty-farty nonsense.[204] There's plenty of nonsense going around, you know? I mean, some real, total, unforgivable crap! Shitty books, for one... You know, shit's never scarce, somehow. Otto Rank's got the bank! ...Maybe it's like farts... Dunno... Do you fart a lot? Just *not* on the bus, okay? ... Oh, come on, I'm kidding! Aren't farts always funny? Like burps, you know? Or people falling on their arse. Or people

---

[202] The *International Cannibal Association* complained about this persisting cheap humour.

[203] The notion of "cool shit" is not to be taken literally, unless turds got frozen.

[204] Not all nonsense is arty-farty. (**Punch**: I'm a sophisticated artist! **Judy**: Kiss my ass!)

shagging... Or shagging *and* falling on their arse. That's just something that makes you laugh like a drain! Not like the arty-farty stuff that bores you to death. That's my meaning.

But there's also some *good* stuff. Like good books, you know? Have you ever read *Utopia*? Or the Russians? They're great, really, especially the epileptic one... What's his name? ... Well, good, real good... I mean, farts can be good too... No shit! Real good. Yeah, yeah: Doctors say so! I mean, for your health. Unless you're on the bus, as I told you... or inside a lift or a small room... Then they're fucking deadly, mate! And a fire hazard! You shoot out one of those and... Ah! That's such a Saddam-like thing to do! Kill-the-Kurds, you know?

3. *Is Today Wednesday?*

Well, doesn't matter. So, I don't know. I can't say if she was any good as a filmmaker or just a lot of rubbish. Doesn't matter, really... John loved her. Shit, he really loved her! Now, to be honest with you, she seemed nice and fun... Yeah... Enough fun. She smiled, she talked, she wasn't shy... And she had a nice way about her... Nice, you know? Cute. Sweet. Endearing, as my hot aunt Iris would say. Not much of a sense of humour, though... But that's just what I recall. Maybe she's a real cracker, if you get to know her, or after a few glasses.

Well, I must have met her three or four times, always in John's company. What was her name, now? Oh, fuck! Not the name, again! Can't recall... Belle or Noëlle... Something like that. Not too pretty. I mean... She was pretty: Hot, almost. Fuckable, yeah, 100%. But not my type. Pretty, she was pretty. But so... *posh*. Skinny, and... Self-important, you know? Like Julia Kristeva coming to Geneva. Or like her snatch was made of gold and she shat diamonds out o' her arse... You know the type. The kind that makes you sniff it forever, and that's it: *Cruel*.

I mean, she could pretend that she had it all sparkling and special. A snatch to be kept in the vault, you know? Or the arse of the month on some dodgy porn site: The hole to vote for! "Vote for this asshole!," you know? Like real politics, thinking about it... So, she was actually real pretty, fancy blonde, and dressed well. Very well. The kind of thing that can give you a boner just by looking: Shirt skirt, stilettos, fine legs, nice arse... That kind of stuff... Hey, Winnicott can be a mott, but *she* was *never* slutty: Too high class. She had money to splash around, you see. So, model-like. Pretty, was pretty. But not so pretty for *me*: Not for *me*.

4. Is Today Thursday?

I don't know how to explain it, really... You know, taste is taste... Not enough meat on the bones for my taste, you see... Skinny, yeah, too skinny... Like a model. All those bones sticking out.... I mean, I like them plump. I like... squeezing... But, fuck, who cares? It's John who had to worry about that kind of shit, not me! Besides, you know, beauty is in the eye of the beer-holder, right? Know what I mean? You can't just get everyone to agree... Or they'd all be busy trying and shagging the same few people... Chaos, that would, be: Total chaos! Like a war of all against all, or a stampede by the Kaaba... Or a Black Friday at the mall!

Anyway, just as he got near Tommy More's Square, just by the Central Bar, the one where they make that famous cocktail with tequila, ginger and green aubergine—not bad, by the way, and, yes, yes, I know, it's funny, but... Well, you know... Weird, but it actually tastes better than it sounds—, well, right past the bar... If you drink too many of those you end up peeing purple piss... And fart like a saxophone! Shit, they can make you fart! Not on the bus, though, ok? That's not cool... The cocktail's cool. They put ice in it... I think. Don't they?

Doesn't matter... You know, brass players fart a lot, because of their job. Crazy, I know! Cool as well, if you think about it, though... Air in, air out... The cycle of life! I know, I know... I mean, farts have their place... Even if they sound crazy, sometimes... Crazy, yes, but, you see, right out of a corner, just like out of the blue, like some kind of lightning, a bolt of fire from the sky, or a big fart without any warning, there you have them: *Three large grey creatures* with long appendages and... sorts of fangs. Waaaahhh! You know? *Three* of them. Shit! All *three* at once... Like Groucho, Chico and Harpo, like a shot, you know? Before you can say "Jack Robinson," or was it "Joan Robinson?" ... Whichever, but scary: Waaahhh!

5. Is Today Friday?

Yes, that's right, mate, scary like fuck! You know, three big thingies, all wobbly and grey and, yes... Grey, for sure. Like... I don't know! The clouds in the sky when it's pissing down. Just fucking big and grey, ok? Scary, mate! ... I guess.... I mean, could they be anything else? Stuff that makes you shit your pants, I mean. Or fart a lot, at least... Like an orchestra.

Think of that: No, not the farting orchestra! Mounds of grey flesh, with tentacles and—at least that's what I was told, mate—*one eye*. One fucking eye! One! Yes, one! Not two, you know? Just one. One! Like the arsehole. I mean: Do you know anyone who's got two arseholes? Come on! Or two dicks? Or two snatches? ... Though that could be fun! ... So, they weren't at all like you and me, or our dogs, or cats, or frigging parrots and budgies, you know, stupid goldfish... Whatever. I mean, gannets, chickens, crows... Fucking blind dodos, for all I care! Weird stuff, really. Like Freud on an asteroid, Jung in a tomb, or Lacan in an ice-cream van!

No, I mean, the *three* of them, like a flash, and *one* eye! Only one! Like Columbo, you know, or Bongo Bongo... Could it be an animal? No, it couldn't! ... Though I don't know if they had two arseholes... Two, can you imagine? Or two snatches? ... That'd be fun!... Well, you see, they see John, smell the flowers—yeah, it was a bunch of flowers, not chocolates—and, bam! *One of these grey wobbly mounds eat' all the frigging flowers in just one bite*—just *one* big bite! All of 'em. In an instant. The time to say, "buh!"... Or fart... Fuff!

6. Is Today Saturday?

...Unless it's a long, smelly one. You know, the sort of Chernobyl-wide fart that makes the people around you giggle and laugh. And mortifies you like shit! It happened to a friend of mine on the bus... He was all red in the face... and stopped taking buses after that. Only walking... May be the right thing to do. Healthy, even. And you've got time and opportunity to fart when you need it, you know? ... But, I mean, I'm sure John was shitting himself... Fuck! I mean. With that kind of... fangs they had inside or around there... That thing. A hole. A mouth. A scary orifice with big fucking teeth: Waaahhhh! A nightmare, you know? Waaahhhh!

I mean, it'd be worse if a snatch had teeth... Woah! Scary, right? I actually think there's a movie about that... I mean, think of it! They made a movie 'bout it! A vagina with teeth! Must have been some pervy dentist... Or was it an arsehole? ... That'd be even cooler, in a way, and freakier... Dental proctology, for one... I mean, you'd run away with your pants still down: "Don't eat my dick! Don't eat my dick!" ... I'm sure you'd make money wi' a film like that. Come on, it would make a hilarious scene! "Aaaahhh! Help me!," eh-eh...

But that's not what was John's problem. I mean, this grey big fucking monster-thing just gulped down *all of his flowers in one big fucking monster-size bite*! Think of that! In the process, you know, the poor man ended up missing his footing, the flowers, three fingertips, *and the bus*! The fucking bus, mate! Total shitshow: Waaaahhhh! Viktor Frankl is in a big fankle! Blood. Bits of finger... A mess. A shitshow! And those big mouths... Fuck me! Anyway. *No* bus, *no* rendezvous... Yep. No bus. Gone. Too late. No bus! None! Heading for the hills, now.

7. Is Today Sunday?

The one-eyed mounds may have had a rocket ship or a flying saucer, for all I know. But John. Fuck! He got no bus! None!... Public transport is important, you know? It's like shitting regularly, but on a much larger scale... Or farting... I'm serious! You know, it's like urban planning. It's important to have places where people can go n' take a dump, for instance... Or a piss, you know? You go to the pub, have a few pints, fill the good old bladder. And then you need to take a bloody leak, mate! You do! ... I mean, also if you're a woman, like John's Belle or Joelle... They have bladders too, you know? Women, I mean... Don't they?

Yep, Joelle... What a fucking bitch, mate! No, really. I'm not being sexist or anything... She was a *real* bitch about the bus... And bitching about it, bitching, mate! I mean, as I said to you, no bus, no rendezvous. Ok? That's a fucking bummer, or not? Ok. Settled. A real bummer. Poor John! Now, there, bleeding... Carrying bloody chunks of his own bloody hand in a bloody handkerchief... Crazy! What can a man do? No fucking fingers, mate! Blood everywhere! No flowers! Eaten by the fucking monsters! Everything got so fucked up, mate! Poor John... And no time to get to the fucking yellow bus, ok? No bus! None. Zero. Zip! Gone, it was. Yep.

Well, in any case, the girlfriend was so fucking mad at him that she broke up with him on the very same day! Think of that! After all that shit that had just happened... I mean... Didn't even go visit him at Saint Stephen's, where they tried to reattach one fingertip... Don't know if they managed, 'cos he's still got three tips missing... Anyway... She was like Melanie Klein in brine, or Karen Horney in a barney... Fucking hell! Blah-blah-fucking-blah! ... John will never hear the end of it... Poor man! He's still suffering from all that shit he got to gulp down his sorry throat. He's so sad... All the time! So sad. So depressed.[205] Cruel stuff, really... Cruel.[206]

8. *What Day is Today?*

I'm telling you: Ranting she was! Mad like some angry ancient goddess... You didn't do as promised.... Come on time... You could

---

[205] Depression is difficult to quantify, notwithstanding the attempts made by psychiatrists.

[206] Unheard, in the distance, the silhouette of a tall, large man sang: "Credo in un Dio crudel che m'ha..."

call... You have a phone, don't you?[207] ... You didn't this and didn't fucking that... John you've got no respect for me... John you can't be relied on... John, you can't be trusted... John you don't know when to give me space... John you've got a small dick... John you're a piece of shit... John this, John that... John you don't really love me... You just say you do... You just want to get in my pants... John I'm not that kind of girl... John I've got my needs... John you don't do it right... John you've got no fucking money.... John you're an arsehole... Shit, mate, she was furious! Hell, she gave him, hell!

Think of that... Girls, I mean... You know? Fucking girls when their knickers get all twisted... Worse than the fucking grey monsters from outer space that come to earth and eat your flowers and bite your fingers off... Think of it! They'd just throw you under the bus, if they feel like it's their fucking right to treat you like shit. ... And that Belle... Poor John... The man was gutted! "Dear John," I mean... It's as old as the world, but from another planet![208]

Postscript For Two Puppets[209]

Punch: Are you still upset?
Judy: Yes, I am!
Punch: Can't you just... ignore them?
Judy: I try, but...
Punch: "But?"
Judy: ...they're so...
Punch: ...Hypocritical?

---

[207] The reader may want to ask his/her phone the following question: "Will technology save us?"

[208] A Croatian explorer claims this planet to be called "Usud." However, he's a well-know prankster.

[209] Readers affected by pupaphobia or generally unnerved by puppets may wish to skip this chapter.

Judy: Hm…
Punch: Phoney-baloney?
Judy: Hm…
Punch: Self-righteous?
Judy: Hm…
Punch: PC?
Judy: Hm…
Punch: OTT?
Judy: Hm…
Punch: Goody-goody?
Judy: Hm…
Punch: Niminy-piminy?
Judy: Hm…
Punch: Apple-polishing?
Judy: Hm…
Punch: Dewy-eyed?
Judy: Hm…
Punch: Forelock-tugging?
Judy: Hm…
Punch: Simon-pure?
Judy: Hm…
Punch: Narrow-minded?
Judy: Hm…
Punch: Janus-faced?
Judy: Hm…
Punch: Tartuffian?
Judy: Hm…
Punch: Uriah-Heepish?
Judy: Hm…
Punch: Pecksniffian?
Judy: Hm…
Punch: Grundyish?
Judy: Hm…
Punch: Pharisaic?
Judy: Well…
Punch: Sanctimonious?

Judy: Yes, that's the word! Where the heck was my old brain, hm: In Florida?

Punch: Isn't sanctimony… normal?

Judy: Sadly, that would appear to be the actual case, these days.

Punch: What did they say, this time?

Judy: That "lame" is "inappropriate." One hysterical chap yelled: "Ableism!" But I was talking of a bloody duck!

Punch: Really? This kind of… concerns, in the 21st century?

Judy: Yes, I know! The same people who watched religiously *Game of Thrones*, *Girls*, *Dahmer*, *Euphoria*, *Vikings*, *Workin' Moms*, *The Gold,* or…

Punch: …*Orange is the New Black, Brand New Cherry Flavour, Da Ali G Show, Veep, The Windsors, Little Britain, South Park*…

Judy: …and adored FAKA's 'disruptive' modern-art performances, Hagendorfer on *Arse Elektronica*, *Wetlands'* torrential humour, or the primeval carnal energy of *Femina Fabula*…

Punch: …or had no problems with Richard Pryor's humour…

Judy: …nor Amy Schumer's, Jim Jefferies', Sarah Silverman's, and the like! Their day's fickle humour sets what humour's fit deontologically![210]

Punch: Hm. I hear you.

Judy: Sorry if I… vent all this… mental crap out, just like that.

Punch: Don't worry, love.

Judy: Thank you, dear.

Punch: I've got one question, though.

Judy: Fire away.

Punch: Why have you replaced the wallpaper in the living room with…

Judy: …throbbing, warm, fully-functioning, intestinal ducts?

Punch: Aye.

Judy: I thought it was…

Punch: What?

Judy: …gutsy!

---

[210] A trendy comedian lost in this footnote observed: "Souls." Then, a mist poured down his online reviews.

Punch: Oh?

Judy: Besides, bowels don't lie: They have no double standards. And then…

Punch: Ah-ah?

Judy: …it's much more informative.

Punch: "Informative?"

Judy: Yes. I mean, when you're at home, how much time do you spend surrounded by the same four walls, every day of the month, hm? And tell me, honestly, have you ever learnt anything useful from those four walls?

Punch: Shit! That's… pure genius![211]

---

[211] Each reader is more than free to agree or disagree with the puppet's gnoseologico-aesthetic appraisal.

ACT TWO: PURGATORIO[212]

---

[212] **Judy**: "Are there authors who are characters?"
Punch: "Are the characters the authors?"

XXI – Aisle of Gentry[213]

One Act:
- *Pierre R.S.V.P. Bowles, a male graduate student*
- *Frank Francis B. Benedict, a male graduate student*

Pierre enters the university library, where his good friend Frank works at the reception desk.

Pierre: (*loud*) Hey, Frank!

Frank: Shh! (*whispering*) It's the library, mate!

PB: Sorry!

FFB: Never mind.

PB: Started early today?

FFB: Yeah, 6 A.M.

PB: Wow! I guess you couldn't drink that much last night, right?

FFB: (*smiling*) No. I had to be… *cautious*.

PB: I understand: No carnival, then.[214]

FFB: No (*sighs*), nothing that holy. Everything was pretty secular and sedate.

---

[213] Refinement has been the humourist's Holy Grail since at least the days of Lord Shaftesbury.

[214] Carnival prepares the ground for the holiest festivities. Johannes Tauler had a green thumb, probably.

PB: Listen, were you 'cautious' also with that girl... What's her name... You know, Monica?

FFB: (*smiling*) Yeah, I had to. What a pity...

PB: Fascinating character, isn't she?

FFB: Yeah, she is! Talkative, ironic... Very pretty... And bloody, bloody, *bloody* clever!

PB: (*smiling*) She always comes up with some brilliant maxim she's invented. She's a sort of sexy genius. I mean, she's read Marcuse, McMurtry, McElroy, Taormino, and Soble. She's unique!

FFB: It's true! Last night she came up with some great quips: "All claims of perversion are attempts at diversion," and "only devils can demonise someone or something that they disagree with." And "atheism is the opium of the elites!" ... Remarkable, don't you think?

PB: (*smiling*) Not bad! ... I recall her once defending Tertullian: "Absurdism is a humanism!"

FFB: Yes, her witticisms! "Neo-paleo-positivists have Darwin as their ersatz Moses," "bosons for bozos," "hard science without the liberal arts is like constipated shitting without the freeing farts," "callus from phallus," and... "if a hard cock stands before you, don't gasp: Grasp!"

PB: (*chuckling*) That's a clever one! (*chortling bashfully*) Offhand, but really clever!

FFB: (*smiling*) Yeah, not bad at all...

PB: (*pensive*) No, no, not bad at all...

FFB: (*as pensive*) Yeah… Just like her body… You see, I don't want to be superficial, misogynistic, offensive, un-pc, Jack-Nicholson-like, or whatever, you know… but… Wow! Just, wow!

PB: (*smiling*) Yeah, really… Can you believe it? (*playfully*) … Brains *and* boobies!

FFB: (*less playfully*) Brains *and* boobies, yes…

PB: (*smiling*) The perfect combination, right? Like Leone and Morricone, or Marx and Engels.

FFB: (*pensive*) Indeed! Like… Adorno and Horkheimer, Fry and Laurie,… Bread and Nutella!

PB: A match made in heaven…

FFB: (*ironic*) …Or purgatory?

PB: (*faking concern*) Suffering, young man? Are you?

FFB: Getting what you want is a rare occurrence, my dear friend!

PB: Ach, well, you know… perfection doesn't belong to man!

FFB: (*smiling*) It certainly doesn't belong to me! (*Jokingly*) Nor to you, silly old bugger!

PB: (*laughing, pausing*) … Maybe it just belongs to Monica!

FFB: It does. I believe it does… (*with theatricality*) She's the golden goddess from Mount Olympus!

PB: (*idem*) The beautiful nymph who bathes in the sacred pool that no man can touch without perishing, dying the most agonising death! (*mimicking an agonising death*) Aaaahhhh!

FFB: She is the bright eye of Venus, who spies the hearts of all mortals in this vale of tears!

PB: The perfect sphere of celestial glass and pure light that only Zeus can hold in his godly hand!

FFB: That's why there's this invisible glass separating the two of us, you see? I'm a mere mortal, my friend! ... Even just by looking at her I get snow blindness, and a heart attack!

PB: (*smiling, pausing, back to normal tone*) ... Was there also that other student, the mature one?

FFB: (*idem*) Iris?

PB: Yes, Iris! That's the name!

FFB: No, I don't think so.

PB: (*morose*) I see.

FFB: (*cheekily*) ... Fancy her?

PB: Come on, mate! She's far too cool and sophisticated for a boy like me. (*with a tinge of sadness*) ... Besides, I believe she's already married... Traditional marriage, you know?

FFB: (*trying to cheer him up a little*) Fancy mature women, then?

PB: (*smiling gently*) I fancy beauty *and* intelligence, my friend!

FFB: (*with fake seriousness*) As we all do. We are gentlemen, aren't we?

PB: (*smiling*) Precisely! (*sardonically*) There shall be no superficiality! (*very friendly*) ... So, Frank, what did you drink, if you had to be so... *cautious*?

FFB: Water, mainly. I must have had a can of beer or two. Nothing else.

PB: (*pensively*) Youth's fount and all that stunt... (*cheerfully*) Well, you know... Next time!

FFB: Next time. (*smiling*) We'll always have tomorrow! (*seriously*) Anyway, what are you here for?

PB: Try and guess.

FFB: (*joking*) A monograph on Descartes' *Coitus ergo sum*? ... No! A pile of theology books, right?

PB: (*smiling*) Yep.

FFB: (*teasing, in fake posh English*) Will it be a pile of Calvinism, my good, hardworking sir?

PB: (*ironically*) Yes, sure: Calvin Major!

FFB: (*laughing*) I don't think they've written many tomes about that poor bloke! (*smiling*) Maybe just a short story in some forgotten book!

PB: (*smiling*) Maybe they should write a novel about him... Or an epic poem!

FFB: Or make a movie!

PB: (*smiling*) Yeah... Can you see F.A.C. MacRunt shooting *The Well-Deserved Loss of Three Oppressive Phallic Symbols*? Or, *If*

You're Late, There Shall Be No Date? ... *Bus & Cuss?* Or what could that be: *Bring Me My Flower or You'll Take a Cold Shower?* ... *E.T.'s Amputees?*

FFB: (*chuckling*) Don't make me laugh out loud here, come on!

PB: (*more soberly*) Alright, mate. So, can I get what I need, then?

FFB: (*idem*) Then what?

PB: Catholic theology... Carmelite Aristotelianism!

FFB: Sounds cool... Many books?

PB: A dozen. Plus three biographies: Simone Weil, Elizabeth Anscombe, and Hans Jonas.

FFB: (*surprised*) And I thought that we historians were the real bookworms![215]

PB: (*amiably*) We're fellow invertebrates, my friend!

FFB: (*joking*) Are you suggesting I'm spineless?

PB: (*smiling*) With all the books you have and read, and work with? Plenty of spine there...

FFB: (*smiling*) Quite right! ... And you know, "you are what you read!"

PB: (*chuckling*) True... And at least we don't have to read about mass and count terms...

---

[215] Apparently, the biggest unreal bookworms are to be found at the City Library of Arrakis.

FFB: Oh yes. There's plenty of stuffier subjects that we could study!

PB: Anyway, I'll go to the theology section myself.

FFB: (*very serious*) I think you should wait.

PB: (*surprised*) What do you mean?

FFB: As I said, I think you'd better wait.

PB: Why?

FFB: (*with fake seriousness, almost martial*) The old general's here.

PB: Oh, I see… (*smiling*) With his sausage-making mistress, by any chance?

FFB: Yep.

PB: Ach, well. I'll wait here, then. He doesn't take long.

FFB: (*back to normal*) No, he does not. But he is persistent, though.

PB: He certainly is.

FFB: And *she* is pretty hot, considering… (*Ironically*) … More mature than Iris…

PB: (*slightly embarrassed*) Well, I don't know… I don't find her, nor them, for that matter, *hot*.

FFB: Too old?

PB: No, it's more like… I don't know… I find them… *Sweet*.

FFB: Sweet?

PB: Yes, sweet. Like two young lovebirds, you know?

FFB: I see… Yeah, I think I know what you mean. Two lovebirds… (*smiling*) Two wee bunnies?

PB: Yeah, more like two wee bunnies, right… You're right: *Cute.*

FFB: (*fondly*) I think they're sweet to come here to snog.

PB: And eat garlic sausage.

FFB: … *And* eat garlic sausage.

PB: Yeah, I think it's a sweet thing.

FFB: Old love's still love.

PB: Yep. Old love's still love.

The two friends stand by the desk. Faint noises come from the aisle, and the smell of garlic.

Curtain.

XXII – The Zamia[216]

Part 1 – Downhill

You might recall a logician who smoked a pipe in his office. Well, you should know that he is an avid collector of exotic Bolivian flowers. He gets them flown over all the way from South America.

---

[216] Please order cheaper flowers. Or learn to make origami. Or merely forget about it.

Quite a hobby to have, isn't it? His husband likes them too, and he doesn't complain about the cost nor the extravagance. Because they are steep. I checked their price online, since I got curious, and I was literally shocked by how much they cost: Shocked!

Incidentally, I think that they make a very nice couple. And they are *so* sophisticated! Probably the most sophisticated couple living in our part of town. I wish there were more people around here with that beautiful sense of tact and… taste. Taste, yes. Impeccable! It is a rare and precious quality to possess. It is tacit, inexplicable, and yet so evident when you spot it in a person, a couple, or even a place. You see it, you know it. But you can't articulate it. Like true humour, which is not just everyday sit-com comicality or cheap laughs, but has that … *je ne sais quoi* that makes it so special. Like real intelligence, charisma, wisdom, or… self-irony.[217]

Well, *I* recall *him*, not his husband, climbing the hill on the northern side of the campus. The one that stretches all the way to the cemetery. You know which one. The one that is always patchy and full of mud. It's by far the biggest graveyard that we have in our town. He was carrying a large object. Bulky. It was a sort of glass box; a fish tank from the look of it, but there was only a little bit o' water inside. Not much. Hardly any. And no fish. None at all.

Now, he had reached the top of the hill, which is not very high, and had just started walking down, very cautiously, slowly, mindful of his steps. The hill, you see, was still covered with snow, for the most part. There could be ice as well, hidden under the thin layer of snow. It can happen. It was the end of winter, after all. And it had been a very cold winter. *So* cold! The air would freeze inside your nose, on the coldest days. Old folks would stay inside for weeks. One of *those* winters. Harsh. Very harsh. Common enough around here, but unpredictable.

Believe it or not, but two white rabbits, hares perhaps, came out of a bush, all at once, and they ran just past him. It all happened in a flash. It was all very, very fast. The hares ran fast. They can do that. I

---

[217] On a parallel ontological plane, the laughs kept wondering: 'Which wise ironists wrote these chapters?'

don't know if the animals touched him, if he got scared, if those curious rodents said something unexpected to him, or… whatever! What I know for sure is that he *fell*, there and then, right on his poor old arse: Bam! But that's not all: He was so unlucky! You see, the big tank went flying into the air and, poor man, it landed *right* on his head: Smash!

As insane as it may seem, he didn't say anything. Not a word. Not a sound. Not even a groan of pain or anything like that. He must have been shocked. Startled, perhaps. Injured, even. What would you do? How would you react to something like that? It wasn't an enviable situation, to understate the case. And he also started bleeding like a fountain. Like the fancy ones that they have in Rome or Florence. But the fountain was… all *red*! Blood, everywhere! Nosferatu would have had a party. Unfortunately, the pale Count was in Romania, not Rome.

The fallen logician had cuts all over himself. All over! That poor man: What a tumble to take! And all that blood: Everywhere! It took him more than a short while to get back to his senses. Well, it took him a long while, actually. He then looked around, aimlessly, like he was lost in a bad dream. Yep. A bad dream. You see, that's the kind of stuff that happens in your worst nightmares. The *worst* ones. The ones where Dracula himself comes and gets you. Like… Christopher Lee, Gary Oldman, Jonathan Rhys Myers… or, I don't know, Bela Lugosi, Udo Kier, and… Klaus Kinski! Yes, that's the terrifying one: Klaus Kinski!

Anyway. That poor, shocked, sliced-up man saw the snow around him. The shards of broken glass. The blood. All that blood! He had literally bled the bloody snow red. Red, I'm telling you! He got a bunch of it in his hands and then shouted—*shouted*, yes—like a madman: "Snow isn't white! Snow isn't white! Snow isn't white!" … What the heck was *that* about?

Part II – Uphill

Having witnessed the scene above, a flower and a giant otter commenced a dialogue:

- ❖ Why do they cut us down?
- ❖ Because they can.
- ❖ Why do they *want* to cut us down, then?
- ❖ Because they want... *you*.
- ❖ Do they... hate us?
- ❖ Some of them do, yes.
- ❖ Are they... jealous, envious?
- ❖ Oh yes, very much so!
- ❖ Why?
- ❖ Because you're beautiful.
- ❖ And they aren't?
- ❖ Or they were, but are no more.
- ❖ Do they realise how much we... *suffer*?
- ❖ No, not in the least.
- ❖ Even if they... *resent* us?
- ❖ Yeah. It's their way: They generally overlook why they do what they do.
- ❖ But they think they've got... *reasons*, right?
- ❖ Oh yes, every time! It's like a pattern, with them.
- ❖ Then, why are they so... smug?
- ❖ Dunno... They've even got names for that... *smugness*.
- ❖ "Names?"
- ❖ Yes, "names," in the plural!
- ❖ Like what?
- ❖ Ach, they keep changing... Once they had "philosophy," then "science," and even then, they disagree on what must counts as this "science" of theirs: "Physics," "mathematics," "chemistry," "biology..." Not to mention "sociology," "economics" or "psychology!"
- ❖ Why wouldn't you... *mention* them, hm?

- Because the alleged "experts" in these fields like... reinventing the wheel.
- Oh?
- They forget what they knew, discover it again, give it a new... name, yes. And then pretend that it's all because they've become more... "scientific," yes! Odd creatures...
- And what about the others, those who don't... hate us?
- Many of them really *like* you, in point of fact.
- What?
- Sure! Some of them even *love* you.
- How so?
- They give you to persons they find... *special*.
- Oh?
- In life and... later as well.
- Do they give us to their... dead?
- Yes. It's a common practice.
- Do they... kill *us*, in *their* name?
- It's a morbid way to put it but, yes, that's how it... plays out.
- It's not a nice game.
- ...

XXIII – Never a Dime[218]

Mehmet had only recently immigrated. He had done all sorts of jobs, while making sure that nobody asked too many questions about him. His official process of immigration was, in fact, bureaucratically undecided, if not decidedly inimical. Besides, back in his country, Mehmet had been a little too active in the local Communist Party than it was good or advisable for him to do, as well as for the overall wellbeing and employment opportunities of his large family. The West, despite its many shortcomings, offered better options. For a while, that is.

---

[218] If you are indeed familiar with the feeling, then I do feel for your family.

Unhappily, and seemingly all at once, some rich fuckers fucked up real bad. As a result, the Big Crisis came. The Tsunami. While the rich fuckers found out that they had more time to spend at home with their kids, Mehmet was left without a job, hence also with no money to send back home and feed his own kids.[219] It was a really tough time. Tough and soul-wrenching. Tears could be seen everywhere. Daily bread, instead, was a mirage.

After walking around town for three days without pause or rest, asking anyone and everyone for an opportunity, a chance, to earn some money, Mehmet found himself outside the town's boundaries. He was sweaty. His feet were hurting like mad. He was covered in muck, dust, and all kinds of dirt. Out in a field, a huge tent. "*Circus*," Mehmet thought, "*... shit to shove ... Elephant shit?.*" Whichever manure it was, he should probably give it a try.

That is how Mehmet got introduced to Lady Masham, or at least that's what the woman was called by everyone else around that strange, smelly place: It was her stage name. "*Beautiful woman*," Mehmet noted, but then he felt ashamed of his lustful thoughts: He's a pious man, sometimes.

It took a good few minutes for Mehmet to explain his whole situation, show her all the things that he could do, and all the things that he could learn to do—for God's sake, he was willing to try and become a contortionist, if that could help! She was attentive, polite, rather unforthcoming, possibly intrigued, and very, very firm. Her eyes suggested rare intelligence and true force of character. After pondering the case under her stylish, greyish, smooth coiffure, she said to Mehmet: "Sorry. There's no job for you here. Go and try somewhere else."

"*Shitshow!*," he thought, "*No luck, again... Ain't a man his job? What am I, then?*"

Mehmet was back on the road. In a split second, at some point in the late afternoon, the sky got dark and grey, and torrential rain started pouring down. Mehmet stopped walking. He sat on a big

---

[219] His well-trained boss loftily said to him: "If you don't go through a crisis, you won't ever see its end."

stone near the roadside. He took his shoes and socks off to let the rain soak his stinky feet, washing off at least some of the mud and, to his surprise, more than a fair amount of the pain which had been tormenting him for hours. It was refreshing. Truly. Mehmet smiled.

XXIV – One Fool's Man[220]

One Act:
* *Donald John Trump, a non-smoking former democratic US President*
* *Rudolf C., a smoking logician*

The former US President is holding a public speech in the main and only square of a very small village in the Ligurian Apennines, northern Italy.[221] The attending crowd comprises a grand total of one *person: Rudolf, an American logician vacationing in that quiet and isolated place.*

Donald J. Trump: (*with all his parodied mannerisms; he smiles after answering each of his own questions*) Is America a great nation? Yeah. It's the greatest nation in America! (*pause*) Is Europe a great nation? Yeah. It's the greatest nation in Europe! (*pause*) Italy's great, isn't it? Yeah. It's great! (*striking a more concerned and aggressive tone*) It's Marxist immigrant fascists who aren't. They're the real threat! … Not all Mexicans, I mean. (*longer pause*) I'll phone up Putin and talk to him. I'll make him stop. I'm the only one he listens to. Don't worry! Really. Don't worry! (*pause*) I'll make Italy great again! (*smiling again*) Thank you, guys! You're great!

---

[220] Can be one sage's child. (**Judy**: Let yourself be eaten. **Punch**: Who said that? **Judy**: An Indian sage)

[221] The White House denies that such a visit has ever taken place. So does a butler in Mar-a-Lago, Florida.

Rudolf: (*clapping*) -

Trump climbs down his box and approaches the logician.

DJT: (*smiling*) I've got to go to the next village. (*pointing*) The other side of the valley.

R: (*slightly embarrassed*) … It's… nice.

DJT: (*serious*) Can you give me a ride, you?

R: (*surprised*) A ride?

DJT: Yeah. A ride. Don't have my car, you see.

R: (*even more surprised*) You don't?

DJT: No.

R: (*even more surprised, louder, spatters a bit out of sheer puzzlement*) You don't?

DJT: No.

R: (*honestly flabbergasted*) I see… (*takes some courage*) Well, my car is parked down there…

Rudolf walks Trump to his vehicle. It's an old FIAT 600. (An old FIAT 500 can also do.)

DJT: (*incredulous*) Is this a car? I mean, your car?

R: Yes, please, come this way (*opens the door*)

DJT: (*struggles long and hard to fit in the tiny car, sweats and squeezes, but to no avail*) I can't!

Act Two

R: (*embarrassed*) ... Well, there should be a bus coming...

DJT: Oh. Ok. I'll take that.

R: See that sign there? (*he points with his left hand*) That's the bus stop.

DJT: Ok.

R: Well, Mr President, I'm sorry but I can't wait here with you. You see...

DJT: (*interrupting*) Yeah. Go!

R: ... Ok ... Well, good night, Mr President. (*leaves*)

DJT: Night.

Trump sits there in silence between 20 seconds and 4 minutes, depending on the venue. He fishes out of his pocket a sausage roll and a book—a copy of Thomas More's Utopia, *in the original Latin version—and starts reading it while munching on the roll.*

DJT: (*looking up*) Rain, (*short pause*) it's raining, (*long pause*) it's pouring... (*very long pause; looks towards the audience*) I'm the greatest president ever. Ain't I?

Curtain.

XXV – There Must Be a Subway[222]

§1 Rudolf's dreams could be unconventional, to put it mildly. They weren't straightforward nightmares. Still, they weren't pleasant, golden, or sweet, as dreams are proverbially wished to be. That night, after meeting with the former US President Donald J. Trump in the Italian village where Rudolf spent his summer vacations, he dreamt of being in a subterranean corridor, probably part of a large subway system somewhere in America. Hundreds of people were coming and going, hurriedly, without paying any attention whatsoever to him, nor the fact that he was still smoking his pipe, even if it was strictly forbidden. There were guards, policemen, armed gangsters. But nobody took notice of him and his pipe. No smoke alarm went off.

Only a child, who was holding a large glass of water with both hands, stopped before him and bluntly asked: "Are you Tomas Masaryk?" "*Who's Tomas Masaryk?*," Rudolf thought. "No, I'm not," Rudolf replied, rather politely. The child left, as sudden and unexpected as it had appeared. Only a vague recollection of the child's brown jumper and the large glass remained in Rudolf's mind —like very old coffee stains on the kitchen countertop. The mind of the *dreamt* Rudolf, for one. But also of the dreaming Rudolf, for another. If they were one and the same Rudolf. I'm not entirely sure of that. I can't be. Can anyone, perhaps, be sure about it? Plenty of people are cocksure about all sorts of things, as though they knew everything. Especially ignorant people. Although arrogant professors exist as well. They can be found in all nations.

Rudolf kept walking. After a while, he stopped smoking his pipe. He had probably run out of tobacco. Or he was deriving no more pleasure from it. It's not clear. After all, it was just a dream. A figment. Like a book of fiction. At any rate, no child was in sight. No

---

[222] The reader is hereby reminded that all characters are fictional, whatever name they have been given.

brown jumper. No glass of water either. Instead, there were more and more subterranean corridors, each one leading into another. Vast. Interminable. Peculiar. A sort of maze. God's guts, perhaps. *"Who's Tomas Masaryk?,"* Rudolf thought once more. *He* didn't know that. And was that passer-by Alfred Tarski? Rudolf didn't know that either. But he seriously suspected it. He did.

Meanwhile, all the other people running around and past Rudolf became fewer and fewer in number, until nobody was left roaming those corridors but Rudolf himself. *"The maker of this place is the maker of the universe,"* he pondered. Upon which thought, however curious or as mysterious as it could be, a mechanical mouse showed up, racing past Rudolf. Intrigued, Rudolf started following it. *"It might know the way out,"* he mused, *"or to the nearest train."* And so did Rudolf keep walking in those corridors, silently, and without smoking ever again.

Rudolf was going to find a way out of *there*. He knew he would. That mouse would help him. Somehow, he also felt that he would meet his friend Otto, at the end of the journey. Otto was waiting for him *there*, wherever that other *there* out of *there* was. *There*'s always an end, in the end. As Otto says: "All sets, including empty sets, are bounded regions of logical space."

§2 Concomitantly, in another lengthy and deserted corridor, a warm female voice could be heard. The voice was reflecting aloud, somewhat lost in thought, and not wholly cogent: "Such are the noteworthy consequences arising, rather spontaneously, from the personal, social, and historical given whereby so many individuals, communities, cultures, and at times official States, having recognised that One Voice spoke at some point in the past, still promise and honestly venture to live according to their acknowledged responsibility to follow the subsidiary voices and scriptures which are held to be recalling the First, Divine, Supreme Declaration. If such noteworthy consequences are logically deduced, then the pious soul, persuaded of the fact, cannot deny them. The tolerant politicians, for their part, if they allow these souls to absorb such a fact, must then allow for the adoption of its consequences too.

The philosophers, if they want to contradict this line of individual conduct and collective organisation, must in turn demonstrate the spuriousness of the same fact. Nor would it be worth anything at all, and could actually prove quite dangerous for both public peace and general wellbeing, to raise an angry clamour against any purported 'affectations,' 'hyperboles,' 'obscurantism,' 'radicalism,' and so on and on… So many cruel disasters have followed angered clamours of this ilk!"

The train of thought possibly implied by the loud reflections uttered by the warm female voice in the lengthy and deserted corridor was very far from clear. Perhaps, it was unintelligible. Whether such an incomprehensibility was intended or not, it wasn't clear either. Arguably, the overall lack of clarity may have been the obvious result of all these thoughts being part of a dream of Rudolf's. Dreams are notoriously unclear, clearly. Unless, of course, obscurity should have been the clear intent at play. Which is unclear, at least at the past stage during which the dream was being dreamt; *and* the present stage during which these lines are being typed. What is more, Rudolf's dreams possessed a potent sense of clarity, when and while they were being dreamt. That clarity, however, characterised the felt side of the dreams' being, or their being experienced by the dreamer, rather than the conceptual abstractions derived thereof—the 'clear and distinct ideas' with which René Descartes was so enamoured, back in the 17th century. Somehow, the dream-like quality of the dreams at issue was not their eerie haziness, as is often supposed or encountered, but their explicit directness, even if at a level of sheer make-believe sensation and fictitiously vivid perceptibility. Yet all of this may be too cerebral. And it may be misdirected and misguiding too. Clarity does belong, in all probability, to another domain or dimension, which Descartes would have never contemplated in earnest as being the place where the inquirer's mind ought to focus upon and investigate keenly and in earnest: *The corporeal.*

Act Two

🕊

XXVI – I'd Rather Be Me[223]

Introduction

§1   My dear ladies, it is a real pleasure and a great honour to be here with you tonight. Many thanks for the kind and thrilling invitation. It doesn't happen very often that I can voice publicly my views in so prestigious a women-only institution and venue, tell my side of the story—so to speak—, and share with naked candour my life experience, which is much closer to your own than many of you may think. You'll understand later why I'm saying this. Believe me!

Your impressive life-size posters of *me* by the hall's splendid entrance refer to a long and daunting *lectio magistralis* that I'm supposed to be giving here, before all of you—and how many you are! Wow! Well, I'll try and do my best, I promise. You've kindly given me plenty of time—quite a lot, in fact!—to deliver my talk, and I'm not even sure that I can make use of all of it. In any case, as I stated before, I'll try and do my best. So, here we go!

To begin, I must be 100% honest with you. Talking to you like this *is* a challenge for me. I'm not a scholar, a politician, or anything like that. At the same time, performing in front of large audiences is not something that is totally alien to me, even if in a very different context. Also, my old, dear, kind father taught literature for many years at the university, so I can rely on some of the wisdom and example with which he provided me. Help me, dad!

I decided to organise my talk in three parts: First, a short sort of autobiography that can explain how and why I made the life choices that I made; second, an even shorter reflection on what I think is the central and most basic value lying beneath, or behind, my life choices and my business world at large; third, a defence of this business—in essence, what I do with myself and my life is, in

---

[223] Rated NC-17. If sexuality, lewd matters, and crass lexicon can unnerve you, even if fictional, then skip this chapter altogether. But remember: It's all humour.

ultimate analysis, *my* business. And then the conclusion to wrap it all up, both in theory and in practice. I'm not Hedwig Conrad-Martius, but I can try my best!

Hopefully, by being so organised, I won't disappoint my kind, dear old, dad. Or any of you, for that matter. I shall endeavour to be thorough, systematic, and persuasive. You've given me the time that is needed to do that, and you expect me to use it well. If I say something silly, though, please be *kind* with me. My tongue is skilled, I know that, but not in the rhetorical arts. Except, perhaps, for tricolons and alliterations, since my kind old dad used them all the time!

First Part: My Life[224]

§2 Let's start from the beginning, because beginnings can often offer penetrating insights into a person's character, choices, and personality. I was born and raised in an affluent, highly educated, loving, and very kind family. My father, in particular, my dear old daddy, was the kindest and most affectionate man that has ever graced the earth. He would spend lots of time with us, joke with us, and he was always there when we needed him. We were very fortunate.

I say "us" and "we" because I grew up with three sisters, who I loved and still love, and with whom I did all the things that young girls do: Studying, playing, fighting, forgiving, experimenting, smoking behind closed doors, telling stories, seeking adventure, being kind, being naughty, being cheeky, horsing around, being tame, being wild—being *together*.

Going to school was *fun*. I loved it. I have always loved books. As I said, my parents were highly educated. My kind dad, in particular, was a poet, and, as I briefly anticipated, he taught at the university: Classics and English literature. Now, I have forgotten most of my Greek and Latin, and you'll have to kindly excuse me for that. Yet,

---

[224] How far can a fictional person's life be taken apart?

growing up, my heroines and role-models were Helen of Troy, Circe, Nausicaa, and Calypso… yes, Calypso!

My sisters and I would go down to the lake and pretend that we were those great women, or that we were naiads and nereids—kind, clever, and sexy water nymphs from the ancient myths. The fantastic stories that my kind dad told us had opened up a sort of parallel universe that my sisters and I were free to inhabit and play with. A safe space where we had the freedom to develop our imagination and let it go in all directions, if we wanted to. And we *did*.

But let's go back to my school days, because they were important. I went to a school run by nuns, from first grade all the way up to the first years of college. Those nuns were the best people that I've met in my life. Kind, generous, always smiling. The happiest persons— the happiest *women*—that I've ever seen in my life. Really! No more joyful people has ever existed anywhere on this earth, I believe. Perhaps only in my business, on occasion.

There was only one subject, one dimension of human reality, that didn't 'work' for them, that put them off, so to speak. It's easy to guess which one: It was *sex*. Whenever anything sexual was raised, mentioned or, God forbid, done in actual reality, they just went mad at us, my classmates, my sisters, and *me*, of course. I found all that strange, unkind, unloving. Above all, I found that *unchristian*, that is, contrary to the spirit of Jesus Christ's teachings.

§3   Yes, I speak openly of Jesus, Christianity, faith, religion, even if it's very unfashionable these days, especially in the movie industry and in sophisticated academic circles like yours. You see, I have always been a church-going, believing, committed parishioner. My local priest, Father Richard—the kindest priest you could meet in real life—was also my best friend; my sisters aside, of course. Father Richard was the man that I could confess all of my sins to, and not just as a matter of confession. You know, I'm referring to the sacrament of confession, which is one of the kindest gifts that we have received from God—and God has given us more gifts than most of us can fathom: This is the *theological* wisdom of my speech, if you like. As to the *psychological* one, well… *Divertissement* cures *ressentiment*… But let's go in good order!

Father Richard was a kind, patient, intelligent man, and he listened. Yes, he *listened*. No matter your age or sex, he took you seriously. You were a *real person*, for him. And that is something that I've tried to do myself ever since: To take each and every individual that I meet as the unique person that they are. Like you are kindly doing with *me*—here, today.

Thanks *again* to all of you for doing just *this*. It's not something that *I* can take for granted. Given my profession, people talk a lot *about* me, and generally in very negative terms. Or they talk *about* me and my profession as if they knew it—but they don't. Worst of all, they don't let me and my colleagues talk, and, if we do, they don't take us seriously. Our voices are cancelled out, distorted, ridiculed, or reduced to something else that can confirm their prejudice.

Maybe, they all would benefit from meeting someone like Father Richard. He always had something intelligent, life-giving, and life-changing to share with you. One point that Father Richard shared with me as a young girl was: "Find God in *all* things." And so did I. It's a traditional Jesuit motto—and the wisest, kindest advice that a young person could get. It still guides my life. And it is also why sex became so important for *me*: Thank you, Father Richard!

§4 You see, as a teenager, I started seeing how much pain and suffering *sexual frustration* could cause. The geekiest boys, in particular, were the worst. Bottled up inside them, sexual desire was making them angry, confused, sad. It was the *devil*'s work. One, in particular, caught my eye. His name was Gavin. He had a funny face, he was as skinny as a pole, he had a weird voice, but he was kind, intelligent, sensitive. I liked him. As I said, I could see that there were boys aching and longing for water that could quench their thirst. But that water was nowhere to be found. In a school run by nuns, what were the chances, say, of being instructed to masturbate, have orgies, or watch porn? No coitus in the syllabus! No rock 'n' roll; no cock at all!

I decided to take matters in my own hands. One day, while I was sitting beside Gavin, I started stroking his crotch. There was already a bulge. I just made it bigger. It was during a biology class, ironically. And I kept going. Then I took it out. What a beauty! Thin, long, pinkish, bent... It isn't actually the most beautiful cock that I've seen, but, back then, it looked like some amazing revelation bursting out in front of me. Like a jack in the box—or a *Johnson* in the box, if you like... Eh! Some of you are giggling already. Like my sisters and I did when we were playing sexy nymphs by the lake. Other ladies are flushed, and gone all red in the face. You see? Sex is *still* a difficult subject to discuss in public. So I made it my mission to do so. To be the kind but firm prophetess of sex in our sad, suffering, cruel, and hypocritical world.

Gavin, when he exploded in my hand, gave me one of the most loving and sincere moments of self-realisation as a Christian that I've ever had. Yes, he *did*. That memory is so clear, as if it were still sticking to the deepest part of my soul. My very core. The hardest, most central part of *me*. Every time I think about that beautiful experience, it feels like some sort of kind embrace from high above that is coming down to reach for me and engulf me with joy and total release. A true blessing. A bliss. A kind and warm sense of acceptance, love, and joyfulness. That's what my partners' orgasms are for *me*. Truly, God's blessings come in many dressings.

From that moment on, Gavin and I became best friends. He was so kind. So sweet. A real sweetheart. He didn't expect to start a serious relationship with me or anything like that. He didn't have so much faith in himself. He also knew and understood that I couldn't be tied to one pole only, you see. Yes, he understood *me*. My personality. My needs. My desire. My longings. My loins. So, he introduced me to a group of friends that he had in school: Kind, shy, geeky boys like him. The sort of young men that my sisters, especially Michelle, but also Dora and Anita, made constantly fun of, without mercy: Ugly, gangly, spotty, chubby, sweaty, jumpy, gawky... Think of an insult or concoct a new slur: Truly, *you* name it!

§5 I'm *not* joking. My sister Michelle *was* certainly doing that—often, eagerly, and cruelly. She called them "nerds," "dorks," "weenies," "dinks," "incels," "swots," "wimps." There are always plenty of terms available to insult, belittle, and victimise victims! It wasn't too hard a thing to do. Think of any physical defect, flaw, or lack of confidence that boys that age can have, and I'm sure that at least one of Gavin's friends had it. They were the sort of young men who, if ignored, grow up into unattractive and vulnerable adults: You probably know the type.

Accumulated libido gnaws at their soul. They drink too much, eat too much, watch too much TV, not exercise enough. They do drugs, at times, or get pills from their doctors. They're sorry, suffering, sad, solitary men. No matter how much stuff they put into their stomachs or veins, they're hollow, because they're eaten away by a deep, unkind, grinding, ingrained sense of futility, self-loathing, hopelessness. All of which stems from *sexual frustration*—the root-cause of all human cruelties, as Marcuse taught us long ago. I call them the "frustrated martyrs."

They are the sort of grown men who try desperately to find online a wife, from some desolate place in Asia or Eastern Europe—and lose their savings in the process; or can only score with prostitutes—and poorly; or are so full of self-doubt that they can only rely on online porn and their own two hands—or some robots, these days: A kind invention, in a way. Erotica as *robotica*… It took centuries, and a bunch of engineers, but finally men have their own dildos!

Truth be told, these robotic companions are much more expensive than our nice dildos, including the fancy multi-speed ones… Maybe it's cheaper to talk to a fictional lover generated by artificial intelligence: She gets to know you, she understands your kinks better and better, and she can give you the thrill that you need for little money. *Much* less money than one would spend on a demanding, domineering, moody girlfriend—or a hi-tech sex-bot from Japan!

Incidentally, *I*'ve my own online avatar these days, if you want to give it a try.

Second Part: All Life[225]

§6 Anyway, I learnt a lot by spending time and experimenting with those kind, geeky boys. They were fun, when you got to know them. They just needed to be given a chance. And I did it. In point of fact, we are still very good friends. Some of them come to all of my shows. Friends like them can make the most loyal fans, you know? Your hardcore fan base.

And, frankly, over time, a strong spiritual connection developed among us. It was by pleasing all of these young men, and by being pleased by all of them in return, that I discovered *my* greatest talent and *my* true vocation. Thanks to those kind geeks, I ended up thinking of all the misfits and unlucky men who can't get any, who have no chance to ever get some sexual thrill and satisfaction. All that suffering. *Human* suffering. *Real* suffering. Martyrdom.

And so I went into the business that has made me famous, or infamous, depending on who's doing the talking. They all have their perspective on things. Including those things that they don't know very well… Anyway… That's not unusual, even in academia, my father told me.

Yes, my father, the 'great' Symonds… Unlike most girls in the business, I kept my first name, Monica, as a sign of love and respect for my kind and loving family. But I changed my last name: I had to make it catchier. I thought of "MacCinderella," as a bit of a joke, but "Wells" sounded much better. Besides, I loved H.G. Wells. I had read all of his books when I was young. He made me aspire to a better future, a *utopia*, a world where greed and need would disappear, and where sex could be as natural, ordinary, kind, and happy a feature in people's lives as eating breakfast cereals in the morning, having tea in the afternoon, or watching movies at night.

And yet, it's even deeper and more basic than that. Sexual release, sexual satisfaction, is as important as the daily bread that we pray for as Christians. It is as crucial for people's wellbeing as drinking water, or getting enough rest. If you think about it, without sex, life

---

[225] How far can a real person's life be taken apart?

itself would *end*. Not just human life. Also the animals, perhaps even the plants, would all cease to exist. Think about *that*! Cool down and think! Without sex, *no* life at all. Without sex, only death.

§7 "But sex is dirty," some of you will say. I've heard it many times. Do you know what my answer is? *Yes*. Yes, sex *is* dirty. But dirt is *good*. Dirt is the ground were the flowers can blossom. Those flowers that kind young men give to their fiancées and that old widows return to those men's graves at the local cemetery—like a belated kiss, or a never-given blowjob. It's real love. It's *kindness*. This is the *philosophical* message of my speech: Dirt is good.

Mirth needs filth, for one. Haven't you played with dirt, ever? My sisters and I certainly did. By the lake, we rolled in the mud, made mudpies, threw them around, and came home covered in muck and grass. Our parents would then kindly help us get undressed and take a warm bath… Beautiful days, which will never come back… And, like my parents, dirt is *kind*. It's just the victim of a bad rap. Just like —please ladies, do pardon my French—shit, *merde*, excrements, faeces… You know, manure. Horrible, right? Well, flowers, wheat, corn, olive trees… *Life* as such finds nourishment and the possibility of growth in cows' and horses' dung, doesn't it? Growth needs filth. That's another important lesson that I learnt by the lake. Neither nourishment nor living growth can be found in rubies, gold, silver, or the purest crystals!

Some of you look grossed out… I'm sorry… I know. Ladies aren't supposed to talk about physiological functions, and even less celebrate the fact that they get laid—and as often as I do; and for money to boot! In *public*, of course. Ladies don't talk about these things in *public*, no matter what goes on in their alcoves. In *private*, who hasn't confided in a kind friend or a kind sister and told her, with great pride, that she got a man totally mad about her, that she blew him with great skill, that she jerked off some big shot or famous guy, that she sniffed her girlfriends' wet panties, that she had great sex with two different lovers, that she can get it in her ass and enjoys it very much, or that she got covered in warm cum and felt amazing?

Yeah, "cum." Disgusting, isn't it? Well, it's just like "dirt." A word, to begin with, and something incredibly important as well. Cum, sperm, semen: They signify *life*. Life itself. Life is liquid. Life is humid. Life is humour. It's very ancient wisdom. But it's also modern science. Humours are at the very centre of God's creation, of all that lives and breathes, and has a life-supporting metabolism. It doesn't matter if it's a plant or an animal. Think about *any* habitat on our planet that can support life and all the creatures thriving in those habitats: Humidity, water, rain, lakes, rivers, seas, oceans, blood, digestive juices, sweat, spit, the plant's sap…

Didn't God Himself mix dirt *and* spit to create the one and only being that the Bible says resembles Him? Introject God, then! Is it a mad idea, a scandal? Read Saint Paul: Jesus' teachings have *always* been meant to be madness to the Gentiles and scandal to the Jews. Real Christianity will always throw you off balance! My faith will always be a divine shock… I can see you gasp: Am I mocking my own creed, my tradition? No, I don't think so. I'm not joking. I'm serious. I'm fulfilling my mission as a believer. Truly, I am finding God in *everything*. Just as I was told to do all those years ago by Father Richard—that kind, gentle, wise priest.

I know it sounds crazy, but God's grace comes also as cum in one's face! Sublimate everything, and nothing sublime will be left for you to enjoy in this life! These are the kind of unexpected paradoxes that intelligent people like yourselves can find humorous as much as insightful—even if wackily so. Many others, instead, can only get confused, or offended. That is why, perhaps, people with a *poor sense of humour* tend to be the most enraged enemies of my line of work. They can be clever people. Some of them were my teachers at the university, where I did a BSc in biology, followed by an MA in gender studies. Still, without humour, you get no humility and no sense of proportion. Above all, without humour, you get a dry desert.[226]

---

[226] A grain of sand lost in this footnote observed: "Souls." Then, a mist poured down its surface.

§8   I've met a lot of these arid people: Bright, often, but with no joy. No self-irony. No irony. Unloving. Resentful. Unimaginative. Literal. Censorial. Uncompassionate. Punitive. Unkind... *Cruel*. Even if they rationalise it all as justified moral outrage and reformist political zeal. Certainly, they're never as cheerful as the good nuns that I was used to as a kid! Not that the nuns were any better, in this respect. They too couldn't and, even now, can't grasp my sexuality, my love of love, my generosity of body and spirit. They could and can only talk about injuries, traumas, risks, infections, venereal diseases—another godly intervention in the world, isn't it? Although a pagan one... It was and is as if *our blood*, the blood of women like *me*, could only be contaminated, and never really be healthy, happy, free, giving, and kind.

And then the *sin* 'thing,' of course! Sin, sin, sin, sin... The nuns would hammer away on that one point without pause: Sin, sin, sin, sin... But without sin, I wondered, where's the fun, the thrill of transgression, the discovery of the limit, the elation of growth, the discovery of oneself? If God is in everything, then He must be also in sin—or in what *looks* like sin to some people, or is believed to be so, but actually is not. Just like some people are disgusted by common, universal things without which life would simply disappear. The most important things, in essence. Bodily humours, like spinal fluid, mucus, saliva, urine, blood, and sperm.[227]

Let's not rush things, though. I stated at the very beginning that my *lectio magistralis* would be as thorough and as academic as possible. Let's give these critics some credibility and look at their most frequent attacks at people like me, my profession, my world, *my* business.

---

[227] A sperm cell lost in this footnote observed: "Souls." Then, a mist poured down its mitochondrion.

Act Two

Third Part: My Business[228]

§9 They say that it's bad for the body, that there are damages, prolapses, illnesses. That's true. It can happen. Sometimes, you really get screwed. Especially if you're not careful enough or don't know what you're doing. Or the conditions you're in are dangerous ones. I've seen it with my own eyes. But the same is true of ice skating, football, rugby, boxing, or classical ballet. Honestly, have you ever seen a ballerina's feet and ankles? Go and take a good look, if you haven't, I dare you! They're literally covered in bruises, deformed, broken, and kept together with wraps and plasters. Rather than 'dance therapy,' there should exist 'dancers' therapy!'

Ballerinas start on this destructive path in *childhood*, surrounded by smiling mothers who clap boredly at their synchronised movements and jumps and stuff. All seemingly happy and yet oblivious, or rather complicitly silent about, the physical damage that is being inflicted on those little girls—and a few boys, of course: I don't want to sound sexist or unkind. Would anyone ban ballet because of that? Or stop kids from going into contact sports or any sport where they can injure themselves? No, nobody would! And reasonably so, I'd argue.

Those activities are *valuable*. In so many ways. They teach discipline, courage, loyalty, cooperation, and many other virtues. They make you strong in your body and will, and capable of reaching your goals. They can cure traumas, not just cause them. Also, they possess inherent beauty, aesthetic force, spiritual kindness, and they can make yourself and other people feel deep, incredible emotions. They can excite you, elate you, and even capture the attention of large crowds, who will then pay attention to *you* and, if lucky, make *you* feel important, or even rich and famous, on some luckier, rare occasion—like it happened to *me* in *my* line of work.

---

[228] What part of a person's life can be deemed fictionally real rather than really fictional?

So, let's treat porn like we treat ballet. Let's have good floors, capable teachers, informed students, first-aid kits at hand, trained therapists. I seriously contend that it's easier to justify becoming a porn actor than a ballerina, because the adult industry, as the name suggests, accepts *adults* only. There are no mothers sending children into it. It's grown men and women who decide to go into it. They may do it for all kinds of reasons, and sometimes the wrong ones too, like it happens in *all* lines of work—I'm not denying that. People can make wrong choices, *all* the time. Normally, they quickly realise it. Other times, it takes decades before they understand it. Or they can be led into recalling their carefree past with contempt, unleashing a deluge of retrospective traumas and pointless self-loathing… People can be cruel in so many ways!

But my point here is that it is *their* reasons that they're following and acting on, not someone else's. If they make porn their business, then it is *their* business. And that's what happened to me as well: I made porn *my* business. Successfully, I should add. I found acclaim, love, admiration, friendship, pleasure, safety, and kindness in it. If I wanted and I still want to do it, then let *me* do it, leave *me* be—don't be needlessly cruel to *me*. It's *my* business!

§10 *They* say it's prostitution. Sex work. Yes, well, *of course* it is. That's true. That '*work*' bit, at least. It's true, almost obvious, to a plausible but only partial extent. For one, prostitution doesn't have the artistic qualities and creative characteristics of the porn industry. It's not glitzy. It's not as standardised and organised. And it is often outside the sphere of lawful business and interactions. Good Lord, that's no small difference either! Much harm, far too much, results from this difference. Being well-regulated by laws and judges is the a-b-c of basic civility!

However, people in my well-regulated business are still doing *sex for money*, if we want to reduce the whole thing to some kind of contract without any other social context—as a matter of ethics and psychology, I actually think that prostitutes, more often than not, have other, kinder motives, feelings, hopes, desires, reactions, longings, all of which go beyond the simple cum-for-cash logic:

That's how orthodox economists and criminal kingpins think, not most people, unless they're forced into making elementary choices between survival and starvation.

Like porn, moreover, prostitution is *diverse*. In the world of prostitution, it can be even easier to guess who's in it for the right reasons, the wrong reasons, and who's being wronged, that is, who's being denied the freedom to choose—*liberty*: An important value. One thing is to be a high-end escort, maybe a part-time fashion model or a former actor, accompanying rich men in Dubai or rich women in Jamaica, and making loads of cash over a five-year period that will fix you for good. You prefer that to being a waitress, a nurse, a teacher, an oral hygienist, or working on a building site? Then be my guest! Plenty of people do so: It's *your* choice.

Another thing is to be a trafficked young woman, raped, beaten, brought to a foreign country, caged, deprived of passport and legal status, squeezed for money by some mafia thug, who also forces you to take drugs, abort your children, make no friends, and untold other horrors. Bastard sons of bitches exist aplenty. And they're much worse and much crueller than the out-of-luck, innocent bitches who spawned them. Sometimes, these bastard sons of bitches are famous captains of industry, rich media gurus, noted financial soothsayers, well-educated stock-brokers, respected business-people, film producers, or even influential pundits and politicians. Who knows? They could even make president of the US, one day. Imagine that!

So, similar reasons and approaches should apply here. Sex work, whether it's porn or prostitution, is *work*. Respect work, then. Respect labour. Give people real job opportunities, a chance to make their own choices, be protected from exploitation, suffer no violence and no coercion, operate in safe and healthy environments—the sort of stuff that any worker, any trade union, or any socialist party in the world would campaign and fight for. One important thing that I've learnt from my kind parents, who were both devout Christian socialists, is that Tories are capable only of *tough love*. And that's not real love. Love is kind. Tories are not. Love is generous. Tories are not. Love is warm. Tories are not. Love is fluid, Tories are not.

For as long as we've got this cruel thing called "capitalism," which requires people to sell their time and skills for money, workers should be given full rights, good wages, benefits, paid holidays, and safe and healthy working conditions. That's love too. That's kindness. And that's the best that we can get right now. The day when we have a communist utopia—which is something that many of you here, in this fancy ballroom, are likely to dread—then we will be making porn just and purely because we like it. It will also be the day when no *stigma* is attached to porn, sex work, or sex as such. The day when Anaïs Nin or Alberto Moravia receive the Nobel prize, or people like me and Stellar Love are allowed to compete with Meryl Streep and Emma Stone for the Academy Awards. But we are a long way from that state of affairs, whether you'd deem it ideal or not, in which my business would be really and only *my* business.

§11 If critics don't know what else to say, then *they* move up high into abstract territory. *They* say that porn is part of "patriarchy," whatever that is, and helps it continue and grow into a threat against "women," as though women were all made out of one and the same mould. Yes, right. Now, patriarchal societies existed and still exist. Go and take a tour of the Middle East, for instance. Or go to China. But those are also the countries that *ban* pornography. Look at the few countries in the world that grant some *real* freedom, some *real* pluralism, and allow people, women included, to make at least some *real* choices about their jobs and lifestyles, and you'll see that they're those that allow porn to be made or, at least, circulate. People are then free to *fantasise*, at a minimum—and people *need* to fantasise, lest they fall prey to passive-aggressive "pink madness," as Hillman dubbed it. I'm sure you're familiar with his work in psychology.

However, don't start me on voodoo stuff like "micro-patriarchy" and "hidden" structures of "socio-cultural violence" or "coercion." I'm a biologist—crikey, I'm a scientist! You either come up with empirically sound categories that we can agree on, operationalise and test, or you'd better stop making up ghosts, which you and your friends take to be the make-up of reality, while other people can come up as easily with different ideas, schemata, interpretations. It's like dealing with orthodox economists, or getting Aaron and Moses to agree on the direction to follow! It's a game of shrewd constructs, but with no basis to sort among them and decide which ones you should take seriously, and which ones you'd better chuck and forget about.

As to the alleged threat against the class of "women," I'm always left puzzled, and a little bemused, by the cheek that some clever people have whenever taking the stand—like me here tonight, ironically—and speaking, as if they knew the inner essence of things. Who the heck are "women"? Who the heck are these people talking about "women"? Do they know each and every one of them? Think of it! Apart from the biological category and the looser socio-cultural conventions developed on it, there exist on our planet *billions* of specific individuals—billions of unique *persons*—and as many noggins, personalities, body types, sexual preferences, subjectivities, hopes, fantasies, kinks, manias, and professional vocations. Including *mine*.

It sounds shocking, but there it is anyhow: Think of all those people who like taking fists up their ass. Aren't they people, *persons*, just like me or any of you? Of course they are! Different individuals have plenty of characteristics. As such, there can be overlap and like-mindedness: Asses and fists are themselves best when they're not from just one and the same person. Still, each one of these men and women is *unique*. Each one of *us* is her own person!

There may be broader stereotypes and general trends. I'm not denying *that*. They're an obvious feature of any human community. No society could do without them. Some of them can be limiting and despicable. There's plenty of stupid, cruel, unkind social and cultural 'rules' that say that girls or women are like that, and only like that, have no sense of humour, are irrational, or they can do this or that, and only this or that. But that's stupid stuff that applies to boys and men too, who are then sent to war, down mineshafts, driving trucks, collecting garbage, sailing on sinking vessels, or straight to the electric chair despite an obvious psychiatric condition. It's the sort of prejudice that makes men expendable, while *we* are not—"women and children first!:" Have you ever heard it? … Hopefully not on a cruise ship!

Also and above all, that's exactly the sort of stiff gender roles that can change and have *already* changed—at least for women. We are no longer living in the 1950s or 1800s, nor the 1990s and 2000s! Thanks to our mothers, grandmothers, and great-grandmothers, women's emancipation has been *won*: Hurrey! Today, only mere remains, traces, *vestiges* of patriarchal oppression are left around—ask the great Laura Kipnis about it! Ruins of a collapsed empire. They are being uprooted everywhere—apart from the Middle East: Those poor veiled women and their burqas! Try wearing one and you'll understand my point even better. You might then come to agree with me on the fact that my business is, or should be, *my* business.

Conclusion[229]

§12 Those people who speak of "women" in so cavalier a way remind me of my kind old nuns, who would claim to know for real what "human nature" is like, down to the tiniest practical details, and, on that privileged basis, argue that something is "inherently wrong" or "inherently right." These kind nuns, and their blessed Church, had access to *the* Law. The others didn't. They alone, in short, could distinguish between good and bad. They alone could reach the deepest grounds of morality, like the best divers. Nobody could question them, their reach, or their interpretation of those grounds themselves. And that's the pickle; for there is a pickle!

Deep *there*, I think, you don't have the Law revealing itself in a definitive, explicit way to someone's pure and well-formed heart, but not to other people's hearts, like Allah or the angel Moroni are said to have done. Down *there*, wherever that is inside you, you get God talking in a mysterious tongue to *you*, *each* of you, each of *us*, as the *unique persons* that we all are. When *your* heart, *your* conscience,

---

[229] Do notice that the Latin etymology of "conclusion" indicates 'joining together," 'shutting up,' and 'enclosing.'

speaks to *you*, you should better start listening. Because, among other things, it's very hard to grasp what's being said to you. It's a real mess, at times!

On the contrary, whenever someone claims to be right *all* the time, no matter what, and, at the same time, doesn't even listen to dissenting opinions about how they want to conduct their own existence, or *yours*, then the *devil* is at work. That's the infernal realm of dogmatism, fanaticism, literalism, repression. It's the bleak universe of the Third Reich, not the kind, loving one of Wilhelm Reich. It's a domain filled with rage, envy, fear, insecurity, resentment, *not* love.

Love listens. Love helps. Love accepts. Love welcomes. Love takes and gives chances. Love is kindness. Love is protean. Love can mean a pearl necklace or a fist up the ass. Love is flexible. Love is supple. It's like life-giving, flowing, fresh water. It's not rock-solid ice. Love is never afraid of pursuing happiness. Hatred, *au contraire*, is so cold and full of fear, that it denies happiness even to the ones who do the hating. Stop the *hate*! That's what I say.

Sometimes, I suspect that all the hatred and the blame that my business unjustly receives has to do with the *self-hatred* of people who are sexually frustrated. Because love is the enemy of hatred. If hatred abounds, then that means that there isn't enough love going around. And if there isn't enough love, then there isn't enough sex, enough kindness. If only people were busy spending hours and hours having weekly orgies and daily sex, even just on their own, they wouldn't have time to kill one another, maim one another, rob one another, or go to war. *Make love, not war*! They had understood it pretty intelligently in the 1960s, hadn't they?

Platonic love will *not* do, for it won't disarm the likely warriors, but only increase their frustration—frustrated young men especially, who have always made the best, cruellest soldiers. People *need* to fuck. And most people don't do it nearly enough. They *need* help, then. So, *fuck* more! Fuck, fuck, fuck like rabbits: Lovely, kind creatures in God's creation; aren't they? Fuck like rabbits, then! Don't be choosy or judgmental, and you won't spend your old age regretting that you hadn't fucked more when you were young and fit.

You may even create a more equal, integrated, and happier society in the process. It's all part of loving others as yourself: *Love* other people, make love, fuck a lot, and love *yourself*. If you don't have a partner, wank or finger yourself aplenty, and then some. Trust me, *I*'ll be there to help you!

§13 Let me leave you with a closing, practical suggestion too. My heart spoke to me a long time ago and taught me that love is *power*. Fucking is power. Possibly, it's the most powerful power that has ever existed. Without love, hence without making love, hence without fucking, hence without sex, hence without sex appeal, life would simply *stop*. The power that we have to stimulate others, titillate them, give them pleasure, or create new life with them, is a power rivalling all armies, all kingdoms, all systems of law, all sciences, and all religions. Pure power!

As for us Christians, love means the pure power of *charity*, in the way Saint Paul wrote about it. Let's use this power, then, as a power to do *good*. Let's do real charity! A hands-on approach is what is needed. Facts, not just theory, or sheer theology! Hence, don't neglect the fact that *ecstasy* belongs to faith as much as sex: Do you think it's a mere coincidence?

In a unique chance to be good Christians, I challenge you to host a series of hand-job *volunteering* sessions around the city. Don't idealise love: Embody it! Dress up sexy, put on your best make-up, get a fancy new pair of pumps, be kind, and invite frustrated men, ugly men, deformed men, lonely men, diseased men, suffering men —and as many women in similar conditions, for that matter—to come to you, thanks to you, for you, with you, in you, on you!

Give them some joy, some relief, some kindness, some love! Make full use of the power that you possess. Be generous. Be kind. Bo good. Be loving. Each and every one of you. Make a kind, good, positive use of your immense, innate, intrinsic power. I've been doing it since I attended the kind nuns' school. I made it *my* business. Now try and make it *yours*![230]

XXVII – Alien Day[231]

One Act:
• *Otto N., a smoking logician*
• *An ensign of* Star Trek*'s USS* Enterprise *(who looks like Gershom Carmichael)*[232]

Otto wakes up. He's aboard the Enterprise. *He doesn't know it. A young ensign approaches him.*

Ensign: (*politely*) You are up, sir! Excellent.

Otto: (*puzzled throughout the conversation*) Pardon?

E: You are up, sir. Awake. That is good.

O: Why's it good?

E: Because you are no longer asleep, sir.

O: Was I asleep?

E: Evidently, sir. You snored, at times.

O: (*embarrassed*) Sorry about that.

---

[230] Only *three* elderly ladies in the audience applauded. For the rest, a loud silence followed the end of her speech.

[231] Also known as "On an Earthly Night." (**Punch**: Why do they like clarity so much? **Judy**: They fear the dark.)

[232] Yes, I confess it, I'm an inveterate Trekkie. (**Punch**: Isn't that clear enough? **Judy**: Eternity beacons.)

E: Nothing to be sorry about, sir.

O: Why's that?

E: That what, sir?

O: Nothing… nothing to be sorry about. Snoring.

E: Snoring is a perfectly natural process of the human body, sir.

O: Have I got a body?

E: I believe you do, sir. Though I have not probed the issue, sir. May I, sir?

O: What?

E: Probe, sir, the issue.

O: Probes?

E: Not that I know of, sir.

O: Not what?

E: No probe was launched, sir. Though I can check, sir.

O: Where?

E: With the ship's steering cock, sir.

O: What?

E: The captain, sir.

O: Who?

Act Two

E: James Tiberius Kirk, sir.

O: Tiberius?

E: Yes, sir. Though I don't think he likes it very much. Never uses it, sir.

O: Who?

E: Tiberius, sir.

O: What?

E: The captain, sir.

O: Oh… The captain?

E: Yes, sir. The captain.

O: (*completely lost*) … Does he snore?

E: I can't say, sir. Though I have heard him breathe heavily, sir.

O: Have you?

E: Yes, sir.

O: Why?

E: I was listening, sir.

O: What?

E: The breathing, sir.

O: Breathing?

E: As we speak, sir. Are you not?

O: What?

E: Breathing, sir.

O: Am I?

E: I would gather so, sir. It would seem logical. *And* biological. Shall I probe the issue, sir?

O: What?

E: Probe, sir, the issue.

O: Probes?

E: Not that I know of, sir.

O: Not what?

E: No probe was launched, sir. Though I can check, sir.

O: Where?

E: With the ship's steering cock, sir.

O: What?

E: The captain, sir.

O: Who?

E: James Tiberius Kirk, sir.

O: (*pensively, as to himself*) Tiberius?

Act Two

E: Who, sir?

O: Tiberius.

E: The captain, sir.

O: Tiberius… Eh?

E: The ship's steering cock, sir.

O: What?

E: The ship's steering cock, sir.

O: What?

E: The captain, sir.

O: Tiberius?

E: Yes, sir.

O: The ship's steering cock?

E: Yes, sir.

O: Steering?

E: Yes, sir.

O: Cock?

E: Yes, sir.

O: Of the ship?

E: Yes, sir.

O: On the sea?

E: No, not exactly, sir.

O: Not the sea?

E: Yes, precisely, sir, not the sea, sir.

O: (*even more puzzled*) Not the sea…

E: Space, sir.

O: Where?

E: Here, around us, sir.

O: Isn't that normal?

E: I suppose it is, sir.

O: I mean, look around you!

E: Yes, sir. It is definitely a spacious ship, sir.

O: Which ship?

E: The USS Enterprise, sir.

O: Enterprise?

E: Yes, sir.

O: Whose enterprise?

Act Two

E: Ours, sir. Our mission, sir.

O: Mission?

E: Yes, sir. Mission, sir. To boldly go where no intelligent-but-without-prejudice-towards-diversly-able beings, be they carbon-, silicon- or other-chemical-based, civilisationally-advanced-yet-without-implying-any-inferiority-towards-other-civilisations-at-different-levels-of-civilisational-development, and technologically-capable sentient creature has gone before, provided that no time-travel-trickery is unduly involved, that is, sir!

O: (*flabbergasted*) ... Who's in charge around here?

E: The captain, sir.

O: (*proud of himself*) Ah! Tiberius!

E: Yes, sir. But, please, do not call him *that*, sir.

O: *That* what?

E: That, sir. The T-word, sir.

O: T-word?

E: T-word, sir.

O: What word?

E: The T-word, sir.

O: That's *that*?

E: *That*, sir, exactly.

O: *"That?"*

E: Yes, *that*, sir.

O: Not "Tiberius," then?

E: Yes, *that*, sir, the T-word, sir.

O: *That*… Ah, you mean "Tiberius," then!

E: Yes, sir. That, sir. Shh!

O: … The steering cock.

E: Steering, yes.

O: Cock.

E: Cock, sir. Yes, sir.

O: Of the ship, right?

E: And left, sir. But we prefer port and starboard, sir.

O: Which port?

E: Any port of call, sir.

O: Call?

E: Yes, sir.

O: Who calls?

E: The captain, sir.

Act Two

O: (*with enthusiasm*) The ship's steering cock!

E: Yes, sir. The captain calls, sir.

O: What? Where?

E: Anything, sir. Anywhere, sir. Unless in violation of Federation Law.

O: Federation?

E: Yes, sir.

O: (*flabbergasted and frustrated*) Oh God… Can I talk to anyone else?

E: Who, sir?

O: The ship's steering cock, for one.

E: The captain, sir?

O: Yes, of course! (*losing patience*) Gordon Bennett! Are *you* sleeping?

E: I would gather not, sir. Highly unlikely. Shall I probe the issue, sir?

O: What?

E: Probe, sir, the issue.

O: Probes?

E: Not that I know of, sir.

O: Not what?

E: No probe was launched, sir. Though I can check, sir.

O: Where?

E: With the captain, sir.

O: (*mixing anger with hope*) Yes, the captain! That's what I said!

E: Yes, sir. (*with pride*) We are not sleeping around here, sir!

O: (*particularly surprised*) Oh! Doesn't he sleep?

E: Who, sir?

O: The captain.

E: The ship's steering cock, sir?

O: Yes, cock.

E: (*in a dreamy tone*) That's the dream, sir.

O: What?

E: The cock, sir.

O: The cock?

E: Yes, sir. The captain's, sir.

O: What?

E: In *my* reveries, sir.

Act Two

O: Where?

E: It's a matter of taste and personal preference, sir. Mostly in bed, sir. But we are not prejudiced.

O: What?

E: In bed, sir.

O: Bed?

E: Yes, sir. Bed, sir. Where one usually goes to sleep, sir.

O: The captain?

E: In bed, sir.

O: Peculiar… Does *he* snore?

E: Who, sir?

O: The ship's steering cock.

E: What, sir?

O: The captain.

E: Where, sir?

O: In bed.

E: Which bed, sir?

O: On the ship.

E: Which ship, sir?

O: Ours... Yours!

E: The Enterprise, sir?

O: Yes, yes! The Enterprise!

E: Yes, our ship, sir.

O: With beds.

E: To sleep, sir. Primarily, sir. But... We're not prejudiced. I'd rather do it in bed, for instance.

O: In bed? Where *I* was asleep? (*bashfully*)... and snoring?

E: Yes, sir. In bed, sir. Not yours, though. Unless inevitable. But... who snores, sir?

O: What?

"Red alert! Red alert!," a peremptory voice is heard: "This is the captain speaking! Battle stations, all hands to battle stations. This is not a drill! I repeat, this is not a drill! ... Red alert! Red alert! This is the ship's steering cock speaking!" Otto and the ensign rush out.

E: (*surprised to find Otto hurrying beside him*) Where are you going, sir?

O: (*still puzzled*) Battle stations!

E: Why, sir?

O: Duty.

E: (*uncertain*) What, sir?

O: Duty. Be responsible. If it rains, be the umbrella. Do the right thing. Hans himself told me.

E: Tiberius, sir?

O: No, Hans.

E: Who, sir?

O: Hans.

E: Tiberius Hans, sir?

O: No, Hans.

E: Hans Tiberius, sir?

O: No, just Hans.

E: (*smiling*) Ah. I see. Hans!

Curtain.

XXVIII – Runes Out of Time[233]

From the Notice Board Aboard on the Broad Forms of Notice Abroad:

Prof Benedict's lengthy account of the Saga of Finn o' Fjord (Fjarðarfinnssaga) covers two distinct periods in the long life of the titular prickly hero, who presumedly lived in southern Norway at the

---

[233] Dead languages are never late. Dead people, for their part, stop worrying about being late. Bless them!

time of the country's adoption of Christianity in the early 11th century. These are also the historical periods covered in those few extant later manuscripts of the Saga itself on which authentic experts have themselves reached unanimous agreement with regard to their periodical authenticity. Many common variants and outright forgeries of the Saga have plagued the varied scholarly community for countless generations, and the work of variable neo-Finnish linguists and former communist experts in Old-Norse philology has been effectively arduous, to say the least, especially after the collapse of the Berlin Wall and other venerable Germanic institutions affected by plagues, plagiarism, carduaceous blights, and analogous breakdowns.

The first period covered in the account is the one concerning Finn's successful creation of his own personal kingdom in the Norse fjord where he had been born and raised—creative archaeological research has not yet been able to determine which fjord it is, exactly. Much space is taken by the detailed and lively description of Finn's life-saving horse, which he is said to have flogged dead. Nearly as much space is devoted to Finn's distinctive direction pole, another sign of distinction for a marauding and pillaging title-seeking Viking of his generation and high social status, although he is equally mentioned not to have been able to distinguish north from south, and to have been cruelly misdirected by a masked wizard who wished him ill. (It is said that Finn peed in the local penal colony, yet walking right past the communal latrine.) Minor attention is given to major ballyragging traits of Finn's and his fine countenance, none of which counted much *per se*, but all of which left Finn conditionally alive both in private and in public, directed him towards county and kingly public distinctions, and made him look unconditionally dead-right, reasonably accountable, unreasonably attractive, and attractively ballsy.

The second period covered in Prof Benedict's massive account is the one concerning Finn's old-age full trimester of effective tonic repentance and affective pentito's atonement at a nearby subdominant convent, where several pious nuns, whose valuable mercy he was at, are said to have convened after each Mass and conveniently implemented the following pitiless pieties, as well as other invaluable means of piety and salvation: Coldly keeping him awake inside the cold keep, tuning his pitched shaping planer with a U-shaped out-of-tune A pitchfork, pickily coaxing him with coaxial pickaxes, caning him on the fly with canine flying bats, hitting him literally on the head and face with letterheads and other effacing types, breaking wilfully his glasses and will with shards of wilfully broken glasses, chucking mud at him while mudding, biting his pointy nipples and crippling him by ill-using his fingertips as useful pointers, feeding him entrails of unwell mice and other well-fed rodents, ironing his tetters in iron fetters, kicking him carelessly in the groin with uncaringly uncured boils, casting spells over him with runes in runes during overcast spells, spitting on him whenever spitting outside, splashing him with icy water while watering their splashy ice flowers, giving him weekly manicures and visage beauty treatments with flowery and visibly weak evasive clippers, and filling his cell with rotting exotic flowers and other cellulosic crafts. All of which Finn endured without saying a word.

The original informed wordy account by Prof Benedict can be found, free of charge and due fees, duly charged on the university website, originated in informatic Word format only.

XXIX – Sod Off He Said[234]

§1 It was Tom's first real job ever: Mail delivery. On that day, he had found an open envelope and, driven by juvenile curiosity, read the mail. Lo and behold, Tom had quickly realised that the message he was carrying was important, very important. Possibly a matter of life and death. No less than that. He had to let the recipient, some Mr Singer, get it as soon as possible! At least, he had to let him know about that message and its contents.

---

[234] Grammarians don't get upset: "Sod off," he said. (Who's the reader playing Ultravox in the background?)

In a deed of unsolicited altruistic concern, Tom memorised the message word by word. Excessive? Perhaps. He did it just in case he should drop the envelope along the way, misplace it while driving his three-wheeled vehicle, or lose it in some other silly way. Tom was still nervous and full of insecurities. "Newbies' nerves," as a gentle and witty teacher of his had aptly termed those butterflies and other youthful worries during a recent, pleasant conversation at the college: A stern but nice man, that teacher—East Asian, most probably.

Tom parked by the right building, which he had recognised for what it was only after standing in front of it. It was located in a rather dodgy neighbourhood. That part of the city was often in the news, and not for pleasing, assuaging, cheery or meritorious reasons. Stabbings, drug dealing, prostitution, freak accidents, the occasional murder—even prosthodontists! There were then silly dark legends being told all over town about those blocks being infested by gigantic grey aliens, satanic covens, half-intelligent zombies, and slimy green monsters!

Not that *he* really believed in any of that stupid and nonsensical lore. Nevertheless, Tom had reasonably concluded that the short message which fate had landed into his two slightly-trembling hands was actually as important as he had been suspecting since the very beginning. A man's life could be a stake! Maybe more than one... "*Time to save the world!*," Tom thought, picturing himself as some sort of big-moustachioed superman or spandex-clad superhero. He briefly yet heartfully smiled within his revelry-prone adolescent mind—silly, yet saintly.

Tom swiftly climbed seven flights of stairs and found immediately the apartment where he was expected to deliver that rather short but crucial message, which he was now carrying with no negligible degree of acute nervousness and upsetting trepidation. The words of the message were running back and forth inside Tom's anxious noddle. Back and forth. Repeatedly, as though those words were stuck in a loop. Tom's heart was beating hard. So hard! He was sweating like a fountain. He could have been swimming in his own sweat. It was just mad!

Act Two

§2 Tom truly hoped that he hadn't arrived late, too late... He knocked on the door. (Why? There was no doorbell.)

"Sod off!," a voice replied from the inside.

"*He's alive!*," he thought, feeling relieved. "Mr Singer!," Tom said, "there's mail for you. Can you open the door, please?"

"Sod off!," the same voice repeated from the inside.

"Mr Singer!," (Tom didn't know that the actual, real name of the recipient was a different one, but criminals often require shrewd stratagems of that ilk.) "Shall I slip you the mail under the door?"

"Sod off!," Tom was told a third time.

"*Weird*," he said to himself. "Well, okay, I'll slip it anyway, okay?," he confirmed.

Tom wanted to be absolutely sure that the envelope, and the message which the envelope contained, reached Mr Singer. Tom was a serious man on a serious mission: This was no joke!

While he was slipping the letter, Tom hit the door with his head—nothing too dramatic: Just a little bump. Nevertheless, it was more than enough for the door to end up being wide open in front of Tom, in a matter of seconds. Just like that. He didn't mean to do it, really!

Tom got a shocking and sudden surprise. He almost got frightened. And Tom wasn't easily frightened. He had spotted a body, in fact. A dead body, of all things. Lying face down on the floor. With a fez still firmly pinned on the head. A candlestick held tightly in the right hand. A broken glass beside it. A puddle of, well, water, probably. And *no* pants on.

"Heart attack...," Mr Singer's chihuahua stated in a matter-of-fact manner, hopping closer to Tom, "... right this morning. Didn't have his tea either."

"Oh," Tom proffered. "That's sad!." Then Tom looked at the miniscule dog and added: "Well, there was no real reason for me to hurry *so* much and deliver him his mail."

"Right," commented the chihuahua. "Will you sod off now?"

"Oh yes," muttered Tom, a little embarrassed, "have a good day!"

"Right," hissed peevishly the dog through its tiny, sharp teeth. And shut the door.

XXX – Him and Aristotle[235]

One Act:
* *Young Aristotle*
* *Aristotle's old teacher (who looks like Zhang Juqian wearing a fox head)*[236]

Aristotle and his teacher have a conversation. Aristotle looks dejected. He walks continuously, up and down the stage, back and forth, waving his hands, terribly agitated, whereas his teacher stands still and seraphic, almost till the play's end (further stage indications follow below).

Aristotle: (*sad*) Master, they kicked me out of sculpture class. And they made fun of me.

Teacher: (*tenderly*) I'm sorry, boy.

A: They said that my works are without any real substance.

T: I see.

A: They said that all the bodies that I try to chisel look deformed. Especially the bipeds.

T: I see.

A: That my family is so poor and lowly that I can't afford the clay on which I need to practice.

---

[235] *Ditto*: "Aristotle and He." Better now? Meanwhile, another glacier has melted.
[236] Fox heads were considered very stylish in the 1970s. Or so some people thought.

Act Two

T: I see.

A: (*hesitantly*) And... I actually had cramps in my hands keeping me from holding the scalpel and the hammer... It was all an accident, but... I was so ashamed!

T: I see.

A: They said that my work is useless.

T: I see.

A: (*meekly but angrily*) ... Just like its prime mover...

T: I see.

A: (*more angrily*) They're all animals!

T: (*calmly*) I believe they are. (*Quietly, as to himself*) ...What's the karma of a pig from Parma?

A: (*softly, pensively*) ... And I am no creative demiurge...

T: (*smiling paternally*) No chance of that, dear boy...

A: (*angrier*) ... And they kicked me out of drama club!

T: (*pained*) Oh!

A: And... they made fun of me. Again!

T: I'm so sorry, boy.

A: They said that I showed no potential.

T: I see.

A: They said that I can't act!

T: I see.

A: That I'm constantly at war with myself: A lot of effort, (*sniffing*) but all's wasted.

T: I see.

A: "Inefficient." That's what they said… "Not your cup of tea." (*pause*) And "a pot of piss…"

T: I see.

A: They said that stupid, stuttering foreigners can act better than me.

T: I see.

A: And dumb slaves too.

T: I see.

A: Even women!

T: I see.

A: They said that I should go and learn with Barbie Fuchsia…

T: I see.

A: … And Dilhy Anne Babe!

T: I see… (*talking to himself*) Unwise, perhaps… Wouldn't be bad, though…

A: … But that I would bore them tits… (*pause, resentful*) Pricks!

T: I see.

A: (*adding sadness*) ... And they kicked me out of the course in creative writing too.

T: Really?

A: At least they didn't make fun of me, this time... (*pause*) Well... maybe... a mite.

T: I see.

A: They complained that I've got no flow.

T: I see.

A: That marble's water, compared to the arthritic flow of my dull prose...

T: I see.

A: ...That eating broken glass is nicer than reading my stuff, especially my stabs at humour.

T: I see.

A: That I should retire in a convent and take a vow of... written silence.

T: I see.

A: That reading my self-reflexive passages makes them want to do hard drugs.

T: I see.

A: That they would rather disembowel one another with spoons than read my intricate shit!

T: I see.

A: That *I* am a load of shit… "Horseshit," they said, or "dogshit"… (*suffering*) Dang!

T: I see.

A: That I should destroy all my scrolls, parchments, tablets, old floppy disks, and hard drives.

T: I see.

A: That I'm all tragedy and no comedy… "Melpomene pegging Thalia," one of them said…

T: I see.

A: That I'm too grandiloquent, Gordian, goliardic, Gonella-like, and Grice-less.

T: I see.

A: That I'm too informal, overinforming, transformist, formulaic, and uniform.

T: I see.

A: That I'm too vulgar, down-to-earth, impulsive, masculine, offensive, plebeian, and ironic.

T: I see.

Act Two

A: That I'm too cerebral, metaphysical, reflexive, feminine, defensive, patrician, and moronic.

T: I see.

A: That when I try to make a priceless joke, it's always the cheapest one.

T: I see.

A: They complained that I'm just too predictable.

T: Are you, now?

A: That I've got far too much 'gratuitous' curiosa in my stories.

T: I see.

A: That I've got far too much 'gratuitous' violence in my stories.

T: I see.

A: That I've got far too much 'gratuitous'... *language* in my stories.

T: I see.

A: I think that it actually means that they don't like something and so they call it "gratuitous"...

T: A plausible inference, dear boy.

A: Inferences, yes... They say that I always leave out some important premises...

T: I see.

A: … And immediately rush to the conclusion.

T: I see.

A: That what I write is *boring*… "Thalia on Valium," the usual funnyman said…

T: (*yawning*) I see.

A: That I'm always describing just one action.

T: I see.

A: That I always compress the whole story and everything else into one day.

T: I see.

A: And that everything takes place always in the same… well, place.

T: I see.

A: Not enough change.

T: I see.

A: Not enough surprise.

T: I see.

A: No flights of fancy.

T: I get the picture, boy. (*Whispers ironically to himself*) As if anyone could create anything new!

Act Two

A: They said that even MacRunt's arty-farty pictures are funnier than my stories!

T: Are they?

A: How could I know? I haven't watched any, yet!

T: I see.

A: They said that I'm "chauvinistic."

T: I see.

A: They said that I'm... "phallo-centric."

T: I see.

A: They said that I'm "gyno-centric."

T: I see.

A: They said that I'm "ethno-centric."

T: I see.

A: They said that I'm... "cosmo-centric."

T: I see.

A: And then they complained that I don't sound "natural" enough! As if their habits... tyrants!

T: I see.

A: They say that my prose is "unidiomatic." Or "unnaked," whatever that is...

T: I see.

A: They don't get the fact that I use the language which I've... *found* around me, all my life.

T: I see.

A: Just because it isn't theirs, you know? The one that they're used to, or used to expect.

T: I see.

A: Didn't Joseph Conrad have the same kind of problems?

T: He did, boy, he did... He had his own insecurities to contend with... And swollen gums.

A: What?

T: Nothing, dear boy. Never mind. Go on.

A: They said that I'm a man and dare have female characters, and write about women, and...

T: I see.

A: ... That I'm a man and have too many male characters, and write too much about men.

T: I see.

A: They complained that my fiction is incomprehensible because it is not realistic enough...

T: I see.

Act Two

A: ... And that my realism is intolerable because it isn't fictional enough.

T: I see.

A: They said that I'm blasphemous because I include too many nuns and clergymen.

T: I see.

A: They said that I'm blasphemous because I include too few nuns and clergymen.

T: I see.

A: They said that I'm anti-Semitic because I include too many Jewish characters.

T: I see.

A: They said that I'm anti-Semitic because I include too few Jewish characters.

T: I see.

A: They said that I'm Islamophobic because I include too many Muslim characters.

T: I see.

A: They said that I'm Islamophobic because I include too few Muslim characters.

T: I see.

A: They said that I'm homophobic because I include too many gay and lesbian characters.

T: I see.

A: They said that I'm homophobic because I include too few gay and lesbian characters.

T: I see.

A: They said that I'm always making the same joke.

T: I see.

A: They said that I'm repetitive.

T: I see.

A: They said that I'm repetitive.

T: I re-see.

A: They said that I'm repetitive.

T: I tri-see.

A: They said that *I* don't know what I'm saying, especially when it comes to possible offenses.

T: I see. (*as to himself*) There are at the moment 1,453 special categories to be kept in mind...

A: They said that my writing style is closer to accounting than real artistry.[237]

---

[237] A Danish accountant recently complained: "I am an amazing artist!"

T: (*smiling*) Oh, boy. Come on! It can't really be *that* bad.

A: That I write like a frigging Chicago economist!

T: (*serious*) Fuck *that*!

A: That I *remind* them of frigging Chicago economists!

T: (*getting agitated*) Fuck *them*! What an insult! ... Odious slander!

A: That George Stigler and Gary Becker are my soulmates!

T: (*angry*) Nonsense, boy, pure nonsense![238]

A: (*sniffing*) Master, (*pause*) ... Oh, gods, I'm a complete and utter failure![239]

T: (*calming down*) Nah! Don't worry. You'll find something else you're good at. It's only logical.

Curtain.

XXXI – Deep in a Load of Shite[240]

§1 Mehmet, Mike and Merab have finally found a way to make some much-needed extra cash. Since they're reasonably fit, and although they're not young men any more, they've kept busy

---

[238] Nonsense stated: "Italy's armored corps invaded the Vatican in self-defense! They were provoked, by Jove!"

[239] Factually, the alleged failure may have been grossly exaggerated. Psychologically, it was devastating.

[240] Motility can affect your bowels: Watch the ways you move. And if crass banter and superficial bigotry offend you, skip this fictional, humorous text.

moving furniture and all sorts of stuff all over the city. This daring feat of entrepreneurship has been made possible by Merab's Renault Kangoo—and an even older, clumsy, repurposed trailer of dubious origin bumping perpetually behind Merab's battered Gallic vehicle.

Today, they've already spent interminable hours loading stuff from a decrepit old house in St. Thomas More's Square and taking it to some accursed flat in a huge apartment block located at 11, St. Jasmine's Alley—what they tragically uncovered to be a twisty, ghastly, narrow, incredibly long lane, zig-zagging all the time, and climbing most murderously up one of the steepest hills ever in the overcrowded eastern part of the old urban centre. The horror!

Badly built, littered with vans, cars, SUVs, jeeps, bikes, scooters, mopeds, unicycles, and litters that get parked literally everywhere there's any available space, however miniscule—or even where there isn't any space at all, to be frank—, driving up there, in that venerable, bearably spacious, yet unbearably noisy and, every other day, nerve-rackingly temperamental bucket-of-bolts belonging to Merab is something that only the valiant can face, or the foolhardy.

Whichever epithet better applies to the three, fit, hardworking men, they've made it all the way up there. In itself, it's already a significant accomplishment. Bravo! Sort of brave-Scott-of-the-Antarctic kind-of-stuff. Sweatier, perhaps. Anyhow, time to unload.

§2 "A fish tank," Mehmet shouts, scrutinising the object.

"And a huge TV set," Mike echoes, trying to get it out of the van. It's really big.

"Me plasma is half the size, man!," chimes in Mehmet—one of his funny comments, in his funny English. "Bought it from Gershom," he adds, "good man."

"A jar of Trump fridge magnets. Cool!," cracks Mike, pretending to be chucking it away.

"Trump… Trump? … Good man," comments Mehmet, inscrutably, while holding a bag with something rattling inside. "*Marbles… or big teeth?*," he uncommonly hypothesises.

Act Two

"Guys! The complete DVD set of Naomee Blacks' *The Cloister Is My Oyster*! Must cost a fortune, for fuck's sake!," laughs Mike, "I didn't see it when we were loading all this crap!"

"Naomee Blacks?," goes Mehmet, "good woman... Native Eve, yeah, good woman too, *Prussian Institute*..." he adds, smilingly, in a half-lost and half-ecstatic manner, as though he was reminiscing about some very-old-yet-pleasant and spiritually-present experience.

"And another jar of... blue liquid?," evidently catching Mike unprepared.

"Me load it," observes Mehmet, "before."

"I'm bloody hungry...," states Mike, changing the subject.

"Me too," grins Mehmet.

"I'd love a sausage roll," Mike specifies, mimicking some fierce chewing."No sausage!," says Mehmet, in a serious tone.

"I know, brother, I know!," smiles Mike, glancing warmly at Mehmet to assuage him. "Chinese?," Mike then suggests.

"Yoh-yoh, wei-wei" Mehmet replies, making a splendid impression of the stereotypical Chinese. Something worthy of Gilbert and Sullivan. Shane Gillis, perhaps. Or worse.

"Who's helping me with this monster sofa?," cries Merab from behind the repurposed trailer of dubious origin, "you bloody bastards..."

"And fifteen large boxes with... Fuck me!," says Mike, "Books! Bloody bunch o' books. Who needs so many?" (Meanwhile he thinks, "*I hadn't actually noticed they were all boxes filled with* just *books. Bizarre... Who's got so many books, anyway? Reverend Bowles? John? Some nutty university professor? Some pretentious artist? ... Or the library monster?*")

"Hey," says Mehmet, "see if there's *Utopia*. I want read it in English!"

"Fuck off!" is Mike's prompt and thought-through scholarly response.

"Look at this," continues Mehmet: "The marble slab, the kind butchers use. It take us how long to load this?"

"Too long," states Mike, trenchantly.

"Think I've seen one like it in Abe's old garage," shouts now Merab, who's literally disappeared underneath the half-burnt sofa that he's carrying, or trying to carry.

"Right," says curtly Mike.

"Right," echoes Mehmet.

"Right," pants poor Merab, squashed by the half-burnt sofa.

§3 Somehow, almost miraculously, Merab manages to activate, for lack of better words, the far-out, sci-fi-like, dark-blue, blinking intercom positioned to the left of the building's main entrance, which is plastered over with successive generations of formerly-bright-coloured stickers and a shitload of unread notices: Over-plastered and overlooked.

A freaky, almost lucent green slime oozes out of the intercom's hollow in the concrete wall, which tacitly indicates an uninviting, unnerving, limited resilience to earthquakes, low-flying airplanes, and peremptory flatulence. Unattractively, most of the intercom itself is physically dangling down, pathetically suspended in mid-air by the half-mangled electric wires, in a visible failed attempt at hardware suicide—or someone's attack of rage against the machine.

"*What a shitty neighbourhood!*," thinks Merab, while waiting for a voice, an answer, a sound, a change in the intercom's ceaseless blinking, a sign of life.[241] Nothing. They wait.

"Fucking posh place," says Mike, with his characteristic subtle irony. They wait.

The three of them look at each other and say nothing. Silence. They wait.

"Somebody?," asks hopelessly Mehmet. No. Nobody. Nothing. They wait.

Merab tries again. "*Broken intercom?*," he wonders. Silence. Nothing. They wait.

---

[241] Worse neighbourhoods exist in town, most notably around Lime Avenue.
Punch: He was a lovely fellow, wasn't he?
Judy: Such a charming drug lord, yes!

Act Two

At last, a deafening buzzing noise is heard, far too well, and it vibrates long and hard throughout the dismal intercom, which now seems to be on the verge of exploding in some kind of nuclear holocaust or terrorist bombing. Then... Nothing. They wait.[242]

§4 After a very long while, a wrinkly midget—sorry, pardon me —a mature little (small?) person (a conspicuously experienced dwarf?) opens the door and looks at the three of them in disbelief— and, above all, at the gargantuan load of stuff piled up in front of the building's main entrance. His face shows a certain sense of alarm or apprehension. It's difficult to gauge which.

"Mr L. Albert, 11, St. Jasmine's Alley, 7th floor, apartment number 702," inquires Merab, reading from a scrap of paper on which he had scribbled down all the necessary information.

"Mr L. Albert, 11...," mutters the aged person of uncommon short stature.

"All things unloaded. Is there a lift we can use?," asks Merab, somewhat hopeful, but also slightly trepidant. Something's off. He can feel it.

"Yes...," utters the wee old man. "But...," he hesitates.

"But what?," Merab asks. Something's definitely off.

"What did you say the address was?," asks in turn the tenant.

"Mr L. Albert, 11, St. Jasmine's Alley, 7th floor, apartment number 702," repeats Merab, taking another look at the scrap of paper and the hastily-handwritten key-data jotted on it.

"I see," whispers mysteriously the diminutive elderly gentleman.

"What?," now probes the more-and-more-worried and less-and-less-confident Merab, looking at the tenant suspiciously, and a bit menacingly. He's smelling a rat, here... No winged unicorns or flying teapots in the sky... Rodents await: Teeth and shit!

"Well, you see," the tiny senior citizen continues, "I'm Mr L. Albert, Lanchester Albert, 7th floor, apartment number 702, yes... at 11, St. *Carmine* Alley. Not *Jasmine*. That's somewhere else. Not

---

[242] A long wait lost in this footnote observed: "Souls." Then, a mist poured down its lethargic untimeliness.

here." And he immediately leaves the scene, like a man who desperately needs to take a leak. (Truth being, they had caught him while watching a clandestine Chinese blue movie, and having his daily wee tug. The wee old man wanted to finish the wee job at hand, understandably, if not commendably or very politely.)

Mike quickly checks the correct address on his phone. "Fuck!," he goes, "it's at least 15 kilometres from here!," and adds, "on top of another fucking Everest!"

Merab looks astonished. He's pale in the face. Literally. He may be at risk of fainting, or having a seizure, or seeing the Holy-Virgin-Mary-Immaculate-Mother-of-God, which could sway him in the direction of the True Faith, should it happen in reality. No vision, though. Only teeth and shit. Or tusks and shit, since the rat was the size of a blooming elephant. All that stuff to reload, and re-unload, and bring upstairs… That's a nightmare becoming frigging reality!

Mike, meanwhile, is struggling not to land a kick in Merab's arse, or a punch in his face. Maybe both. Wouldn't that be nice, for a change? But he just whistles through his lips: "Merab, you fucking Paki, fucking cunt, fucking piece of fucking shit, fuck, fuck, fuck…"

Only Mehmet smiles: "Don't mind exercise, man. Me guns get bigger and bigger! Like big groper Nazi governator Arnie of USA. Let's go, men!"

And so they go.

§5 If the three of them survived that unforeseen new trip, we can't say. Maybe they argued among themselves, maybe not. Merab's mistake was a real pain in the ass for all concerned. Still, the three men did usually take things lightly. And they joked a lot, most abrasively we should add, among themselves. They did so all the time, like friends or close co-workers tend to do—if they honestly trust one another. Some snotty people could call them, disparagingly, "ordinary gentlemen," but we won't do it here. They're ordinary good men, if anything at all.

In any case, who knows what they did? It's a good question. But we don't have an answer. We're worse than the broken intercom… It's pretty sure that it was raining a little, that day. Did they get wet?

Act Two

We don't know. We don't even know if the three men actually reached the right destination in St. Jasmine Alley—with their cargo intact, preferably. Let's hope they did. Smartphones can be useful, for that kind of stuff. Especially when your smarts betray you.

Intrusion By Two Puppets

Punch: How can you know that?
Judy: What's "that," man?
Punch: That your smarts betrayed you.
Judy: Did they?
Punch: I don't know!
Judy: Then, why are you saying that?
Punch: What's "that," woman?
Judy: That your smarts betrayed you.
Punch: Did they?
Judy: I don't know!
Punch: Then, why are you saying that?
Judy: Because you said that!
Punch: I only said "that!"
Judy: And isn't that enough?
Punch: How can I know that?
Judy: Because you said "that," that's how!
Punch: Is there a... measure?
Judy: You've certainly filled mine: I've got no space left!
Punch: Do you mean... you're upset?
Judy: You bet I am!
Punch: You're not... detached?
Judy: No, I'm not!
Punch: Your heart is... awake?
Judy: Fully, fuming – like Pulcinella's Mount Vesuvius – and screaming!
Punch: Then that's that.

Judy:	"That" or that "that?"
Punch:	The latter, I believe.
Judy:	The latter of three?
Punch:	"Three" what?
Judy:	"That's"
Punch:	Shouldn't it be "those?"
Judy:	It may well be. But then who understands that?
Punch:	Is "those" that, then?
Judy:	It may be that, but not that "that."
Punch:	…Are you still… upset?
Judy:	Not as much as before.
Punch:	Has that calmed you down?
Judy:	"That" or that "that?"
Punch:	Either.
Judy:	Out of three?
Punch:	Well, one of those.
Judy:	"Those" or that "those?"
Punch:	I'll have to think about "that."
Judy:	Only "that?"
Punch:	You are correct: I'll have to think about "those."
Judy:	Correction is my forte.
Punch:	Are you a prison warden?
Judy:	I can be one, if it's needed.
Punch:	Is it needed though, in here?

Judy: No, that penal art is not needed, in here: Books are still free spaces, and people can laugh *with* authors or *at* authors. Or stop reading: It's their choice.

Act Two

XXXII – Understanding[243]

§1 Guys, listen to this kooky message I got from Hella. Is it a prank? What the heck is it?

"A thin, fluorescent, disc-like green monster is following me everywhere I go. It's got a large mouth with sharp fangs, and three black-olive-like eyes that move around its body—a disc of bright green goo that slides under doors, passes through cracks, and wants to eat me alive. So far, I've managed to escape. It doesn't move very fast. But it moves! It's… alive![244]

"It must be hungry. I've seen it eating mice in the building. A few cats have disappeared as well. A parrot, a hamster and a chihuahua are missing too. I know it sounds incredible. But believe me, please. This is no nightmare. It's no delusion. I'm not going mad and seeing things. That creature *is* here, in this building, now, looking for me or, at least, posing a threat to me, my neighbours, their visitors, anyone who steps in here. Don't be duped by all the quiet!

"I think I know where it comes from. There's a dodgy guy, in this block, who's been done for drugs and other shady dealings. I think he spent a few years locked away in a cell. When he came back, he stopped going around much. He's always at home. He's making all kinds of noises in his apartment. Loud and… bizarre. Like he's building something. Or he's experimenting with something… I know it. Because… Because I've seen it!

"Two weeks ago, I went to his place. I knocked on his door. It was the middle of the night, and he was still hammering and making a terrible racket. Mr Racket was there too, with a bunch of sausages in his hands. Probably, he had had the same idea as I had. When he saw me there, though, he just said 'good night' and left. He thought I'd

---

[243] Please recall that, somewhere in Prussia, *Verstand* is not *Vernunft*.
Punch: Why are puppets important, dear? **Judy**: Are puppets important?

[244] Two readers have recently testified to having seen such creatures in an elderly neighbour's basement.

take care of it. I'm pretty sure 'bout that. He's also a bit shy. Strange guy... Looks a bit like God, or Daniel Dennett, but with a dribble... I don't know. There seems to be only strange guys in this building![245]

"Anyway, nobody was answering. I knocked and knocked... Nothing. I gave a gentle push to the door and, well, it opened: It was open all that time! The lights were off, but I could see anyhow, because there was some sort of powerful green fluorescence coming from the bathroom—I knew it was the bathroom because all apartments here are built the same way.

"I went to take a look. And, oh Lord! Please believe me: There, in that bathroom, there was a brain, a huge one, in a vat. Yes, a huge brain in a sort of gigantic fish tank, made of thick glass, filled with a sort of blue liquid, and emanating a sort of green light. It's hard to explain. Really. The brain was covered in wires and tied to some kind of machinery. Computers. Monitors. Power banks... Stuff! Plenty of it. Like an old episode of *Doctor Who*. My friend John would have felt at home... The poor guy! He still misses three fingers...

"Anyway, I didn't touch the brain or anything else, or tinkered with anything. I was just too scared. Well, no, not scared,... *shocked*, rather. Who'd expect to find something like that in your neighbour's apartment, right? You can have weird neighbours, but that's different... Mr Racket, for one. The retired provincial leprechaun, for another. Or that doddering old general... Weird neighbours are actually a common occurrence: Much more so than brains in a vat!

"Well, ... it doesn't really matter. I was *so* shocked. *Then* the fear grew inside me. Yeah, I began getting scared. Seriously scared. Was I in danger? You see, I would have panicked right there, on the spot, freaked out. I was probably going to scream, or vomit, or... loosen my bowels, you know? Yet, unexpectedly, a bizarre thought came

---

[245] The reader might benefit from knowing that one neighbour from Eurasia screamed abuse all day and night: "I don't want to understand! I want everything to mean what I'm told it means! You are monsters!"

into my poor old skull. And I found it soothing. It calmed me down, almost immediately. Thank God for that!

"What was the thought? Well, I think you'll find it stupid, but that's what I thought and found reassuring. Really reassuring... Maybe that's all I needed in that moment not to freak out: A reassuring, funny thought... You see, there and then, all at once, I thought, 'well, if it's a huge brain, then something intelligent will come out of it.' You see? So I left it undisturbed and went back to my apartment. The noises stopped a couple of minutes after that. Complete silence after that. 'He got the message,' I said to myself. Or maybe Mr Racket spoke to him too...

"I was calm, again. I managed to sleep. Strange, isn't it? The day after, I went back to talk to my neighbour. The door was shut. Got no reply. Then, someone shouted 'sod off!,' and the green round monster started slipping under the door. I froze. I had never seen anything like that. I expected to find something very strange in that apartment, after seeing the big brain, the wires, the green light, and the blue liquid in that huge tank... But I didn't expect that horrible monstrosity. Some kind of gelatinous abomination.... Horrible! Just horrible!

"No, not the brain! The... disc! The green creature made creepy noises as it crawled towards me. The carpets on the floor seemed to be slowing it down. That gave me the time I needed to get back to my senses and, well, run like mad! Would you stay there, with that being, that thing, that... horror? I thought I would be safe locked away in my apartment. So far, I've been safe. I filled the cracks all around the main door. That has been enough. However...

"Well, I know it sounds stupid, but it isn't. I mean, I have to go out, you see, to get the groceries, you know? I must eat! Water's here abundantly. But I have a stomach to fill too! Also, I have a job. I've got to go to the library. And check on Alice's progress... I mean, life goes on, even with big brains and green slimy discs around... And then that creepy thin plate, that sort of gooey dish, started following me! It almost managed to get through the lift's doors, once, and it surely went easily under the fire doors, despite all the carpets. Crawling and squelching...

"Please, guys, come and get me. Send in the specialists. Call the T. Hobbes Institute for Psychic Research. There's a real danger here. This green thing is slow, but it's dangerous. And how many people live in this building? Think of that. Think of it... So many people!

"Please, help me! Help us all!"

Guys, let me put it mildly: Hella's gone totally bonkers. The stress of the past few weeks must have been too much for her. You've heard her message. I think you'll agree with me that this is utter nonsense. She's clearly hysterical. Something bad must have happened to *her* brain. Something really bad. Truly, big brains in vats and green monsters... For crying out loud!

There's only one possible line of action. I'm going to talk to Hella, bring her to the station, and request a full psychiatric examination. She needs help. And she will get it: I promise you that much! I've already alerted Dr Penderecki. She will take good care of Hella. Just like she did with Hella's mate Alice in the past. She's a capable and experienced shrink.

That afternoon, Hella's chief went to visit Hella at her place. She had to talk to Hella and convince Hella to follow her and go with her to the station to be examined by a professional.

That afternoon, Hella's chief left and went to Hella's place: It was raining.

She never came back.

§2 *At her own place, on the bedside table, the following enigmatic note was retrieved:*

"An institution devoted by both vocation and profession to the public education of all classes and all age groups may perhaps be astonished to be singled out as a token of those who wish to impede any such education. Similarly, its members will be even more astonished to see a Continent chosen for this illustrative purpose where, by dint of an odd wizardry admired only by the blind and the wicked, real human beings were turned into appetitive machines.

Indeed, instead of teaching about geometry, philosophy, poetry, and other such absurdities, the modern European schools have taught their pupils to innovate, produce, compete, and eat and drink and enjoy themselves. The eager instructors were the promoters of these new norms, and they get furious when they are led to realise what the eventual result of their didactic efforts has been."

"What does it mean?" asked a bereaved colleague.

"Ain't any clue," replied another, "but the chief was a curious woman."

Two days after this seemingly inconsequential exchange, the latter bereaved colleague began musing on a phantasy which, as she subsequently realised, was not only going to be recurrent, but almost obsessive and, from her subjective point of view, as fascinating to her intellect as it could, on occasion, become emotionally overwhelming:

The old wise man had wisdom aplenty to share with all the villagers. He carried it inside a large sac, which he was ready and willing to open for anyone who should ask him to do so, if only to peer inside the sac out of mere curiosity, when not to partake in its valuable contents in a more constructive manner. Such contents consisted in precious human creations that the old wise man had been gathering since infancy and, by then, preserving for days, months, years, decades, centuries, or even thousands of years, making sure that all such precious human creations would not spoil nor damage mutually inside his sac.

The most ancient items had been fashioned, however, by cooling stellar masses, fallen asteroids, active volcanoes, lightning bolts, earthquakes, roaring oceans, mysterious early plants, gigantic rhizomes, and long-extinct animals. Then, chronologically, there followed the numerous creations brought forth by gods, cyclopes, fauns, spirits, nymphs, satyrs, and demons. Such creations had later been joined by those invented and given shape to by innumerable generations of human beings, from the most primitive ancestors of today's humankind to the latest comics, action figures, holograms, and videogames. Finally, there were gadgets and trinkets designed and manufactured by the old wise man himself, who truly enjoyed making new things, tinkering and toying with the immense cornucopia of models, starting points, hints, inspirations and suggestions which he carried in his large sac.

At the presupposed bottom of the same sac, there shone light itself, as well as a chaotic and rarely-touched assemblage of copper-zinc and cast-iron rings, glass marbles, and black-and-white granite eggs. Around them, there whistled an unheard gust of wind, which the old wise man had thrown into his large sac when he was still learning to control his bladder and bowels. Around the same time, he had also added to his early collection boulders of many different colours, exsiccated nests and beaks, and the colossal dry vertebrae of immense dead serpents—dragons, perhaps. When asked about those bones, the old wise man smiled ironically and would only say: "I've always been a dirty rascal."

Nobody believed him. Nevertheless, had she still been around, his mother would have probably agreed with the old wise man's self-disparaging remark, and smiled too. For one, she could have told the incredulous listeners about how much the old wise man, as a boy, loved spitting, screaming, vomiting, urinating, pooing, and ejaculating into the sac. For another, she could have added that the old wise man, as a boy, was still capable of experiencing dread and sobbing, longing in earnest for the days when his mother took care of all his needs and allowed him not to have to think for himself. Even now, after millennia of existence, the old wise man would sometimes fantasise about vanishing inside the protection of his large sac.

At some point in his now-distant youth, though, the old wise man's mother had forced the boy to listen to his stomach, throat, kidneys, heart, liver, lungs, milt, testes, rectum, and muscles. Similarly, she had taught him to hunt, sing, ferment the juice of grapes, assist others, speak, pursue justice, laugh, and dance. In parallel, she had also taught him to become prey, be quiet, abstain from drinking, steal, lie, commit injustice, blame others, and break legs. Gradually, the boy had become a man, though not a wise one yet. Gradually, the boy had become a man, who later grew into a husband and a father. Gradually, the boy had become a man, who eventually mastered the ever-elusive art of being himself. His beloved mother, in any case, was now somewhere inside his large sac.[246]

Inside the sac, the old wise man's mother and a shaggy, hairy bogeyman are chatting:

- *What's that, in your mouth?*
- *What, my tongue? La-la-la-la...*
- *No, not that: The other... stuff.*
- *What "stuff?"*
- *The white stuff... May I touch it?*
- *Alright, that way I'll understand what the heck you're asking me about!*
- *This stuff... here: UGH!*
- *Ah! Now I see.*
- *Yes?*
- *Teeth. These are... teeth, yes.*
- *Do I... have them too?*
- *Open your mouth and let me take a quick look.*
- *Ah-ah: Aaaaaaah...*
- *Yep.*
- *Oh? ...Many?*
- *Enough.*
- *"Enough?"*
- *Yes, like... the right number, more or less.*
- *"Right" for what?*
- *For all the things you can do with them. Or must do, at times.*
- *Like what?*
- *Munching, for one...*
- *Hm.*
- *...biting...*
- *Hm!*
- *...smiling...*
- *Is that good?*
- *What?*
- *"Smiling."*

---

[246] Russian sacs are capable of laughter, especially in the conducive, jovial, punning company of co-sacs.

- It depends.
- On what?
- If it's genuine.
- Why, can it be... not?
- Normally, it isn't.
- "Normally?"
- Yes. Most of the time, smiles are... fake.
- "Fake?"
- Yes: Politeness, publicity, public relations, prudence...
- Isn't that... bad?
- In a way.
- Which "way?"
- We rarely are what we... are: We... wear masks and... pretend.
- Like... actors in a play, eh?
- Very much so. Though the stage can be our life and the characters... us.
- Isn't that... good?
- In a way... Let's see if I can show you...

❧

XXXIII – Duchesses[247]

One Act:
- *Michelle M.D. Symonds*
- *Monica P.H.D. Symonds*

Two college-age sisters play foolishly together, putting on old-style wigs, lots of make-up and fancy costumes, while pretending that they are two naughty noble women at the luxurious court of Marie Antoinette—and sipping on Grand Marnier. They speak their own argot, *though not the 'official' one. They only have high-school-level French. They are very cheerful, and tipsy.*

Michelle: (*with a mock French accent, laughing*) I am ze Duchess de Pompierdur, la Marquise de la Pipe!

---

[247] Rated R. If sexuality, lewd matters, and crass lexicon can unnerve you, even if humorous and fictional, then skip this chapter altogether.

Monica: (*idem, a tad less clownishly*) And I'm ze Duchess *du Feu au Cul, la Marquise de la Cramouille!*

Mi: *Noblesse seulement ici, comme au château de Périgord et Bordelais!*

Mo: *Bien sure, madame!* Princess Sophia and Catherine ze Great have been our assiduous guests…

Mi: I am *more* noble zan you, *chérie!* So much more!

Mo: *Non, non… Je suis* ze real aristocrat! (*lifting a teacup with her pinkie stretching out*)

Mi: *Je suis* ze ROYAL aristocrat! … *Ma modalité aristocratique est absolute et nécessaire!*

Mo: Your head will roll before mine, *alors! Ta modalité est ta fatalité!*

Mi: *Oh, non!* My poor, poor, beautiful head!

Mo: *Oh, oui!* … Beautiful… beautiful head!

Mi: Beauty! Oh, beauty… (*sighing*) Somezing beautiful to give—to ze world!

Mo: (*dreamy*) … Head… *à tout le monde!*

Mi: (*faking horror*) And zey chop it? *C'est terrible!*

Mo: (*idem*) Chop, chop… Ze terror, ze terror!

Mi: Ze pain in ze head!

Mo: *J'ai* ze pain in ze *tête*!

Mi: (*perplexed*) ... Ze pain in ze tits? ... *Mes deux gros seins*?

Mo: (*sharp*) *Mais non*, in ze *tête, stupide*! *Tu es toujours*... llulled into a false sense of computability!

Mi: (*faking rage*) *Mon Dieu! J'ai* ze pain in ze ass... *Vous, Madame*!

Mo: (*clownish*) Ass, ass... asses, assess... And horses, *très bien*! We need zem here! We're animal lovers! Aren't we? Bring us ze animals! And sing with me! ... *Timide*! Are *vous pas* ze main singer *de l'opera de Paris*? (*on the melody of the Marseillaise*) ... *Les animaux de la patrie*...!

Mi: (*playful*) *Pourquoi chanter*? For what? Ze races? Ze war? ... *Vive la France! Vive le roi!*

Mo: (*idem*) *Mais non*! Don't you understand? *Pas pour le roi! Pas pur l'ancien régime*! Ze king can just join ze rebels, for all I care! Or get his head chopped off, like Thomas More, for all we like! We want ze loving animals *pour mon bon cul, ma chère duchesse! La culture est mon amour*!

Mi: Ze *cul*? *Oh là là*!

Mo: *Mais oui! La plus grande activité physique est, ma chérie, l'activité érotique! Aussi avec le cul!*

Mi: Ze *cul*, ze *cul, parbleu*! (*giggling, without mock accent*) ... Shall we call Dora?

Mo: (*without mock accent*) Invite Dora? No! Not in a million years! She's got no sense of humour! (*scoffing*) Boring cow! She's the *real* pain in the ass... And a constant headache too!

Mi: (*without mock accent*) I know, I know! You couldn't believe she's our sister. Could you? I don't know what went wrong with that one: Always talking politics and boring stuff with her friend Fiona! No self-irony... Only (*gesticulating pompously*) blah, blah-blah, and blah blah blah!

Mo: (*back to mock accent, mocking Dora and laughing*) *Mon Dieu! La bourgeoisie!*

Mi: (*idem, in a ludicrous crescendo of French expressions*) *La patriarchie!*

Mo: *L'aristocratie!*

Mi: *Les armoiries!*

Mo: *La tyrannie!*

Mi: (*with mock seriousness*) *La démocratie!*

Mo: (*idem*) *La technocratie!*

Mi: (*back to laughing and general silliness*) *La phallocratie!*

Mo: (*still in a mockingly serious tone*) *La théocratie!*

Mi: (*laughing*) *La pornocratie!*

Mo: (*back to laughing and silliness, in a naughty tone*) *La putasserie!*

Mi: (*fake seriousness*) *La toxicomanie!*

Mo: (*idem*) *La tulipomanie!*

Mi: (*ad lib*) *Les néo-nazis!*

Mo: (*idem*) *Les paparazzi*!
Mi: (*idem*) *Les tabagies*!

Mo: (*idem*) *La barbarie*!

Mi: (*panting from too much laughter, without mock accent*) Shall we call Anita?
Mo: (*smiling, restraining laughter*) No, no. (*lifting a glass*) She's fun, but she's too young for this!

Mi: (*clearly joking*) Shall we call mum? (*ordering teacups and glasses as for a military inspection*)

Mo: (*roaring with laughter*) Yes! (*ironic*) And then she'll make us read a book by Poullain de la Barre, or we will learn the names of all French kings and queens since Charlemagne!

Mi: (*laughing, in silly French*) Like when we learned ze names of all ze *présidents américains*?

Mo: (*faking an American accent*) You got it, sister!

Mi: (*less sarcastically, no fake accent*) … Dad?

Mo: (*smiling, no accents*) Would be nice… *He*'s fun! He's at the lake, though. He's always there!

Mi: (*back to fake, silly French*) *Il-y-a seulement les deux duchesses*! Ze two Duchesses!

Mo: (*back to fake, silly French*) Ze glorious aristocrats! *Nous, nous deux! Bon Dieu!*

Mi: *Les plus grandes…* ehm… noble women in ze whole of *la grande et magnifique France*!

Mo: (*less clownishly*) *Les deux plus grandes et magnifiques salopes de Versailles*!

Mi: (*ad lib*) *Ma chère Marquise de la Cramouille, Baronne de la Chatte, que plaisir*!

Mo: (*idem*) *Le plaisir c'est tout*! ... (*triumphantly*) *Le plaisir c'est moi*!

Mi: (*just having fun*) Have you received my latest gift for you, my dear *Marquise*?

Mo: (*idem*) Ze lacquered blades from ze Orient? *Les bâtons du Japon? Mais oui*!

Mi: Lovely. Aren't zey, my dear *Marquise*? Just like ze real zing, but wizout a boring man attached to it! ... Real gentlemen make you come wizout having to be entertained zemselves, *n'est pas*?

Mo: Yes, lovely. Just lovely. *Mais... Longueur et largeur font l'amour...* You see: Too small!

Mi: (*faking shock, sniggering*) *Quoi*? Too small?

Mo: *La bite du Nippon est trop petite*! Ah! *La bite japonaise est comme la neige congolaise*!

Mi: (*faking shock, chuckling*) *Parbleu! C'est pas vrai*!

Mo: *C'est vrai, c'est vrai! La petite verge ne peut faire jouir que la jeune vierge*! No good friction means dereliction! *On dit aussi en Italie que les bâtons du Japon ne sont pas bons...*

Mi: (*faking shock, laughing*) *Mon Dieu*!

Mo: (*laughing madly*) *Et aussi mamma mia*! (*in a silly mixture of mock French and mock Italian*) ... *Il bastone del giappone suda sì, / ma serve solo a fare la pipì, / perché sforza ma suona alla breve, / è cerino su montagna di neve!* ... It's traditional wisdom down zere, you know?

Mi: (*faking shock, laughing riotously*) Racist!

Mo: (*with exaggerated innocence, in mock French*) *Moi? Moi je? Pas possible!* ... (*back to the mixture of mock French and mock Italian*) *Mamma mia! Mamma mia!* ... *La condizione umana / ti fa bruttissima donna, / ti fa regina, campione, / ti fa gran bella puttana, / non ti fa metter la gonna, / ... non cresce cazzi'n Giappone!* ... (*pompously*) Quantity matters: Categorically!

Mi: (*persisting*) Imperialist! (*now trying her luck at mixing mock French and mock Italian, descending into belly laughter*) Vivaldi! Bernini! Garibaldi! Maldini! Bellucci!...

Mo: *C'est pas vrai... Je sais la vérité*, my dear *Marquise*! ... *Parce que* we are what we fuck!

Mi: (*still wild*) ...Verdi! Mazzini! Togliatti! Armani! (*back to mock French alone*) *Colonialiste*!

Mo: (*faking a Scottish accent*) Lassie, a small bite is a big shite!

Mi: (*crying out of laughter*) ... Scoto-*phallo*... Gallo-*centrique*!

Mo: (*laughing, back to mock French alone*) *Moi*? Ze truth *est que je suis la plus grande orientaliste de la France*, my dear *Baronne*! *La plus grande suis moi je! L'Asie est ma bonne amie*!

Mi: (*jokingly, less roaringly*) Because of all the manga you read and the anime you watch, or *la semence orientale qui vous pipez, Baronne? La semence qui est bonne pour ton visage et ta conne?* You know ze truth? Yo're disgusting! *C'est la vérité, Baronne*!

(faking a posh English accent) Awful, my dearest dear, awfulsomely awfully awfulestly awful! Good Lord! Awful!

Mo: *(faking offense and a serious tone, but in mock French)* Good Lady! My dear dear dear Duchess, *(gradually descending into wild laughter)* *l'art du Japon* is the best. But art is only a part. I need ze real thing: Ze *chose réelle*! *Couchez, enfilez la queue*! ... *Mais enfin* I don't mind at all ze *fruit naturel de la jouissance humaine*: *Jetez, jouez, mes bons amis*! ... *Et vous*?

Mi: *(taking no notice of the question, back to mock French)* And why would that be, *ma bonne Duchesse*, dearest dear, *madame l'orientaliste*? What's ze secret secret of all zis... *qualité*?

Mo: *(following without trouble)* Because it's steeped in ze archetypes, my dear dearest dearer dear!

Mi: *(sarcastically)* Don't you start with your crazy psychobabble, madame ze *professeur*! *Ma chère Baronne*: *Jamais*! *C'est pas scientifique*! Ah! *Descartes et les Lumières* would be horrified!

Mo: *(smiling, but firm, no mock accent)* That's just scientistic obscurantism. Look at the actual art: All archetypes are represented and worked out, every single time! The Japanese got it *so* right!

Mi: *(no mock accent, sarcastic)* *Art*, yes! Because you are the right person to talk about art! "Tart," rather... *(back to mock French)* *La grande tartiste*! Ah-ah! *Tartisme est ton théisme*!

Mo: *(no mock accent, kind)* I know it's hard to define art, or talk about it, but it's not so hard to... *feel* it. You feel art, you feel the... excitement. *(back to mock French)* ... My dear *Baronne*, ze aesthetic domain *n'est pas seul* a question of ze brain! *Mais aussi de conne*: *L'irrationalité*!

Mi: (*no mock accent, kinder*) Hm… But doesn't art become totally subjective, that way? (*now back to French*) *Tu sais, subjectif?* Beauty is in ze eye of ze beholder, and all zat *merde*…

Mo: (*smiling*) Of course it does, *Duchesse*! *But* we are also one and ze same subject, ze same person!

Mi: (*puzzled*) Oh? *Quoi?* … How's zat come about? I don't get ze… relation.

Mo: (*serious, though in mock French*) We share languages and cultures, which are conscious, and we share instincts and archetypes, which are *unconscious*. And ze unconscious is also…

Mi: (*ironic*) … *Collective*! I know, I know… you've told me a thousand times! What a nonsense!

Mo: We dream each other's dreams, *ma chère*! We see each other's visions! We just don't know it, most of ze time. We half-remember ze same jokes, ze same stories, ze same archetypes! … Ze soul has a top but, unlike *moi et toi*, it has no bottom—*la pauvre!*—hence it embraces us all!

Mi: (*back to mock French*) And *you* know all of this, *ma chérie*?

Mo: (*inspired*) Yes, *I* do! And each of us is a thousand persons at ze same time! We have countless secondary personalities inside: Ze little people of ze soul! *Tout le monde est dans la tête!*

Mi: (*more friendly*) Yes, I know, I know… You are ze expert in ze field… (*Then cheekily*) Ze only one you know any better than your friends' dicks at school, my dear dear dear dearest dear! (*laughing*) Dicks, dicks, dicks! (*shouting clownishly*) … Nixons! Nixons! … Johnsons! … Clintons! …Bubbas!

Mo: (*smiling, in an exaggerated mock French*) And what's wrong with that? I like it. Zey like it. *La bite bien-aimée est ma chose préférée.* My dear dear dear dear dear dear. *C'est... l'amour! La vie! La gentillesse! Le bonheur! La vérité charnelle! La gloire du monde et du ciel*!

Mi: (*cheerfully*) Yes, yes... (*still laughing and then stopping suddenly, smiling only*) ... Let's go and take a swim in the pond. I'm bored now!

Mo: (*happily*) Ok!

The sisters are bubbly and happy. They take off their wigs and costumes, hold hands, and leave the scene together, in perfectly good humour, taking the bottle of Grand Marnier with them.[248]

Curtain.

XXXIV – Eating While You Breathe[249]

§1   Alice had to wait an exhaustingly long time before making it into the skyscraper's lift. There was a huge queue of people needing it, like never before. Some of them would even give up waiting, after a while. They would then disappear in the nearby confectioner's, for the most part. Coffee and cake. Cake and coffee. They looked delicious. Those big cakes in the window, that is. They did. They really did. You could see it from there, at a distance.

But they are bad for you, you know? All that sugar. And fat. And God knows what sort of chemicals they put in those cakes. And the

---

[248] If Grand Marnier is not available, another suitable French liquor can be selected and utilised.

[249] Don't try it at home, which is where most human, all-too-human tragedies unfold, almost daily.

coffee, you know... Where is it coming from? Has it been ethically produced? And the blood pressure? Not to mention how coffee makes you tense, anxious, edgy, and nervous as well. Tea might be better... It would be much wiser to follow the few brave ones who leave the queue and take to the stairs. But it's tiring, especially if you've got to go to the sixth or seventh floor—"*and I'm so tired*," Alice thought.

After a very long while, Alice made it into the lift. Squashed and squeezing around her, a group of other people. Not that she herself took much space. Rather, her baggy clothes and her large hood made her look like some sort of chubby, sweaty, disgruntled teenage boy. And self-respecting people try not to interact too much with young individuals of that allegedly unpleasant ilk. Sexist and ageist prejudice can come handy, at times.

Funnily, all the persons in the lift were women. That's an unusual thing, Alice realised, and she got curious. Normally, Alice wouldn't stare or look around that much. It is a confined space. People require their little bubble of privacy. She knew that. She was very private herself. And then, if you meet someone you know, you have to go out with them, or invite them to your place, and dine with them, or take lunch together, or eat those cakes, you know... They're good, but they're bad as well. For your health, clearly.

§2   Another funny thing is that most women in that lift were nuns. Yeah, nuns! Catholic ones. Can you believe it? These days, in the 21st century, there are still nuns in the world... Bizarre! Still, they were there. Eight or nine of them. There's no denying. They *do* exist in concrete reality, quite obviously. Also, they weren't silent at all, the way you'd imagine them to be. They actually chatted quite amiably among themselves. Quietly, yes, but they did chat nevertheless. Whispering something about something. Not praying at all.

Alice caught a sufficient number of words and gestures from their friendly murmurs to figure out, or maybe just plainly imagine, that they were talking about movies. Movies, yes, films, motion pictures. Incredible, isn't it? Something to go see together later that night, or some other night. "*I didn't know nuns went to the cinema,*" Alice considered in her mind.

But she didn't know much about nuns in general, as she realised in that precise moment. Seriously, who does? Nuns are neither rich R&B singers nor dental practitioners. We all know much more about these other types. Or, at least, we tend to think that we know much more, or at any rate something of some relevance, about them. "*Do we?,*" Alice wondered, surrounded by all those chatty nuns and other women, "*what do we really know about anyone, in truth?*"

Of these other women inside the elevator, five caught her eye in particular, that is, apart from the whispering nuns. Like her, all those women were probably the only non-nuns there—inside that hot, artificial, plasticky, and smelly lift—, she logically and a tad tautologically judged. One of them was a stunning blonde, with the kind of body shape and sexy, powerful, head-turning self-assurance that you can see exhibited in Stellar Love's classic flicks, which were Alice's favourites. "*She must be living at the gym,*" Alice briefly reflected.

That gorgeous woman was probably foreign—and Alice was actually correct on that point—whereas she ignored everything else about such a light-coloured, remarkable creature, starting from her vey name—her current one, that is, which is Martha. Also, this well-dressed and well-attended-to constellation of female forms looked like she had… fake tits… You know, breast implants. And that was true as well. "*Does it matter?,*" Alice asked herself.

§3   Martha felt great. Shew knew she was stunning. She did. She felt sexy. She really did. Above all, she felt incredibly and overwhelmingly *powerful*. Oh yes, she did! Martha, some years prior to that casual and impersonal encounter in the lift, had begun sculpting her body to become as alluring and as attractive as possible —to men, and men alone, since she didn't care about women's erotic longings. That demanding self-imposed artistic mission was not a vanity, nor a caprice. It wasn't a sexual or sensual thing. Not as such, that is. Not *per se*.

Quite the opposite, transforming herself into the standard ideal object of average male sexual desire was a sensible, calculated, effective socio-economic move. The sort of considered commutative move that mainstream economists presume we all do, repeatedly, on a daily basis, *qua* straightforward matter of human rationality. The end-result was crystal-clear to Martha, and it explained her choices in an axiomatical manner, on top of an aesthetic one: She wanted to marry a *very* rich husband. The richer he came, the better she'd make him come. If he was going to make her happy, then she would make him happy in return—tit for tat, tat for tit.

Martha had decided to get exactly *that* sort of spouse when she was very young. Young and poor. Concomitantly, she had equally decided that she didn't want to have to live the shitty life that her mother, aunts and grandmothers had endured, back in their native and eternally 'transitional' country. "*I'll have no onions and potatoes,*" Martha was still weighing somewhere inside her fascinatingly symmetrical, singularly Friedmanite skull. *That* was not the life that she wanted to lead, even if her relatives had all been caring and well-meaning. That was *not* the sort of husband that she wanted to land either, even if her father, uncles and grandfathers had all been nice, warm, affectionate, inconstantly-employed blue-collar workers.

Martha didn't resent or hate any of them at all. She loved her family. She loved her father, uncles and grandfathers. Those men made good, excellent husbands, but in a poor sort of way. They were men who didn't drink too much: Just a little. Men who took good care of their families. Men who loved their children and taught them how to live, that is, how to survive. Men who died almost happily in bed, surrounded by loving people that they, in turn, loved dearly. Yet Martha didn't want one of *those*, nor the legion of sprogs that she would have been required to spawn with *one of them* in some cold, small, and stinking room. No, thank you!

All of this, we should add, even if Martha knew that her five siblings had all survived the harsh winters that are still typical of her native region. How many childhood friends, though, had Martha lost to TB and pneumonia? They turned so pale, as white as snow, long before being dead. Their tiny corpses, at the funeral, would actually look healthier and pink, almost red, and with more life running through their veins... They would stop playing with you. It's not that they didn't like you. It's just that they couldn't run, jump, skip, laugh, ... breathe. Her mother had explained that to young Martha: Her friends still liked her, but they couldn't play with her anymore. Their frail, little, brittle bodies couldn't take it. They were sick.

No, nothing like that. No more. Not at all. No! No fucking onions and potatoes! She'd rather fuck an onion, or a rich man who looked like one. She would and will have none of that dingy poverty which she saw all around her, and felt inside of her, for far too many years. None. That's decided. Once and for all. *"Lucky women from rich families don't know shit the way I do,"* Martha reasoned, *"they know no shame, like we do, and they go on telling you what to do, what's right, what's wrong, that you've been duped, and shit... Easy for them! Too easy!"*

None of that, then, no. Martha knew shit *and* shame. Or she thought she knew shit and shame. And she didn't want any more of *that* shit. None. She wasn't ashamed of herself and her choices. Not anymore. She was past that barrier. She will have a big villa on the Riviera, instead. She will have jewels, nice shoes, and the grand, glorious power that comes with having lots of money. No more onions. No more potatoes. She would wash away the stench and the sad taste of all that poor food. Poor people's poor food. Poor memories of poor people's poor food.

Martha had evidently had enough of that particular fare to last her for three lifetimes, or so she would often claim when talking to her local droll acquaintances and, far more seldom, surviving relatives back home. *"Give me cocks that have lots of stocks,"* or *"I'll have white cum and black caviar,"* she would frequently joke with herself —and, on occasion, with few select acquaintances in her prosperous adoptive country: The drollest ones; those who still had a sense of humour. In any case, inside that particular elevator, Martha started nibbling on a new protein bar that her fitness instructor had recommended to her, with a touch of unusual enthusiasm.

§4 Another woman, somewhat older than the commanding blonde, but in many ways no less beautiful than the former—Iris is the older woman's name, incidentally, but Alice didn't know that, and she still ignores it—was standing close by. Focussing upon her own mental processes, Iris was busy trying to think about three snappy, witty remarks that an intriguing new instructor had made in class. What was their meaning? What were they intended to do, teach, cast light upon? She was genuinely engrossed in those academic cogitations.

The class at issue was part of a new multidisciplinary course that she had just started attending at the university. It was, essentially, a methodology module for all aspiring humanists and the numerous social scientists in-the-making, that is, people like herself. It was a well-attended course, but it is also true that attendance was mandatory for all the undergraduates registered in the pertinent disciplines. Had it not been mandatory, it would have been carefully and studiously avoided by half of its present cohort. There was "too much to read," many beginners had complained, on a cyclical, foreseeable basis: They had to read *two* whole books!

The new instructor had said that "the only useful psychologists are the great artists," and Iris believed that she had actually managed to grasp the meaning of that clever remark. She herself, in order to make sense of her choices and emotions, had repeatedly compared her own life experiences with those of the fictional heroines in, say, Tolstoy's or Eliot's novels. All the cold pressors and reaction times with which she had been inundated in her other psychology classes were of no consequence at all, in that spiritual respect. They seemed quite aimless, in fact. Any silly reality show, for that matter, was far more insightful than any experimental study in which she had participated. Even soap operas and pop songs were more perceptive.

But then the instructor had added two more crafty cracks of that kind: "Behaviourism is psychology for the autistic," and "religious faith is the extra beat in a Genesis song." Now, she had a vague, very vague notion of what "behaviourism" meant. And she knew what condition autism was. As to the third remark, she had *no* clue whatsoever as to what her instructor meant. Wasn't "genesis" a section of the Bible? Were there songs in the Bible? Or was the instructor talking about some traditional chant or epic poem about the beginning of the cosmos? And what in heaven or earth had beats to do with all of that? Iris was puzzled.

Notwithstanding such salutary obstacles, Iris liked her studies and pursued them with great eagerness. Very much so. She also liked being around other students, younger students. She liked the cute attentions that she had been receiving from a pretty shy boy attending the same courses as she did. It reminded her of her own youth. It was sweet. And perfectly innocent. A mere faint memory of flirting, in a way. Nothing more. Just a small, beautiful game. Nothing compromising. Amusing, rather. Maybe a little cruel. It was purely a minor test of the residual power that she still possessed and, at times, enjoyed deploying at her own command. That pretty shy boy, in a manner of speaking, was hers to toy with. And who doesn't like playing?

Unfortunately, while she was trying to recollect the features of that gentle young man's handsome face, Iris kept being distracted by the notion that her husband might be coming back home in a bad mood. Iris dreaded that. Truly. Of course, there was no good reason why he should come back angry or resentful on *that* particular day. Probably, things were going well for him at work. Possibly, even better than just well. "Gloriously," as he would sometimes say, while describing his many and seemingly unending professional accomplishments.

By so doing, Iris was trying to reassure herself. Her husband was a wealthy, envied, brilliant man. Everybody respected him. He was important. Imposing, even. The sort of tough man who can conquer a kingdom for himself, were we only living in the days of Henri VIII and Thomas More. *But* what if he was in a bad mood? What then? How would he address her? How would he behave? Where would she find shelter? He was tall, strong, dangerous, and… cruel. That pretty shy boy, instead, looked like nothing but a morsel off a sugar cube.

§5   There were then a mother and her bubbly two wee girls—Alice didn't know that they are Mrs Symonds and her two younger daughters, called Dora and Anita, but these details are secondary at the moment—, who kept talking about some masked Danish-Mongolian rapper or groundbreaking penta-sexual pop icon that they liked so much. "God, please, kill us all!," Alice mumbled at one point—she'd rather listen to Rota's *Godfather* theme on an eternal loop!

The two girls' mother seemed prone to make them stop and be quiet, but without much conviction, nor any real success. The lift resonated with her two daughters' lively comments and livelier giggles. In truth, Mrs Symonds herself was somewhat preoccupied, if not simply busy: She was daydreaming. Something which she was keen on, as a matter of those small yet significant daily habits that a person can exhibit, and whether that person herself is even aware of those habits or not. Mrs Symonds was picturing herself in a universe of her own creation, where she could spend hours experiencing a different kind of daily existence. A refuge.

Specifically, Mrs Symonds could see herself at the helm of a flourishing enterprise—the sole and supreme top manager of a successful newcomer in its competitive business area, or the wealthiest CEO of a transnational corporate juggernaut. She would be its bold captain. The woman at the helm. The boss. She would wear power-suits and ridiculously tall high-heels. She would treat all subordinates and inferiors with ice-cold contempt, especially younger male ones. Men would get a taste of their own medicine, for once! It would only be poetic justice, and an ample dose of retribution. They all would live in fear and awe of her, and respect her.

Mrs Symonds really liked that particular fantasy of hers. Her voice would be God's voice. Her will God's will. Her hand God's hand. No joking, no laughter, no humour would be allowed. *Her* business is meant to be a serious enterprise! It's a place where people work to make *her* money, as *she* orders them to do—while also keeping the shareholders sufficiently happy by means of dependable distributions of more-than-adequate dividends. What mattered most, however, is that *her* workers would live under constant terror of being fired by *her*, and *her* alone. "*That's real power*," she thought, "*almost as good as the ancient* jus vitae necisque."

Nevertheless, *there* she was. Inside that elevator. With her two noisy daughters. She was taking them to see a physician, the family physician: A competent but queer GP, who liked dressing up in her kooky aunt's old curtains, or the old-fashioned wallpaper that you could still find, and be aptly horrified by, in fewer-and-fewer greasy spoons in that neighbourhood. Her daughters complained that they "had water" in their ears and couldn't hear well enough at school. "*Maybe they shouldn't go all the time down to the lake*," Mrs Symonds opined, in her own mind, blaming her husband for that inconvenient aquatic pastime of their daughters.

Unbeknownst to the three of them, Alice was also thinking about the greasy spoons in that neighbourhood. Terrible places. All that fat! The fried food. Clogging your arteries. Killing you slowly. Dreadful, really dreadful! "*Why don't they ban them?*," she wondered, "*don't they know that they are actually murdering people with that kind of food?*." What a callous system! "*They put money before people's health, and that's that*," she thought, whilst a bothering sense of bitterness filled her mouth and her soul. Bitterness, yes, even if she couldn't actually recall anything that tasted bitter. What's bitterness like? Can anyone describe it?

§6 Gradually, floor by floor, the lift emptied. The garrulous nuns were the first ones to leave. In the end, Alice too got to her floor. Only a young brunette was still inside the lift, that is, after Alice herself had stepped outside. It was a petite, dark-haired girl called Simone. Alice had failed to notice her, and so had everyone else. It was as though she didn't exist or had no material body, even if she actually did. She had been inside that lift all that time, after all.

As to what sort of thoughts and emotions were roaming around Simone's mind or soul, it is impossible to say. She has always been inscrutable. Even today. Even for the author of this book. I am really sorry about this limitation. Yet nobody can see what goes on inside

Simone's heart. Only God can, if He or She exists. Which one hopes is the case, generally speaking.

It's not even certain that Simone herself understood or understands her own feelings. It can't be ascertained. You see, some people are just like *black holes*: Dark, dead, and potentially deadly stars. They're there, they affect the cosmos around them, you can find out that they're there, but you can't really see them, nor peek inside them. At the same time, they can draw you in and destroy you. That too is part of the cosmos' array of amazing powers.

Conceivably, Alice had herself fallen into one of those deceased astral bodies. It was many weeks, in fact, that she had been obsessing about pursuing a healthy and "wise" lifestyle, as she liked connoting it and presenting it to herself, whenever some nagging doubt dared arise in her consciousness—there's *no* worse enemy than your own conscience: How cruel it can be!

Alice knew that it was a hard thing to do and accomplish, but she was determined. She knew that she was a strong, free, educated, independent, powerful, modern woman. But she would attain an ancient ideal: That of living coherently and consistently like a mouse, reducing everything to sheer survival. "Natural needs only, like Diogenes," she would utter on her own, sometimes. That way, she would not be tempted by consumerist toxins and unwholesome foods.

To better avoid temptation, Alice had duly removed her old fridge, the gas cooker, the dinner table, and sold the empty chairs that used to crown it. No canned pork, no pasta, no sugar, and no dry goods of any type could be found in the kitchen's cabinets, or anywhere else around the apartment: They were industrially manufactured. Her house was gloriously empty of all of that: *"Blow thy shelf!,"* she would joke within her head. Even the so-called "organic" stuff was absent. It was all a *lie*. It is all a lie! A cynical, Machiavellian, bloody scam! What Alice had actually been eating for the past few days, it is quite a mystery. *If* she had eaten anything.

§7 Had Mrs Symonds' eccentric GP seen Alice, she would have immediately diagnosed her with *anorexia nervosa*. Alice, however, had made sure that no GP, no physician, no medic, no nurse, no professional, no neighbour, no colleague, and no friend could set eyes on her vanishing body, which she kept hidden underneath ungainly piles of baggy clothes. She had learnt the tricky art of making herself *inconspicuous*, if not completely and utterly invisible. That sort of prodigious feat was still beyond her current abilities. One day, perhaps.

Alice didn't trust any so-called "expert." Official science was in cahoots with the food industry, according to her, that is, the large corporate manufacturers of venomous products, the greedy ruffians that were destroying the planet, killing the bees, murdering the elephants, massacring the chimps, and making trillions of profits every week by reinvesting their financial capital into the armaments and pharmaceutical companies that benefitted from the ongoing annihilation of Planet Earth. Criminals. All of them. Without exception. They're all vultures!

Alice would *never* give her own money to such callous bastards. People without a shred of conscience. People who, sooner or later, would unleash a… zombie apocalypse, for all she knew, because of their cost-saving and profit-making experiments and chicaneries. She would *never* let them have her body. Or her soul, for that matter. Better dead than defeated. *Never*!

Fathomably crabbit and committed to pursuing her noble goal at *all* costs, Alice had been neglecting her domestic duties for months. Her flat may have looked fittingly despoiled, hence devoid of stuff and appliances, but most wooden struts and, say, the old mangy wallpaper could have benefitted from some maintenance. The same considerations apply to the wirings, the spent lightbulbs, and the many squint and dangling electrical outlets peppering the otherwise unsavoury apartment, in which only a red daybed and an unplayed piano survived as furniture.

Even more crucial would have been to fix the obvious *crack* in her living room's ceiling, which corresponded to a tiled section of a lower rooftop running around the outside of the building where she lived—and starved. Over the past few weeks, the crack had become wider and wider. The wind could be heard whistling through it.

Sometimes, you could even see the Sun shining through it, although in a somewhat pale, minor, lukewarm, almost feeble fashion.

§8   On that day, though, the Sun was *not* shining at all. It was a grey, rainy day. One of many. The town, albeit welcoming and charming, is definitely *not* a famous tropical destination. "Wolves complained about the weather," recites a local, common, self-ironic hyperbole. The citizens, in any case, are quite used to it. That is why, in all likelihood, they tend to avoid having cracks or other major material deteriorations in their ceilings and, above all, their roofs.

When it rains, rainwater can accumulate and rush into an actual dwelling, causing no insignificant amount of damage to the extant property. It is the sort of damage that would get many people to quarrel with their insurance company, which would standardly refuse to pay for that kind of moist destruction. "Negligence," they would always say, "and blah blah blah…"

Alice could clearly see the trickle of dirty water running down from the ceiling and creating a large puddle on the living room's floor. The carpet was damp and mouldy. She could have put a bucket there, but she owned no bucket. Not anymore. Or maybe she did, but she had forgotten where it was kept. In the meantime, the revolting reek of rotting textile and decaying wood could be perceived without impediment. It was growing. It was pervading more and more corners of her apartment. It was like a toxic cloud or vapour. In truth, Alice still had a working nose. She sensed it too. Her nares were not clogged. But it is not the nose that saved her life.

At one point, Alice felt a strong kind of *compulsion* inside her. A bit like when you avoid instinctively a hurtful collision with a fast-moving object. Something that happens to you. Not something that you decide to do. As though your body still pays attention while you don't. It was like an impulse or some deep-seated intuition. She couldn't explain it. She still can't.

What matters, however, is that Alice approached the trickle of dirty water. She opened her dry, thin mouth. She pushed forward her whitish, trembling tongue. She let the yellowish water run over her extended tongue and drip down, slowly, into her parched throat. And then another funny thing happened. She sensed something that she had almost forgotten: Flavour. Yes, *flavour*! Tasting the flavour of something. And she realised that she badly needed to eat.

⇘

XXXV – Quiet Plumbers for the Whisperers[250]

§1 Some people had tossed out the idea that zombies are but a corny fantasy, a fiction, a horror story. Others had tossed out the possibility that zombies are a clever and perchance subtle cultural allegory of class polarisation and class warfare. A few people, even if it is difficult to say exactly how many of them are left now, had denounced zombies with gusto as an immoral, indecent, disgusting, despicable token of cultural appropriation of Afro-Caribbean folklore by Western and Eastern filmmakers—and artists at large.[251] A large, willing, worldwide feat of egregious callousness featuring much blind greed, which should be better tossed out.

Whether or not all of these out-tossers overlooked something important, or had a morbid penchant for letting their legal advisors overlook their wills, nearly all of these living people are currently dead, or zombies—which means both conditions, actually, as confirmed last night by the born-again Christian Nosferatu. Regrettably, the alarm went off when it was too late, and nobody has been able to turn it off yet: *Listen, oh ye people of Earth! The zombie apocalypse has come in genuine, lived reality; and it has not yet gone away—if it will ever go away!*[252]

---

[250] The movies show that the living dead don't know they're living and ignore they're dead.°

° Crosses are frequently associated with the living dead, but are unwelcome in note #254.

[251] An artist, disconsolate, stated before being eaten alive: "They really can't laugh, none of them! Not even at Borat or Hugleikur Dagsson!"

[252] Some people did prefer the apocalypse to whatever normality they actually had before said apocalypse.

Meanwhile, considering the general unpreparedness, nobody had truly gone for the zombies, not even the armed generals—that is, apart from those who truly did go for the zombies, but without proper consideration, and henceforth lost their arms, limbs, life, life and limb, limb and life, and more. It was a bloody bloodbath, according to some cold-blooded observers who saved their skin by the skin of their teeth—many of them being bloody dentists.

§2 Human civilisation has tragically collapsed, hence the lights are out all over the planet, whilst only a handful of resilient survivors can now see with any clarity when the lights are out—and whether or not such an outward celestial spectacle leaves them filled with any inner light, like classical tragedy would do, classically. Human civilisation is effectively finished, but so is equally the much-awaited hearty recuperation of the Earth's ecosphere. Without further anthropogenic activities being furthered and covering the world in layers of chemical and toxic dust, there are no longer any new pollutants to dust—only old ones, e.g., radioactive waste in the ground and microplastics in the seas. A totally-dispirited *Zeitgeist* may be a tad untimely.

Custom-made commercial goods have become a distant, almost forgotten memory, and novel customs and traditions have been developing among the surviving pockets of human beings who outsmarted the sufficiently brainless zombies and succeeded in keeping our species going, and without having to empty their pockets in the process. Fascinated with occult matters, ancient humankind may have consulted the augurs to process the signs, and the assigned augurs could have then consulted their ancient fellows. Yet, the enlightened and ageing people of the modern age were not prepared at all to face the apocalypse's ugly face in any sort, way, mode, respect, form, manner or shape. Their well-prepared top-executives, Wall-Street oracles, mega-tycoons, AI-programmers, super-gurus, techno-logists, and prostho-dontists had prepared more than well the end of the end: Even their best, most definitive LLMs spelled worse than lame.

As the ensuing and perduring global chaos came to pass, all manners of bad manners proved passable, if not good, locally, and on occasion—even those that would have caused someone to be sued, back in the days when corpses and parts thereof were no mobile threat to anyone, for the most part. The much-desired rigorous veneer of moral civilisation became as desirable as Venereal diseases, or *rigor mortis*. Some mortals saved themselves by bolting from their homes. Others yet by bolting their homes. Once again, as stated, and in any case: *Few left*.

§3 The sadly weathered population that weathered said apocalypse has even managed to restart, here and there, some semblances of community life and complex social interaction, but only in rare and noteworthy cases. To this end, even if the end was near, the dead gave a hand—a dead hand, but a hand nonetheless. (Albeit nobody demined the many mined minarets.)

Unlike the zombies that were screened in the old, happy, unhappy days of, say, F.A.C. MacRunt's experimental cinema, the unlikely creatures from whom (or which) the surviving survivors have had to screen themselves ever since the apocalypse was occasioned by some mischievous spirit or divinity are not entirely stupid and—if you run experiments, communicate with them, hit them with deadpan humour or a poker in the face, drop spirited bombs, or brainstorm in earnest a little—they can occasionally leave you, your poor peers, and the rest of us in a likely state of uneasy peace—though not really easily rest in peace themselves, given their stupefying arrested development and somewhat unnerving, fated, non-fatal cretinism.

Newfangled rules and regulations have been heuristically sanctioned to cope with the zombies' sufficient insufficiency of brainpower, while other brainy rules and regulations have been realistically sanctioned. Survival requires endurance, intelligence, skill, spam, creativity, imagination, courage, and flexibility, doesn't it? Indeed, it does. Does it not? It does, it does! New rules of thumb have thus thumbed their nose at thumbed old rules that kept billions under the thumb: They were now all thumbs. Clarifying clarificatory new papers have been clipped together to the same end, doing all that which could be done, while vast branches of the old tree of human legislation have been ended by clipping them altogether—they were done, though not well-done, and so were this and that as well. Sometimes, you've got to be cruel to be kind, or kind of cruel to be kind, or cruel to be kind of kind, or kind of cruel to be kind of kind.

§4 In the derelict old city, old Tom, old Gershom and three old Johns had held fast to a fast Oldsmobile of their youth and, in a secluded and well-protected distant valley, they eventually succeeded in surviving—exactly in the way in which countless ripe old men have often done since youth: By living conclusively quiet lives apart, until the dying part is quite concluded.

Formerly bound by all kinds of mediating, binding, and well-sorted social conventions, as well as by all sorts of unkind and ill-sorted conventional social media, those five unique breathing persons expected now to be equally bound for an unkind spiritual conclusion that none of them, in their inspirited youth, would have ever anticipated or been able to fathom *qua* material possibility for any real human being in real existence in any real part of the real world, or the real entirety thereof: Exhaling their last breath on a planet that had been quickly overrun by slow-moving zombies, who (or which) only seemed to be coming out of some B-movie, but could not be let be or become something else but overrunning slow-moving zombies in real reality, for that is what they really were—no matter how unrealistic this matter could seem.[253]

Picking mushrooms and seeding a cultivated field with watermelon plants to cleverly water and cleave, and cultivating the clever art of seeding ripe watermelons, those five brave men fed their bodies for very many years—whilst leaving room for a modicum of cultivation among themselves verily prevented their brains from going to mush and producing mad books. All of this,

---

[253] As Count Dracula said to one Ms Carrie Xmas: "They don't believe it until they see it."

moreover—and you don't have to keep quiet about it unless you madly want to—, by keeping quiet all the time, so as to attract as little attention as possible, i.e., by being attentively quiet and paying attention to the well-attended quiet. Much wretched plumbing was thus done by using plumes instead of wrenches. Still, most effort still went down the drain.

Lastly, it must be affirmed that all five lasting survivors who were left there learned there-and-then from such apocalyptic events one important form of eventual wisdom that they had never fully formed before in their minds, that is, not even in drama class nor at right- and left-wing party rallies: A clear sense of the right priorities; e.g., knowing how to cast the seeds of watermelons is truly much more important than knowing how to throw a truthful seedy party.[254]

XXXVI – Dine and Shout[255]

Two Scenes:
- *Rev. Pierre R.S.V.P. Bowles (only in the first scene)*
- *A masked friend, with and without a dog*
- *The author (only in the second scene)*[256]

It's carnival time. Rev. Bowles and a masked friend with a dog on the leash are having a good few drinks at the local bar, which looks like an American diner from the 1950s. They observe the people sitting at the other tables, especially the masked characters who come into the bar, and converse amiably—all of it while being fairly well-stewed. They're in a very good humour.

---

[254] As a known political aside, knowing which identifiable side one is on is not a side-issue in identity politics.

[255] On many occasions, the latter may be as important as the former. If intoxication and chauvinism unnerve you, skip this rowdy comedy.

[256] Please notice that the fictional author's author is not fictional, unlike the author authored in this fiction.

FIRST SCENE – *Superheroes*

Rev Pierre Bowles: Look at a' 'ese shuperheroesh! I guessh shuperheroesh need drinkin' too!
Masked friend: You must drink a lot to as-beer to become the kind of guy who saves the world!

PB: Beer can be 'e drink of shalvation!

MF: The salv-actional beverage!

PB: We should toasht dddo 'at, right?

MF: Or boast about it?

PB: Be'er 'an ge'in' busted…

MF: What d'you mean, mate?

PB: Well… It's a bi' embarrasshing, but you shee… Lasht time we were 'ere. D'you 'member 'at?

MF: Aye, well… Some of it! I had to spew only a couple of times…

PB: Ok, 'en… When we decided to go home, and 'ank God for 'at… 'member 'at?

MF: Yeah, well… More or less! …I do recall a plastered couple waltzing around… So?

PB: I just couldn't hold i' in, you know? So I pished in the park in fron' o…dde…'ouse… me 'ouse!

MF: No, man! You didn't!

Act Two

PB: I did, I did… Gosh, I wa' like a 'enaisshance fountain! 'ey should pu' mme in a big shquare in Rome or Florensh, you know? Psssshhhh! Pssssshhhhhhh!

MF: The pissing reverend goes irreverent! Ah!
PB: I was bustin', mate! My bla'er, you know… Boom!

MF: "Better out than in," my wife would say…

PB: Wise woman, 'eally wise… A bi' like my frien' Frank, truff be dold… Hey! Wonder woman!

MF: Well, okay. She's great, I know that well, but she's no wonder woman! And I love me wife…

PB: No, no' your missus, you looney! Ddde 'able down 'ere! Cannn… you shee her?

MF: Ah, right. That table there! … (*more soberly*) Have I seen those girls before? I think I have…

PB: Hm… I know mosht peoble 'round 'ere… Le' mme shee… Hm… That's 'e youngest girl o' the Shymondzszzz 'amily… Sheeesh…mmmondsh… Nishe beople, by 'e way… the Shymondsh… (*muttering*) Dde fathersh looksh a bi' like Walter Benjamin…

MF: Yep. Anita. That's her. You're right… (*pause*) Fuck me backwards! Grown into a fine, good-looking, and bloody *hot* young woman, hasn't she? Wow! … Model-like material!

PB: Wouldn' know. You shtop loo'ing a' girls 'at way, when you're in…me line o' work, you know?

MF: Oh my: The reverend can't even look! …Any emotions that aren't socially mediated, hm?

PB: Well, it's not 'at … Oh, bolloksh! You shee… You learn… bounce the eyes off 'em.

MF: Like priests and nuns, you mean?

PB: Yeah… And vishishiansh too, I 'ink. You know… dogtorsh… at the 'oshpital… and kliniksh…

MF: … And dentists, I guess.

PB: No, 'loody 'entists 'on't do that… Ne'er!

MF: Ah! Dentists… Evil people! Cavities… emptiness… evil, evil people!

PB: Aye… Aye, 'eal evil. (*makes two horns in front of his forehead to mimic the devil*)

MF: Well, anyway, that's not my problem. I'm in no religious order, praying 24 hours a day! And I'm no doctor, asking my patients to disrobe, or probing and prodding inside their private holes! My profession doesn't prohibit looking. And I look. I have a *right* to look. I *choose* to look!

PB: You bloo'y univershidy professhorsh are a' a 'unch of creepsh, my dear!

MF: Not at all! First, our students are *adults*. Like us. Second, beauty is… *beauty*. Like art. Or nature. Blessings from God. Your beloved God! … Third, I must keep in touch with current humankind and know very well what it's like. I am professionally devoted to the scientific duty of careful, consistent, repeated, repeatable, and, sometimes, caring *observation*! Ah! … Fourth, my *gender* entails special privileges, whether you like it or not. I may be a dirty slut or a cheap hooker, but never a dirty pig or an old creep: That's *your* bad luck! You'll be sued and called to court. I'll be called "sophisticated" and courted. Ah! You can only become Trump or Berlusconi. I'll be... Colette, Zsa Zsa Gabor, Annie Ernaux, Madonna,... Ranvir Singh,... Brigitte Macron! 'Cos we can only be the pishing people that our pishing society allows us to be... Ah, again! How's that as a knockout argument, eh? (*burps*) ... And consider that I'm as drunk as a skunk!

PB: ... Well, if you *obsherve* sho well, who'sh de o'er one, 'e one beshide... wonder woman?

MF: I do, my poor, pious, o-blinding friend! It's her older sister Dora, who's dressed as... what's that? Oliver Cromwell, I guess... I met her a few times, with her friend Fiona. Remember her?

PB: Aye... I do.'e one who's an art...arshtisht... yeah, aye... (*more quietly*) Ah, 'e Shymondsh!

MF: What about them?

PB: 'Ey're really good beoble, you now, but... well, wi' 'eir own problems... 'ard onesh... 'oblems!

MF: Like everyone else, you mean: (*very ironic*) Who doesn't have problems?

PB: Exactlily! Like everyone elshe... poor 'uman 'eings... Id's so 'ard ddo be a 'uman being!

MF: Aye... I mean, look at the two of us!

PB: Wha' dddjyou mean?

MF: Well, for one, our youth's gone... done for... skedaddled!

PB: Yep. I 'now... We're old an' fa'... 'at'sdrue!

MF: Must be all the beer we drink!

PB: May be… But, (*burps*) … who cares?

MF: Well, *I* do. I'd like to stay young… Or look youthful. My wife wouldn't mind that… I think.

PB: Ach! You women are all 'e shame! Alway' 'zhinking a'out how you look!

MF: Come on! You can't deny *that*. Beauty *is* power. Think of Evita! And youth is more powerful than the rest of us, in *that* respect, which is decisive in *so* many ways… Isn't that important?

PB: Nah, no' really. No…

MF: I don't believe you! You're just being a pig-headed hypocrite… I know you know better than that! And so do you! Anyway, what's really important, then, oh my dear pished and pisssshing Pope of all beers? Oh, our great Roman fountain of wisdom and cannae-hold-it-in pish?

PB: (*laughing*) 'Ank'you, 'ank'you… (*smiling*) Well… Goo' 'ings ge' be'eer with age, you know?

MF: Like what, you silly fat bastard and prophet of the glorious pishing inheritance of the arse?

PB: True love, for one. Ever sheen 'ow shweet ol' goubles are?

MF: … Ok, ok… Old couples loving each other… I give you that one…

PB: Friendshshipsh is 'no'er oon: It doesnae age. Id ge' be'er with age! Like us, you silly old bin'!

MF: Right, ok. Friendship... I grant you that one too... But, what else?

PB: Fucking Scotch, you eejet! The wa'er of life! God's grea'esht gif' do greaturesh of ddhe flesh... With bladdersh to bloody empdy shomewhere, addimes... Like Roman fountainsh! Psshhh!

MF: Ah! Scotch! ... You win, ya basa! ... (*after an apt pause*) Shall we get a couple of drams?

PB: Uuuuhhhhh... Oh, yesh, my friend!

They get their whisky, raise the tumblers, and toast aloud.

PB & MF: To friendsshhipsh!

Curtain.

SECOND SCENE – Minor Villains

The reverend and his masked friend are totally sloshed, hence the former has conveniently disappeared inside the bar's crowded toilets. The dog is also gone – probably urinating in the bar's car park or the adjacent area. The reverend's masked friend keeps drinking and talking to herself, primarily, until she catches the eye of a man sitting alone at another table.

Masked friend: (*drinking and singing an improvised variation on a well-known football chant*) Wonder Woman, Wonder Woman / She likes the power ring, she likes the power ring! / Wonder Woman, Wonder Woman / And then the lasso n' sting, and then the lasso n' sting!

Author: (*observes with obvious curiosity*) -

MF: (*continues*) *Wonder Woman, Wonder Woman / She's got the bomb ear-rings, she's got the bomb ear-rings! / Wonder Woman, Wonder Woman / And then she crushes things, and then she crushes things!*

A: (*continues*) -

MF: (*continues*) *Wonder Woman, Wonder Woman / She's got the flyin' shoes, she's got the flyin' shoes! / Wonder Woman, Wonder Woman / And then yer baws she chews, and then yer baws she chews!* (*N.B. depending on the venue repeat all verses once, twice or thrice*)

A: (*continues*) -

MF: (*engaging the audience with the eyes and gesticulating vividly to invite the spectators to sing along all three verses in whatever order is desired*) *Wonder Woman, Wonder Woman / She's got the bomb ear-rings, ...* (*ad lib., depending on the responsiveness of the crowd.*)

A: (*continues smiling*) -

MF: (*stops abruptly and addresses very aggressively the author*) ... HEY!

A: (*smiles*) -

MF: (*very loud, to end any residual chanting*) HEY, I SAID! YOU! (*pointing at the author*) THERE!

A: (*smiles*) -

MF: Yes, YOU!

A: (*smiles*) -

Act Two

MF: YOU, at that table! What are you looking at?

A: (*smiles*) -

MF: D'ya think I'm funny? Ah! (*grabs a half-full beer glass from a table*)

A: (*snorts*) -

MF: Sure I'm funny, ya fanny! (*slowly and unsteadily approaches the author's table*)

A: (*smiles*) -

MF: What the fuck is there to look at, ah? Do I make you laugh, you perv?

A: (*smiles*) -

MF: 'Cos that's what you are, you fucking perv! Sitting there, watching… sayin' noffin'!

A: (*smiles*) -

MF: Look at you, ya perv! You and yer fucking stupid face and greasy hair!

A: (*smiles*) -

MF: I bet you're a fuckin' zip, a bloody wop, aren't you? Ya sweaty Pavarotti! (*splashes beer at him*)

A: (*chuckles, dries off some of the beer with a serviette*) -

MF: Do I make you laugh, ya wonder bread wop? (*she slaps him mildly across the face*) ... Ah? You seedy macho whopper! (*slaps him again, harder*) Go and kiss Harlequin's ass, you dog!

A: (*laughs briefly*) -

MF: Did 'at make you laugh, ya Tony, ah? Wha' 'bout this one, you fucking wallione! (*she punches him in the face*) You bastard oily spider! (*in Daly-like Itanglish*) How taste it, ya comica man?

A: (*sore, but laughs a little more than before*) -

MF: You bastard of a spaghetti-twister, what are you laughing at, ah? (*she punches him again, hard*) ... Fucking pervy salami! (*punches again, harder*) ... You low-down Pulcinella! (*slaps*)

A: (*sore, starts laughing loudly*) -

MF: You... What the fuck are you laughing at, you goddamn rizzo (*she punches him again*) ... filthy provolone (*slaps twice*), you mangy mingia (*punches him hard again*) ... Eat your own teeth, you dirty, lecherous pig! (*punches him twice very hard in the mouth, always hard from now on*)

A: (*even more sore, starts an unrestrained belly laughter*) -

MF: (*perplexed, even angrier*) What... What the fuck! You filthy meatball! (*slaps once*) Small-cock Mussolini! (*slaps him twice*) You fascist gnome! (*punches*) Rotten Marconi! (*slaps thrice, then punches him again*) Black-shirt pizza-muncher! (*punches him twice in the belly, slaps, punches in the face*) Ah!? Eh!? Machiavelli (*one slap*), Berlusconi (*two slaps*), Salvini (*three slaps*), Meloni (*four slaps*)... What the... Eh!? (*she is getting tired from beating the laughing author*)

A: (*in agony, laughing uncontrollably*) -

Act Two

MF: (*furious*) What is it, ah? What's to laugh about? (*punches him twice*) You horrid Mario! (*punches once*) … Horrid Super-Mario! (*punches twice, slaps once*) … You sick, no-cock, stupid I-tie! (*slaps twice*) … What the… (*getting tired, agitated, raging wild*) WHAT?!? (*punches once in the belly, very hard*) … You hothead macaroni! (*panting, slaps four times*) … You dodgy Guinea pig! (*punches twice, she's getting extremely tired*) … WHAT?!? (*punches once in the face*) What the fuck… You! Sexist, tricoloured, freak, son-of-a-bitch! (*slaps twice, misses once*) … AH!?

A: (*in agony, laughing uncontrollably*) -

MF: (*idem*) What the fuck are you laughing about, you bastard, toothless grape-stomper! (*punches him three times*) What… Stop, you… (*punches*) STOP! AH! You, you… Fucking… (*punches twice, getting ridiculously tired*) sweaty greaseball, cock-sucking homophobe! (*punches three times, more and more tired*) … WHAT?!? (*she looks at the author like he's a total loony*)

A: (*in agony, laughing uncontrollably*) -

MF: (*idem*) TELL ME! You… (*punches once, not too hard, she's tired*) You… (*punches him twice, but weakly, because she is very tired*) … fucking bleeding impotent gina! (*punches three times, but ineffectively and with great effort*) WHAT?!? (*punches hard four times, panting and wheezing*) … You shabby garlic-breath Fonzie of my shitting arse! (*punches once and misses*) … WHAT?!? TELL ME! (*misses again*) … Ya bastard, stinking ginny! (*punches poorly twice, getting exhausted and exasperated*) AH! You degenerate, fucking maniac! (*pants*) …WHAT?!?

A: (*in agony, laughing uncontrollably*) I… I'm…

MF: (*idem*) "I" WHAT?!? (*slaps four times*)... AH! TALK! (*punches and hits well*) You fucking racist, fucking rude, fucking harassing, fucking dago! (*punches him twice, less well*) TALK!

A: (*in agony, laughing uncontrollably*) I'm pu... pu... pu...

MF: (*idem*) You... WHAT? (*slaps twice*) You fucking dagowop rat! (*spits in face, punches once*) ... STOP LAUGHING! (*punches poorly*) STOP IT! (*punches and misses*) You ass-whoring, papist, pasta-making, bigoted paisano! (*spits*) ... WHAT!? WHY THE FUCK! (*slaps in the face*)

A: (*in agony, laughing uncontrollably*) ... leg...

MF: (*idem*) WHAT'S THAT? (*punches twice*) WHAT THE FUCKING FUCK! (*very poor punches and slaps ad lib.*) STOP IT! You dirty Bologna, bloody geep, ass-rimming mafioso! WHO THE FUCK ARE YOU LAUGHING AT? (*clownish violence ad lib.*) STOP IT! WHAT'S TO LAUGH ABOUT, you blasted, ball-licking... *pater familias*! ... YOU FUCKING GINO!

A: (*in agony, laughing uncontrollably*) "I... I'm... I'm not... I'm not Italian!" (*keeps laughing away like he's totally demented, spitting blood and teeth from his mouth*)

Curtain.

XXXVII – Grounds for Confusion[257]

§1 Mrs Symonds woke up, which is the only known viable alternative to death, coma, and comparable vegetative states.

---

[257] Elusive woolliness can be logical, but elucidations are insufficient or excessive depending on the audience.

Nevertheless, she could hardly believe that she had woken up. She was in her usual bed, in fact, but her house was… gone. *Yes*, gone! In lieu of her familiar and familial house, now there stood a… forest around her. A forest, yes! Some kind of forest. Woods. Vegetation. All was green around her. Verdant. Fresh. Not too cold. Quiet. Just a gentle breeze and the rustling leaves, which were not immediately reassuring, surprisingly enough.

Mrs Symonds got up. She felt mildly agitated. Somewhat unsettled. Who wouldn't, given the circumstances? She was wearing a long, white nightgown. Her house was a tad chilly. Besides, her husband seemed to like her better when she was, well, covered, so to speak. But he wasn't there. She couldn't wake him up and ask him for help. For she needed help. Or at least she felt she did. That forest was a very bizarre place in which to find yourself. Especially if you can't recall at all how you and your own bed got into that unknown forest.[258]

Mrs Symonds looked down. Her slippers were on the floor, or ground—it was covered with green grass, as a matter of fact—, and put them on, as she would normally do. She started walking. In which direction, she couldn't say. Any direction was as good as any other, probably. The ground was grassy and soft. The trees around her… Birch, probably. The sort of tree out of which the kind nuns of her old school made the thin canes used to punish the naughtier kids. Those who laughed too much. She missed those days. Childhood's always a happier time, for almost all of us. While she walked on the grass, she wondered: *"Is this the Island of Reil?"*

§2 Mrs Symonds reached the end of the forested area. In front of her, as though it had been dropped there from the sky, there appeared an enormous city. Buildings of all sizes, skyscrapers, spires, domes… *Prima facie*, it looked like a mixture of Metropolis and Brasilia. But it was *so* orderly. There was a transparent structural rhythm in the whole urban space, which she could grasp with ease

---

[258] An elf of the forest said: "This is not my forest." The elf was lost.

from her vantage point. That is, standing at the edge of the mysterious forest.[259]

Mrs Symonds was genuinely marvelled. It was as though the painting of a Renaissance ideal city had just been printed in 3D, or there had been a magical materialisation of one of the many planned towns erected on the blessed, imaginary island of Utopia. Had it been irregular, it would have turned into an interminable, labyrinthine plexus of winding crossroads. As it stood before her eyes, it looked like a gigantic Roman *castrum*, or a strangely habitable chessboard. It also reminded her of a videogame which she liked as a young woman: Tetris, it was called.

Mrs Symonds felt curiously reassured by all that neatness and regularity. It was and it felt clean, agreeable, predictable, and comforting: The art of building can produce such effects. If it was an alien city, then the aliens had a sense of taste, as well as some competent and capable architects. The alien engineers had probably studied the works of Vitruvius, Alberti, Palladio, von Hildebrandt, and Boullée. That well-ordered metropolitan domain exuded a potent and uncommon feeling of comprehensive evenness and all-encompassing equilibrium, as though the city were the premeditated, monumental reification of the rarest of virtues: Impartiality.[260]

Mrs Symonds was not *entirely* reassured, yet. That which the alien city lacked in the most evident manner possible was the most obvious component of all cities: *Citizens*. That humongous place was empty, or looked empty, from the location where she was at that moment in time, whenever that was. So patent a tranquillity and so loud a silence could have scared and worried many people, but she was not overwhelmingly afraid. On the contrary, those features too were relatively assuaging, and almost pleasurable. All in all, she was now acceptably serene.

---

[259] An elf of the forest said: "I can't smell my forest." The elf had caught a rather nasty cold.

[260] An eccentric, incensed reader screamed: "It's not fair! It's not fair!"

Act Two

§3   Mrs Symonds decided to keep walking and reach the city. "*It shouldn't be too long a walk,*" she speculated. And it was not. After a short while, she was exploring that peculiar yet peaceful place, enjoying the beauty of its many and diverse buildings, as well as the overall geometrical composition of the apprehensible urban space. Signs of life were present. Both vegetal and animal. Trees, but also creepers, flowers, insects, sparse small birds, a swan, and numerous small rodents. Mice, perhaps. Or hamsters. Not porcupines… Weasels? Or could they be lemmings? She wasn't sure about those little mammals. There were very many of them.

Mrs Symonds was able to explain to herself why there could be all that life in such a place, whether or not her explanation would really stand the test of logico-experimental reason and proper scientific inquiry. There were thin, soothing, narrow blue brooks running throughout the city. The streets of that fantastic metropolis were criss-crossed by rivulets and streamlets. "*Wherever there's water,*" she rationally inferred, "*there's life.*" Occasionally, there were even small ponds, and a few frogs or toads could be spotted. Although not very many. She had always liked amphibians, for some reason. There may have been fish too, but she didn't see any.[261]

Mrs Symonds started hearing a different kind of noises, at one point. She was well into the belly of the city, after all. There had to be *someone* in that gigantic place. It was only logical. The noises weren't the breeze, nor the animals, nor the creeks and burns carrying life—and the potential for life—wherever they ran in that surreal, trancelike, well-arranged metropolis. The new noises were mechanical, almost bell-like, or so she hypothesised. They had to be produced by metallic objects clanging, or something like that. And there where heavy thuds, albeit not loud ones. Something or someone was whining too, like a shrill cry, a neigh, or a child's scream.

§4   Mrs Symonds entered a huge square—much huger than any square that she had ever seen before. Not even the Red Square in

---

[261] An elf of the forest said: "I can't see my forest." The elf was blind.

Moscow or Tiananmen in Beijing were that big. Not even the two of them conjoined, she gathered. It was quite simply the most enormous square upon which she had ever gazed. Therein there moved, slowly, very few creatures which she had not yet discovered while visiting that mystifying urban domain. Some were humans: Persons. Others were not: They were shiny, cubic, metallurgical objects ambulating on stumpy artificial limbs. They looked like bulky robots from some antiquated science-fiction story. And she had never liked that literary and cinematic genre very much, unlike two of her four daughters.

Mrs Symonds shuddered. Where were her daughters? Why weren't they there with her? Were they lost? Had anything bad happened to them? Was their father with them to help and protect them? The mental image of her four daughters quickly visited her mind, but flew away as quickly, back to that unconscious realm whence all thoughts originate. Somehow, she got awfully distracted by something—or interested in something—all of a sudden.

Mrs Symonds was amazed: There were large animals as well! Not many. But large, and visible. Two elephants, several horses, two zebras. A lonely kangaroo. Even a wild boar. And she had always liked large animals. Perhaps because she had grown up on a farm. Or maybe for some other reason. She would have been unable to explain with any degree of intersubjective intellectual certainty *why* she liked them. But she knew for sure that she liked them. She did.

§5 Mrs Symonds approached one of the horses. It was the closest large animal with respect to where she was located at that moment in the city's huge square. She asked the horse: "Who are you? What place is this?" The horse replied: "I am your son-in-law, *dura mater*, don't you recognise me?." "Oh yes, you are right! Silly me!," she commented, "but what place is this?," she asked once more. The horse answered flatly: "I don't know! We just live here: It's our city."

Mrs Symonds was honestly and maddeningly perplexed. *"What sort of an answer is that*?," she considered, a bit peevishly. At the same time, however, she had the candour required to admit to herself that the circumstances were most peculiar: Not only was she in the

Act Two

largest square of a large city that was largely uninhabited, but she was presently holding a conversation with a horse, as though she were Saint Francis talking to the wolf of Gubbio, or Mr Gulliver.

Mrs Symonds kept looking around. She saw two black-and-grey chimpanzees. They were mating. "*Odd*," she thought, "*it shouldn't be done in public*." And she walked hurriedly past them, whilst trying to ignore the unfamiliar noises which they made while copulating. The ground was covered in light, off-white dirt, a kind of fine fawn sand: "*An ancient Roman arena*," she concluded. It was quite pleasant to tread on it. Enjoyable tactile stimuli mattered to her.

§6 Mrs Symonds' slippers felt more than comfortable. She had no difficulty exploring that new environment in those indoor shoes. Taking a stroll of that type was almost a luxury for a busy, pious family mother and hardworking housewife such as herself. She didn't mind having the opportunity to take one. Unexpectedly, a hare hopped towards her. It was dark-brown and cream-white. It was shedding its fur. The hare looked at her, opened its mouth, and emitted a series of sounds. It was as though the animal was trying to communicate with her, but the language which it used was totally unknown to her.[262] After that, the hare ran away.

Mrs Symonds was disheartened by her inability to converse with the hare. Still, she went on roaming around the gargantuan square. It was beautiful: Orderly, sunlit, levelled, and neatly geometrical, thanks to the many well-aligned buildings that guarded its orthogonal perimeter. The few living creatures scattered over its surface did not ruin the overall sense of peace and tidiness that she perceived so distinctively. Suddenly, however, she heard some kind of human voice not too far from her. It was a moan, a lament. A squeal, perhaps. But human.

Mrs Symonds looked to her right. Close by, at the mouth of one of the myriad of big, small, and medium-sized streets irradiating out of

---

[262] It was reported by now-defunct students of pre-Adamic dialects that the hare had stated what follows: "The brain isn't a computer. Humans are animals, not machines. Even perfect imitations aren't the genuine artifacts."

that huge square, there stood a man, sobbing, leaning against one of the many well-designed buildings of that immense ethereal city: It was an empty synagogue, from the look of it—the Egyptian door and the façade's large Star of David signalled its likely religious function, along with a circular plaque carrying an improbable and obscure Latin inscription: "*Posthac animata lex*." The weeping man seemed to be alone and disconsolate, if not desperate. He didn't quite belong in that eerie yet calm urban scenario. He was out of place in that out-of-place, Daliesque place. Like a sad story in a funny book.[263]

§7 Mrs Symonds approached the crying person. She looked at the weeping man intently, and with more than just a drop of curiosity, mixed with sincere apprehension: "Who are you?," she asked. He didn't answer. He didn't even react. It was as though he had taken no notice of her amidst all that irregular spatial regularity. "Who are you?," she repeated. Nothing. The man did not respond. He didn't even gaze in her direction. It was as though she was invisible.

Mrs Symonds observed him carefully. He was dressed like… Wagner's Rienzi! And he was in pain. The groaning, whimpering man was nursing a bleeding hand close to his chest. "Are you hurt?," she inquired. Nothing. The man didn't reply. It was as though she didn't exist.

Mrs Symonds looked at his bleeding hand. It was badly wounded. More than that, it was missing three fingertips. As though they had been bitten off by a dog or, who knows, a hungry wolf. "What happened to your hand? … Can I help you?," she questioned him. Nothing. The man didn't acknowledge either her or her question. It was as though she wasn't there.

Mrs Symonds began very carefully to move again, trying to get physically close to the haemorrhaging man and, hopefully, aid him in some way. "*I'm a woman*," she considered, "*he won't take me for a*

---

[263] An elf of the forest said: "I can't read this funny book." The elf had forgotten his reading glasses.

criminal or a creep." Then again, as soon as she stepped nearer, the crying man ran away, vanishing around one of the many street corners available to him. He ran fast.

Mrs Symonds looked for the sobbing and bleeding man in all the immediate alleys: He was gone. Nobody was there. No animal of any size either. Nothing. Quiet and stillness were everywhere. Even the blue streamlets seemed motionless and silent. Only the tidiness of that city's mute architecture persisted with any perceptible intensity. Stony organisation trumped all living organisms. It was as if the weeping and haemorrhaging man had never been there.

Mrs Symonds felt impotent, ineffective, insignificant, and incapable of doing anything constructive or positive. Life, often, seems to be a mere exercise in frustrating futility: Endless chores and dull drudgery till you callously become nothing but a cold corpse. Saddened as much as baffled, she kept walking along the edge of the cyclopic sandy square. She started feeling an unpleasant hint of loneliness sprouting within her heart's humid soil. She didn't like it at all.

§8 Mrs Symonds changed her initial direction. Cautiously but steadily, she advanced into the titanic middle section of the impressive khaki square. Slowly, another human shape entered her visual field. She moved towards it. After a while, she came upon a man, probably Persian, who was flogging a horse in the most brutal way that any civilised person could ever imagine. A few more minutes of such an unrestrained flogging, and the horse would have surely died.

Mrs Symonds took a better look. Right beside the martyred horse, there lied the carcass of another horse, a dead one, which had just been skinned. The Persian man saw her coming near him, and shouted: "Me need feed me starving children!." "I understand," she responded, "but why don't you start with the other horse? It's already dead. It's been skinned. And it doesn't look maggoty, rotten, or anything like that. Use *its* flesh. Leave this one alone. Leave it… alive."

Mrs Symonds was not totally unused to being listened to and obeyed. She would have surely enjoyed getting much more of that kind of control over other people, and probably more than it would have been good or healthy for her to possess, but she certainly didn't get none at all. Her four daughters and one husband lived in an everyday state of supremely-vigilant and virtuously-submissive fear of God—that is, of *her*. However, she could not expect this stranger, this Persian man, to take her as seriously as her own family would have done—not to mention to do exactly as she had just told him to do. Which he did. Right on the spot. Without any sign of reluctance. As though a decorated general had issued a direct order to a humble infantryman.

§9 Mrs Symonds perceived a small yet appreciable surge of strength and self-respect in her breast. "*Curious*," she pondered, "*but there may be a chance of doing something around here, or getting it done.*" Reflecting on that specific, novel, empowering thought refreshed further her previously unquiet spirits, and gave her a substantial, neat, and reinvigorating sense of hope. It wasn't stereotactic surgery, after all, nor finding angels' eggs. It could be done: *Something*!

Mrs Symonds's reaction was not particularly surprising. Being able to affect the people and the environment that surround you is a prime and primal urge that is felt by nearly every human being, if not the immediate consequence of a deep-seated animal need, the continued unfulfillment of which would lead to deficiency, deprivation, disease, disaster, and death. Those who cannot or do not want to modify at all their lived circumstances or any other person's behaviour are either asleep or mortally wounded, whether in their body or in their soul.[264]

Mrs Symonds took a long, deep breath. Wherever she was, she reasoned, she could still be herself. Even in that dreamlike city and

---

[264] Somebody whispered to another: "Soulless!" (**Punch**: Chichikov's called! **Judy**: I ain't dead souls to sell.)

nightmarish situation, *something* could still be done. *Her* power was not nil. And any power can be used to do evil as much as to do good.

Mrs Symonds smiled. "*Let's get cracking*," she concluded.

XXXVIII – Saving Lights[265]

§1   Mike had no money left in his bank account. Worse than that, he had no money left in his wallet. Worse than that, he was in serious debt. Worse than that, it was not a bank that he owed money to. Loan-sharks are carnivores, as the name suggests. In a few weeks' time, Mike's flesh may well have ended up feeding his stern creditor's dogs, or her hogs, which the money-lender would spend hours describing in fine detail, calling by first- and second name, explaining the pedigree and bloody aristocratic lineage of, summoning up the worthy exploits of, talking senselessly about— philosophising, even—, extolling the "unjustly unseen and unappreciated virtues" of, prophesising the future full ethical and political rights of, and praising for their remarkable intelligence— superior to that of most persons she knew, she would say, mixing her manifest porcine fondness with concealed insults and subtle threats to her interlocutors.

That was the *only* thing that she would gladly spend without any hesitation whatsoever: Time. She was never in any hurry. She could wait. She had a genuine interest in the passing of time. "*Let it elapse*," she would think in her well-organised, calculating mind, "*and fall in my lap.*" She knew that she owned the time of dozens of other human beings like Mike: The lives and livelihoods of many ill-omened citizens in that same town where Mike had first come to work and, later, become unemployed. Episodic vagaries of a well-ordered, dynamic, rich, and bountiful modern economy—that's what plenty of university-educated people stated repeatedly in the news:

---

[265] Christmas is indeed a sacred festivity. (**Judy**: What is love? **Punch**: Baby don't hurt me, no more.)

Cycles. Like catamenia. Something normal, natural. Nothing to worry about.

Right! The collapsed, corrupt banks which had denied Mike a mortgage and a loan to buy a tattered old van had been promptly rescued by the most-solicitous State, whose governing bodies had been throwing busloads of taxpayers' money at the incompetent, crooked bankers. No such lifelines had been thrown in *his* direction by the much-concerned public authorities. Somehow, as Mike came eventually to comprehend, if you are very rich you can't be allowed to get poor. If you are very poor, instead, they won't allow you to get rich. Lawfully, that is.

Unlawfully, substantial amounts of money could actually be made by a few poor people. Not many, though. The bankers themselves led by exemplar: Bloody paragons of inverted virtue. The nations' leading kleptomaniacs had shown how psychopathic indifference to other humans' suffering, Machiavellian scheming, infinite shameless selfishness, and outright sadistic pleasure in causing others to hurt and grovel before you can be a positive boon. "Be like them," said the implicit message: "Have no heart, no scruples, no conscience, and you can make a killing."

§2 The shifty loan-shark, who had followed the bankers' lead and developed her own small-scale financial operation, was just a very good pupil of theirs. A stellar one. A shining derivative. The more money she made, the more hogs she bought. The more hogs she bought, the more sausages she could sell—another source of income. "Better safe than sorry," she would often say, smilingly, "that's why a discerning modern entrepreneur needs a diversified portfolio." Discernment could then be said to be one of her distinguishing characteristics.

Mike felt completely powerless in her presence. That woman had *de facto* claims on anything and everything that he had ever possessed. She had already taken his car, his moped, his bicycle, all of his savings, his only wristwatch, his petty jewellery, his granny's gold teeth, his old wedding band, his father's older medals, and the

TV set that Abe-the-butcher had found for him at a fire sale in the town's wild west side. Whenever she talked, Mike had to listen.

Mike's auditory duties were pretty self-evident, even if the loan-shark talked complete and utter rubbish about her bloody lovely frigging whiffy blasted noisy hogs—which she turned into goddamn sausages anyway, so much she loved 'em pigs! She had already taken everything from him, and now she enjoyed taking his time—Mike's last remaining asset. Hours and hours, wasted. Bloody swine, pigs and piglets! Mike couldn't afford that sort of waste. He needed to go out, walk all over town, and find some scraps of a job, some money, or some bread to eat.

At last, he was off the hook. That is, as far as knowing what Tina Porker, Frankie Lardon, Betty Fankle, Jane Raw, Jimmy Bristle, Mariah Carney, Lola Banger, Britney Spots, Ted Red, Justine Porcine, Tommy Hammy, Bella Teats, Johnny Chops, Miley Trotter, Terry Snout, Sarah & Donald J. Rump, Courtney Hock, Gavin Bacon, Henriette Masseter, Gina Barrow, Gigi & Taylor Gilt, Lenny Blanket, Jo Crisp, Ariana Gambon, Moe Pig and Edgar Allan Pork had all been up to. The blessed, stinky lot of them! She had finally left. The usual courtesies, the usual threats—Mike knew the drill. Far too well. She couldn't afford to feed him to her pigs. Not yet.

Phew! *That* was something. Much better than nothing. Mike still had *some* time. Not an enormous amount. Hence, he left his dingy quarters as soon as she and her fancy hybrid pink car had disappeared from view. It was finally the hour for tracking, stalking, snaring, and killing.

§3 While hunting for the sort of employment for which thousands of other desperate men and women were also hunting, Mike found himself in More's Square. It wasn't the prettiest neighbourhood in town, to be perfectly candid. But there were worse ones, especially during hard times such as those. Besides, near the old church, there were some cheerless Christmas stalls. Nothing fancy by any stretch of the imagination, but brightly-lit. A sheer shy hint at the memory of genuine joy against a vast background of grim, harrowing depression.

Mike decided to go and take a look. There were all sorts of knickknacks and children's toys. All Made-in-China, of course. And there were tempting loads of different sweets, candy, cakes, rolls, and even soups and kebabs. He was *so* hungry. What is more, Mike was also "free to choose," as he recalled being told by a piece of old, traditional Reaganite propaganda in his youth. Bad TV. Bad principles. Bad advice. Bad policies. Bad seeds. Bad harvests.

Mike knew far too well the mocking liberty of Hobson's choices. The sort of choices that hypocritical tyrants are so keen on kindly granting to you: Despots, mothers, markets. There he was, reaping the results of the social experiment that had been conducted on, or against, his generation—and a few others too, but Mike tended to focus on the plight of his own generation, understandably. Too much to choose from. Too many goodies to buy. Too many artificially-created urges to satisfy. No jobs. No money to pay for anything. No purchases. No goodies.

Mike's mood was getting darker than the squalid and grimy buildings encircling the square. He would have eaten two bricks for supper, had he had any bricks. Someone caught him wandering aimlessly and dejectedly amid the uplifting stalls. "Hey you," Mike heard, "get this. It'll do you good," and he was given something warm to hold in his hands. It took Mike a while to figure out what was going on. The warmth itself had distracted him. Beguiled, almost.

Mike hadn't realised how cold it was, on that horrid day. He hadn't paid any notice to the falling snow. He was too engrossed by and preoccupied with his growing heap of problems, and interest payments. Who could blame him? And then, in addition to the warmth, he perceived the smell. It was a lovely scent, a veritable fragrance. It was real food. He looked at his hands: The left one held a plastic cup with pumpkin soup inside it; the right one a roll—with sausage, naturally. "*Hogs*," Mike considered, "*poor devils…*"

§4 Mike sat on the steps near the church's main entrance. He couldn't really glimpse at the candles blazing inside the temple, even if the main door was open, nor spot the few paintings that were still

Act Two

hanging on its deteriorating walls. Somebody had told him that there was a cool one showing a headless John the Baptist… "*Pity*," he judged, and he started drinking his soup.

It was a good soup. Mike then took a bite off his sausage roll. It was a good roll. Good bread. Even the two short, chunky, greasy sausages were good. The church looked nice. It was a bit like the one where they had held his father's funeral. A firefighter, his father was. He had died rescuing three foreign kids living in some sort of rickety shack. All those years ago…

Who had given him that food? That was a sensible question. Mike wondered about it. Yet, he couldn't say. He tried hard to flash on the moment when he was given the food… The man's voice was… Ah! Nothing. Not enough. His memory failed him. "*Pity*," Mike thought. He would have very much liked to thank that kind person, who had shown him unprompted and much-appreciated generosity. But it wasn't possible. No matter how hard he tried to remember the chain of events that had led him to having his two hands blessed with warm, fragrant food, nothing came back to his mind. "*Pity*," Mike thought once more.

Mike had been in a sort of gastric trance, a mystical reawakening of the salivary glands, and lost all notion of the surrounding environment and people. Everything had happened so fast, so quickly, and without prior notice. Only his financially-mandated fasting had lasted for any notable long time, if anything. "*Pity*," Mike estimated a fourth time, and drank some more soup. "*Better man than that fat tosspot… tried buggerin' me in prison*," he pondered, and took another bite off his roll. It was a good roll. It really was. The sausages too.

Seen from that angle, the square didn't look bad either. The church wasn't ugly, for sure. Not even the dirty, decrepit buildings around it looked bad. They had some kind of cluttered, derelict, historic charm. The sort of pitiful yet 'authentic' look which some refined foreign tourists may even appreciate, and pay for. "It all depends on how you look at things," Mike's oldest aunt used to say to him when he was a boy, "and they'll show you a very different side." "*Fallen angels*," Mike considered, "*poor devils…*"

§5 The square's vista and the church's architecture kept appealing to Mike. They deserved being eyed and enjoyed. He had never been an art lover or an expert in any BBC-documentary kind-of-stuff. Nevertheless, he could easily recognise and applaud beauty, as well as faint traces thereof. "*I'd like to show this place to Duck,*" Mike realised all of a sudden, while smiling and chewing heartily at the same time, "*on a day like this, wi' this light and this church, I think he'd turn 'nto a bloody Christian, that silly ol' bloke,*" and he kept smiling and chewing with no shortage of heartwarming enthusiasm. "*Or he'd end up runnin' a blooming nudist camp in Iran, for a' tha'!,*" Mike joked with himself, and smiled even more heartily than before.

Stopping by the stalls, sitting by the church, savouring the food, and seeing the edifices around him were all good things. And good things are always welcome. Especially when they are the exception, rather than the norm. Mike's norm had been a painful one. He knew that fact in the very core of his whole being. "Not too bad," Mike repeated a few times, almost inaudibly, as though gently pushing those words through his lips. "Not too bad." There was something… *radiant* about that particular place in that precise moment. Something… important. What it was, Mike couldn't really guess, or get. It was more like an intimation, the very beginning of a distant hunch: A big secret hidden under a thick mound of grey ashes, or brown leaves.

While resting there, Mike also started reflecting on a delicate existential point that had been torturing him for a while—more or less since he had lost his last job: "*Am I a failure?.*" It was a painful point in question. And a worse possibility. A depressing probability, even. And yet, his friend Duck used to argue that truly wise people are *never* successful, because they're too well-balanced to pursue anything in the mad, obsessive way which is needed to thrive and triumph, typically by trampling over other people and crushing them into dust. Only maniacs become great entrepreneurs, famous professors, orbiting astronauts, Olympic champions, Nobel-prize winners, academic firebrands. Only cruel, cunning nuts make huge sums of money and surround themselves with fancy cars, jewels, villas, designer clothing and… blasted hogs.

Besides, *"less is better, innit?,"* Mike reflected, *"what horrid savage I'd be, if I had a' those bloody pigs she's got!."* He swallowed the last bit of sausage. *"Better bloody poor than bloody pig,"* he reasoned, *"rich people,… poor devils…"*

XXXIX – Ashbound, Part I[266]

§1 *"If I talk to the press about it, then…,"* Michelle thought. Her shrewd head spinning around, trying to figure out the best way to take *her* down. That pretentious, pompous, phony, pathetic, petty, preposterous, promiscuous, putrid, pestilent, pernicious, punkish … poseur! Michelle couldn't stand *her* hypocrisy. Not one bit. Not the most infinitesimal, tiniest iota. Not even remotely. That horrible woman! That traitor! Making fancy 'art,' making grand gestures, and parading *herself* everywhere as some sort of international champion of the great feminist cause, emancipation, equality, justice, and womankind at large at that, and then being such a… hypocrite. Really, a lying, lecherous, lurid, low-lying hypocrite!

Apart from those unpleasant and somewhat ungenerous ruminations, Michelle's day had been nothing short of fantastic. What a glorious day! New contract, new clients, new clothes, new cosmetics, and a pair of smashing Louboutin high heels that would make her look hotter, and possibly taller, than any of her sisters, particularly the hot tall one! She felt proud. She was proud. She had

---

[266] *Warning*: The "Ashbound" narrative duo is possibly the most disheartening tragedy in this book. Sexual violence is monstrous. However, for a literary-philosophical work to engage with "cruelty" proper, its most common, blatant forms can't be left out. In this case, Franca Rame's courageous artistry has been of pivotal inspiration. This book's ultimate author was exposed to her art by his mother—a parent of boys—in his formative years. For which thing he—a parent of boys—is still grateful to her: *Sometimes, a punch in the guts is worthier than any argument*. Also, if you think you or someone you know is a victim of sexual violence, consider contacting the police or a dedicated hotline.

accomplished something important. Her parents would be proud of her too, or so she believed, at least. And she cherished that notion. It warmed her heart. Her sisters would be proud of her as well, eventually. A tad envious, probably. They're still sisters, after all. Love doesn't preclude contest. If anything, it makes it even more enjoyable.

"*If I send a carefully worded email to him, then...,*" she realised, "*maybe after tea.*" But that realisation had to be shelved. Not to mention the course of action that sending any such email implied, and implementing the course of action itself, which would inevitably result from taking that first electronic step—that much being perfectly clear to Michelle's logical, capable mind. Postponed. Everything. Why? Because life interfered. Or better, Michelle had to face the dreadful, cruel fate that countless women have had to face since the dawn of history.

While she was standing in the subway carriage, she was assaulted. [Writing about "cruelty" proper requires imagining and depicting instances of harrowing cruelty, not least one of its most common and tragically notorious forms: Male-on-female rape. This cruelty exemplifies and expresses an archetypal dimension of sexual psychology and sexual politics that, following the late Andrea Dworkin, can be argued to reside at the core of patriarchal institutions. The "Ashbound" duo was thus designed and meant to serve this thematic literary-philosophical purpose and instantiate such a Dworkinian perspective—and on three of the four key hermeneutical levels characterising each and every numbered chapter in this book. As such, said duo was intended *ab initio* to fit logically, ethico-politically, and psycho-dynamically within the broader framework of the present literary-philosophical investigation. Building with the greatest respect and deeply-felt gratitude upon Franca Rame's groundbreaking monologue "Lo stupro," which had been so impactful in his formative years, the ultimate author of the present book endeavoured to produce a short section providing a brief chronicle of the assault itself. This being a chilling section that in no way would sensationalise the traumatising monstrosity of sexual violence and that, hopefully, could serve as a morally instructive punch in the guts of all those persons—especially but not solely young men—who could find themselves perpetrating such a monstrosity—basically, an Anglophone way to recover and pay tribute to Franca Rame's Italophone legacy. After battling with his own conscience, experiencing the well-known mismatch between creativity and morality, and considering in earnest the huge spectrum of unceasing ethical and socio-political debates encountered on this dismal subject while working on the much-more-aloof scholarly tetralogy *Humour and Cruelty*, the same ultimate author decided to give up on finalising those descriptive passages, notwithstanding having prepared *ab ovo* the present reader for brutal encounters with unmitigated cruelty in this book's very pages, and being himself familiar with artists and intellectuals who had no qualms in utilising the most graphic imagery, e.g., the aforementioned Dworkin, Snoop Dogg, Eminem, Stieg Larsson, Jonathan Kaplan, Pier Paolo Pasolini, and the Marquis de Sade. At any rate, notwithstanding this conscious act of self-censorship, which some readers may deem confusing, contradictory, or even cowardly, enough horror—indeed, enough cruelty—may still be inferred from the rest of the story, also with regard to the measure of retribution suffered by the cruel rapist. Hopefully that not-too-subtle illustration of Dante's *contrappasso* will serve as an adequate punch in the guts. And in any case, as the already-mentioned ethicist Philip Hallie had acknowledged and discussed in detail in the last century, no silver-bullet solution has yet been found in order to prevent cruelty from emerging in human life, including the seemingly innocuous and secondary sphere of literary and artistic pursuits, where the telling paradox of *in terrorem* techniques keeps reasserting itself, sometimes only partially, as a cruel means to avoid worse cruelties.]

§2 It had been a full, feral, ferocious "treatment," as the local police's jargon characterised those extreme but not-extremely-infrequent violent events. One of the reporting officers, incidentally, was also the one that, by pure coincidence, stepped into the carriage and intervened to apprehend the cruel monster that had attacked Michelle.

The clearest and sole recollection that Michelle had of the entire event had nothing to do with any police officer, criminal, and penally-relevant factor or detail. Hidden in that corner of the subway carriage, Michelle, her soul, her mind, her consciousness—whatever *that* was, which was also her true and deepest self—had smelled the ash and the strange, acidulent odour of old cigarette butts. Albeit forbidden, plenty of people still smoked in the subway. Especially at night. And then they would drop litter all over the place. It was peculiar, to say the least, but Michelle had never realised how comforting the smell of spent cigarettes could be.

§3   That is also the very first thing that she told to her counsellor two years later, when she discovered that she could cry again—since no tears had been shed by Michelle after the assault, for all that time. Blank, inexpressive, catatonic at times, she had been a sort of living dead after the incident. Her parents had to send her to a special clinic in another city. St. Stephen's wasn't equipped for that. Luckily, they could afford to do it. Michelle's own savings were ample too. Money, on occasion, can be of real use. Those who don't have any, instead, must suffer a long sequence of supplementary sorrows, some of which expire exclusively after death. As to Michelle's liquid rediscovery of her own inner affects, it happened in a rather unique manner.

Such being, at another rock-bottom, all that is known about it, inasmuch as a tall male nurse working at the clinic gave a brief first-person account of the whole incident to Michelle's curing physician. Apparently, Michelle was busy doing one of the few actions in which she seemed to express any interest after suffering her dreadful and cruel trauma, and recovering from the injuries and lacerations that her battered body had endured: Cleaning windows. Force-fed at times, because she wouldn't eat her meals by herself, Michelle seemed always ready to clean the windows around the hospital. She did it especially if she was prompted by someone else, but sometimes she did it also out of her own initiative. Not very often, though.

On that specific occasion, Michelle was cleaning one of the windows in the canteen reserved to long-term patients. She could see the northern part of the large park extending in all directions from the clinic's site, which was situated at the then-current northern edge of the ever-sprawling urban centre. The tall nurse said that Michelle saw a wild sow coming out of the bushes. The animal was not alone: A light-brown furrow of lively little piglets came out in the open as well, hopping sprightly behind their corpulent mother. Michelle smiled, apparently.

The grey-haired, lanky, and generally well-liked tall nurse caught Michelle's smile in a clear reflection on the large window which she was busy cleaning—slowly, but steadily. Then, Michelle started laughing. Softly, in the beginning, but afterwards louder and louder. Suddenly, she stopped. Her guffawing became a dry, warped howling: A shriek, almost—like a discordant, grating oboe, or a strident glissando by a *cor anglais*. It was the sound of thunder announcing the coming rain, which started pouring copiously on Michelle's bony, ashen, exhausted face.

The tall nurse stepped closer to her and gently asked the then-crying Michelle if there was anything that she needed. He wasn't just doing his job. He wanted to be helpful. That is why he had chosen that career path. Michelle, with her pale, gaunt cheeks covered in salty tears, said to him: "Counsellor." The tall nurse understood, and took Michelle to see and, hopefully, talk to the in-house psychiatrist. Which she did. Michelle enjoyed those conversations with the boyish young doctor. They made her feel lighter, sane, and somehow clean. Three weeks later, Michelle left the clinic and moved back to her parents', where she still resides at present.

XL – Ashbound, Part II

§1 Abraham didn't know what to do. They all said that he was too old, and that they were looking for younger or more experienced workers. It made *no* sense. How the fuck could they be younger *and* more experienced than he was? And what did they mean by "qualified," for fuck's sake? Wasn't he qualified enough? After breaking his back and, a couple of times, his legs, working on construction sites all over town, being a stupid rich guy's stupid bodyguard for two years, slaughtering screaming animals at the local abattoir, and even shoving fucking elephant shit at a fucking filthy circus… What more did they want? Fuck!

And if those excuses weren't sufficient, then they would proffer the ominous, dark, demonic curse of the current age: "Unemployment." That's what they kept repeating. A fucking voodoo mantra, for all he knew: "Unemployment." What more did they want? Fuck!

He thought that it all had to do with the colour of his skin. No, he wasn't Black, African, or, as he would callously say to his sparse, irregular, and comprehensibly shocked and intimidated drinking mates: "I'm no [self-censored]!." Abraham was just the wrong shade of brown. Not too dark. But dark *enough*. His grandad had immigrated in the last century's early years. Abraham had grown up in that ungrateful town. He spoke like anyone else who had been born and raised there. He hated the right kinds of inferiors. He was a reliable racist. He *was* a local. What more did they want? Fuck!

It didn't matter. Or, at least, that's what Abraham thought. And that's what matters. They may have called him "Abe" and sounded nice to him, but he knew that it was all pretence: A fucking charade. Nobody respected people like him. He knew it in his heart. He wasn't as good a citizen as the others. Or *they* believed that he wasn't, at any rate. That's why the police stopped and searched him much more often than they would stop fucking rich, fucking white, fucking privileged, fucking entitled people. It was a fucking persecution. Daily, weekly, monthly, annual, and year after year, throughout his entire childhood, adolescence, youth and adulthood. A fucking sham. A fucking pain in the arse. An officially-allowed, fucking pogrom in slow-motion. A clever, cruel means for distinguishing between sub-humans like him and fucking rich, fucking white, fucking privileged, fucking entitled people. What more did they want? Fuck!

He hated *them* for that. All of them. *They* were all fucking rich, fucking white, fucking privileged, fucking entitled people. And their women in particular. Whores, all of them. But especially the pretty ones. Sluts. All made up, like they should go to some fucking show at the fucking opera house, or at the fucking movies. Maybe they did. Slappers. Some fucking shit by that idiot MacRunt, or even worse, if possible. Shouting fat men and obese old women being applauded by closet faggots and their cheating wives. If only he could punish *them*. If only he could have his revenge. A droplet, a lick, a miniscule taste of fucking revenge. Charles, Clint, Chuck, Liam, and Sly fucking Gardenzio fucking Stallone always get their revenge, don't they? But, guess what, they're all fucking white, aren't they? What more did they want? Fuck!

God, dear God, how he hated *them*! *They* had all the fucking money, and they kept all the fucking jobs for themselves and their fucking friends. He was no friend of theirs. No, he wasn't. They were no friend of his. No, they weren't. There was no friendship between them. There was no love. Only constant reminders of all the shite that he had been chewing on for far too long. Shitty flat, shitty neighbours, shitty yellow buses, shitty school, shitty services, shitty bureaucracy, shitty jobs, shitty wages, shitty taxes, shitty immigrants, shitty politicians, shitty bankers, shitty depression, shitty layoffs. What more did they want? Fuck!

§2 While pondering and ruminating, almost obsessively, about his cruel situation and the ill-starred town where he had had the dreadful misfortune of being born, Abraham got onto a deserted subway carriage. Despite being a routine passenger, he wasn't even sure that it was the right line, that time. *"Fuck knows?,"* he wondered, very briefly—appropriately, perhaps. Still, he felt quite stupid. And feeling stupid is not something that he could tolerate. He hated that.

It was night. It was late. Nobody was around. Only Abraham and his resentment, his rage, his hurt, his loneliness, and his self-hatred.

Hatred is like alcohol, you see. You can get so used to it, that you gulp down litres of it every single day of the non-working week without even thinking about it. You just imbibe it. And it is like drugs, you know? You get a kick out of hatred, but then you need more and more of it each time, just to revive a dim memory of that first potent kick. And then you need hatred not to feel like shit. So shit, in fact, that you can't even find the strength in you that is needed to hate—at least, to hate! It's powerful stuff. Truly powerful. It's addictive. And addictions can be stronger than your own will. He hated that.

Like drugs, you can *overdose* on hatred. You get so much of it, too much in fact, and your system goes tits up. All of it. You can die from it. If not physically, certainly within your soul, your mind: Your "psychology;" one of those fancy words they had taught him at school. It's not hard to explain, though. It's just a kind of massive heart attack, but of the mind, or spirit. Only bloody psychopaths are safe from it, 'cos they have no real emotions inside. Or that's how Abraham felt about it, anyway. He would have very much liked to be like those psychopaths. On that day, at least, and in that precise moment as well. On a different day, the fact of being devoid of emotions would have been a dreadful thought. No feelings? Like that crazy old aunt of his, where he stayed for an entire summer as a child? No, thanks! He hated that.

Abraham was wrong, by the way, on a number of issues. But that's not relevant. What's relevant is that he was wrong about *one* particular issue: He wasn't alone. In that same, smelly carriage, littered with cigarette butts and other junk, there was a woman. Gorgeous, she was. Fucking gorgeous. Fucking high heels, short skirt, tight top. Fancy hairdo. Model-like material. "*Whore*," he thought. She was a fucking whore. Nothing but a filthy whore. He hated that.

How could he be wrong about that woman's fucking work? All the merchandise was there, on display, available to those who could afford to pay the sort of extortionary price that a high-end hooker like her would charge. She was some chic pro for sure. She must have been making in one hour what he used to make in a month. She was not one of those cheap junkies with whom Abraham had had some transactions when he was much younger. Not many times, though. He felt sorry and dirty after each time he had come inside one of those thick, whiffy, rubbery condoms that they made you use. He didn't like that at all. He hated that.

§3 After that point, Abraham could and did swear a million times within and upon his soul that he didn't know what the fuck had happened. Not that he did know. Or that he didn't know. It isn't clear. To him or anyone else. How can people interpret the past, if they can't access it? Our souls or minds can sometimes be like an impenetrable and irredeemable black box.

Perhaps, it doesn't really matter. What matters is that *they* still say that he assaulted the woman travelling in that subway carriage, and raped her—in that subway carriage. Violently. Ferociously. Brutally. Viciously. Cruelly. *They* still say that he punched her, or slapped her, and tore her clothes, left bruises all over her body, scratches on her breasts, and ripped her hair. *They* still say many things. And because of all the things *they* still say, he is still locked away inside a small prison cell, where he has done nothing but crying, praying, and being bullied and abused by other inmates, whose faces he doesn't recognise, whose names he doesn't remember, whose actions he wants to forget—and succeeds in forgetting. Almost as though he had found some secret switch inside his own beleaguered, accursed cranium: His personal, private black box.

They also say that, between the time when he was apprehended by the police and the time when he started muttering incomprehensible prayers inside his dingy cell, he spoke only *once*. No more than that. No less. And it wasn't even on his way to court, or in court, or with any judge, lawyer, constable, bureaucrat, clerk or psychiatrist that he met. He had met many of those people. But he had told them nothing. No speech. No words. His mouth was a black box.

Abraham wouldn't even speak to that white-gowned butcher, one Ms Isaac or Ms Jacob, who visited his prison, smiled only with her mouth but never with her eyes, and fixed Abraham's teeth, which some fellow-prisoner had smashed into a reddish powder. Why the inmate had done that to Abraham, it's not known either. It just happened. Like many other ordinary horrors taking place in that prison. Maybe that's why they built the penitentiary outside the city's official boundaries—out of sight and out of mind. That prison is meant to be like a black box.

What was it that he said, that once? The local lore is that, about two years' time into his unusually-long penal sentence, a guard took him to the showers. Somehow, Abraham would often forget to wash, and the other inmates would start complaining about the wretched way he smelled. Understandably: They had noses. The guard took him to the showers. No roughing up. Just taking him to the showers to get washed. They say that *that*'s one of the nicest guards that you can meet in the local prison, if not the nicest one. The sort of guard who hasn't forgotten completely that you are, after all and anyway, a person, a human being, an animal of the same species as the rest of us. The nice guard helped Abraham to disrobe and get into the shower. The water started running. A minute later, it stopped. It was time to dry Abraham's massacred body, get dressed, and walk slowly back to his dirty cell. All of which they did without any difficulty. And so was Abraham back to his tiny black box within the larger black box.

"Good boy, Abe," the nice guard said to him, while taking his leave from Abraham. "The devil made me do it," he replied. "The devil what?," the startled nice guard asked him. Nothing. No reply. No answer. Not a single word. Nihil. Silence. Abraham didn't repeat what he had just said. Nor did he seem aware of what had happened. The nice guard told his superior, his superior reported to the warden, and the warden called for a specialist. Some kind of shrink-in-training came to the prison a couple of months later, and tried to converse with Abraham and get him to repeat what he had said—or say something, anyhow, anything, for mercy's sake! Nothing. No reply. No answer. Not a single word. Nihil. Silence.[267] Nothing else came out of his mouth. Ever again. Only the senseless muttering of

---

[267] On a parallel ontological plane, the silence kept wondering: 'Which black boxes wrote these chapters?'

endless, probably hopeless prayers inside his mouldy prison cell. A purportedly witty Iranian inmate called him "the mumbling imam." Abraham didn't laugh. He didn't say anything. It was as if Abraham was lost inside a black box.

Interlude For Two Puppets[268]

Punch: Have you played with styles and references?
Judy: Oh yes!
Punch: High and low? Eugène Labiche and Chris Rock?
Judy: Yes, both.
Punch: Old and new? Terence, *Dulcitius*, and the latest jackass craze on the internet? A few cringe memes and rare orphic truths?
Judy: To some extent: Everything's already in *The Odyssey*…
Punch: I know; still, one tries… Real and virtual?
Judy: Very much so.
Punch: Hypothetical and categorical? Alternating them, like day and night? Comedy and tragedy? Caresses and punches?
Judy: Yep. Even if real life is mostly bites…
Punch: Peripheral and focal? Repetitively: Like a machine gun?
Judy: Indeed, I have: Aye. At some point, some readers must get it!
Punch: Do you feel any better, now?
Judy: A bit.
Punch: Just "a bit?"
Judy: Yes, "just 'a bit'."
Punch: Why so… little?
Judy: Because I fear…
Punch: What?
Judy: …those who obsess about scoring points, or guessing which side you're on. No pity, harsh… totemic ruth at best.
Punch: Anything else? Outright fascists aside, of course.

---

[268] Readers affected by pupaphobia or generally unnerved by puppets may wish to skip this chapter.

Judy: Well… I do fear… misunderstandings…
Punch: Hm.
Judy: …misinterpretations…
Punch: Hm!
Judy: …misconceptions…
Punch: Hm…
Judy: …mistakes…
Punch: Hm?
Judy: …and anything else that starts with "mis."
Punch: "Mischaracterisation?"
Judy: Yes. Like turning compassion into conflict or competition.
Punch: "Misogyny?"
Judy: Yes, very much indeed.
Punch: "Misandry?"
Judy: As much, for sure: It's a matter of equality.
Punch: "Misguided" people?
Judy: Oh yes! It's like a medieval siege!
Punch: "Misdirected" ones?
Judy: Yes. Especially those who fight heroically for Pure and Great Ideals! Everything must shine: They can only see surfaces!
Punch: "Misfiring" ones?
Judy: Yep. Those too. Though many of those are just callous and cynical egotists. Bunches of bloodhounds…
Punch: "Miserable" ones?
Judy: Above all! Their spleen becomes the only reality that they can perceive! They can only share anger, not joy, not… mercy. It's tragic.
Punch: "Mistique?"
Judy: Oh? I guess… Is that a new French brand?
Punch: Why's there so much… *cruelty*?
Judy: The hell I know!
Punch: Do you think *we*… are cruel?
Judy: Who, the two of us?
Punch: Yes.
Judy: Certainly! Even if we ain't stuffy literalists…
Punch: Why are *we* cruel, then?

Act Two

Judy: The hell I know!

Punch: Didn't you say that before?

Judy: Yes, I did.

Punch: Why?

Judy: The hell I know!

Punch: Isn't that... repetitive? You know: Unnecessary, pointless, neo-literalist?[269]

Judy: Only for the clever people who've already guessed where we are going.

---

[269] Literal-minded readers are hereby absurdly invited not to literally mind the present book's absurdism.

ACT THREE: PARADISO[270]

---

[270] **Judy**: "Who's the author?"
   Punch: "Must there be one?"

XLI – Evidence of Spring[271]

Three Scenes:
* *A senile, semi-retired old General of the glorious National Army*
* *The Devil*
(N.B. Stage direction can play at will with the advice provided by the dramatist.)

SCENE ONE – The Basement

The old general is wandering anxiously in a labyrinthine basement, talking aloud to himself, and eventually meeting a strange interlocutor. A lectern stands in the middle of the stage.

The General:
(*upset*) A men's club, they said! A gentlemen's club! Our town's own Blacks Club, or Sloane Club... The city's Arts Club. Blessed Annabel's... (*ironic*) Definitely!

The Devil: (*softly*) Psst!

G: (*startled*) What was that? ... (*angry at himself*) Old fool! Now you'll start hearing voices! ... (*frustrated*) Blimey, where's the way out of this awful place!

D: (*softly*) Psst!

G: (*pretending hard not to have heard anything*) They said they wanted "a general." "An esteemed member of our leading elite." "A monumental pillar of the local community." "A distinguished representative of the ever-noble army." "A much-admired war

---

[271] Nature bounces back: It's like a law of... Nature. (**Punch**: Where are we? **Judy**: That's the real question.) If you are afraid of the dark, skip this chapter.

hero." "A paragon of virtue for all future generations"... Nonsense! They're after my money. That's what they're after... Scoundrels! I'm sure of that! My money! That's what they want... (*timidly*) If not worse...

D: (*softly*) Psst!

G: (*shuddering, still pretending*) The madness, the madness of it all! And those looks...

D: Psst!

G: (*afraid*) W...?

D: Psst!

G: (*terrified*) What? What's that? Who's there? Show your face! ... (*trying hard to impress*) I'm a decorated general of the nation's standing, glorious... standing army... in semi-active status ... If there's a war, you know... Well, in case of conflict... You know, if an invasion, or a foreign power... Well, I'm a *decorated* general, and you shall address me as... You know what I mean!

D: (*not showing itself yet*) How could I not?

G: (*afraid, but strangely lured*) What? ... Not what?

D: (*suavely, and a little bored*) Not know whether or not millions of people are murdering one another. It is my precise duty to involve myself in such... delicate matters.

G: Who are you?

D: You know me already, dear general. Do not be shy, please. You were never intended to be coy, demure, ... sheepish.

G: Sh… sh… You, you… Hm… Sh… Show your face!

D: Only if you promise me not to scream and do foolish things, such as invoking… well (*with a disgusted expression*)… some high power or anything like it. Do not do *that*, please. And do not scream, dear general. I only want to talk to you. No screaming.

G: Screaming? … What? No, no, young man, I… I… I won't scream. What do you think I…

D: (*more coldly*) Why would you think that I am a man?

G: (*afraid, lured, and a little puzzled*) Well… Why not? The voice, I guess… Yes, yes, the voice!

D: (*talking in a distinctive female voice*) The voice can be *changed*. Toyed with. Faked.

G: Well, yes. I guess it can… I suppose… You… you must be an actor then. Or an opera singer!

D: I do like Boito's work, that much is true.

G: Boito? … Bo… Bo… Well, young woman, or man… Show yourself!

D: Will you scream, if I do?

G: (*all of the above, but offended as well*) Scream? A general? Who do you think I am? I'm a *decorated* general! Generals are no… s… s… si… sissies! … What do you think I am? Ah!

D: A mortal—a mortal man, ephemeral: There you are, and then you are not. A meritorious mortal. A martial and magnificent member of the military. Yet an ephemeral, mortal man nonetheless.

Act Three

G: (*panicking*) A mo... mortal... (*finding some composure*) Well, yes, I am a mortal man. But... But so is Socrates! And if he is mortal, then... Well, all men are mortal... (*trying again to impress*) It's a *modus ponens*, you know? Not to be confused with affirming the precedent, or denying the... (*sheepishly*) consequences... (*with some annoyance*) You know what I mean! (*angrily*) It's a *modus ponens*!

D: (*humorously*) I am fond of the *modus... de-ponens*, logically.

G: (*serious*) ... I don't, don't know that one... (*confused*) Did you study logic?

D: I did. With two local teachers. Fascinating subject. Magmatic. And similar to law. Plenty of details in which to hide at will: Small metonymic inroads into the world's inherent chaos!

G: Chaos... (*going into total confusion, once again*) Sorry, did you say... *local* teachers?

D: Yes, local. They teach at the local university. Boring people, though. Unadventurous.

G: Well... Logicians, you know... They are not ad... ad... adventurers. We soldiers, instead... We, we, we can be very, very, very... *dangerous*, you know? Young m... woman? We soldiers, soldiers like myself, m... me... members of the mi... military... we can be lethal weapons!

D: I know *all* that perfectly well, dear general. Dear *decorated* general. That is precisely why I wanted to meet and talk with *you*.

G: (*petrified*) Me?

D: Yes, *you*, dear general.

G: Why *me*?

D: Please, dear general, do not be *so* humble. It is almost embarrassing. You are well past such affectations. You do not have to pretend, truly. Not with *me*. No fake humility, please! Besides, humility is, quite frankly... *overrated*, in more than one way. More than one... *You* are a glorious, *decorated* general and, in your long and impressive career, you have taken many life-and-death decisions. Life and *death*... *Decisions*. Take pride in what you achieved!

G: (*with a touch of pride*) Well, yes, I know... Well, I know... But... it had, it had to be done, you see... You see... A capable mi... mi... military officer ... He must be ready to do what *needs* to be done... Needs... (*long pause*) Now, young... person... Well, *you*, show yourself!

The devil shows itself. Its face is monkey-like and smiling. It is dressed impeccably. Very stylish. Red and black, primarily. It sports a sparkling-new top hat and a fancy walking stick.

D: Here am I, my dear *decorated* general.

G: (*going pale, and on the verge of screaming*) But... B...b...b... b... But...

D: Tut-tut. No screaming we said, did we not?

G: (*calming down a little, not much*) But you are...

D: Yes, of course I am. Who else? Am I not the sort of expert who would take an interest in your notable profession *and* professional history? It is not just innocent psychotics and the most gifted dentists that admire the skill and the efficiency of great military men such as yourself! People who would dream of merely... approaching the heights of terrific... talent that you attained in

Act Three

your long, honourable, distinguished career... Life in the Army is no tea party!

G: I... I... I... I... guess... I guess, guess you would... (*pause*) Dentists, yes... (*puzzled, as though to himself*) Dentists? (*pause, back to 'normal'*) ... Tea... But wouldn't...

D: (*warmly*) Do *not* worry, please, my dear general. It does not become you. A *decorated* general!

G: W... What can... well, will, well... But... What is it that you want, young...?

D: Please, let me show you around. I am asking you only *that*, for the moment. You see... There are very interesting places here that none of the present residents remembers. Nor makes use of. And *that* is a veritable shame. So much... pent-up energy. A shame!

G: Res... residents? Which... resid...ents?

D: Yes, residents. The fatuous members of your exclusive gentlemen's club. You are quite right not to pay much notice to their entreats. They mean well—and that is already quite worrying. But they are also harmless, for the most part. Mouths without teeth. They are not worthy of *you*.

G: W... w... worthy? (*a sudden smile*) Of *me*?

D: Of you, my dear general. *You*. Who else?

G: W... w... well, if you put it this way. I... I think I can begin to... understand you.

D: That is excellent, dear general. Excellent. Understanding is excellent. It is sometimes preferable to mis-understanding. But it is also in order to avoid *mis*understanding that I wish to show you around, if you shall allow me, dear general: People, praxes, and places, to be shown to you.

G: W... what places, then... Sh... s... show *me*?

D: Would you really mind following me in this dun... basement. Please, dear general, stay close. I shall help you to... navigate it, dear general. It is *so* easy to get lost, in the dark.

G: It is quite dark, that's true... Quite dark... D... ark.

D: Come, dear general, please! Here is the first secret chamber, where my worsh... worried friends and associates congregate. A few perv... persistent, punctilious,... pious souls are still using it, without anyone paying any heed to their activities. It is a very private affair. (*in a self-praising tone*) ... It is all rather ingenious, actually. One could even say... *diabolical*.

SCENE TWO – The Corridor

In what follows, the devil shows the general what is inside a number of different rooms, the described contents of which are not to be played nor displayed on stage, but only inferred from the conversation occurring between the two characters. A doorframe stands in the middle of the stage (depending on the venue, openable doors can be included in lieu of the sole frame).

(N.B. Scene two is the play's main and longest scene. It can be subdivided into separate scenes, if the stage direction and resources allow it.)

SCENE TWO – The Corridor – First chamber

G: (*peering in a state of shocked curiosity*) What... what are they doing? ... Who... How many ...

Act Three

D: Those... acolytes are the most numerous group. My own... disciples, so to speak. Loyal followers. (*proudly*) I am the original *influencer*, you see: A master of... differing perspectives.

G: Infl... Per... Ah?

D: Well, these... supporters are bona-fide customers of mine, you might say. They are all very consistent and considerate individuals, in a way. Concerned citizens, almost. Commendable.

G: C... co... ci... Yes, yes, I... I see, but... but... why?

D: They come and bring me... *gifts*, dear *decorated* general, so that I may... *help* them.

G: Gi... gifts?

D: Yes, dear general, kind gifts: Their partners' tears, the blood of enemies, the scalps of casualties, the chains of prisoners, the teeth of patients, the foreskins or even whole genitalia of deluded boys, the torn hymens of poor girls, the barren bonds of scorned suitors... All duly *archived*! Or elaborate new concoctions: Cluster bombs, suicide drones, credit default swaps, Bitcoins...

G: Bit...s... So... speculation, finance... crises?

D: Of course, dear general! How can you forestall the utopian peace and the happiness of the Epicureans and all other ancient... troublemakers? You litter their garden with addicts' needles and alcoholics' broken bottles. How can you forestall the utopian peace and the happiness of the Keynesians and all other modern... socialists? You litter their economy with financial mines and boobytraps. Human ingenuity! What can it do, with just a little assistance from... below.

G: Assist...ance?

D: Dear general... Please, dear general, do not think me greedy, for I am not. I am nothing but a generous friend, a helper, a conscientious counsellor, a benefactor. I am compliant with all standards of corporate governance. I am socially and environmentally responsible. Someone who cares about other people's dreams and hopes. And I am keen on fair trade too! So, you see, I accept much simpler things as tokens of... respect, proximity, and... *friendship*.

G: Fr...iend...?

D: Friendship, dear general. Can you see? Look at all those gold watches, for instance, and the large wallets, the bright pearl necklaces, the cute amphetamine pills, that pile of MBA degree scrolls, the dry fish tanks, and so many empty flasks and flagons! So many! (*with mock self-pity*) ... Where will I store them, one might wonder! (*with a more serious tone*) But it does not matter. There is little which I would not to do to help them... Such tremendous individuals!

G: He... help them?

D: Yes, *help* them. You see, dear general... You may have heard of the popular expression "the evil eye." I am pretty confident that you must have. It is a silly expression. Something that no expert ophthalmologist or occultist would ever use. But, like all forms of popular lore and folk wisdom, it does contain a grain of truth: A grain. ... But without grain... No bread to eat!

G: Gr... grain? Br... ead? ... Truth...?

D: Dear general. If it were not for *my* involvement and intervention, which is something that these convened... devotees so ardently beseech of me, why would anyone be the... misfortunate victim of so many, so many, sorry, very sorry accidents, injustices, trials, tribulations, sorrows, crimes, and unforeseen vicissitudes? Why is the wheel of fortune a breaking wheel? Have you ever wondered or reflected on such a fine point of… existential vagary?

G: Va… vagary… Yes, vagary… Ex… Well…

D: Please, dear general, let me show you another secret chamber. I believe that it will be of your liking. Something closer to your… marked personality and considerable military experience. Are you not a *decorated* general? Oh yes, you are! …You shall see…

SCENE TWO – *The Corridor – Second chamber*

The devil opens another door.

G: (*with awe and astonishment*) But this is… this is…

D: It is, dear general.

G: … this is…

D: … A battlefield, dear general: The adytum of martial virtues…

G: …A… a… a… battlefield!

D: Yes, dear general, a battlefield!

G: (*pointing towards someone or something inside the room*) Look, look at those…

D: Oh yes, dear general, are they not… magnificent?

G: All those soldiers, that… carn… kill… terr… action, operation, engagement… All that…

D: … *Freedom*, dear general… Freedom! Can you recall the elation of pure, undiluted freedom?

G: F… f… fff… freedom?

D: Yes, freedom, dear general. The most important value of all! The one for which I… Pardon my immodesty… For which I myself devoted all of my… talents, energies, aspirations…

G: They, they…

D: Yes, general, they *do*. They *can*. They *may*. They *crave*. They *wish*. They *will*. And they *do*!

G: But *jus in bello*… The rules of engagement…

D: A fiction, dear general, a diversion. You know that yourself! Who controls anything, really, in the mayhem of warfare? Only *decorated* generals like yourself have a modicum of control… just a modicum. Like a snowflake in a flaming pyre: Swoosh!

G: Well, yes… B…b…. but…

D: Look at all those lifeless bodies, dear general. Look at the mutilations, the murders, the rapes!

G: I see…

D: And look at all those soldiers, dear general!

G: B… b… but what army is… Who… Who are they?

D: Soldiers, dear general, troopers, fighters, *warriors*. Like yourself. Maybe not serving in the army in any official capacity, as you still do, but… active, operative, engaged… 'out and about,' so to speak—if you allow me to indulge in the somewhat silly parlance of our times.

G: Not… n… not, in… in the army?

Act Three

D: Not officially, no. Not... bureaucratically. But they are all warriors in spirit: Unruly, hardened, unbending. Soldiers fighting for the fight itself, not for illusory triumphs or empty ideals!

G: Who are... are... those, those women?

D: Dear friends of mine.

G: F... fff... friends?

D: Yes, dear general. Marvelous individuals who had... an interesting approach to, say, prussic acid, motorways, new forms of... (*grinning*) religious regression,... but also bathtubs for their little children, yet-untried pedagogical techniques, pouring kerosene, food preparation... Some experimented with new strategies in infant- and elderly care. *Friends*. One or two of them came up even with new forms of soap-making. A nice Italian family mother, for instance...

G: Soap... soap-mmm... making?

D: Yes, dear general, soap-making. My friends, when duly inspired and incited, can be very... creative. They just require... a whisper in a discreet corner of the mind, a gentle nudge...

G: Nnn... nn... nudge...?

D: You must forgive me, dear general, I do not mean to rush you, but I would very much like to show you another chamber, if you will only be so kind as to follow me. Stay close, please. I know how... *enticing* this particular room can be, that is, for a distinguished military man such as yourself. But please, dear general, let me help you get a better sense of what I can... offer.

G: Yes, yes... Of course... please... Ahead...

SCENE TWO – The Corridor – Third chamber

D: Come, dear general, this way... (opens another door) Look, dear general, a banquet!

G: (with even more awe and astonishment) Incredible!

D: Is it not, dear general? Is it not?

G: Well... Those plates...

D: Gold, dear general, solid gold.

G: And the cutlery...

D: Gold, of course. Gold, dear general.

G: And the wines...

D: The best ones, dear general. Only the best ones. And any other exclusive beverage of which an outstandingly-sophisticated connoisseur such as yourself may ever dream! It is all there!

G: But the food... the food...

D: Yes, dear general, the food. It is delicious.

G: Yes, of course... But aren't those... those...

D: Yes, they are, dear general. Would you expect anything else?

G: Well... I suppose... But who? Where?

D: My dear decorated general, is it not obvious?

G: What... what do you m... mean?

Act Three

D: Think of all those wars, dear general, and all those beautiful, cyclical waves of currency speculation, and the cost-saving chemical pollution of the streams whence poor families draw their cooking water, or the addictive fats and sugars in commercial breakfast cereals, and the generous tax breaks for the super-rich, the underfunded healthcare services, the taxable wealth disappearing in remote fiscal havens... I am nothing but business-friendly, dear general!

G: Do... do... do they, now?

D: Of course, dear general. There are so many ways to destroy families, murder little babies and young children, and provide... well, suitable ingredients to my excellent cooks. The best chefs whom you could find in the whole world, dear general! ... Only the very best, for my friends.

G: (softly) All... all, all those... children... All that... blood...

D: Please, dear general, let me show you more. You seem so interested. So captivated. It is a real joy to be your... cicerone. An honour, I would dare say.

G: (confused) Not Virgil? ... (as though he's had a pathetic insight) Ah! Yes, yes... Of course...

SCENE TWO – *The Corridor – Fourth chamber*

D: (*opening another door*) Can you see in here? I know it is a bit dark...

G: No, no... I can, can... see...

D: Can you see that young man, for instance, down there?

G: Oh yes, yes, I do… I can…

D: Look at the adoring females kneeling in front of him…

G: They are… they are…

D: Yes, dear general, yes! They are indeed!

G: Su… sss… Serving… Servicing… Him? All *three* of them at once?

D: Three, yes. But, please, do not be *so* modest, dear general. Please, a man of your experience! A Casanova such as yourself! Shall I mention the promising scent of garlic sausages, perhaps?

G: (*a bit surprised*) Do you… do you know? … Well, I… I…

D: Of course I do, dear general, of course I do. I consider it my sacred—I could say *fiduciary*—duty to be… informed about the people whom I can credibly… befriend.

G: And, and… Friends…

D: *My* friends, dear general! They are the raging masters of the universe, the bright stars of cinema and music, the trailblazing new artists and Nobel-Prize winners, the burning firebrands of all fashionable academic branches, the magnetic presidents, the mesmerising captains of *Fortune-500* companies, the many millions of stern domestic matriarchs, the innumerable cruel bosses on the workplace, and all fiery kings of lore and shining emperors that have ever existed…

G: And… the… g… generals?

D: Those too, dear general. If it is their greatest wish. And if they… behave.

Act Three

G: Behave? What do you... (*suddenly distracted*) Is that... Is that... Is that *Alexander*?

D: What an eye, dear general! Yes, he is: Your personal hero! And look, beside him, in that bundle of flesh, between those Nubian odalisques: Napoleon! And Tamerlane too, to their right, with Idi Amin, Plato, Michael Jackson, and those three young boys! And look, further left, you see?

G: An.. a... a... airplane?

D: Yes, an airplane. The "Lolita Express," they call it. What an apt designation! See how many illustrious royals, rich magnates, important presidents...

G: B... bu... but that's...

D: Oh, yes, that is indeed! You recognised *him*, did you not, dear general?

G: Why? ... Why is he... here... there?

D: Who do you think helped him have the brilliant career which he had and enjoyed so much? Success and fame can never be attained, unless you have some... *friend*, like me, who is willing to assist you in your... plans.

G: I understand...

D: Of course you do, dear general. But let me help you *deepen* your understanding.

G: Wha... what... what do you mean... deepen?

D: Please, dear general, let me show you. It is so much easier. Clearer. Like crystal!

SCENE TWO – The Corridor – Fifth chamber

The devil opens another door.

G: (*incredulous*) C... C... Cro.... Crosses?

D: Yes, dear general, crosses. A major invention. Civilisation at its highest!

G: Wha... Whe... Why?

D: My dear general, please, look well. Look at those crosses: They are not even upside-down!

G: But... but... Are those...

D: Yes, dear general, yes!

G: They... they... can't... can't be!

D: Oh yes, they can, yes they can, dear general!

G: N... nuns? And... and... monks?

D: Yes, dear general, they are. They are indeed.

G: But... but... Why?

D: Dear general, some strengths are weaknesses. Some weaknesses are strengths.

G: Wha... What?

D: Dear general, did I not promise you that I would *deepen* your understanding?

Act Three

G: Ye... Yes, I... I think so.

D: Good, dear general, good. Thinking is all that is required, right now. And you are a thinking, even thoughtful I would dare say, rational individual. Almost *scientific*, if I may be so bold.

G: Scient... ific?

D: Yes, dear general, scientific. Ah! Modern science... Another great moment in humankind's history and civilisational achievement. It made me less... famous, of course, but I do not mind. I do not aim at being... conspicuous. I am not vain. I just want to be a good *friend*, dear general.

G: But... but why all these... clerics... and nuns?

D: Consistency is like kindling, dear general. And all burning desires can lead to me and my... dwelling place. That is, if the burning is... intense enough.

G: In... tense?

D: Yes, dear general, intense: The springboard being an internal tension, quite appropriately.

G: But... Why, why they? Them? Of... of all the people that... why?

D: Purity can be the most powerful object of human desire, dear general. *Purity*, and its flames.

G: Pu... puberty?

D: (*laughing*) No, dear general, not "puberty!" Although that can be hellish too, of course... No, I said "purity," dear general: The cleanest shroud of nothingness.

G: Purity?

D: Yes, dear general. A wish of being so enlightened, so pristine, so clean, so perfect that... Well, one does get to the light, but a little too close. Like a moth lured by a burning fire.

G: A mmm... moth?

D: Yes, dear general. A moth. A Middle-Eastern, desert-dwelling, locust-eating moth...

G: A... moth?

D: Yes, dear general. If you approach the Sun, or stare at it for far too long a time, you... suffer, and... perish.

G: P... pp... perish?

D: In a manner of speaking. Astronauts alone run that risk, in physical reality—that *limited* side of the cosmos, of course... But for most people, well, the Sun is more... metaphorical.

G: Mmmm... metaphorical?

D: Yes, dear general, metaphorical. Figurative. Allegorical. Poetic. Lyrical... Mystical.

G: Mmmm... mystical?

D: Mystical, dear general. These persons dream of joining (*disgusted*) something high... A pure, supreme some*thing*, or (*horrified*) some*one*. They wish it *so* much. They work *so* hard to get it!

G: And so...

Act Three

D: And so they think, or foolishly believe, that they are *there*, that they climbed up *there*, that they succeeded in becoming one with... (*disgusted, again*) well, *that* one thing or... yes, something.

G: Are they... Aren't they?

D: Of course they are *not*, dear general! No water, no... cleansing, no blessing, no thin cannibalistic wafer nor any superstitious ritual can remove the original stain, or straighten the crooked timber. None, dear general! Believing yourself to be pure, high, good is by far the surest malice!

G: And so... these religious people...

D: They become arrogant, dear general, arrogant and blind. Blinded by the same light after which they lusted so passionately. And so they cannot see the evil that they do, the persecutions, the prejudices, the petty-mindedness, the harsh reactions and projections. (*gleeful*) Marvelous!

G: Mmmm... arvel?

D: Yes, dear general. All the evil that is done in the name of goodness. The cruelty that is perpetrated in the name of kindness. The inequality promoted in the name of equality. The wars fought in the name of peace. The shackles imposed in the name of freedom. The injustices committed in the name of justice. The dystopias realised in the pursuit of utopias. The purulent stigmata carved into other people's hands in the name of one's own handy, pristine dogma... All of it in good conscience, for goodness' noble sake, and in goodness' sacred name!

G: Gggg... goodness?

D: Yes, dear general, *goodness*. The lure of the highest moral standing, the pinnacle of virtue, the holier-than-thou ability *and* duty to watch, rank, condemn, and chastise others. Ah! And the tacit excitement that comes from exacting the chastisements! ... Unless one becomes *jaded*.

G: But... ?

D: Think of the evil, dear general, and the self-righteous *thrills* of deeply-frustrated people who get offended, outraged—and their secretly ill-wishing claims, critiques, campaigns, corrections, coercions, and cancellations, which they pursue without mercy! They go around in search of scandals because they repress their barbaric inner vandals. Ah! Martinets and their mallets! True believers and their sharpened sabres! Theirs are the blackest chiasmi: Censorship for pluralism, oppression for emancipation, negation for affirmation, oblivion for memory, oil for food!

G: O...oil... But... but... but ill... ill, you know, ill... and *evil*?

D: *Evil*, dear general? Do you want to see sheer evil? Do you want to... comprehend sheer evil?

G: (*strangely intrigued*) Evil... Sheer... *Sheer* evil?

D: Yes, dear general, unadulterated, uncompromising, patent and blatant evil. *Perfection.*

G: (*strangely curious*) Oh.

SCENE TWO – The Corridor – Sixth chamber

D: (*the devil opens another door*) Look, dear general, and let your eyes and soul imbibe nothing but *absolute* perfection, which is to reach into their deepest recesses and change them forever. Feast eagerly on the eager feast which you are allowed to contemplate in this august chamber!

G: What! What! ... Who? Who?

D: An alluring sight, dear general, is it not?

G: Yes... No... Yes... But?

D: That young brunette, dear general, that petite woman: *She* is meaning. *She is... perfection.*

G: How... What... But she...

D: Yes, dear general. Can you see how she is slicing her left breast, so as to feed her suitors? And how another suckles at her bleeding wound, as though he were a cruel infant reaching for, and biting at, the sore, reddened nipple of her nursing, suffering mother?

G: Yes... But how...?

D: And look, dear general! More flesh is being carved from her sides and buttocks! More lovers and adoring partners are getting nourished! And more blood is drunk in the golden cups... What a unique and grandiose spectacle, my dear *decorated* general!

G: But... But... Why?

D: Dear general! Is it not obvious? Think only of the joy of a full, complete, total communion with *me*, dear general. The sempiternal. The superhuman. The free and unpolluted Will that all defies and all challenges, without fear. Any fear. Without boundary. Without limit. Without end!

G: Like... God?

D: (*loud and terrifying*) DO NOT UTTER THAT... AH! That pompous, know-it-all crackpot, who munches all things into mulch while saying that he loves them! ... DANG! I hate it! AH!

G: (*in the most everyday tone*) Oops, sorry!

D: (*getting back to its malignantly jovial attitude*) Never mind, never mind... You are new around here, dear general. It happens. You will learn how to... conform, in the end... And use no g-word!

G: (*shocked, trembling*) Ah, eh, well... But all this...

D: All this, dear general, makes *you* into an idol, a totem, a golden calf: The One True Way! The Active Intellect! The *Natura Naturans*! The Pineal Gland! The *Substantia sive Natura*! The Ultimate Monad! The Master of Noumena! The Absolute Spirit! The Will to Live, or Power! The Vital Impetus! The Omega Point! The Instant! The Termless Rhizome! The Event!

G: Yes, yes... But, but... Cutting off... Chopping... Your own...

D: Feeding adoring incubi with your own body is just *one* possibility, dear general: Only one. There are many paths available. Hers is just one among many. It is, after all, her independence, her autonomy, her agency, her will, her subjectivity, her choice, her body, her... soul.

G: One... Only one p...p... ath?

D: Dear general, human imagination is limitless. Entire *universes* live therein, dear *decorated* general. *Universes*. Think of that, dear general. *Universes*! Only ignorant people and dogmatists fail to realise how infinite is the power of our mind, if we only give it full... abandon!

Act Three

G: Oh?

D: And pay *no* attention to academics! They all say that they stand for 'Socratic dialogue' and 'critical thinking,' but in reality they fear and despise them both as much as real businesspeople fear and despise actual 'free markets' and 'competition.' Because *reason*, when followed through, corrodes and destroys every invention and institution, and leaves only *desire* unaltered! Such is the wry irony of *recta ratio*, dear general: It is nothing but the vapid logic of stiff asses.

G: Yes, yes... But... why does she... chops, slices... nurtures... Why?

D: Each and every person has her own destructive drives, filthy itches, murderous motives, crazy cravings,... shadows, dear *decorated* general: The caged shadows of the soul! And all shadows need release. They are alive. They need food. Here, with me, the shadows can eat anything and everything that they have always wanted. Can you see it? Shadows stepping into the light!

G: I see what she... And she... But she...

D: By nourishing those loving cannibals, she nourishes herself.

G: But blood, bleeding... The self-maiming...

D: Sinister glees, grisly aspirations, and *all* cruel reveries become reality in this place, dear general, *my* place of choice and... entertainment. *All* things can happen here, far from the laws of physics, biology, medicine or... whatever! We allow no cathartic fiction, no compensatory subterfuge, no artful simulation, no purgative game, no superficial laughter. Only Real Evil!

G: Real... evil?

D: Yes, dear general, Real Evil! ... Here, dear *decorated* general, any laws that you may wish to break or violate can be broken and violated! (*bombastic*) Broken *and* Violated! (*dramatic pause, more matter-of-fact, friendly*) This privilege, however, is reserved to my... *friends*, dear general. Only to my friends. The friends whom I strive to help and assist. In all ways possible.

G: All... ways?

D: Yes, dear general. *All*. All of them. If Eve gave the deadly pome of knowledge to Adam—an innocent practical joke of mine, I should add, which I repeated later with an odd English gentleman and an ambitious American undergraduate—so can the young woman give her own flesh to these hungry sycophants, and all of them shall live—herself as well. This is Evil, dear general. The stain. The darkness. The malevolence. Pure. Unadulterated. Alive. And *forever*!

G: Forever?

D: *Forever*, dear general. Because she is no mere woman. She is no mere... murderous child-minder or furtive arsonist. She is the Serpent, the Visitant, the Conjurer, the Merchant, the Witch, the Conqueror, the Libertine, the Dollar Sign, the Fanatic, the Carper, the Positivist, the Stockbroker... She is eternal. Because she is *through* me. *With* me. *In* me. All the time!

G: All... time?

D: All of it. Always. She is the Will, the will that breaks all laws and reigns supreme!

G: Lll... laws?

D: Yes, dear general, all laws. The laws of... (*with recalcitration, pointing towards the sky*) *that*. The laws of nature. The laws of

Act Three

man. The laws of woman. The laws of children and kindergartens. The laws of clerks and administrators. The laws of high justices and tribal elders. The laws of great emperors and petty bureaucrats. The laws of Zipf and Murphy. *All laws*! Because *I* am absolute. *I* am licence. *I* am my own orthodoxy. *I* am willing for willing's sake!

G: (*in an oddly light-hearted tone*) You can be very lyrical, at times, you know?

D: (*angrily*) Of course I know, general! Do you think I have only studied logic? Bookkeeping? Or (*in a disgusted tone*)... odontology?

G: (*apologetically*) Sorry, sir. I didn't mean to offend...

D: (*back to its cheery malevolence*) Do not worry, dear general. We all make mistakes...

G: Yes, yes... You are... very... very kind... It's just that...

D: "Just that," dear general?

G: That it's all so... well... a little... yes, you know...

D: "You know" what, dear general?

G: Well... Overwhelming? If that's the right word... I don't know... Over the top, perhaps?

D: Dear, dear, dear... my dear *decorated* general! Please, do not panic. Do not be... unduly concerned! Ah! My dear general! What you have seen is simply the obvious result of playing out in daily reality that which is normally left to poems and dramas, myths and fantasies, faint dreams and pale imitations; or even videogames and films, in our modern, technological age.

G: F… fff…fantasies?

D: Yes, dear general, fantasies, dark fantasies. And such would they remain if I were not to assist you, humans, as imperfect and timorous as you are! Without my help, most people would daydream, write haywire stories, shoot or watch dodgy flicks, or play violent computer games…

G: Games?

D: Means of psychic hygiene, dear general, but not of communion with *me*. A mockery. A travesty. A simulacrum. A fiction. What a waste! What an insult! Why taking ablutions in the icy water, when you can bathe in the fire and… exalt your own individual and unique self above all else?

G: Sorry… But… *Hygiene*?

D: Yes, *hygiene*, dear general. The regular expulsion of waste, leftovers, unused proclivities, forbidden dreams. *Catharsis*, if you are classically-minded. Inevitable components of all minds. The result of a much-welcome… descent, a long time ago. A good yet only partial fall.

G: I had never thought of that…

D: Some people did. Some have thought of it long and hard… (*resentful*) They have even found and recommended outlets to live with such fantasies: Blasted priests, artists, and therapists!

G: Thera…pists?

D: Bigots, academicians, and cranks mistake images for persons, words for objects, utterances for actions, offences for harm. But they are *not*. Form is *not* substance. Simulation does *not* end

Act Three

suppression. Living *with* dark fantasies is *not* the same as living *in* them, nor living them *out:* Crying "wolf" bares no wolf!

G: Living... out?

D: Yes, dear general. Living *in full*, living *through* something, and letting it live *throughout* yourself. The shadow subsisting as the sole totality of your being. A triumph of malevolence, egotism, cruelty, and... *liberty*. (*politely*) My most precious gift to humankind, modestly.

G: Liberty... You? ... liberty?

D: Yes, general, I de-regulate, over-rule, and liberalise: I deliver *liberty* to all who wish to have it!

G: But... but...

D: Please, dear general, do not be taken aback. Especially when you can be taken forward. Of all people, you should be the last one to be shocked or repulsed by any of this. What we do here is mere child's play compared to what you achieved on the battlefield in your illustrious career!

G: Ca... ca... career?

D: My dear *decorated* general! Just think of the thousands whom you sent out to maim, kill, ravish, pillage, destroy, humiliate, imprison, torture. *And* in turn be maimed, killed, ravished, pillaged, destroyed, humiliated, imprisoned, tortured! (*ironically*) I could learn a few tricks from an expert such as you! (*dreamy*) Wars are like bright shadows under a black sun! They are like ethics taught by counterexamples: Wars feed the Tree of Knowledge with carnage and corpses!

G: I... I... I know... know, but...

D: (*more menacingly*) You have *always* been with me, dear general. I have *always* been with you. Be *through* me, *in* me, *for* me! The time has come: Join me! Join my... associates. Realise *all* your dreams! The most secret dreams! You have already come so far: Take the last step!

G: Last... s...s...tep?

SCENE THREE – The Entrance Hall

A bigger door frame and a small, tall table stand in the middle of the stage.

D: (*back to its cheery nastiness*) We will make a pact. A simple contract.

G: Con... tract?

D: Bureaucracy, dear general, bureaucracy. (*ironic*) One of my best inventions.

G: Bu... you? Invented? Oh?

D: Of course I did, dear general... (*sterner*) Anyhow, please, a *signature*, nothing else. And then...

G: Then what?

D: (*charming*) ... You shall have *anything* you want, dear general!

G: Any... thing?

D: Yes, dear general. Desire would be... your subordinate...

G: Any... *one*?

Act Three

D: (*grinning*) Oh yes! Are you thinking of a younger sausage maker? You old devil! ... Her daughter, perhaps? ... Or both of them? Ah, dear general, what a lovely and loving mind do you possess and set to work! Of course, dear general! As I said, you can have *all* and *everything*!

G: Every... *All*?

D: Yes, *all*. For all is mine to give: Ascendancy, gain, frenzy, relish, rapture... *All*!

G: Yours to... *Give*?

D: Yes, dear general. *Give*. Will you... *take*, then?

G: *Take*...

D: Any, every, thing, one, or... *body*... At your complete disposal, dear general.

G: Body... *Bodies*?

D: *Bodies*, yes. Bodies above all, dear general. Young, healthy, alluring... bodacious.

G: Bo... bo... bo... bodies?

D: *Yours* to do as you please, dear general. After all, you deserve it...

G: *Any*... body?

D: *Yes*, dear general. Your own included! You shall be young, healthy, fit, muscular, virile... Your erections will be like the pharaoh's obelisks. Obelisks, dear general! To penetrate, please, pervert, punish, and possess any woman, man, animal, robot, pumpkin, doll or dental hygienist that you may desire. Any sausage maker. *Any body*. I promise you, dear general. *Any body*!

G: Any... Wow!

D: Yes, dear general. Any colour, size, age, height... and gender, species, country of origin, native planet, respiratory chemistry or physical shape. Any income bracket, social class, institutional background, agency degree, postcolonial condition, countercultural belief, socialisation level, Gini coefficient... *Your* imagination will be *your* reality! *You* will be whatever *you* want to be!

G: In... teresting...

D: Dear general, you shall have command over everyone and anyone. *Anyone*. The choice will be *yours* and only *yours*. Supreme. Imperial. Dictatorial. Tyrannical. You shall be a king, an emperor, a CEO, an alpha male, a top dog, a president, a captain, a leader of millions, a finance minister, a university rector, a cardinal, an ethics committee... *Anything* you want! And all to enjoy the greatest and most unlimited forms of power and pleasure: *Your* power and pleasure.

G: Mmmm... mm... my...?

D: Yes, dear general. *Your* pleasure will be my command. I shall arrange everything, so that *your* reign may commence. I shall bestow power onto you like no Caesar, king, emperor, Pope, Tsar, Tory Prime Minister, governmental minion, CEO, chief accountant, or resentful Post-Office clerk has ever enjoyed... (*pause, in a more matter-of-fact tone*) I simply need a *signature*.

G: (*lost in the previous chunk of conversation*) Any... colour? ... Planet...?

Act Three

D: And sexual preference, self-identification, olfactory capacity, nose length... And *anything* else which you may wish, dear general. (*smiling even more*) ... Even a whiff of garlic, should you want it, and whenever you desire it (*again, pause and more prosaically*) ... Just a signature.

G: I... I...

D: *Pleasure*, dear general. And *power*! So much power! (*flatly*) ... A signature.

G: I... I...

The devil fishes out of a hidden chest pocket a long scroll of parchment and a beautiful golden pen. He shows them to the general and places them carefully on the small, tall table.

D: (*enticing*) Here, dear general... just here, (*pointing*) a *wee* signature...

G: (*still lost in the previous chunk of conversation*) I... I... Any... size?

D: Yes, dear general: Your fantasy as your fabric, your life as your loom! (*flatly*) ... A signature.

G: F...fff... form?

D: Yes, dear general: Think of all that stifled, unlived life to be unchained; reach for it! ...Sign!

G: I... I...

D: I know what you want, dear general. I know what you wish. We have been together...

G: To...gether?

D: ... Since the day you were born...

G: I... I...

D: Dive into my sovereignty, dear *decorated* general: Your will is my will! My will is your will!

The general looks like he is going to sign the contract. But then something unexpected occurs.

G: (*finding a sudden surge of fighting spirit*) Well, old devil, you know what I think? I think that... Well, if you are here, then... Well, God is here too. (*the devil covers its ears*) ... And if there's evil, then there's ...good too. Some good... And if there's low, well, there must be... high. A roof, I mean... And if there's right, then there's... wrong... left... wrong... Well, you know what I mean... And if there's night, then... day will come. And if there's a sunset, then a sun...rise... will... rise... follow! If it rains, if it rains... sunshine will come back... And... if there is Winter, yes Winter... so there is also Spring, and Summer... and Autumn... But that doesn't matter right now... And if there is a bad mother... what was that one that Professor Freud was hammering on? ... Yes, if there is a bad mother, then there is also a good mother... And if there's Papa Bear, well, then there's also Mama Bear... and if there's Lady Mustard... Well, well... Well, you know what I mean! (*and he leaves the premises, most forcefully and impressively, marching bravely and martially through the larger doorframe on the stage.*)

D: (*utterly surprised*) What the hell was that about? ... (*pause*) Did he mean Lady Marmalade?

Curtain.

Act Three

XLII – The Return of the Giant Insight[272]

One Act:
- *Rudolf C., smoking logician and part-time clown*[273]
- *Otto N., smoking logician and part-time clown*

Two logicians enjoy their shared hobby and charitable enterprise: Improvising comical routines on stage, dressed like circus clowns, and misbehaving in the goofiest ways. All revenues are earmarked and set aside, to be wired at the end of the theatrical season to the bank coordinates of the International Society for the Protection of Rabbits and Undetached Parts Thereof.

Rudolf: Good day, Dr A.A.A.A. Cabral y Ortega!

Otto: Good day to you, Dr K.K.K.K. Cioran-Kaunda!

R: Are you on your merry way?

O: I don't know. Do you?

R: Do what?

O: Know.

R: Know what?

O: Which way it is.

R: For what?

---

[272] Smaller insights can also be beneficial, not least when dealing with humour and cruelty.

[273] Readers affected by coulrophobia or generally unnerved by clowns may wish to skip this chapter.

O: The merry.

R: The berry?

O: Where?

R: On the way.

O: Where to?

R: The merry.

O: Is the berry on the way to the merry?

R: How would I know?

O: What?

R: That which I know.

O: What is that?

R: My knowledge.

O: Do you have knowledge?

R: I suppose I do.

O: Knowingly?

R: How would I know that?

O: I'm not sure…

R: Don't you know?

Act Three

O: No, I don't know, I suppose…

R: Are you entertaining doubt?

O: Yes, well… maybe. I don't know!

R: Know what?

O: What *for*.

R: *What* for?

O: Does doubt need entertained?

R: I doubt it.

O: That's not funny.

R: Do you know a funny thing?

O: I knew one, but… I've forgotten it.

R: That's a pity.

O: It is.

R: What is that?

O: That.

R: That what?

O: That *that*.

R: Oh, I see.

O: What?

R: That which I see.

O: What is it?

R: It is *it*.

O: Is *it*... *that*?

R: I have to think about that.

O: What do you think?

R: That I have a hunch.

O: Really?

R: Really.

O: What does it tell you?

R: That I know.

O: Know what?

R: That it *is* that.

O: What is *that*?

R: *It*.

O: "It" what?

R: How to find the way.

Act Three

O: Which way?

R: To be merry.

O: I see.

R: Do you?

O: Do I what?

R: See.

O: See what?

R: That you see.

O: Let me see…

R: Can you see the way?

O: Which way?

R: To be merry.

O: I go fishing. That makes me merry.

R: Did you go fishing, today?

O: Yes, I did.

R: What did you catch?

O: A cold.

R: Cod?

O: Cold.

R: Cold cod?

O: If uncooked. Or left to cool down…

R: (*with anger*) I'm not nervous!

O: I think you are.

R: What do you mean?

O: That.

R: That what?

O: *That* which I said.

R: And *what* was that?

O: I don't know. I don't remember.

R: Neither do I.

O: Why is that?

R: I'm nervous.

O: Oh.

R: Oh?

O: "Oh" what?

R: Is that all you have to say?

Act Three

O: What?

R: "Oh."

O: "Oh?"

R: Yes, "oh."

O: Oh yes.

R: Yes what?

O: "Oh."

R: What "oh?"

O: "Oh."

R: Oh!

O: Yes, "oh."

R: Oh, yes.

O: Ah!

R: (*relief*) … Eh!

O: "Eh" what?

R: Eh?

O: "Eh" what?

R: Ah! "Eh."

O: "Ah" or "eh?"

R: "'Ah' or 'eh'?"

O: Eh?

R: "'Ah' or 'eh?'"

O: "Eh."

R: Ah!

O: "Ah?"

R: Eh?

O: "Ah?"

R: "Ah," yes.

O: Ah! "Ah"

R: Yes, "ah."

O: Ah! "Ah," not "eh."

R: Yes, "ah." Not "eh."

O: Ah!

R: Ah-ha!

O: Ah-ha-ah!

R: (*as though being challenged*) Ah? Ha-ha-ha!

Act Three

O: (*laughing*) Ha-ha!

R: (*laughing*) Ha-ha!

O: (*rolling on the floor, laughing like a barking lunatic*) Ha-ha!

R: (*stopping suddenly to laugh*) How did you find it?

O: (*jumping to his feet; not laughing any more like a barking lunatic*) Find what?

R: The fish.

O: By fishing.

R: Where?

O: In the lake.

R: Which lake?

O: The lake.

R: I see.

O: What?

R: The lake.

O: Where?

R: At the end of the way.

O: Which way?

R: The way to be merry.

O: How do I find it?

R: Follow your heart.

O: My heart?

R: Yes.

O: Not, "your heart?"

R: No, not "your heart," *your* heart.

O: I see.

R: What?

O: "Your heart."

R: Where?

O: Nowhere.

R: Really?

O: Really.

R: Am I dead?

O: No, you are not.

R: How do you know?

O: I am talking to you.

R: So what?

Act Three

O: You are replying to me.

R: I see. (*pause*) So you are not dead either.

O: I suppose not.

R: That's good.

O: What is good?

R: You.

O: Me?

R: Yes, you.

O: Why?

R: Because you are my friend.

O: And you are mine.

R: Thank you.

O: You're welcome.

R: Thank you.

O: You're welcome.

R: Thank you.

O: You're welcome.

(*Ad libitum*)

Curtain.

The clowns keep the closing routing going behind the curtain and let it fade away as they leave the stage in the same direction.

ᘿ

XLIII – Woman on the Corner[274]

§1 Gershom E.I. Carmichael had been told a lot of bull by his cellmate, the noted and feared Mr John 'Steeple'… or 'Spyre?'… Millar, when he was counting time at the local joint. Not a vacation, that one was. None at all… However, he had been told some sense as well by that sort of… criminal celebrity, who seemed to know all aspects of the local mores. All in all, that Millar had proven to be a cool guy, despite his shortcomings—and there were loads of those!

How could it be otherwise? Steeple, or Spire, or whatever… He was his *cell*mate—yes, *cell* mate, as 'mate inside a prison cell'—at the penitentiary, for pity's sake! Not some goofy classmate at school! What's more, S… Well, *John* Millar, he was always ready to help him, even if he hardly knew Gershom. Somehow, that jailed kingpin and peculiar history buff took Gershom under his wing right from the start, and newbies need friends like John in dark places such as the one in which Gershom had landed—because of yet another argument and physical confrontation,… and the waving of a shiny blade, they say… But they say many things.

Life there was hard. It was no child's play. Not by any stretch of the imagination—and of the arse. In any case, Gershom's fate there had been much more tolerable and humane than the one that he had seen being suffered by the weird guy, probably a foreigner, who kept crying and praying in the cell beside his, and never spoke, nor actively interacted, with anyone else—not even the guards or the

---

[274] Aka "Woman at the Corner." Either way, someone is waiting for somebody else, somewhere.

young-looking visiting psychiatrist... An empty shell, that one... Not the shrink, of course: The weird guy, the weird guy!

That guy was *so* depressed. And so fucked up. Mentally as well as physically. Passively, in fact, that weirdo had plenty of interactions, especially with the worst of the worst in that bad place... Horrible... He became an easy bum to be shagged, and a quiet punchbag. They would bugger him, beat him up, and he wouldn't react in any way. None! Incredible... He would just lie there, until they were done with him. They left him for dead, a couple of times, but he kept breathing... In any case, he was already dead inside, according to Gershom, who had *never* seen anything or anyone so sad in the course of his life—which had been no walk in the park.

One possibly good thing is that that poor, dejected, wounded nobody was released before Gershom himself. The weirdo was free... As such, rare and probably distorted news about him reached the prison very late, confusedly, and without any order. No order. That is how Gershom came to know that the weird sob, who everybody there called "Mum" or, sometimes, "the mumbling imam," had ended up living in the street, begging silently for bread, incapable of 're-entering society,' or whatever noble goal the local penologists and social workers thought that incarceration could eventually and miraculously produce. What a lot of ludicrous bollocks!

Perhaps, what later happened to Mum was a blessing in disguise. The rumours were that a bunch of masked kids, on a Halloween night, doused him in petrol and set him ablaze. Blahm! Like that... A human torch! Fffffhhhhhh! What a way to go... Mum had been left there to burn by those cruel masked pranksters and, hadn't it been for the pouring rain, they would have never found his body, or been able to determine who that torched stiff was. So cruel, so... pointless. All of that in cold blood! But again, maybe it was a blessing in disguise.

§2   Prison makes you really face the worst that there exists in the world, whether it happens inside or outside. Somehow, being a detainee marks you for life, even if you just spend a few months or a few years in there, and do your best to become a 'viable and employable law-abiding citizen' once you get out of prison. It's like a chronic disease. A form of modern leprosy or a skin disorder that you can't cure in any way, and the visible signs of which stay with you, as though you had been branded, or you had had the bloody smallpox and survived... Like a big mark on your forehead that says: "Ex-con!" People's focus can then be as scorching as fire.

Nevertheless, being outside was *better* than being inside. That is what Gershom had concluded, after going through the joint's revolving door his fair share of times. For one, you could get better food, even if not all the time. And food is important. Not only to survive, but also to lead a life that is worth living. For another, being outside meant that Gershom could visit the secluded little corner between Jonas Passageway and Hobbes Alley, not far from Tom More's Square. There, he had time and opportunity to purchase his favourite happy pills, which were sold eagerly and reliably by an oddly-dressed and half-crazy woman who, no matter how full-mad this one sounds, reeked of garlic sausages. 'Tis no joke! It was as though that woman had been grown like a plant in a vase filled to the brim with garlic sausages!

For some extra money, that weird, malodorous creature would also give him a very nice foot massage, read his fortune, tell him stories, serve him black tea, and entertain him with her two trained hamsters. Funny little rodents... He had never seen hamsters do tricks before. It was actually quite a show. She also made passes at him, just a couple of times. She probably wanted to take him to her place and... get going. However, Gershom had no desire to follow her anywhere. That street corner and their commerce were more than sufficient for him. He didn't need to go with her God-knows-where, and maybe get some nasty warts or stinging beasties on his cock, or worse. Moreover, he didn't feel entirely safe, when he was in her company. There was something off, something dangerous, about that spry, odd, ever-beaming woman. And not just that dreadful garlicky miasma that hovered around her all the time!

Gershom's happy pills couldn't be found easily. They weren't expensive. Rather, they weren't fashionable. And yet, they gave him just the buzz he wanted. They relaxed him, and made him *see* things. He could be transported by them to a distant, different, *better* universe, where he felt that he truly belonged, and where it didn't matter that he had been in prison numerous times, or that he had a bad temper and much displaced anger. Just like his old dad, who his mother had almost beheaded with a big shard of broken glass… Sure, 'twas just another happy family. Like so many in the neighbourhood where Gershom grew up. So happy!

§3 Notwithstanding the inconspicuous and arguably frequent transactions between them, Gershom didn't know the name of the woman selling him those happy pills. Still, he knew that she called them "the pills to breathe underwater," and that they were allegedly made out of a natural and "100% organic Tibetan magic drug" that Big Pharma didn't want to be known around the world, because it would ruin their profits, shares, dividends, and the whole palaver… He didn't believe a single word of what she said about those happy pills, of course, but it was fun listening to her, because she really sounded as though *she* believed in all that horseshit!

Besides, that stinking, bizarre, and somehow sensual old woman seemed to enjoy being listened to and, in her crazy mind, taken seriously by her customers, especially a habitual one such as he was. A trusted client. When describing the frigging Tibetan drug, she was full of energy, elated, almost ecstatic. It was fun to watch. And Gershom didn't want to deprive her of that sort of joy either. Somehow, she reminded him of his own mother. But he had never seen his mother smile in the same gung-ho way that unusual pusher smiled when ranting about Big Pharma, Wall Street's "coming vultures," or extolling the virtues of her Oriental pills to breathe underwater. He wondered what his mother would have looked like, had she ever smiled like that. Perhaps, one day, the pills will make him *see* that. He would have liked it very much.

Gershom wouldn't consume the happy pills right away. Instead, he would go home, take a bath, get completely naked, fill a tumbler with water, gulp down two of those Tibetan means of chemical salvation, and lie in bed. There, he would be visited by the most diverse, astounding, spiritually-enriching, and meaning-giving visions that he had ever experienced—and that he would ever experience in the course of his troubled existence: There was never a nice park.

Those chemically-induced visions could be scary, at times. Certainly wacky. But he didn't care. When he was having his trips, which could last up to ten-twelve hours of out-of-this-world distraction, sleep included, Gershom was far *away*. Truly away. Away from prison, away from life outside and after prison, away from his childhood's memories and traumas, away from all the horrid music that latches onto your brain and never leaves you, away from the shitty neighbourhood in which he had spent so much of his life, away from the company of unsavoury characters and punks, away from any crazy notion that either of his parents might still be alive, away from the reek of garlic sausages, away from rancour, away from all that blood, away from… everything.

§4 On that occasion, Gershom was visited by a humanoid and imposing masked being, which sported two thick, opaque, very wide wings. Not bird-like, though: More like a giant bat. Gershom couldn't see any telling signs that this winged creature was either a man or a woman, and his badly-tripping head resolved that thorny issue by deciding that the masked entity was actually neither—or maybe both—but most definitely *not* a mere male, nor a mere female. In his wandering mind, Gershom started calling it "Batter." Why that was the case, nobody knows.

Gershom himself would have been unable to explain it. Perhaps, the name "Batter" had to do with the bat-like wings: An alternative to the more common and probably copyrighted "Batman." Or, maybe, it was some sort of tacit association with the word "better," or "butter," which Gershom preferred to margarine. Another option is that the creature reminded Gershom of his very few days of employment in the printing business, which was cut short by his deplorable and impulsive stabbing of an overweight, overzealous employer. That odd moniker might also have been related to cricket, which Gershom played when he was young—and was crap at. Or maybe it was just some secret Tibetan motto that meant "take these pills and you'll feel stronger than a bull." Gershom couldn't tell.

As he would have stated under the circumstances: "Fuck knows." Well, actually, fuck *doesn't* know. For all the shadow-contents that those magical Himalayan happy pills unlocked inside the escape-seeking man's brain, his visions rarely presented him with outright, titillating, and pleasing sexual content. Or, if they did, it wasn't like some kind of dirty or sexy movie; not even the half-cocked, half-baked, arty-farty type of films that had made that phony F.A.C. MacRunt a constant, highfalutin, overblown, ball-breaking presence in the country's TV and internet shows for so many years... Too many years! "*Stellar Love's much more honest,*" Gershom had always thought—the refined movie buff that he was. Whether you agree with him or not, that was his confident, sincere, and supposedly well-reasoned assessment of the matter. Aesthetes go hang yourselves in the bathroom, in short.

Rather than sexual, the contents of Gershom's visions were... Who knows? They were far too mad, messy, and mish-mashed to be easily described by a single label or category of thought. For those who grew up in the 1960s and 1970s, "psychedelic" might carry a lick of appropriate connotative insight. And yet, there were none of the colours and vividness that one would normally associate with LSD, or with analogous hallucinatory drugs and mushrooms. Gershom's oneiric voyages were both chromatically simpler and affectively more distant than anything produced by LSD and the like. Aldous Huxley and Susan Sarandon might be interested in trying those happy pills, for a change. Unless they already have, that is... Have you?

§5 Batter picked Gershom up, holding him from behind and sliding its strong arms under the latter's armpits. It wasn't an impressive or dignified way to start lifting him and then taking him flying into the airy void. Gershom realised that. But Batter was no soaring eagle, nor a bloody hummingbird. It wasn't even a pelican, a skua, or an ostrich. It was some sort of giant bat. Part human, part insect-slurping rat, big and scary... You wouldn't expect much sense of beauty, elegance or jaw-dropping panache from a creature like that, right?

Flapping its large wings, Batter flew Gershom onto a tall, thin spire, which extruded from some haunting, half-collapsed Piranesian cathedral in Thomas More's Square. None of that existed in reality, and Gershom acknowledged that much, but it didn't matter at all. First of all, he had to make sure that he wasn't getting impaled by mistake, or that his still-virgin rectum would not be compromised by Batter's deficient foresight and wrong choice of trajectory. Secondly, the view of the city that one could get from up there was quite spectacular. "*It's a pity no spire like this exists*," Gershom judged in his own dreaming, dreaming, dreaming head.

"What is pain?," Batter asked him, out of the blue.

Gershom looked at it. He didn't recall that Batter could talk. After all, has there ever been a talking bat? At the same time, this giant bat was no ordinary bat. And it was talking to him. In the fourth place, it was a bloody vision! Who said that there can be no gigantic flying-and-talking bats in a drug-induced vision that ask you medical or metaphysical questions? ... My point exactly! So, in this vision, this good goliath, a sort of pumped-up relative of Michael Keaton, George Clooney, Christian Bale... and all the rest—you know the lot —well, it queried Gershom, who was busy admiring the whole town from above, like some tourist on the leaning tower of Pisa, or the CN tower in Toronto. Plenty of towers, around the world, if you think of it... Ancient obelisks too... Are they all phallic symbols? Or is it just a matter of engineering?

"Pardon?," did Gershom reply, rather formally. He hadn't caught Batter's words all that clearly. Nor was he sure that he had understood them correctly. Besides, in that way, he could give a little more thought to the answer itself. He didn't want Batter to think of him as an eejit, or an ignorant bastard. Gershom would have found that humiliating. And a little unfair.

"What is pain?," the incredible creature repeated, with a cavernous voice that made it sound like the villain of a million B-movies. "*Not even MacRunt would have a character like that in a flick!*," Gershom considered, while trying to come up with a sensible response. He didn't want to disappoint Batter. For one, Gershom felt a sense of gratitude, even friendship, towards that outlandish, ominous, yet Gothically-captivating creature. For another, he feared that a bad, poor answer could get Batter all riled up, make it fly away, and cause Gershom to be stranded on that cool but scary spire in the middle of the sky.

"Well," Gershom began, while licking his lips vigorously, so as to reduce his own stress levels. "Pain is... Stress, for one... Yeah, like... Now, for me, were you," he laughed nervously, "to abandon me here, in mid-air... Ah...," and continued: "But pain is also, like a signal, an impulse that goes to the brain. It runs along the nervous system and... Well, your brain, your brain says: 'That's pain!' And it ss... starts...ss... screaming. Yeah, screaming... Like, this yell that goes through your bones, your head, your... skin, even... I mean, it depends on the pain... Sometimes it is in a certain point of your body, or even your mind, soul... consciousness... whatever you want to call that thing that is *yourself* inside of you... Or it can be all over the body, or soul, or even both... Yeah, that's the worst kind... Then you aren't only stiff, sore, fatigued... It's not just headaches or a bleeding cut in some sore part of the body. Then, it's anxiety, sadness, depression... All sorts of symptoms, everywhere, all at the same time."

"I understand," Batter replied.

§6 In that precise moment, Gershom felt exactly *all* of the components and characteristics of pain that he had just tried to describe and explain. The effect was shocking. He didn't care anymore where he was. He didn't care about Batter. He didn't care who he himself was. He didn't care about falling off the spire. He might have liked it, in fact. That is, had he fallen down and destroyed himself. Being dead. Feeling nothing. That would have been *so* much better than to go on experiencing all that pain, even for just a fraction of a millisecond. It was unbearable.

There are no words to describe the intensity of the pain that Gershom endured. He lost all sense of time. He lost all sense of self. He started hallucinating. Having visions within the vision. Batter, now, was nowhere to be found. Instead, Gershom saw only a barren white hall, possibly at St Stephen's Hospital. He was inside it. He looked around. There was... Gershom... Yes, another Gershom! There were two of them... Or maybe not, wait... Gershom realised that he was looking at *himself*, from the outside. His mind, his soul, his... consciousness, his *self*, well... It, he... Whatever! It had left the body and was observing it from the outside.

The body was not lifeless though. It was not one of those out-of-body and hovering-around experiences that Gershom had read about in an old book when he was a teenager. He wasn't lying on some hospital bed... The body was... alive, yes, breathing, blinking, heaving... you know, all the signs of normal life were there: All of them! Also, it seemed conscious, or, well, conscious enough. That body was... in pain, yes! Pain! That's what it was. Gershom was looking at himself being in pain. But... How was that possible? And how did he know that?

Gershom, without even thinking about it, focussed a little more on his suffering self and, well... He 'found' himself back into... *himself*! Yes, there was no 'outside' Gershom anymore. No doppelganger. No 'other' self. He was inside his body, again... And Gershom didn't like it at all. Oh no, not at all! The pain levels were excruciating. They were gruelling, torturesome... All his limbs, his back, genitalia, mouth, neck, forearms, fingertips, knees, hips, ...his guts... All of them were aching, hurting, burning. They were... afire: He was ablaze.

All his nerves were sending screaming messages to the brain. The brain itself was flooded with wave upon wave of primal fear, interminable guilt, horrible shame, the deepest sense of grief, and a paralysing feeling of impotence and utter, utter tiredness. It was the deepest and most devastating sense of exhaustion that a person can experience: Total, pure horror.

This veritable volcanic eruption of unlimited anguish and infinite aching went on for two or three eternities. Or so they seemed to Gershom, who didn't know what to do, nor how to get back to his former vision... At least, had he only been able to step once more out of his own body, his suffering self, his pained personality... And so, he did. He was *out*. Again. Looking at himself from the... outside, yes. For there was no other way to describe it but that one. "*What a big nose*," Gershom also happened to think, briefly, while observing his other self.

Batter was there as well. Funny. Gershom hadn't noticed it flying back. He was probably too distracted by all the angst and hurt that he had been going through. Maybe it was a sign of hope. Friends are still friends, even if you are... hurting. Or maybe *especially* when you're hurting. Isn't that the adage? The proverbial wisdom? Good friends should show up when you are feeling low, low, low... So low, so very low... Shouldn't they? Don't they?

"Please, Batter... help me," prayed Gershom.

"No," said a voice. It was Batter's voice.

§7   That brusque refusal made Gershom panic. Not only did he find himself back inside his tormented self, but new torments were added: Hopelessness, infernal dread, the very notion that God may exist and be... *evil*. Gershom started confessing all his sins to that evil God, even those which he hadn't committed, or that he thought nasty people could attribute to him in particular, or to any former convict in general—like Gershom was, and *felt* he was. He prayed and prayed. He beseeched that evil God to be... less evil; yes, less evil... towards *him*, at least. That evil God could go on tricking people into believing in their five senses and fewer hard sciences. That didn't matter. Only pain did. It was just too much. It was as if a thousand surgeons kept carving up Gershom's body and performing bone grafts all over it, without anaesthesia.

"God, please, take me away!," Gershom uttered.

"No," said Batter.

§8   "*Is it the devil?*," Gershom thought. Perhaps Batter was Satan. I mean, it looked quite... demonic. Didn't it? That's, at least, the new line of reflection that Gershom had started spinning in his own whirling mind, while suffering all varieties of psychological and physical torture and extreme distress. Kinaesthesia was of no relevance to him. The fear of damnation was. "*Does he live in my heart?*," Gershom wondered, assuming the devil's gender...

... "*That's not very PC*," he then reflected, and a faint, remote hint at a wry smile could be perceived, even if most tenuously and in the weakest possible manner, inside his poor soul. Someway, a trace of humour could still be retrieved, somewhere, notwithstanding the ongoing agony and the unending pain. It was a patent sign of despair, in all probability, as well as of social conditioning—one level of it, at any rate: Pavlov and Skinner scraped only the surface.

Gershom went over all his sins, errors, crimes, and misdemeanours. He did that a million times. He didn't have any spectacular failure to recount, but he had made many mistakes in his life. Also, other people, bad people, misguided people, could have easily accused him of terrible things... Yes, they could have... Being innocent, yet accused. Like Jesus, Socrates, Thomas More, and that 'Hurricane' boxer! How many people have been accused of terrible things, when they were innocent! All those poor victims of 'moral' panics, mass hysteria, online piling-up, prejudiced persecutions... How terrible! That was a dreadful, paranoid thought that came back to him and haunted him, again and again, like a powerful wave crashing against the pier in the local harbour, where Gershom was now... standing.

"*Shall I jump?*," he asked himself, while looking at the black, cruel sea, which might have been a source of annihilation, non-existence, peace, the end of all that pain, and cruel dis-order. Moreover, a silent whisper kept telling him that he *should* jump. Was that the mandate of hell? Satan's fancy? "*I hate disorder*," Gershom thought, as though that thought had come into his mind without asking his permission. But that's actually the way all thoughts appear: Out of nowhere; and inside our minds—like a sudden lightning. Or a lightbulb being switched on: Pop! Cartoonish... Nightmarish too, at times. "I am order!," Gershom shouted, "fuck the id!"

Somehow, a minimal, distant memory of psychoanalytic readings had resurfaced. Go figure... All kinds of junk, nonsense, trivia, bric-a-brac, dregs, residues,... flotsam and jetsam seemed to be stored within Gershom's... consciousness, mind, soul... and they were all showing up in the most chaotic manner... A mental kaleidoscope reeling out of control.

"Stop this! Stop this! Stop this!," he implored.
Silence. And pain.
"Stop this! Stop this! Stop this!," Gershom implored once more.
Nothing. And pain.
"Stop this! Stop this! Stop this!," he implored a third time.
"No," was Batter's answer.

§9   Gershom was lying on a wooden patio. It was Spring, or Summer, or early Autumn... Unclear... *"Am I just biochemistry?,"* he wondered, somewhat pleased at the sound of an erudite term inside his own tortured, aching being. *"Are the laws of nature just like faces in the clouds? Or is there an actual order? ... Shall I see a priest?,"* he added, feeling uncomfortably... medieval, yes, *medieval...* "Why isn't it enough?," Gershom asked, in a soft, humble tone, fighting the spasms and cramps tormenting his tongue and larynx. "Why?," he insisted, "why?"

Another potent surge of physical punishment and mental devastation took over. He felt like a log being tossed around by Neptune's cruel whim in a stormy sea. *"I liked the Odyssey,"* Gershom remembered, in the thick of all that confusion: Armand Assante, Bekim Fehmiu, Kirk Douglas... Monteverdi... Childhood memories... All those memories: Images, intimations, fragments, crumbs, shreds, shards... The past, blended together in a cacophony of flashes.

"Is this what Alzheimer feels like?," he pondered briefly. *"It must be terrible,"* he added, moved by a genuine bout of compassion for the elderly. One of his uncles had died of it, or so he had been told when he was a teenage boy. Gershom hadn't seen him in the final stages, but his father had told him that it was a sorry sight. A sorry one indeed: Pitiful, and painful.

Suddenly, all quiet. Well, almost. No more storm. No more sea. No more flashes. Not even compassion. Neptune had fucked off. Gershom was alone, in a white place, maybe the hall that he had visited before. The body was still aching horribly all over—all the sorry way from what felt like a glowing 21st-century phossy jaw, down to the lower limbs' ghostly elephantiasis. His soul, however, was engulfed by one feeling and one alone: *Self-loathing*.

Gershom *hated* himself. With all of his heart, all of his will, all of his own... self. "*How can they love me?*," he queried, "*I'm so pathetic, so imperfect, so inconsistent, so worthless...*" He would have cried, if it had been possible. Yet, his lachrymary glands were swollen and red, as big as acorns, and they were hurting *so* much. The tears were all clogged up inside, blending with the mucus and making it hard for him to breathe: A man *can* drown in his own tears.

An already-frail balance had broken down. Totally. Uncompromisingly. Gershom had broken down, and apart—and even up with himself. He didn't love himself. There was no self-love left. Not an ounce. Not a gram. Not a drop. Nothing. Hatred. Hatred. Hatred. Hatred. He hated himself. "*I don't want my children to be like me*," he yelled inside his own head, even if he didn't have any children. "*I don't want to be like my father*," he continued, "*I don't want to be a bad example... I don't want to think that it will all be fine... I want them to be freer than me... less frustrated... less weighed down by... life.*" ... "*I hate life*," Gershom concluded.

"Kill me, please!," he begged.

"No," said Batter.

§10 Gershom was kneeling before an altar. He was inside a church. Which one, he ignored. He hadn't been to Mass or anything like that since the latest funeral... Fifteen years ago. He didn't care about religion. He didn't believe in God and all that crap. He wasn't a child, or a peasant from some bleak, rainy, muddy valley in some remote corner of Europe during the Dark Ages... Or maybe he was... Nothing was clear or evident, apart from the pain, which had come back in the most complete and merciless way. Pain's fiery reign was present, and supreme.

"*Why can't I sense my dead relatives around me?*," Gershom wondered, "*why can I only feel melancholy, all the time, and someone hiding inside it?.*" He had no answers to give. "*Why isn't it*

Act Three

enough to ask for forgiveness?," he went on, "why is everything just like it was before?." No idea. No reply. "*I'm completely mad*," he joked—to some extent. "*But I can function*," he thought. "*Is it worth it?*," he added. "*But worth what?*," he queried. He didn't know. "*Am I only a dick, meant to make babies?*," he pressed on, "*to let the species... evolve, into nothing?*"

For all his faults and penal troubles, Gershom had been a clever kid at school. He spoke good English—to the point that, in prison, a funny guy called him "Einstein." Above all, he still remembered a few interesting things from his studies. He had liked reading Schopenhauer, for one, and he believed that people like Darwin, Freud, and that insufferable Richard Dawkins had actually stolen everything from him, without acknowledging their intellectual debt to the noted German pessimist. "*Isn't it all pain?*," Gershom speculated, "*just like he said?*,"—that "he" meaning Schopenhauer, of course—"*and boredom, if you're lucky!*." Gershom grinned, even though only internally. "*I know I'm* more *than that*," he pondered, "*but why can't I* feel *it?*"

The pain was interminable. It was seemingly unendurable, cruelly systematic, and all-encompassing. Nevertheless, some minimal, truncated reasoning processes could still take place. "*Why didn't she like it?*," Gershom wondered, "*why didn't she trip away with me?*." Who that 'she' was isn't clear. Not even to him. Gershom had been with many women, but he had never had a stable relationship. He didn't know why. Life, in all likelihood. "*I'm alone*," he thought, "*I'm alone with my feelings... I'm afraid of my feelings... I don't want my feelings... Is this all... an obsession? Is it a symptom? Is it a punishment? What is it?*"

Gershom recalled a couple of sorry psychos that he had met while enjoying yet another cheery stint at the local prison. He didn't want to be like *them*; like *those*. He didn't want to lead the inconsolable, tormented existence that *those* poor guys had to go through on a daily basis, fighting constantly with the contradictory voices, the terrifying images, and all the other torturing contents of *their* own poor, pained heads. They were worse than the brainless zombies populating countless TV shows. "*Is* this *madness?*," Gershom kept asking in his own troubled, aching mind. It was a scary notion. He was scared of it. *So* scared. Terrified. Was he crazy?

"God, tell me!," Gershom cried.

"No," said Batter.

§11 Gershom was inside a room. Small, dark, yellowish, filled with cigarette smoke and the stench of stale beer. The TV was on. His father was sitting on an armchair, watching a porn flick, wanking. "*Is that Stellar Love?*," Gershom wondered. "*I guess she is*," he replied to himself: Nice girl. Beautiful eyes. Wondrous legs. Beauty could still be grasped, oddly enough, even in the midst of the terrible maelstrom that he was in. "*Better than zombies*," he added, in yet another faint, instinctive surge of humour. His lips couldn't bend into a smile, though.

"Go and fuck as many girls as you can!," he heard his father say out loud. Gershom turned towards him. His father was standing one or two metres away from him—to Gershom's left, to be exact—looking at Gershom with a stern gaze, a sinister smile, and a shrewd and determined look on his pallid face: "Youth's fucking short, boy! Fucking short!"

"The innocent is wrongfully accused and crucified," Gershom heard someone else say.

He looked in that direction. It was a weird-looking guy with… Was that a fake beard?

"Jesus is man's sole true role model," the creep stated, "that's what you must seek!"

Gershom was perplexed. And in *so* much pain. So much!

"Unjust punishment is a lavation of all sins, especially the sins of others," the short and freakish priest added—because he *had* to be a priest: What else could he be? Besides, "*only priests speak of Jesus, these days*," Gershom considered. "*But what the fuck is a 'lavation?'*," he honestly wondered. He had never heard that word before. Or so Gershom thought, at least.

"Hey, you," Gershom said, trying to start a conversation with that hairy and perchance holy Danny DeVito: "Why can't I have peace and quiet? Why all this pain? … Why am I afraid of black cats?" The

Act Three

diminutive, peculiar, shamanic fellow smiled. It looked like he may have actually winked at Gershom. But he vanished in an instant: Poof!

Gershom was alone inside that room. His father was gone as well. *"What if I can't sleep anymore?,"* Gershom wondered, *"is this what is going to kill me? ... Let's hope it does,"* he concluded. Anything, but death especially, was preferable to the state of all-pervading bodily and spiritual distress that he had been experiencing. Ending that wild narcomania, disappearing into nothingness... What a blessing! "I want to sleep!," Gershom yelled, to no avail.

It just wasn't possible. He couldn't fall asleep. Gershom could *hear* everything, in fact. *Any*thing, perhaps. Even the faintest of noises. What was that about? Have you ever heard the sound of leaves falling onto the ground? Have you ever heard a car approaching from ten kilometres away? Have you ever heard the way a sparrow breathes? Or the heart pounding inside a cat's chest? Or the rustling sheets of someone sleeping in a distant, separate bedroom? Gershom could hear *all* of that, and more. So much noise. Noise, noise, noise, noise! It was all *so* loud. So very loud. He couldn't sleep, as a result. Who could?

And all the pain on top of it. All that pain. Pain, pain, pain... It was just too much, too much. Unbearable, *almost*—for he was still there, was he not? Maybe, but only maybe, he could bear it, after all... All insects are capable of transforming their entire bodies. Some jellyfish repeat their life-cycle. Brains rewire themselves in adolescence...

"Can I be this strong?," Gershom briefly pondered.

"No," said Batter.

§12 Batter wasn't done. Not even remotely. Not at all. But Gershom didn't know that. He could only hope it—in vain. "What is pain?," Batter asked, once more, in its distinctive villain-like yet surprisingly amiable tone of voice, which had just a hint of a known accent.

"*This* is," Gershom promptly replied. And as he said that, he suddenly realised that much, most, almost all of the pain was *gone*.

Like that. Whoosh! The well of guilt, shame, horror, dread and fear was… dry. The limbs were still stiff, the back a little creaky, the fingertips and the gums somewhat sensitive, the scrotum burning, the head dizzy, the liver pulsating... Overall, though, also the physical pain seemed to have… receded.

"Did you *cure* me?," Gershom inquired.

"No," was Batter's terse rejoinder.

§13 "Thank you, Batter," said Gershom, "thank you anyway…," and he smiled. "Thank you, God," he continued. "And thank *you*," he uttered, picturing the face of the half-mad lady who sold him his happy pills. *"I'm sure your cooking must be good*," he thought as well, God-only-knows for what reason or to what purpose. Gershom had been seized by a sudden wave of universal gratitude. It was a good feeling, for a change. It was like being dipped into a calm ocean of pristine love. Was that a taste of God's blissful embrace?

Out of the terrible maelstrom, Gershom had also more energy to try and think: *"Can we absorb or communicate one another's pain and self-loathing?,"* Gershom asked himself, *"subconsciously, like… like… like animals do? Sensing things, smelling, watching… feeling the environment around, feeling the other animals… But we can't measure human dignity."* It was a flaky train of thought, but there were no discernible rails around that place, wherever it was.

There is a certain sense to senselessness. Trips are trips. They don't have schedules or itineraries. They just go on as they do. Gershom knew that. He had tripped before. But never in so dramatic a fashion. Above all, he had never experienced so much *pain*. The pills weren't happy ones. Not this time. *"I need… sleep,"* he considered, *"a little bit of work… and helping others… helping helps."* He pictured the old Leon Trotsky in his mind, just like that, without any warning whatsoever, as though anything could exhibit any coherent logic. *"Mexico City is bad for your brains,"* Gershom joshed within himself, and smiled, but not yet with his lips.

Gershom felt his own stomach rumble and growl. Even if he was inside a vision, he still had a body—a body that could suffer a lot, moreover. He realised that he must have been hungry. "Fuck off, you

Act Three

Satan!," Gershom mumbled, like some disgruntled friar, without any special explanation or motive. And he burped. He was growing an appetite. That must be a good sign!

"Can I go home?," Gershom asked, like a child seeking permission to leave school.

"No," was Batter's strict reply.

§14 "Bizarre," Gershom cogitated, or maybe proffered, "I can hear my own thoughts, the sound they make, like internalised dialogue..." Perhaps *that*'s what was keeping him awake...

Gersham didn't know. He just couldn't. He was also hearing his own breathing, like an incessant series of complex noises. Strong ones. Not faint at all. Not the way you might imagine them, unless you go through the same cruel ordeal as Gershom was going through. Which is something that you might happen to wish on your worst enemies. That is, if you have any despicable person in real life whom you hate that much and wish the worst possible ills of. A foe. An adversary. A nemesis. A total pain in the ass. "*Ah! Asses too can get so fucking sore!*," Gershom conjectured, out of context, like a total ass. Another internal smile occurred.

After a short while, his mind started to get... thinner... yes, thinner, thinner and thinner. "*I'm like HAL being dismantled bit by bit*," Gershom pictured in his head. There's less pain, though. "*Maybe it'd be good to die this way*," he considered... But then the aching and the anguish returned, even more potent than before. It was like an explosion, or a gunshot: Bang!

Once again, Gershom's lived cosmos felt like it had been made out of a dark fabric: Pain itself, pure pain, unadulterated, quintessential, deep, archaic, primordial, archetypal... Just pain, pain, pain, in all forms and shapes, in all domains and sectors, in all nerve endings, in each and every neuron of his suffering, probably crazy, disconcerted brain. Pain. Nothing but pain. Einstein, Fermi, Dirac, Giacconi... None of them would have been of any assistance there.

"Help me God!," Gershom cried out, "I'm just a sinner, a sinner... One of your stupid children...," and he started crying, his swollen, acorn-size glands allowing it for a short while. A very short one. Gershom looked around. His eyesight was impaired. He didn't know by what. It wasn't because of the tears. At any rate, he couldn't see very well. He noticed a small, simple, cheap table. There was a silver crucifix on it, rather bulky. He grabbed it. He put it against his chest, and started praying, like he had been taught to do as a child.

A tiny particle of him found all that one-man liturgical theatre very silly, silly indeed. At the same time, it all felt quite natural. And soothing. Besides, that droplet of momentary soothing was better than nothing. Much better. And certainly better than all that monstrous avalanche of physical and psychological pain which had blanketed him and did not let him go.

Gershom felt like a broken machine. But also more, and less, than just *that*. He felt a remote hint of sexual urge, and then the shame that comes with it. "*We are body, mind, and spirit,*" Gershom summoned from some dusty corner of his consciousness. "*We need a force, a wind, an agency that sets our body and mind in motion,*" he went on, "*without it, we are dead. Cadavers. Nothing ... The breath of God is that wind,*" he reflected, "*which no anemometer can measure, because the most important domains lie beyond the scientist's measured reach.*"

Why had he started musing on such theological nonsense was a real mystery. Maybe it was all the fault of that silver crucifix, which he held like a teddy bear, or a stuffed animal. Gershom had a little bunny—a hare to be exact—which he liked intensely, when he was a small child. He would talk to him, with him... Yes, "him," because it was his special friend Mateo, from South America: "*If you want to know someone, you talk to them, you don't run an EEG.*"

"Can we fly to Brazil?," Gershom nervously suggested.

"No," said Batter, and smiled—a chilling smile.

§15 Gershom woke up. "Am I in Portugal?," he muttered.

He was not. He was in his bed. Naked. Sweaty. Finishing his trip. Unless something came back and the merry-go-round restarted. It happened, sometimes. It was actually quite nice, normally. Gershom wasn't wishing it, though. Not *that* time. That time he had had enough. Much more than enough! But no human being is in control of this type of mad shit, once it gets commenced—maybe that's why they tell kids not to do drugs. It is like shooting a bullet: After you've pulled the trigger and fired, you can no longer decide what will happen to the bullet.

A flashback hit him. *"Fuck!,"* he just had enough time to utter in his broken mind.

Floating around the spire, Gershom saw himself in the small room with his father. It was as though Gershom could be in two or three places at once—ubiquity being a divine attribute, they say. His father was still there, in that small room. The TV was still on. Gershom couldn't see if Stellar Love's flick was still on. *"Pity,"* he thought, *"she's a beautiful woman."*

"Pitilessness" would have been a more appropriate concept. The two men in that small room were both in incredible pain. So much pain. Terrible pain. The pain that Gershom had just been experiencing in its full force on his own. And unlike boring cinema or bad chronicles, that type of pain is never repetitive, redundant or tiresome: It hurts like hell each and every time.

Weakened and wrecked by all that pain, the two suffering men were trying to hug. But it was very difficult. *So* very difficult. They had limited control over their aching bodies. The paroxysms, the involuntary contractions, the sudden bursts of pure and total physical distress… And all that fear, the paranoia, the anxiety… All of it was back, and more. And all of it felt pitch-black, engulfing the mind and the heart with infinite blind horror, while the physical realm bestowed onto their bodies nothing but unalloyed pain. No beauty. No peace. Pain only.

"Accept it," his father whispered to him, grinding his teeth, "accept mistakes, chronic conditions, limited betterment, paranoia, belts, the paranoia of paranoia, fragility, mortality, humiliating imperfection, chains, being loved, needing help, eyes, giving help, strings, being weak, being innocent, suffering injustice, ears, being forgiven, threads, hoping, any strength you're given, love, self-love, ropes, and *duty*—all of it, son, all of it, mine as well as yours!"

Gershom didn't know what to answer. His father had never spoken to him that way. It sounded like some crazy beatnik book. He looked at his father. He loved him. He glimpsed at a reflection in his father's eyes. It was Gershom's mother. His father's one and only wife for longer than forty years. Gershom loved her. His father loved her. They both loved her. They just weren't very good at it. "*Where do you go and learn how to love?*," Gershom wondered.

"Can I be with her?," Gershom supplicated, dry tears filling his blood-shot eyes.

"No," said Batter.

§16 "Birth's a life sentence," Gershom's mother calmly asserted: "All mothers are killers."

"*What does she mean?*," Gershom thought, for a brief moment.

"You shall spend your time hurting, because you're good," she whispered.

"*What?*," Gershom asked himself, being completely lost and bewildered.

"They'll always toy with you," she added, "they're cruel. All of them... *We all* are."

"*Who?*," Gershom wondered, "*what?*." Nothing made sense. Yet there he was... with his old, long-dead parents. Or were they still alive? He wasn't sure of anything anymore.

"There's only one real thing in life," she coldly stated to him: "Pain."

Gershom was terror-stricken and dumbstruck. He had his heart—and his bowels, in all likelihood—in his mouth. "*Is she my mother?*," he wondered, feeling deserted and doomed.

"You have always been nothing," his mother whispered, "since the very start."

"Can I start anew?," Gershom heard being said. But where? And by whom?

"Anarchy. Chaos. The universe," his mother listed—and she grinned, guardedly.

Gershom stared at her. Was that woman his mother? She certainly looked like her...

"No answers. Only questions," she murmured—her guarded grin becoming a smirk.

All of a sudden, a male voice began repeating the previous question, but *inside* his brain: "Can I start anew? Can I start anew? Can I start anew? Can I start anew? ..." Nobody answered.

A phone rang. That too was inside his head. "*I hate phones*," Gershom thought. The phone kept ringing. The noise was deafening. The phone kept ringing. Nobody answered.

"Can I start anew?," Gershom repeated once again, but *outside* of his pulsating, hurting, swirling, ringing, deafened head—he still had a voice of his own, in spite of all that chaos...

"No," said Batter.

§17 "*I'm not so useless as I thought*," Gershom somehow meditated amidst all that physical pain and mental anguish, "*sorrow, sickness and death will always come.*" He even managed to smile this time, "*but we can do something along the way... something good*," he added, "*and whatever fear we have, we can feel it and yet know that it isn't real.*"

"But what if you're wrong?," another voice interjected, as though someone had turned on a wireless set inside his brain. There were other noises too, and voices. Some sounded clearer than others. "Lower your standards," his father asserted, "it's a survival technique... Perfection means self-destruction." And the agonising old man finally succeeded in embracing his son.

The two men would have cried out of joy, but they were already crying out of anguish. Moreover, neither of them could shed any tears, because their lachrymal glands were even more swollen, and the ducts even more clogged, than they had already been up to that point. It was all so unnatural, and simply unendurable. The pain, the fear, the hurt, the paranoias... Gershom heard a melody... But what was it? It sounded familiar... Was it Bellini, Rossini, ... Andrini, Basini? ...No, it wasn't. There was something more... electric... Gershom didn't quite nail it.

While being surrounded, submerged, shaken, and remorselessly subdued by incessant confusion and primitive excruciation, father and son kept hugging, holding fast and firmly to each other amid swelling throbs of desolate yet genuine love. Above all, they went on suffering. But without any visible, tangible, liquid, humorous signs of their heartfelt, copious crying. So many hooks in their flesh. So many probes in their brain. So much pain. So much dread... Father and son... Tearless sorrows in sinking boats... What was that melody?

"Stop the pain, please! Let us breathe, let us rest, let us... be!," Gershom barely managed to groan out of his collapsing, aching throat. His uvula was a bead of incandescent lava. He was despairing. He was gasping for air. He was drowning in a sea of pain. He was adrift.

"Save me!," Gershom implored.

"No," said Batter.

§18 "I'm so tired, dad," Gershom sighed at one point.

"Me too," his father replied. "We all suffer, boy. Terribly. Sometimes it lasts years. Other times a lifetime. But we're not allowed to tell others that we suffer," he said to Gershom with paternal tenderness, "we can't show our weakness. Not even to ourselves. We are *men*, boy. Men, you know? We must be *strong*. Strong. Strong... Strong and stoical, boy. Like soldiers on the battlefield. We've been expendable since the dawn of time, boy," and he started shouting: "Save the women, boy! Save the children, boy! ... We're fucking drones!"

"How can I save myself?," Gershom asked.

His father looked at Gershom with a splenetic and sarcastic look on his face: "You *can't*. Do you think any girl would pick a crying lad? ... Even the lassies who say they want a 'sensitive guy' or 'a modern man,' you know?," the father snorted, "ah! ... What a fucking load of hypocritical pish! Bullshit like there's ever been any... Lies, lies, lies! They'll rather have a monthly check from the child- and family services than a sad, weak, broken man in the house!"

Gershom was speechless. He was terror-stricken. And he was exhausted.

Act Three

His father chuckled, weirdly energised or maybe simply pushed forward by the torturing inertia of his torments. But he was dead-serious too: "It's always the same stupid circus. Cultured gays and lesbians want babies and families, don't they? Just like your illiterate shit-covered ancestors: They can change the form, the shell, but the substance's always the same... And the substance is shit! *Shit*, boy! We're still animals. We're still pathetic primitives... We've had to go through the cruellest selection methods since we were small rodents! It still goes on!"

Gershom was still speechless. Still terror-stricken. And he was even more exhausted.

And so his father added: "Selection... Selection *and* competition... Even today: From leaping off the cliff to risking harassment lawsuits, unless you're Banderas, Clooney or Brad Pitt! Ah! How many o' *those* men can you see around here, eh? But *those* are the men that really turn on the ladies. *Those* are the hunks that the ladies think about when they're busy shagging their well-squeezed, hard-working men... See if they'd have a poor Steve Buscemi, or the geeky guys from school, for fuck's sake!," and he smiled at his son, "no, boy, the rest of us have to prove their worth by shoving shit, taking shit, eating shit, and doing 'n saying no shit! Heaps, mounds, and mountains of shit, boy! *Shit*! That's a man's stinky legacy to his sons!"

"*Shit*!," Gershom gloomily surmised. "*Is there a way out*?," he wondered.

"No," said Batter.

"Never found one," added Gershom's father.

§19 Gershom's father smiled with his eyes too, this time... There was in them a panicky gleam, as well as a buffoonish sparkle. Plus, as also experienced by his son, signs of an infinite amount of utter pain and helpless tiredness: "Unless you've got *lots* of money, of course," the father said, "but that's like having the biggest club, the thickest furs or the driest bloody cavern! Uh-uh!," the old man went on, sounding and moving around like some kind of prehistoric man, "real fucking progress, innit? ... While the rest of us have to fight for scraps, or be left to die like a fucking nobody, a bum, a loser, a failure, a bin-man, or a hairy truck driver who's totally invisible to the ladies, or disgusting... And if you look at the ladies, these days, then you're a creep, or it's an 'hostile environment'," he snorted, "for fuck's sake!"

In spite of all the persisting corporeal hurt and spiritual sorrow, Gershom laughed with sincere gratitude and palpable affection at those very harsh words and very oafish antics. Hearing his father's booming voice, his unique accent, his colourful way of phrasing things, his funny way of thinking, his wild exaggerations, and his warm and loving curses... That was *him* well enough: *His* old dad! It was so... *sweet* and... *caring*, especially after all that time. After all those years. After all that suffering... And throughout all that ongoing suffering too.

"Da'," Gershom began a sentence...

"And then you get no bloody 'thank you' from no one, because that's your fucking *duty*, boy! Your fucking *duty*!," his father interrupted him, "'cos *duty* is your only birthright!"

It didn't matter. The two aching bodies and tortured souls embraced each other once again, even more fondly and more forcefully than before—and then again, again, again, and again. That way, the two men were also bracing for impact, because they could feel that new humongous waves of pain were going to come crushing down onto the both of them. It was an everlasting tempest of overflowing torments from which they couldn't escape. It was a limitless universe of essential pain that nobody can even begin to fathom, unless they have visited it themselves—and suffered. It's the most consuming, annihilating force that there's ever been.

"... at least I'm here with you," Gershom finished his sentence.

Gershom and his father had never hugged each other like that in real life. They had never done enough of... *that*, as simple and as basic as hugging or being physically affectionate may be in other families. *"What a shame!,"* Gershom realised, *"what a shame!"*

Father and son were totally and abysmally depleted. And so they kept holding each other tightly. Their bodies had never been that close to each other in real life. Not longer than a few seconds at a

Act Three

time, that is. It wasn't done in those days, and in those parts of the world. It wasn't proper. It was stupid, weak, effeminate... or something like that. No warmth, please! No open displays of affection. Nothing of the sort, here! Real men are as tough as rocks. *Hard* as rocks. That way, their women know that they can rely on them. Isn't that what all women want from their men, in the end: Solid rocks to keep under their feet?

"Demolish me!," Gershom-the-rock beseeched, sighting no hope in front of himself.

"No," said Batter.

"*Duty*, boy!," added Gershom's father.

§20 "What can I do, dad?," Gershom asked, with a child's innocence sculpted right at the *very* centre of his *very* being. It was as though he had never grown into an adult.

"I don't know," said his dad, and grunted noisily, while looking at his boy with loving but melancholic eyes, "I don't know... *that*. I wish I could... But you can't know *that*. Nobody can. So, all you do... You do what you can... Your best... Your *duty*... And then you fall off a roof while fixing tiles, get electrocuted while fixing wires, get a stroke while filling forms, get driven over by a bus, a car, a motorcycle while going to work... Hit by a lightning bolt out in the freezing fields, under the pouring rain, or out at sea.... You crash the lorry that you're driving at night and lose your legs... Or get abducted by aliens that bite off your hands, for all I know! ... All of it, boy, 'cos that's your *duty*!," and he chuckled. "At best," his father added, "you chew on Prozac, smoke crack in a rotting basement, or drink yourself to an early grave," and gave his adult son a vexing look, "it's hard enough as it is, and without even a Saviour..."

Gershom didn't know what to reply or do.

"But you've got it worse than me," his father continued, still wearing a snarky smile on his face, "'cos you're *Swedish* now, boy! ... Self-flagellating *Swedish* scapegoats choked by semantics!"

Gershom looked at his father. He was puzzled. "Swedish? What d'you mean, dad?"

His father chuckled, again, despite the vast and powerful currents of unending pain that were submerging the two of them, crushing pitilessly their very essence: "You've got to cook, boy, and clean, and do the laundry, and wash the dishes, and fetch the kids, and get them ready for school, and make sure they brush their teeth, and get them ready for bed, and read them Papa Bear stories, and take them to the rides, and pay for all that stuff, and work like a fucking horse to pay for all that stuff, and be polite, and be kind, and be respectful, and give the wife her space, and let her have her moments, experiments, career, and say always the right thing, and bite your lip, and bite your bloody tongue off, and be rebuked if you go out to the pub with your mates, and wait for when she's ready, and do it only when she wants, and only how she wants, and dream of or watch no fucking porn flicks 'cos that's an exploitative sexist shame, and it's... oppressive, or whatever it is... and be ordered about like a pawn, and do as you're told, and grant them more and more of that 'power' that they talk about so much and apparently have never enough of, and then listen to their rants about equality, injustice, the double burden, their... powerlessness, mysteriously, and, what's the other one... yes, patriarchy! What the fuck is *that* around here?," and his father exploded in a tortured yet potent roar of laughter, as only a desperate person is capable of doing, or a tearful jester at an unforgiving princely court.

"Fucking Saudi Arabia and fucking Taleban, ok," the old man remarked, "but not *here*. No more. If there's ever been anything... Have you met any patriarchs? Ah! It's old slogans and new scheming. Vacuum activity at best... And then rants, rants, and divorces, plus kids and cars and houses and savings if they stop liking you, or get a better offer, or a younger dick! Where's men's fucking power, boy?," his father chuckled once more, "have you ever seen power down a mineshaft? On a merchant vessel? In all those cubicles eating men alive? Inside a lorry at night? And still you get no 'thank you' ever, because you're just being 'decent,' you know? Just 'normal,' boy, 'cos that's expected. It's your *duty*! Your *duty*, boy!," his father repeated, "and don't you dare complain, boy! 'Cos you're in the *first* fucking world, you've got a roof, and you're not starving like your grandparents, so you just stop it! Ah! You've lost one leg, not two, right? So, hop along, you privileged, entitled bastard!," and his father roared again, "They're afraid of saying that you too can have it bloody hard, as if by admitting that plain truth you took something away from them—like you're stealing their money or denying their pain… 'But what about me!?,' they'll say… Why are they so cruel? As if it wasn't possible for you to hurt like the lot of them do—like hell, that is—or worse. Or know the taste of shit in the mouth! All 'cos you've got a dick! So, no gratitude. No 'thank you.' It's just your *duty*, remember that!," and his father laughed roaringly a third time, "but a new one too. A new bloody stack of new fucking *duties*! On top of all the others that you've inherited with your stupid pecker!"

"Can you rescue me?," asked Gershom, sensing the futility of his own question.

"No," said Batter.

"I'm the one who needs rescued, boy!," Gershom's father bellowed.

§21 Pain. Heartache. Suffering. Desolation. Sadness. Anxiety. Struggle. Depression. Torture. Humiliation. Pain. "Who gives birth to himself?," inquired a male voice, which then flatly asseverated: "Everything *is* and *is not* at the same time, *here* as much as *there*… Living means dying." Pain. Loneliness. Terror. Angst. Vomit. Bile. Noise. Cramps. Rue. Fright. Pain. "My soul drops deeper than myself," that same male voice said—or was it an indirect question? Pain. Angst. Vomit. Fear. Melancholy. Rejection. Insomnia. Agony. Pain. "Not even freedom from starvation has made humankind happy," another male voice commented. Pain. Bile. Paranoia. Joylessness. Hurt. Effort. Pain. "You are what you are," Gershom heard being whispered by a female voice, "nothing can change that, for nothing can change nothing." Pain. Harm. Dread. Guilt. Strife. "They say they want reconciliation, but all they're after is remonstration." Pain. Drudgery. Horror. Blood. Dejection. Pain. "Contradictions chase one another," the same female voice averred, loud and solemnly this time, "forever and a day!" Pain. Slander.

Sweat. Mockery. Blood. Pain. "What are we?," the voice queried, "... *are* we?." Pain. Shame. Guilt. Shame. Pain. Vomit. Bile. Grief. Pain. Shame. Guilt. Conflagration. Annihilation. Pain. Pain. Pain. "You mayn't say that!" Pain. Pain.

"Noooooooooooooo!," screamed Gershom.

"No," said Batter.

"No," added Gershom's father, in the most heartbreaking tone of voice.

"*No!*," discerned Gershom's terrified, exploding, obliterated mind.

"No," repeated Batter.

"No," repeated Gershom's father.

§22 Gershom was aghast. And utterly wrecked. He had no energy. No trace of any strength.

His pitifully dog-tired, suffering old father started ranting again: "You're Swedish, boy! 'Cos you must do all the things your mum and gran' did, but you're still the same old soldier who gets sent to die by some infernal general and his cunning mistress, and gets selected by a woman, if he's lucky, but only 'cos he *provides*. Just like your old dad and his own da' before him. But you've got no room for error, boy! Ah! You must be *reliable*. More than ever. No jokes, then! Especially about blondes, boobs, sex, rapes or any nasty stuff, 'cos that's lese-majesty, it's oppressive, and it's *toxic*... As if one couldn't see when you're joking and when you're serious! Or distinguish between reality and fiction, or use and mention! What a load of bollocks! ... So, work hard, boy! Don't ever let any one of those bastards down, *not once*! And remember that you're *still* expendable, but *more* than before! No moaning, 'cos that's pathetic self-pity: Male tears! Victimism! Don't you cry, boy: 'Cos even *that* is toxic!," and the old man chortled bitterly.

Gershom didn't know what to say—no spirit left anyhow. So, he kept listening.

"They go on telling you that you've got 'all the power'," his father proffered, "they invent all sorts of new 'isms' that *you*'re guilty of 'cos you've got a cock, but then all of these alleged powerless victims can get you to starve, cast you out of your own home, and never show you again your kids. Ah! Instead of banding together and punching the fucking general and his mistress in the teeth… No! They want to *be* the bloody general, that's the truth! And when they've become that, they keep telling you that they're the victims! Hypocrites! But, well, I'm the one ranting here, ain't I? Have I become as bad and insufferable as they are? I'll better get me a glass of wine," and he winked at his son—or was that just a spasm?—who kept listening to his father, puzzled yet strangely pleased, "not even ranting are you allowed to do, boy, 'cos you're a fucking man, and that's whinging, moaning, and it's mansplaining, it's disrespectful, and so on. But the naked truth is that it's *unmanly*, and the ladies don't want to hear a whining little boy who cries, even if he's being kicked in the face by a bunch of mean girls! Masochistic Swedish scapegoats you are… If you want to complain, come back Tuesday next year, but make sure you've got a big nuclear bomb up your arse, 'cos then they might, just might, take you seriously: Boom!," and his father guffawed, mimicking a mushroom cloud with his hands.

Gershom watched his theatrical father with a child's loving tenderness. And the most hopeless hope of any hope. His father smiled. "Do you have a fag on you, boy?," he asked. "Ah, no," he immediately corrected himself, "smoking's bad for your lungs!," and sniggered.

"Am I you?," Gershom questioned his father.

"No," said Batter.

"You wish!," added Gershom's father.

§23 "*Irony*," Gershom thought, "*humour*," and smiled as well. A family trait. Something that Gershom loved and appreciated. Something that could keep him afloat. Even in that sick, spooky place, if lucky enough. But it required energy. A faint trace of it. And he was *so* tired!

"Thank you, dad, thank you!," Gershom fondly ejaculated. His father smiled.

Gershom smiled back, even more warmly. "But what if I'm afraid?," he inquired.

His father replied: "Son, don't worry. We're all afraid. Fucking afraid. All the time. Everywhere. Life is a fucking threat. People hate you. Parents hate you. Children hate you. Wives hate you. Colleagues hate you. They're all after your bloody throat...," and while he was saying that, a wound opened on his father's neck, and copious red blood started pouring out.

Gershom was terrified—that is to say, in addition to all the misery and ill-being that he was already enduring at that insane point. "Dad, I beg you, don't die!," he shouted.

His father smiled. "We all die," he said, "and thank God for that!," the old man added.

Gershom's father looked up, as though he was now communing with God Himself, and reached for his wound with his right hand, opening the large cut further, letting more and more blood come out of it, without pause nor any visible further distress. Had it been water, all that gushing blood would have looked like some overrated Renaissance fountain that Chinese and Japanese tourists go photographing and throwing coins into. And that Arab terrorists would surely want to blow up. "*Bloody terrorists!*," Gershom envisioned, for a segment of a segment of a segment of a millisecond. "*Prejudice too is always with you*," he comprehended as well. "*Another thing to accept and cope with*," he concluded, "*because we are imperfect.*"

His father's red blood filled the bedroom. Gershom peered around: He hadn't been awake. He was still tripping. It was a trip inside another trip inside another trip. Perhaps he was in Portugal, after all. Or was he still up on the spire, held by Batter? Gershom couldn't tell. And he was suffering. *So* much. Without a milligram of vigour left in his martyred being.

"Stop all this noise!," Gershom yelled. "Stop the pain!," he cried —to no avail.

Gershom was so tired. *So* tired! And he was in so much pain. *So* much pain! Everywhere in his body. And everywhere in the deepest recesses of his anguished soul. Pure pain. He felt pain. He envisioned pain. He tasted pain. Nothing but pain. He *was* pain.

Act Three

Sore, horrible, pitiless, unjustifiable, relentless, uncontrollable, screaming, fucking pain! And more still. PAIN! PAIN!

"I'm sorry, God, I'm sorry!," Gershom sobbed, lost amidst neuroses and psychoses.

He would have liked to go to a church or a chapel and throw himself onto the ground and beg for absolution—for him, his father, his father's fathers, and their own primeval fathers. But he inspected the space around him: There were no doors, no windows, no sign of any trapdoor or means of escape. It was like a sealed box. A coffin. A casket.

"*Am I dead?*," Gershom speculated.

"No," said Batter.

§24 Exhausted, Gershom looked wistfully to his right. His father was painting a… bloody Renaissance fresco on the wall! What the fuck was that, now? With his own red blood, that is, which Gershom's father was using as red paint and red pigment. "*Horror and art can be mutual companions*"—an unexpected yet clear hint at a genuine aesthetic insight quickly flashed within Gershom's confounded mind. All kinds of incredible things can happen inside the mind, which far too many fail to mind.

The father's red fresco was intelligible, even though solely from a certain distance: All things make sense only at specific levels of generality. There were red shapes, red figures, very much like red statues, emerging out of the red ground, like half-covered or ruined red temples in some Mediterranean archaeological site. Some of them were easily discernible: There were Jupiter, Hera, Saturn, Hephaestus, Mars, Apollo, Mercury, Venus, Eros, Priapus… and then a gigantic bee, a drone, a spent drone. The drone also looked like a phallus, with no foreskin on. "*Who's bloody circumcised?*," Gershom wondered. "*I'm not*, he then added, "*… is it harmful?*"

On the right end of the red fresco, his father had painted a tall spire, and at its summit there was something like a red light, a red star… Was it the Sun? God? What was it? Gershom was curiously attracted by it. He peered intently. Somehow, his eyes were functioning better than normal, at that point, even if they were still as sore as being cooked alive. Gershom saw a symbol inside that elevated red star, a bright badge or coats of arms, some military insignia... shaped like... "*Fucking Star Trek!*," Gershom realised, "*what the fuck is* that *doing in this vision? ... It's anticlimactic, isn't it?*," he joked with himself. "*Still, being Mr Spock...*," Gershom appraised, "*would be nice, maybe... I could* control *some of this pain.*"

"*Am I Mr Spock?*," Gershom hypothesised.

"No," said Batter.

§25 While he was meditating about the bloody cool-blooded Vulcan, Gershom found himself 'inside' Hephaestus. Well, actually, he *was* Hephaestus. He could see the other statues, the sky, the spire, Spock-the-light, and everything else as though he were that particular statue, that... *being*, 'cos he was breathing, and moving, and thinking, and feeling, and... suffering. Suffering, yes, like Gershom had been suffering, but from Hephaestus' vantage point, so to speak.

Gershom-Hephaestus looked around himself. He started contemplating the other statues. He could focus on them, while reducing a tiny bit the terrible pain that he, it, or they, was or were experiencing at the same time. Just a tiny bit. Yet better than nothing at all. *Much* better.

Each time Gershom-Hephaestus managed to reach a certain level of concentration—though Gershom himself would have been unable to explain how much—he 'moved' into the particular statue that he was thinking of. Little by little, as though he was learning to ride the bike or play a new videogame, Gershom started getting the knack of it. He was then Jupiter, Hera, Saturn, Hephaestus, Mars, Apollo, Mercury, Venus, Eros, Priapus, the gigantic bee, and also the many amorphous red statues that were shyly popping out of the red ground.

This was no form of entertainment, mind you. For each and every red statue into which he moved, Gershom would experience—also and above all—the many pains and varied sorrows characterising each of them. Gershom came to know intimately what distress and

Act Three

ill-being can afflict Jupiter, Hera, Saturn, Hephaestus, Mars, Apollo, Mercury, Venus, Eros, Priapus, the spent drone, and everyone or everything else into which he could transport his consciousness.

That way, Gershom came to know all the extant varieties, modes and forms of pain, both physical and mental, both human and superhuman. Still, since each red statue was a different being, each presented a limited and specific set of pains and torments. Somehow, that condition was *better* than the one he experienced when Gershom was just 'himself,' that is, outside of *any* statue, hence wandering as Gershom-only around that lunar or Martian landscape. Except for when he was Mr Spock. Then, as a Vulcan, Gershom felt decidedly better. *Much* better.

"Can I become Mr Spock?," Gershom queried.

"No," said Batter.

§26 Aloof, isolated, and located in a much higher position than the rest, Mr Spock—because that is how Gershom had decided to keep calling it, given his limited imagination and the fact that he was still suffering like hell—felt *less*. Less pain, obviously. But not just that. Spock felt less of any emotion, any feeling, as though he or it possessed some kind of switch with which the passions of the soul could be turned off. Gershom liked that very much, for he was knackered and had suffered far too intensely for far too long a time, but he also knew that Mr Spock was *less* than Gershom himself. It was just *part* of him. Gershom couldn't be *just* that.

The red statues, on the contrary, had plenty of pain to offer. Superhuman pain too. That wasn't much fun, if one wishes to use a mild euphemism. At the same time, each of those statues had longings, knowledge, and potential pleasures to offer as well. Gershom 'hopped' repeatedly across the statues, and he got to know better and better their constitutive pains and pleasures, their minuses and their pluses, their costs and opportunities. It was a demanding, draining, and dismal process. The pain was not lessened much by 'playing' such a peculiar dissociative game, yet Gershom had almost become used to suffering constantly and continuously—that is, to being in a place that could have been easily described as the red pit of hell.

At one point, while he was crossing between statues, and seeing the world itself from a multiplicity of different and mutually irreconcilable perspectives, Gershom found himself in his bed. Maybe he had just stopped observing his father's bloody fresco. He didn't know. In any case, he was there, now. He looked around. No windows. No door. A coffin. *The* coffin. He was still tripping. The pain hadn't really stopped. Gershom had just been effectively *distracted*, for a blessed, almost blissful, yet also bloody miniscule instant.

"Make it last! … Just a little longer!," Gershom pleaded.

"No," said Batter.

§27 Anguished and suffering, Gershom checked out his own two feet. They weren't there. Where were they, he didn't know. Instead, he could see two demons clubbing a young man into a pulp with big mallets made of stone. The chest was sunken and opened widely. The fleshy innards spread everywhere, The limbs squashed. The bones splintered. Surprisingly, the demons hadn't smashed in the young man's head, yet. Maybe they kept it intact for the final popping blow. Who knows how demons think? Or how they amuse themselves? But it is likely that demons favour the marshy, dark affective glebe whence both laughter and horror proceed.

Out of that unbroken young head, Gershom could make a profile, a recognisable face. It belonged to an old acquaintance of his. It was… Who was it? … Yes! That reddened, blood-soaked, dead face belonged to a pale, lanky, timid, taciturn Icelander, whose name was… Those names aren't easy to remember… Björn Þór… Baldursson, Baldvinsson, or something like that. Karlsson, perhaps? He just couldn't recall it.

That quiet Icelandic boy looked always sad. He *was* always sad. Even if he came from a good family and a prosperous country. What was there to be sad about? And yet, the humours flowing inside the boy's strained veins and arteries were black and dense, like thick ink or crude oil. That's the gunky sludge which his lonely, lost, and bleary Viking heart was pumping around the colourless body. "*Good for him he's dead, poor soul*," Gershom remarked in his own lonely, lost, and bleary British consciousness.

Undeterred by the ghoulish and gory sight of that pulpified pale cadaver and the two delirious armed demons, Gershom turned his face very slowly and scanned the room to his left. His father was there. This time he was not painting: He was *writing*. A sort of shopping list. Or some kind of decalogue to be imparted to the children at Sunday school. It wasn't clear. That is, it wasn't clear until his father completed it and, reaching further into his wound, disappeared into his own self, like an imploding star, leaving once more his son alone, consumed, writhing.

"End this! It goes on and on and on and on and on! It's too much pain!," Gershom cried.

"No," said Batter.

"*Is this a nightmare?*," Gershom conjectured, knowing already the answer.

"No," said Batter.

§28 Gershom scrutinised his father's writings on the wall. And he read out loud:

> "Keep hydrated.
> "Eat well.
> "Rest aplenty.
> "Do no harm.
> "Do good.
> "Have friends.
> "Love.
> "Honour God.
> "Keep going.
> "Trust your visions."

Gershom woke up—perhaps. He couldn't be certain. He saw blackness, for the most part. There was only a faint stripe of light filtering through, at the bottom of his visual field. He then remembered to open his eyelids. He looked around, cautiously. There was a window. The door too: In its proper place. His feet were there. No devastated Nordic remains were in sight. There was no gory fresco. No blood-inked shopping list or whatever. No blood at all. No endless pain. All gone. Just tiredness. Nothing excessive, though. The mind was surprisingly fresh and responsive. The body grumbled: Gershom had a yearn for eggs and garlic sausages.

His father wasn't there either. Pity! Gershom loved the extravagant old guy, and he had never told him that enough times, he realised. His mother... neither. Damn! Gershom loved her too, and she should have been told so by her crazy son far more often than he had done. Missed opportunities, which never return. An old cliché, perhaps, but also a sore truth. That's probably why sore truths become clichés, which are known facts that nobody can really stand and wants to think about in earnest. Maybe only incoherent, utter nonsense can never become a cliché.

"Are you there?," Gershom inquired.

"No," said Batter.

§29 Apparently, Batter wasn't there. What a shame! Gershom liked that winged creature, even if it was a weird being with bat-like features, a cruel penchant for denying you whatever it was that you wanted most, and was far more tight-lipped, laconic, and stereotypically Scottish-like than Gershom would have liked it to be. Still, it was a cool sort of guy, or being, that Batter. It could fly, for heaven's sake! It didn't laugh, but it possessed a wicked sense of humour. It might have been from Glasgow... But Batter wasn't there, anyway. Gone. Vanished. *"Where's it flying, now?,"* Gershom wondered, feeling lonely.

Gershom went over a string of... commandments—as he reasonably guessed at that point—which were stuck in his post-trip, trauma-filled, chaos-prone, and ever-more-unreliable brain: "Keep hydrated, eat well, rest aplenty, do no harm, do good, have friends, love, honour God, keep going, trust your visions." What were they? Gershom kept weighing and ruminating. Was that *the* Law? It wasn't obvious at all. Not to Gershom.

Still, it didn't make *no* sense either. As basic and as vague as they could be interpreted to be, those commandments possessed an enticing, terse artlessness and a vigorously direct tone that, quite simply and as inflexibly, *demanded* that they should be taken seriously and seriously entertained. "*Maybe there is a Law, after all. It's just that grasping it well is, well… it's no easy stroll in the park!,*" Gershom began intuiting, genuinely puzzled as much as fascinated by those commandments. There seemed to be something valuable within, behind, beneath, around or about them. And no intelligent person can do without a measure of experienced guidance.

In truth, those commandments had come from the father. Hence Gershom felt like he could put some trust in them. Above all, he felt that *he* could trust his own father: His old, imperfect, loud, flamboyant, sour, clownish, bombastic, sharp-tongued, keen-witted father, whom Gershom loved so deeply and so dearly, warts and all. Just like Gershom loved his cheerless mother: That grey, worried, inscrutable creature, always hidden in some corner of her own enigmatic yet ultimately caring heart. Gershom missed her too. He missed her very much. He loved her. Besides, if you can't trust your own parents, who can you trust?

§30 "*Funny,*" Gershom thought, "*but there can be wisdom in madness.*"

XLIV – Bad-Bum Boon[275]

One Act:
• *Mike J.J. 'Tinder' Lewis*
• *A police officer, who looks eerily like Calvin 'John' Major*

---

[275] Fallible human beings need second, third, fourth, fifth, sixth… multiple chances.

Mike is going to stand trial. On his way to the court of law, he exchanges a few words with a police officer escorting him. The police officer speaks in a funny way.

Mike: (*sighing*) Here we go.

Police Officer: Firs' time?

M: (*sad, speaking softly*) … Never this big before.

PO: Mone', eh? (*cleans his left ear with a key*)

M: Not really…

PO: Luck' you!

M: (*puzzled*) Why?

PO: No job' goin' around, the' day'.

M: Right… Got a few friends looking for some… (*pained*) Tough period!

PO: Tough, tough. Ye' (*cleans his right ear with the same key*).

M: Yeah, *tough*… Been on the shelf before… Long time… No bread. Horrible time… Tough.

PO: I know tha'. Me too.

M: You too?

PO: Ye'. Life's shi' fo' a' o' us, sometime'.

M: (*with a tinge of honest humour*) But this is *my* time…

Act Three

PO: Kil' anyone?

M: (*shocked*) No, I'd never do something like that!

PO: (*smiling*) Cu' anyone? (*cleans his left nostril with the same key*)

M: (*smiling*) No, I'd never do something like that either!

PO: (*smiling less*) Kick' anyone?

M: (*smiling less*) No, c'mon!

PO: (*serious*) Shagg' anyone? … Underage? (*cleans his right nostril with the same key*)

M: (*very serious, offended*) No! Do you think I'm a crown prince?

PO: (*smiling*) Stol' a car? … Or jus' a few pineapple'?

M: (*smiling*) No.

PO: (*smiling more*) Goo' to know… So wha'?

M: (*serious*) The legal papers read: "Hubris and indiscriminate throwing of ripe fruit."

PO: (*pause, puzzled*) … "Halitosi'?" (*cleans his teeth with the same key*)

M: No, no! They said: "*Hubris*… and indiscriminate throwing of ripe fruit."

PO: (*surprised*) Real'?

M: Yessir.

373

PO: Go' hel' you!

M: (*smiling*) Hope He does: I need all the help I can get!

PO: (*much more serious*) Di' you do i'? (*runs the same key through his own closed lips*)

M: (*with candour*) Well... I *deserve* my punishment... (*with hope*) But I'll come out a better man!

PO: (*serious*) We are wha' we do ... (*in a hopeless tone*) Fruit' o' you' labour'...

M: (*melancholy*) Aye ...Hm... Fruits* of my labours...

Curtain.

* Two coconuts are having a heated debate:

- One is one and everything.
- One, when thought, becomes two.
- And so, from two, spring out the many?
- Exactly! Plurality is truly a singular phenomenon!
- Won't the two and the many be so different as to deny the one, though?
- Not unless difference is their background commonality.
- Is difference the underpinning basis of unity?
- Of oneness, yes. That's why it endures. It's a ceaseless event!
- How can difference be not... different, though, each time?
- It's like a regular vibration. You know: I feel it in my fingers...
- A string? Or just a silly song?
- A quantum: All battles are fought over it, and with incredible energy!
- A wave? Like the lion's sea in the effing light?

Act Three

- And a particle. At least partially. Discretion ain't compartmentalisation.
- A monad, then?
- Have you ever met anyone or anything that was *not* a monad?
- Probably not.
- Precisely my point!
- I'll make a point of your precision... *One* point?
- Yes, one, to start with. Which becomes two and, then... many.
- And yet is or remains a point, nevertheless. Even one on top of another!
- Since it is non-dimensional, I should duly add, quite logically.
- Yet it's the starting... point of all viable engineering: Amazing!
- Bull's eye! Now go and build me a bridge within budget... He-he!
- Targeting practice, hm? Or merely... creative accounting?
- It's more like theology, rationally. Besides, it's only natural.
- It does sound logical, yes. It makes sense. Or maybe it discovers it.
- Yes... Mathematical, almost. It's like a logical function of thought reality.
- Is it... Metaphysical? And not just for keeping the shelves in order!
- At the end of the road, everything is metaphysical: The shelves as well.
- All things in good order and the right place. Like... a line?
- A line is a but direct consequence of all of this: It's a series of points.
- Seen from a... point of view.
- Like everything else. What's not relative? Reference systems make reality!
- Maybe... What of ultimate ontological necessity, though? Say... Aseity.

- Inevitability, yes… That's why detailed, rich descriptions are so valuable!
- Who or what established this complex system?
- God knows!
- Does He?
- *He* does.
- Do *you* know?
- I don't know.
- Is it a point of contention?
- Not for me. But I shall think about it.

XLV – Ophelimity and the Off-worlders[276]

The handwritten[277] note reads as follows:

"My name is Walter W.I.I. Farmer. I work as a tourist guide. My wife is a qualified physician. She's a well-respected GP. I am not mad. Unlike my mother-in-law. (This is not a trite joke. The old woman is seriously ill.) Call a graphologist, if you're in doubt. I write these notes so that a document is left for someone, anyone, to read. *I* don't know who. I don't know when. If I had a phone or camera, I would use it, but I don't own any. These few notes will have to suffice.

"Last Monday, while coming back home from one of the many tours that I lead around the city almost every day of the week, I saw three aliens from outer space roaming the streets. They were grey, big, had long appendages instead of normal arms, a small head with one big eye in it, and a large mouth with sharp long teeth. One could use the word 'monsters' to describe them. But I don't know what they are, exactly, apart from the obvious fact that they originated

---

[276] This chapter addresses planetary issues: Its author's got balls.

[277] The handwriting is commendably legible. (**Punch**: Can you still read? **Judy**: Only if it's on a screen.)

from some other planet. Nothing like that has ever existed on our Earth. I'm sure of it.

"The following day, I started finding unusual business cards in my apartment, in very strange places. One in the living room, another in the kitchen, the master bedroom, the loft, and even the bathroom. The business cards are rectangular, all the same size—the normal, usual one that business cards have—and they differ only in colour. Some are a dark shade of red, others a lighter one: Like the colours of cardinals and bishops walking out of some papal conclave. Each card carries on it the shape of an acorn. That's all. Just an acorn. Etched in golden ink.

"I searched online to see whether anything exists carrying that particular logo, or something similar. Nothing. Two days later, I started receiving worried phone calls from friends, colleagues, acquaintances, and neighbours. They all told me that they had been approached by some person, or persons, and asked about me, my family, daily habits, job, and so on.

"A plumber I had called to fix a broken pipe reported to me that he had been allowed inside my apartment by someone, who the plumber thought was me. However, it was not! I returned home twenty minutes later. I had made a simple mistake in recalling the exact hour of the plumber's call. The other 'me' was gone. Someone had got into my house and impersonated me! And they searched through my stuff, personal records, and books. They stole some of them. *Micromégas*, for one. And *The Mind and Society*. All four volumes! Why?

"I know that they are watching me, following me, trying to get me, or at me. I feel them. I know that they're there, skulking in the shadows. They're trying to hurt me, somehow. Why they want to do that, I don't know, though I suspect that it must have something to do with the grey aliens that I saw in town. I can't be certain. But I will find out. If I make mistakes, like I did when coming home late to open the door for the plumber, so must they. They are human beings, or at least some of them must be! And if they are human, then they are fallible.

"If they make a mistake, then maybe I will have a chance to disclose who they are, what they want, and what the acorn means. Even in the most desperate situations, there is always a way out. It's not happiness, I'm well aware of that, but at least it's hope. And hope is much better than nothing. Sometimes, it can be everything."

XLVI – Follow Me Follow You[278]

And so did John speak onto his four young daughters:

Tale #1 – While Holding Anita's Hand

"My dear girls, this is why the centaurs became *extinct*, like the headless men of Libya and the singing sirens of Phoenicia before them. Whenever the centaurs went to see a doctor, the doctor would refer them to a veterinary. And whenever they went to see a veterinary, the vet would refer them to a doctor. Either way, nobody tended to their injuries and illnesses. Little by little, they all died, one by one, uncured, when all they needed was an unguent made of myrrh, silver-grass, cassia, nutmeg, and edelweiss, such that any old lady in the village could prepare!"

Tale #2 – While Holding Monica's Hand

"Here is another story that I want to share with you: The bears' family, which you know so well, had to cross a river, not far from the lake where you like so much to go and swim! But the youngest bear didn't want to cross it. He was so afraid! The water was high, and he couldn't swim well. It was understandable. It is right to be afraid, sometimes. It can save your life, even.

---

[278] As long as readers can follow. Ironically, in the age of followers, people's ability to do so may have declined.

"Papa Bear, at one point, after explaining why they had to cross the river, grabbed the little frightened bear by the collar of his neck, and crossed the river with him. The little bear was so scared! He got splashed on the muzzle so many times! He thought that he was going to fall and drown in the cold water of that cold river! He feared that his father might drop him by mistake! He didn't want to be eaten alive by the fish: They have nasty mouths and very sharp teeth! At one point, he even thought that Papa Bear hated him and wanted to kill him!

"Nothing bad happened. In the end, even if all wet and trembling, the little bear made it safely on the opposite side of the mighty river. Yes, safe and sound. Papa Bear had helped him cross the river, even if it meant that he had to grab the little bear and force him to do so. It wasn't very nice, it was a bit of an adventure, and it taught the little bear to have less fear of big rivers: Because they can be crossed, if there is someone who can help you. Above all, the little bear learned that, at times, *guidance feels like coercion*: It's an important lesson to be learnt."

Tale #3 – While Holding Michelle's Hand

"I don't think I've told you about a young soldier, who was so worried about his performance at the annual military parade that he spent hours and hours training in the woods. He would march up and down along the brook, surrounded by birch trees and a few buzzing insects. There was no birdsong, because the young soldier's marching had scared the birds away. In a similar way, no other animal approached him, even if a somnolent badger and a sly old fox kept an eye on that bizarre creature, which was so big and noisy as to be impossible not to notice. 'I'll march perfectly, like a Dutch automaton,' the soldier would sometimes puff out, while in his heart he kept thinking: '*My friends will respect me. My father will be proud of me. My brothers will be proud of me. My sisters will be proud of me. My mother will love me.*'

"One day, while marching along the usual brook, the young soldier saw something incredible: The waters of the brook had turned red and glowing! Driven by curiosity as well as some half-forgotten thirst, the young soldier approached the bank of the small stream, kneeled down, and took a very good look at the red and glowing waters. What he saw amazed him. The river wasn't just red and glowing, as if some strange substance had been accidentally poured into it or a brightly-coloured strand of algae had blossomed on its surface. The waters of the brook were literally afire: The familiar streamlet had turned into a river of fire. It wasn't magma, by the way. There had been no volcanic eruption. The waves had become flames: That's what had happened. The young soldier had no explanation for that metamorphosis.

"All of a sudden, a bulky creature started emerging from the fiery waters. '*It must be a phoenix,*' the young soldier thought. As it lifted itself from the brook, very slowly, the young soldier had time to make out its features and realise that it was not a phoenix. After all, whilst there were flames aplenty, there were no ashes to be found around there. The young soldier was puzzled: '*Could it be a pelican?*' Yet, that guess too was mistaken: The young soldier had seen a long sac-like segment of the creature's long body and, still influenced by the idea that it could be a phoenix, he had continued to try and interpret that vision as if it were or had to be some kind of bird. It was no bird, though. The strange creature was a fish. It was a big salmon.

"'What are you doing here?' The young soldier asked. 'Showing you the way home,' replied the fish. 'I know the way home,' said the soldier. 'No, you don't,' the salmon asserted, sounding both wise and ironic, 'that's why you keep marching up and down in the woods!'."

Tale #4 – While Holding Dora's Hand

"In that very same forest, unseen and unheard, there was a wise old woman. She had left her home, family, village, and the land of her ancestors many centuries ago, because she hated their many sins and countless imperfections. In the forest, all alone, she communed with the plants and the soil, the sky and the rain, until she became a living fig tree, covered in green moss, rooted deep in the earth. At last, she had found true peace within her aching heart, and her love for the world would no longer hurt. Because *even love can be cruel, in this world.*"

"Good night, my darlings."

🌶

XLVII – Visible Touch[279]

One Act:
• *Alice C. Ponyrev, police officer (carrying a water bottle)*
• *Hella B. Lutwidge, police officer*

Officers Ponyrev and Lutwidge are busy sorting and archiving forensic evidence in a veritable forest of numbered cardboard boxes. It's a repetitive and tedious job. Almost machine-like. While seeing to their duty, they exchange a few considerations and reminisce together.

(N.B. The actors are expected to improvise with the props at their disposal.)

Alice: (*bored*) A blank income tax return form…

Hella: (*idem*) 55/31-7

A: (*stores away*)… A piece of… burnt… human foreskin?

H: 61/8-9

A: (*stores away*)… A pair of broken glasses…

H: Same… (*pointing*) And those silver crosses too …

A: … And the glass eye?

---

[279] Touching moments may seem silly. Sillier yet is not being touched by such unseeming moments.

H: Yep. Same. Next to the pineal gland. You don't need to check again the diagram, do you?

A: (*shakes her head to say "no", stores away*) ... A subscription card... half of it.

H: 86/66-9

A: (*stores away*) ... Two tourist brochures. One's on Japanese teahouses...

H: 55/6

A: An old CD (takes a look) *Antarctica*, by... Vangelis?

H: 44/9

A: (*stores away*) ... Three cartridges... Hunting rifle?

H: Let me see... (*she scrutinises them quickly*) Yes, 44/12-14. I'll put 'em away (*and she does*).

A: (*starting a parallel conversation*) Remember that day we went to see Paganini's birthplace?

H: (*more enthusiasm*) Oh yeah!

A: (*idem*) It was lovely, wasn't it? (*she sips water from her water bottle*)

H: Yes! The most beautiful city I've ever seen: The sea, the mountains, the art, the churches...

A: (*more bored, a little surprised*) Three... fingertips? (*As to herself*) ... Bloody?

H: (*idem*) Oh, there they are! 22/6-7. The one with the old kymograph, or whatever that was.

A: (*stores away*) ...Now, Paganini...

H: Yes, yes, lovely. I really enjoyed it! ... Who was the artist of the Arendt-versus-Rand debate?

A: What, the huge pile of cigarette butts, and the dark slime?

H: Yes, that one.

A: Biggi, if I remember correctly, ... Luigi or Renzo, something like that. Local.

H: Yes, right! Clever, very clever... I liked that exhibition: Plenty of irony and cool ideas.

A: (*bored tone of voice*) Bus ticket here.

H: (*bored tone of voice*) 7/6-7

A: (*stores away*) ... What's this bottle? (*she shows it to her colleague*)

H: Martini, Red. 32/8

A: (*stores away, more enthusiasm*) ... We didn't drink any alcohol back then...

H: (*smiling pensively*) I know: One of your phases! (*softly to herself*) "No hypocrisy!," you'd say...

A: (*taking no notice, back to a bored tone of voice*) Pipe. (*pause, sniffs*) Smelly... Turmeric?

H: (*idem*) With the broken tumbler, please. And the foreign book.

A: Right-o! (*puts in the right box; then softly to herself*) God bless people who still read books!

H: (*bored tone of voice*) More?

A: (*idem*) Plenty! (*she sips water from her water bottle*)

H: (*idem*) Ok, ok… (*softly, to herself*) No end in sight, today…

A: Louboutin pumps? (*observes with interest*)

H: (*also interested*)… Leave them aside. I'll double-check the right file later on…

A: Ok. (*does as told*) … A map. "Utopia," it says. (*As to herself*) … Norway?

H: I know the box… (*fetches and stores away*)

A: PlayStation… 6? (*softly to herself*) … How many versions are there?

H: Cool… Same as the earlobes. (*fetches and stores away*)

A: (*dreamy*) We went to a rock concert in that small theatre when we were there, remember?

H: Oh yes! And you were mesmerised by the white gloves of that singer… What was his name?

A: (*pause, then enthusiastic*) Steve Hogarth! … Ah! Unforgettable, simply unforgettable!

Act Three

H: Yes! Tenor voice, soft, lyrical, mellow, sophisticated. As stirring as Peter Gabriel: Real poetry!

A: (*short pause, back to bored, louder tone of voice*) Anal plug!

H: (*less bored*) 68/1 … (*takes a good look, surprised*) *That* big?

A: (*stores away*) "Expert model," it says… Dilhy Anne Babe's "Wondrous Instruments" line.

H: (*smiles, more enthusiasm*) Like Paganini's violin…

A: (*idem*) What was it called?

H: "The cannon," I think.

A: Cool name.

H: Yes. Cool. And cold…

A: Yeah… It was cold then, wasn't it? We didn't expect that, even if it was wintertime…

H: Yes, it was *cold*. Especially when we took that little train on the mountains, north of the city…

A: That was a blast! (*she sips water from her water bottle*)

H: (*smiling*) Yeah… I enjoyed it. Marvellous… What a view! … (*dreamy*) Remember the snow?

A: (*smiling*) Yeah! Totally surprising!

H: You know… It's maybe banal, an old chestnut… but it's true...

A: What's true?

H: Remember counting the snowflakes? Watching them fall? Losing ourselves in their dance? Waving goodbye to the melting snowflakes?

A: I do… (*smiling*) Yes, I do!

H: (*dreamy*) Well, isn't that God's hand? … You know, immense beauty in the tiniest things?

A: Yes, it is! You're right. Beauty's everywhere… (*long pause, back to work*) *Another* foreskin?

H: (*matter-of-fact*) … Burnt?[280]

Curtain.

XLVIII – Puke's End[281]

§1 H.S. Racket's trip was over. He had finally come back home. And he didn't like it one bit. He was depressed, to say the least. No funds. No support. No help. No show. Nobody cared about his plays anymore. Only provincial theatres and amateur companies. The glory days had dismally expired. And mercilessly so. He felt like puking. Life is so revolting, at times: He was an old man. His bright age of blazing innovation and acclaimed ingenuity belonged to the past.

---

[280] If safe enough, a disquieting smell of something burnt can be spread around the theatre.
    Punch: Why are puppets unimportant, dear?
    Judy: Are puppets unimportant?

[281] Only devotees of stenchy Roman showers have complained about it.

Act Three

"They say that time is an unfeeling, cruel master," he mused, *"and that fame is a fickle, cruel mistress... Why is it that arseholes are always the ones who are in charge around here?."*

That was actually a good line, he realised, so he jotted it down. Because H.S. Racket—"the quiet magician of contemporary drama," as he had been called in better times—went on writing, no matter what. It was his vocation. His muse. His demon. His fate. His curse. His addiction.

Nonetheless, it was pretty obvious to him that he needed some sort of change. Something that would bring novelty and, perhaps, excitement, back into his life. Thus, on that day, H.S. Racket decided that he was going to do something 'crazy' which he had kept postponing for far too long. Too long. It was the moment for experimentation. The day had come.

Following the advice of a long-lost and somewhat eccentric, on-the-spectrum friend of his, he would go and visit the Church of Hymna Jenga Gabhrish. *"They'll all be out watching the eclipse,"* he thought, *"it should be tranquil, and private... It's better to avoid rumours."*

§2 His prediction was correct. As he entered the New-Age temple, which was located on the second floor of a dismissed abattoir near More's Square, he saw only three other human beings, in addition to himself. They were two women and one man. The women looked like... space dancers from a 1970s bad music video. They wore golden catsuits, which comprised a golden hood covering their head and hair. They looked sinisterly attractive, but also pitifully fatigued. *"They must have been doing too much boogie,"* H.S. Racket cracked with himself.

The man approached him. Short and wearing a far-too-long white robe, while also sporting what looked like a fake grey beard—though it might have been authentic, mind you—he greeted H.S. Racket: "Welcome, my son!" The man's voice was shrill and juvenile. *"I could be his grandfather and he calls me 'son,' for Pete's sake!,"* the famed yet frustrated dramatist couldn't prevent his aging self from thinking. He tried to smile at that groovy minister, priest, celebrant, or holy man of sort, who smiled back at him—and with a vigorous honesty that didn't go entirely unappreciated. *"The zen monk Budai?,"* Mr Racket wondered, humorously.

The smiling *empireocatcher*—for that was his official title in the temple—addressed H.S. Racket once again: "Welcome, son! What can I do for you?." Mr Racket didn't know what to say. "Have you come to pray with the *pirocastresses*," and he pointed at the two drained gleaming women who were reclining on a white plastic bench, "our dear sisters?." Those two poor women gasped, as though they would have rather murdered the visitor than helped him with his spiritual needs—*"or carnal needs?,"* the playwright wondered, while coyly surveying those females' well-wrapped and lustrously-shimmering bodily forms.

"No, not really," he promptly replied to... "Cleanthes," as the celebrant later introduced himself to the protagonist—even if his real name is actually Aristotle III, Jr., according to some ridiculously unreliable sources. "I don't know why I'm here, to be honest." After which the two dear sisters went back to reclining onto their shared white plastic bench. One of them started to snore, as a matter of pneumatic fact. She did so in the key of C major, mostly.

"A searcher, a pathfinder, an inquirer!," uttered merrily Cleanthes, who was probably keen on the idea of doing something in there, if not something entirely good or thought-through.

§3 "How did you know we were... here?," Cleanthes asked him, bowing gently in his direction, with a rather pleasing, courtly, almost adulatory sense of reverence. "A friend of mine, an old friend...," and so did Mr Racket whisper the friend's name into the cleric's ear. Cleanthes promptly lifted his head, looked at the playwright straight in the eyes, and said, in a high-pitched, surprised, and probably much-irritated tone of voice: "A *friend*... of yours?"

H.S. Racket balked. "Well, more an *acquaintance* than a friend," he hastily replied, "someone I met because I needed to... borrow a copy of... *Walden Two!*." Good choice of words: H.S. Rackett could still think on his feet. "I see...," continued Cleanthes, "I'd be surprised to know that a man such as he can actually develop any

Act Three

bond of genuine friendship with another human being." It was almost as he had just called that old 'friend' of Mr Racket's an outright bastard and a rotten scoundrel. *"Bitterness galore!,"* the dramatist considered.

"What did he do?," the aging artist couldn't avoid asking, at that point—his curiosity and instinct of self-preservation having been piqued and activated, perhaps a little too much. "Dishonesty, dear son," Cleanthes stated, in a softer, colder, truly pained tone of voice, "disheartening and patent dishonesty towards me, the dear sisters," both of whom were happily asleep on their white plastic bench, "our enlightened community, and the *empireum*'s Supreme Intellect, the *Unus Mundus*, the *Primum Quantum*, Whose Will we revere, adore, and serve."

"What did he do?," Mr Racket asked once more. "He stole all our money and ran," Cleanthes curtly answered. "Damn!," Mr Racket instinctively exclaimed. "Hope so," was the *empireocatcher*'s uncompromising and plausibly ill-wishing response to that churlish, spontaneous exclamation—spontaneity being so very often the sworn enemy or propriety. "And he didn't have to," stated then one of the two spangly… nuns, who had evidently woken up, perhaps because of the conversation occurring between the two men, or simply because the white plastic bench was just too small and uncomfortable for both women to really manage to rest on it for any lengthy stretch of time.

Mr Racket turned towards the *pirocastress* who had spoken—*"she's really pretty,"* he quickly thought, *en passant*—and put a direct and candid question to her: "Why not?." "Because he's a filthy-rich university professor and doesn't need *our* money," she said. "Yes, he's got a very nice house, a fancy wife, and even a giant tropical bird," the second *pirocastress* added, thus completing the not-so-commendatory picture upon which Mr Racket was left to reflect.

§4   "How can *we* help *you*," Cleanthes interjected, airing an earnest spirit of compassion and genuine brotherly concern. "As long as you're not here to ask for money," one of the gilded *pirocastresses* hissed viciously, feeling probably less charitable and kind-hearted than her quaint *empireocatcher*. "No, no money...," the perplexed author and stage director immediately replied, "... meaning!"—hey, he had just found out what he was there for! That's progress... "Meaning," he repeated, "*which neither physics nor chemistry can grasp*," he also happened to speedily rehearse in his highly-educated mind, "*since semiotics is irreducible to them*."

H.S. Racket then went on, "but before we tackle that issue," and he joined his hands close to his chest as in an act of contrition, "please tell me more about my... acquaintance, if you can, because I believe that knowing those facts may help me make better sense of the sort of... *meaning* that I can unbury here, if I'm not being unfair in any way." He didn't really know why he had said that, but it all sounded quite reasonable, now that he had blurted those words. "*I'm curious*," Mr Racket realised, "*...maybe it's more than neurotic conduct, or boredom.*"

Cleanthes looked at him again, took a deep breath, and stated: "Power comes in many forms, my dear son, but your... acquaintance could see only one. He wanted *money*. Because with money you can buy influence, bribe judges, fund politicians, silence tongues, launch mud-slinging, hire assassins..."—"*assassins?*," Mr Racket wondered, "*and I'm the melodramatic one!*"—"... and commit all sorts of crimes, unpunished."

"What other forms of power are you thinking of?," the dramatist then asked the funny-looking cleric, who listed, without having to think about it, a fairly convincing litany of suitable candidates: "stamina, ingenuity, charisma, youth, fierceness, beauty, dexterity, good health, seductiveness, strength, wisdom, agility, intuitiveness, speed, intelligence, maturity, eloquence, good humour, patience, will-power, nobility, determination, virtue, steady luck, joviality, good taste... and exquisite food-making." "*Impressive!*," thought H.S. Racket.

"Your fr... acquaintance was *sick*, dear son," added Cleanthes, "and I do hope that, if he can really avoid damnation, he then may find a path to redeem himself, to *cure* himself... No matter how unlikely, there may be a chance for redemption and healing at some point for all of us, hence even for people like him, if not *especially* for people like him: The more diseased you are, the more urgently you need your medication!" After proffering which, the *empireocatcher* covered his face with both hands, as though contemplating some profound mystical truth. He looked convincing, even if a tad silly. Perhaps, that's wisdom too: It looks silly, yet it isn't.

§5 Mr Racket was strangely moved by that brief verbal exchange. He didn't expect to find anything of any real value in that bizarre place. He approached the white plastic bench and sat on it, right beside one of the two extravagant priestesses. "*Pretty, yes, and smells nice,*" he swiftly processed in his mind, unprompted. The swanky and curvy female friend of the blessed *empireum* put an arm around his shoulder, like a sister or a good friend would do. Mr Racket liked that. He had needed it for some time—and it's been said that to be human is to be sensitive.

"Imagine things are different, and you will live in a different world, because the world is in your mind," she whispered in his ear. He didn't feel like puking at all, H.S. Racket came to realise, to his pleasant surprise. He hadn't unearthed any rare joys in that unconventional church yet, nor any divine elation or sublime ecstasy. But there was some *warmth*. A warmth that he had known before. And it wasn't difficult for him to identify when, where, or with whom. That warmth was still available to him: He had just forgotten to approach it for a while.

Basically, Mr Racket started feeling excited at the notion of going back home, where he knew that he would meet, once again and as on countless days before that one, his long-time partner and wife, Stella. "*The woman that the annoying blind dodo wouldn't stop talking about,*" he briefly cogitated, "my *woman!*." "Ah, women! A man's blessing, or curse, depending on where *he* is along his journey," his father had once said to him. His father may well have been right on that delicate matter, H.S. Racket now realised in his own mature years, "*as usual.*"

"We never stop growing, hence we never stop feeling growing pains," the other *pirocastress* asserted. *"How do they come up with this stuff,"* he thought, *"… I might use it in a play…"* And then he wondered: *"Is she reading… my mind? Weird…"* "Tell us about the woman whom you love, dear son," she continued. "Yes, enlighten us!," added the other glittering vestal. Cleanthes came near and stood there, close to him, smiling and ready to listen.

§6 "What can I say… Stella and I… we go back a long way. We met in high school, of all places… And we've been together ever since. She was, she is, kind. I was… mesmerised by her from the very beginning. She was beautiful, of course, and she will always be; but she was also… *so* clever, and *so* good, you know? Morally good, with good values, good… traits of character and… *inclinations*, for lack of better words. And she had, and has, a fantastic, caustic sense of humour: The more she loves someone, the more savagely she bites them!

"Don't get me wrong. She's no saint. Nobody is. Who's perfect? Besides… were I to tell you what she did for a living, you wouldn't believe me… You see… For a good few years… Well, that was a long time ago. It doesn't really matter. It never mattered. Not much. Or, maybe, you see… since I'm an artist, a playwright… The fact that she was alternative, unconventional, brave, courageous… that she was *herself*, yes, above all… She was and is and has always been *herself*, like no other person I've ever met… She's always been like… water. Yes, water!

"Also, Stella taught me the meaning of joyfulness, even during periods of financial difficulty or personal stress… She taught me the meaning of generosity… generosity of spirit. Whenever I was having a hard time, fighting against my own demons, my… depressions… Well, she was *there* for me. She helped me to walk again. She saved my life. And why? Why, I sometimes wonder, honestly… Why would such a marvellous being spend her time and energy helping someone like me, so imperfect, so pathetic, so pointless, so… ridiculous?

Act Three

"Above all, Stella taught me the meaning of *innocence*. Yes, in spite of what superficial people and right-thinking conformists may say, *she* is the most innocent person that I have met in my life. Innocent, yes! Innocent in her instincts, innocent in her dispositions, innocent in her actions. Never lying, never. Not to others, not to herself. Her innocence made me realise how narrow-minded *I* was. An arrogant young man who thought he knew everything! How stupid of me! Although learning that other people may understand things better than you is something hard to swallow for any person, especially when you're young... Stella helped me to do that.

"And then all the small, pretty, funny, *meaningful* things about her... I don't know anyone else who would listen primarily to Varèse, Ligeti, Nono, and Bulgarian chalga. Or that would play and dance at home some silly K-pop routine! Or... or, her... well, her complete inability to do anything useful in the kitchen. I am the cook at home. Not because I'm any good, but because she would burn down the whole place, if you left her unattended in the kitchen!

"Now, I must be completely honest with you: Stella would listen occasionally to other music, including Baroque opera, which is *my* favourite genre. However, she would never come to the opera house with me. She said, and she still maintains, that she's... *scared* of it, which is an unusual thing for anyone to say, but especially for her, because she doesn't seem to be afraid of anything... Still, even in these odd moments, or probably because of them too, she was... she has been... so, so... so extraordinary, and so sweet, and so special, and... lovable..."

§7 Mr Racket *loved* Stella. Cleanthes and his two flashy assistants could read it on his face, if not in his mind. "Love others as yourself," Cleanthes said. "It's not original, but is still good." He smiled. "Son," he said to H.S. Racket, "you love your wife. Don't forget to love yourself as well. She does. Why shouldn't you do the same thing?," and he continued: "Far too often we are imprisoned by our own constructions, our thoughts, our preconceptions. They are the given checkerboard of the world, and the world is in bad hands, very bad hands, for the most part... Money, money, money... The calculating mentality that forces you to use people as tools, means to an end, even those whom you love most and are closest to you. How cruel! How stupid! And the surest way to forget how to cultivate humility and selfless generosity: Wisdom's death!"

"*Heavy-handed,*" H.S. Racket judged. Then, he stood up and, without saying anything, he hugged the short, quirky, and rarely-bearded celebrant. The two of them allowed that male embrace to continue for a long while, until one of the *pirocastresses* asked: "Hey, can we join in?" "Of course," said Cleanthes. "Of course," Mr Racket echoed him, "*and yes, please, sister!,*" he chanced upon as a genuine, exuberant, and totally-unrehearsed enthusiastic notion which had popped up inside his brain as soon as the twinkling priestess had begun signalling in a tacit way that she was positively interested in moving in his direction. "*Why's there always so direct a communication line between my brain and my dick?,*" Mr Racket wondered.

As way-out as it may have looked to an external observer, that glimmering four-people embrace filled Mr Racket's heart with cheerfulness and a renewed sense of purpose. Above all, he was ready to go home. "Aren't you going to stay for the evening rites, dear son?," Cleanthes asked him, when he noticed that the unexpected pilgrim was now on the verge of leaving those somewhat desolate yet surprisingly welcoming premises, "brother Florian will be playing for us," the *empireocatcher* added—and smiled affectionately with his entire face, hands, arms, belly and... large body. "No, father," H.S. Racket replied in a courteous, grateful, yet very firm manner, "thank you for everything. Truly. But I must go. I think I've just had a *revelation.*"

Act Three

XLIX – Deflation[282]

§1 Tom had been at Mass. He went every Sunday: An old habit from his Coptic childhood. He wasn't really sure that he believed in any of that mumbo-jumbo, especially all the stuff that you recite in the credo, but he liked the cheer and the chats after Mass. Everybody would gather, have coffee, eat some cake, and talk plenty of lively and funny rubbish. It was sweet, warm, welcoming. It was a vibrant community, mixing people coming from different countries, ethnic backgrounds, educational levels, professional paths… It was like the cosmos condensed into a parish hall, where all ways of life and possible personalities met one another, and found ways to be nice, sociable, kind, charitable, and even generous and friendly.

But that was *that*. Tom had an appointment *after* Mass. He didn't want to be late. Lonely and fairly well-off, his old Chinese teacher had told him of a special place which Tom-the-wealthy-bachelor might want to visit and, perchance, become a *regular* visitor of. A sort of secret association of like-minded aesthetes: "An exclusive and classy *club privé*," as Tom's kind, polite, and very reserved East-Asian teacher had positively described it.

"*Why not?*," Tom thought. "*It could be fun*," he speculated, "*in one way or another.*" Another way to explore humanity, himself, and hedonic pleasure—if all went well, that is, and the place wasn't just chock-a-block with old creeps and sickly prostitutes. Tom was in no mood for anything seedy and disgusting. He had *class*. He had *money*. He had *taste*. And his old Oriental teacher seemed the kind of man who knew what he was talking about.

It was a rainy afternoon. "*Better indoors than outdoors*," Tom concluded. He reached *the* special place, knocked on the door in the way the old instructor had told him to do, and was allowed inside. Albeit dimly-lit, the club did look classy: Antique furniture, late-

---

[282] The wind erodes the soil… If lewd topics unnerve you, even if humorous and fictional, then skip this chapter altogether.

Baroque and rococo paintings, leather-bound books on mahogany shelves, enormous Persian carpets, crystal chandeliers, crimson velvet sofas, the best Scotch readily available at the bar... Wow!

This was really an élite and probably expensive club to join. "*If its members are half as well-sorted and good-looking as the ambience is... Well, it may be worth investing some money in it,*" Tom conceded, whilst a measure of hopeful sensuality started taking root inside him.[283]

§2 "Welcome," a high tenor voice uttered, "we've been expecting you."

"Have you?," blurted Tom, instinctively—and more than a lick defensively.

"Oh yes, we have indeed," pointed out a not-so-tall, rather-robust, finely-dressed, and outmodedly-polite middle-aged gentleman, who smiled almost reverently at Tom: "We always know who our potential... members can be. Mr C told us everything about you."

"Mr C?," Tom queried, a bit nervous.

"Yes," replied the courteous man, "Mr C, your teacher... We all have... abbreviated monikers in this club... Tradition, you know? It's important to us."

"I understand," whispered Tom, and nodded delicately, almost apologetically.

"You shall be *Mr T*, for now and,... if you join us... and, that is,... if you are accepted, onwards too..." the gentleman elucidated, with a well-mannered but resolved intonation.

"*Accepted...?*," emphasised Mr T, genuinely puzzled.

"Yes," the refined gentleman asserted in a confident manner, "*accepted*. You know: Medical certificates, financial viability, non-disclosure agreements, further letters of recommendation... Bureaucracy!," he concisely specified, "you can't escape it, not even here," and he graced Mr T with another more-than-friendly smile.

"Of course!," observed Mr T, whose doubts had been so swiftly cleared, "and you..."

---

[283] Fleetingly, Tom recalled in his mind a poem by D'Annunzio.

"Mr W," he promptly answered, "at your service," and smiled again, endearingly.

"Mr W?," Mr T repeated, to make sure that he had actually caught that man's moniker.

"Yes, Mr W," the obsequious gentleman confirmed. That's who he was, apparently.

"Well… It's a pleasure to make your acquaintance, Mr… W!," said Mr T, feeling reassured, and with growing eagerness and fascination about that peculiar place.

"Likewise," replied Mr W, who bowed towards Mr T, most politely. "Shall we?," he added, pointing towards the long corridor to his right, "we all call it 'Pauliska'," he purred.

"Of course," commented inanely Mr T, not knowing what to think of that feminine denomination. "Show the way, please," he then correctly pleaded, yet with more than merely a tinge of incipient lust mixing with his intense, gripping, expanding curiosity about… Pauliska.

§3 "The greatest happiness for the greatest number… of members," Mr W said, grinning a little, while starting the guided tour of that mysterious place, "that's our… motto, Mr T."

"Interesting," Mr T muttered, a little uncertain about the motto itself.

The female-named corridor was so long that Mr T couldn't see the end of it. The apposite faint illumination had something to do with that optical phenomenon. There were doors and additional corridors showing up discreetly, almost startingly at times, to both their right and left, as they walked together, very slowly, and descended into the secret bowels of the club.

"All members are sworn to secrecy," Mr W whispered, "obviously."

"Obviously," repeated Mr T.

"Here's our first stop," murmured Mr W, while gently opening an unpretentious little door: "It is our… filling station."

Mr T looked around the glistening and beautifully-decorated room. Once again, he was taken aback by the antique furniture, the elaborate small tables, the valuable *objets d'art*…

"Original," interjected Mr W, "French, mostly from around the blessed year 1767…"

"Remarkable!," exclaimed Mr T.

"We are quite proud of it, to be perfectly candid with you, quite proud…," said Mr W, communicating a dab of self-effacing modesty and a concomitant sense of accomplishment.

On the many diminutive yet venerable artisanal miracles of gilded ebony scattered around the room, there stood golden and silver cups of many different sizes and shapes. All of them were gorgeously decorated: "*Superior period pieces!*," Mr T thought, visibly intrigued.

"We also have a Cellini's pre-baronial bowl…," breathed excitedly Mr W.

Mr T looked at Mr W. "*Cellini!*," the former considered in his mind, speechless.

"Please," continued Mr W, "my dear Mr T, do inspect the cups."

Mr T did as prompted. He was even more surprised, and impressed. Each cup contained a different type of… drug. Yes, drug. Not only illegal ones, but also perfectly legal drugs, which any physician or, more rarely, even some specially-qualified orthodontist could prescribe.

Mr T looked again at Mr W, almost dumbstruck.

"*Stimulants*," explained Mr W, "to make sure that our members can extract as much satisfaction as possible from the excitements, events, encounters, soirées, and many other… carnal joys and spiritually-enriching opportunities that our exclusive club so liberally provides."

"Stimulants?," wondered Mr T, in a very soft tone of voice, while being led by Mr W to sample a whiff of a particular white powder, which was not entirely new to Mr T.

"Obviously," replied Mr W, while straightening a small silver teaspoon.

"Obviously," echoed him Mr T, robotically.

Act Three

§4   Mr W and Mr T left that exquisite room filled with purported stimulants, and began walking together, once more, along… Pauliska, the main corridor.

"How… Where… You know, you… gather all those…," stuttered Mr T, still astonished by the unusual, lavish, and penally-indictable display that he had just witnessed.

Mr W beamed, rather graciously, and stated: "Well, Mr T, since we are all sworn to secrecy… Let me just say that a… highly-qualified Mx S makes sure that we receive only the best and safest… stimulants… in exchange for a hefty discount on the membership fees."

"Fascinating," noted Mr T.

"Indeed," concurred Mr W, clasping his hands with candid enthusiasm and looking most delighted about the whole situation: He had probably judged that he was doing a good job.

A few seconds later, Mr T was being introduced to a different room, and a noisy alcove.

"Please," proffered Mr W, beautifully blending politeness with directness.

"Oh!," was all that Mr T could articulate.

"Two of our… loveliest members," Mr W asserted, in a slightly unctuous tone.

"Who…," mumbled Mr T, with an evident interrogative expression on his face.

"Mr G and Ms C," replied tersely Mr W.

"I see…," said Mr T, who had been presented with the torrid spectacle of two bodies—a muscular young male body and a not-so-fit female one—engaging in a loud, unrestrained, and remarkably athletic act of sensuous posterior entanglement. The elderly woman was on all four, spreading her legs and buttocks as much as she was capable of, shouting and howling aloud like a crazed and goatish gothic werewolf, while the much-younger, well-built, strong man pounded her with rhythmic precision, holding a full set of dentures in his left hand, and perspired in so profuse a quantity that he reminded Mr T of the imposing Oceanus in the Trevi fountain.

"Ms C is our oldest member," Mr W clarified, "a loving and lovely woman. Always very… charitable. Generous. Giving, almost. Skilled like no one else in the arts of oral… encouragement… And eager, most eager. Almost insatiable… A true force of nature!"

"And… Mr G?," asked Mr T, his voice trembling a little.

"A young… member," Mr W stated, "reliable, strong, virile… and loyal, to the utmost!"

"The utmost?," uttered Mr T, baffled by that description.

"Obviously," enunciated Mr W, stressing that particular point by lifting both eyebrows.

"Obviously," repeated mechanically Mr T.

"Can I share a little, innocent secret with you?," inquired politely Mr W, who was starting to grow fond of Mr T, possibly because of the latter's endearing insecurities.

"… Of course," replied Mr T, a touch hesitant at that point.

"Ms C is… well, that attractive and selfless female bundle of passionate love and sexual proficiency is…," and he lowered his voice, "my mother-in-law! … Would you *believe* it?," emphasised Mr W, pointing gently towards the hazardous terrain of tonal irony.

"Mother… in law?," queried Mr T, genuinely puzzled by that revelation.

"Mother-in-law," repeated calmly Mr W.

"And do you ever…," inquired Mr T, who had suddenly become quite curious about that atypical family arrangement.

"Oh no, never!," answered promptly Mr W, "I am in charge of the place, you see, but I don't partake in its… cornucopia of fleshly amusements."

"Don't you… Ever…?," continued Mr T, quite incredulous, and a dash disappointed.

"No, sir. I just work here," Mr W cut him short.

§5 As the guided visit proceeded farther into the club's ornate and absorbing architectural intestines, Mr T was shown an array of "earthly delights," as Mr W immodestly described them. A brief and partial summary may give the idea of what these earthly delights consisted in.

Act Three

A stunning middle-aged brunette, called "Ms I," was happily defecating onto several naked club members, all meticulously tied to the cold, hard, chequered granite floor. Their mouths agape, they awaited eagerly the disturbing meal that she was going to provide to each and every one of them, controlling with great skill her anus' tight, finely-tuned muscles. As Mr T was told, Ms I started engaging in that positively outgoing erotic practice after going through an acrimoniously negative divorce; "and she never misses!," Mr T was also duly and somewhat smugly informed by Mr W, who added: "Coprophagous individuals tend to be demandingly fastidious." "... *No shit!*," Mr T couldn't avoid remarking in the intimate, secluded chamber of his own mind, while also trying to ignore the dubious bouquet pervading that 'delightful' room.

A masked, skinny old man, possibly of Asian origin, was lying prone on a monumental bed, while about a dozen young women, all of Asian origin, took turns fisting him with gusto and, one should add, the appropriate degree of penetrating care. The man didn't emit any sound, not even the faintest moan, whereas the bubbly Asian girls giggled and chatted amiably among themselves, as though they were but a group of schoolgirls spending an afternoon at the rides. Mr T forgot to ask Mr W what the old man's moniker was. Mr T was somewhat distracted. That scene was highly unusual and... as his inner 15-year-old self comically suggested, *"real badass!."* Mr T smiled at his own joke—*en passant*, of course, but also with honest admiration for the old man's silent stoicism, which rivalled the mythical composure of the ancient sages.

A middle-aged lady, to whom Mr W referred reverently as "Ms F," stood on a golden chair or makeshift throne, and, from up there, screamed and urinated abundantly over a small crowd of stylishly-clad, fake-tan-sprayed, well-combed, much-much-younger males. As Mr W explained, and probably recited from memory at one point: "Ms F considers her golden showers a theo-political statement. She argues that her bodily humours evoke the life-giving powers of the Great Mother and remind all men, but especially the younger and handsomer ones whom she so greatly favours, of their natural *inferior* status, because all men were... created by Nature Herself, the motherly She-Goddess, in order to provide and purvey for, protect, perpetuate, pleasure, pamper, and play second fiddle to the world's women, who are the true daughters and mystical sisters of Nature Herself, the motherly She-Goddess," and so did Mr W exhale with relief. "... *What a lot of pish!*," Mr T privately observed.

Another chamber was being used by a grinning short woman wearing a full-body, head-covering, leather-and-latex catsuit and some ludicrously-elevated platform-shoes—"Ms S," Mr W commented, "a gifted PhD student in zoodermic grafting... and our *best* dominatrix"—and two naked men, who were ardently receiving a furious thrashing. Their backs and buttocks were covered in red marks from the lashes which they had so delightfully suffered, whereas their shaved chests were covered in blood and, as Mr W elucidated, Ms S's saliva, which the two "slaves" regarded as some kind of "sacred humour." "The two gentlemen are Mr E and... well, Mr X, let's call him that," chuckled briefly and rather tactfully Mr W, somehow amused by his own irresistible wit: "The former... well, a former military man and...," Mr W then breathed out his comments in a hardly-audible tone of voice, "the latter, ... a famous banker, and... tax fraudster!." Mr W's eyes were gleaming wildly and vividly with abandoned glee: "He's our *trusted* accountant," he also noted. "... *You bet!*," Tom jibed within himself.

A medium-sized alcove hosted an elderly man, quite chubby, and with the most peculiar orange-hued hair. He stood alone in front of a tall mirror, gazing at himself, and masturbating frantically. "Mr D," said Mr W, "our wealthiest patron... And former president. God bless him! God bless us all!." Mr T didn't know what to think or say of that unexpected spectacle. Was it a form of intellectual reflection? Or was it just an erotic practice? What was happening? And what was that carroty-headed wanker thinking about? Was there anything special going on inside his cranium? Mr T would have very much liked asking Mr D about that perplexing solo action, but he correctly concluded that *that* moment was probably not the most propitious. Mr D would have had to be interrupted. That wouldn't be nice. Mr T hated being indelicate.

Act Three

A separate locale, which could only be reached by treading carefully along a lengthy, dark, narrow, twisty side-corridor for quite some time, was populated by... farm animals. It was a stunningly large and noisy chamber. Probably the biggest that Mr T had visited or seen up to that point. Hay, grass, pebbles, dirt, large tubs filled with water, corn, acorns, seeds, pellets and turds of many different shapes and sizes were scattered all over the marble floor. Portraits of one and the same English gentleman abounded on the walls. One in particular caught Mr T's probing eye, since it depicted that gentleman sitting in a wheelchair with a hat on his head and... another head... lying squint on a plate placed between the legs! As odd as it sounds, that sight was familiar to Mr T. "This paradisiac sanctuary is for hardcore utilitarians," Mr W explained.

§6 It took Tom some time to get used once more to the bright light of the sun, even if it was already the late afternoon. Almost evening, in fact. Outside the exclusive private club, the world was going on as usual, apparently unaffected. Tom didn't know what to think. It had certainly been an unusual and interesting experience. Humankind can be diverse. Very diverse.

All of a sudden, a small door screeched open. Tom took instinctively cover behind a parked car: It was an old Renault Kangoo. Mr G, Ms C, Ms I, Ms F, Ms S, Mr E, Mr X, Mr D, the previously-garrulous Asian girls, and a few furry specimens from the hardcore utilitarians' pleasure-maximising menagerie were exiting the club's well-disguised premises. Tom caught the face of a mere handful of those exiting people, while ignoring altogether the much-noisier farm animals. Perhaps, it wasn't rationally advantageous for him to do that then. Undoubtedly, he wasn't consciously discriminating against those compliant, hardworking quadrupeds.

"They all seem wabbit, but..." Tom reflected, "... almost flustered and... almost... sad."

Tom started walking back to his place. The sun was definitely setting. The air looked suspiciously pinkish—a sign of poisonous contamination. Tom looked pensive. He *was* pensive. He knew how important it is to have habits that can give you a kick, or at least the memory of a kick. At the same time, his old Chinese teacher had once said to him: "Ethics and aesthetics never coincide." Tom was starting to understand the meaning of those words—for words have *many* different meanings. Those meanings which we take most seriously give shape to the world that we indwell, for better or for worse. But who decides which is which? And why?

Extrusion By Two Puppets[284]

Judy: What are you piling up there?
Punch: All the bad things.
Judy: "Bad?"
Punch: Worries, fears, traumas, wounds, heartaches, irritations, paranoias, sasses, irritations, guff, jingoisms, arrows…
Judy: It looks like you've got plenty of those… "things"!
Punch: I've lived a fairly long life…
Judy: So have I! I'm not… ignorant about that.
Punch: …and I've been trying to be a good, capable, moral, Kantian person…
Judy: So have I! And without wearing any veil!
Punch: …but, objectively, I made a terrible mistake!
Judy: Really? What mistake was that?
Punch: I became *serious*.
Judy: Is that serious?
Punch: Very much so.
Judy: Why? I wouldn't have counted it as much of a… principle.
Punch: Because if you get seriously serious, then you laugh far, far too little.
Judy: Is that… serious too?
Punch: Oh yes!
Judy: Cripes! I might well be shafted!

---

[284] Readers affected by pupaphobia or generally unnerved by puppets may wish to skip this chapter.

Act Three

Punch: I know... Scary, isn't it? It's like... skipping desserts. Unconscionable!

Judy: Is there... a cure?

Punch: Yes, and a natural one to boot: *Humour*.

Judy: Like... staying hydrated?

Punch: It's the same principle, basically. Fairly neutral, right?

Judy: Is it... easy? You know... like being an egoist, or envying others?

Punch: No, not like that. On reflection, it's *less* easy than I expected.

Judy: Why?

Punch: Everyone around me wants me to be... serious.

Judy: Do they?

Punch: Yes. Laughing is allowed only on special occasions. Lest you're an outlaw!

Judy: "Allowed?"

Punch: Yes. Seriousness is their fundamental idea, not being humorous!

Judy: No, I meant... do you really need their permission?

Punch: Yep. It's like having... puppeteers: If you disobey, they shame you into guilt.

Judy: Did you... sign some contract with them?

Punch: Implicitly.

Judy: What does that mean?

Punch: It is a... social contract. A kind of waltzing to be done by standing still.

Judy: That's quite... an original position to take!

Punch: It's burdensome, to be frank... Yet, we all do it!

Judy: *Implicitly*: I can see how that happens... It's some seriously nasty shite!

Punch: So much intolerance: Where's the individuality that we were told about? And the freedom?

Judy: I'm so sorry for you... And for us all! It's... unjust.

Punch: So much repression: Where's the happiness that we were promised? And the authenticity?

Judy: I'm so sorry for you... And for us all! It's... unlucky.

Punch: You know what we ought to do, love?
Judy: What, dear?
Punch: Go to a puppet show! There may be more utility in it. Or, at least, some fun!

L – Wrangled[285]

One Act:
• *Young Dora D.D. Symonds, sister of Monica, Michelle, and Anita*
• *A loving parent of the sisters*

Dora: (*angry, all the time*) No respect! That's what it is, mum. No respect at all! None. For nobody. Not for you, not for dad, not for me, not for her sisters, not for herself, and not for *women*!

Parent: (*sits in the dak and speaks gently, except for the last line*) I understand, darling, but you see…

D: Read! Read it! Read the filth my sister has just published! Filth! Filth! … I'm telling you, mum. Nothing but filth! Ah! … Read the horrible garbage she's written, mum, read! IH!

P: I understand, darling, but you see…

D: It's nothing but an embarrassment for herself, me, my sisters, our family, you, and *all* women in the world! All of them! Shame, shame, shame! Mum! Nothing but shame! OH!

P: I understand, darling, but you see…

---

[285] This family provides familiar parody, which is recommended to philosophers.

Act Three

D: Listen to her nonsense! Just because she knows foreign languages she thinks she's *intelligent*! Mum! And don't you try to defend her! Rather, find a place where we can burn this filth. AH!

P: I understand, darling, but you see…

D: (*reads from a small piece of paper*) *Evviva il Re di Francia / colpito da una lancia / lamenta il mal di pancia / e accusa un'arancia* … What sort of stupid idiocy is this? Eh, mum? Aren't you ashamed of your daughter? And this one here: *Se sei davver cretino / non leggi l'Aretino.* Ah? Mum!? Don't you realise that this is *cultural appropriation*, among other things!? EH!?

P: I understand, darling, but you see…

D: (*reads from a small piece of paper*) And then there's this one: *Si vous aimez beaucoup le poisson / faire très attention au mercure / Préserfatifs et du bon ton / Et assurez-vous que soit dur!* UH!

P: I understand, darling, but you see…

D: She's intolerable, mum! She's immature, childish! She's got *straw* in her skull! Straw, straw, straw! And all this *sex* she's writing about! Mum, you must do something! It's obscene, outrageous, and… oppressive! She identifies with the aggressor! It's the gaze in the mirror, mum: The evil gaze, the male gaze! And She's not even 21: Her brain's not fully formed yet!

P: I understand, darling, but you see…

D: Listen to this one (*reads from an enormous piece of paper*): "Philosophy for Wankers. Chapter 1. Oh My God! On the Judeo-Christian tradition and its Islamic continuation" … Blasphemous, even… Disrespectful! … Mum! "Chapter 2. The Biblical Story: Onan and the Church Fathers. Snippets of Origen in particular." What's that about? Ah? Isn't that transphobia? And then "Chapter

3. St Thomas' Lists of Sins and St Francis' Animal Love." Ah! ... Speciesism!

P: I understand, darling, but you see...

D: (*continues*) ... "Chapter 4. How the Enlightenment Went Wrong: You Kant!" Ah! How does she dare? And she thinks she's *clever*! Mum! She thinks she's being... blooming *clever*!

P: I understand, darling, but you see...

D: (*continues*) ... "Chapter 5. Tissot: Watch Your Wrist! Chapter 6. Hillman's Pink Madness. Chapter 7. The US Evangelicals & Sex-Negative Feminism: Inane Bedfellows." (*even more furious*) How does she dare? How, mum, how!?! She justifies misogyny, patriarchy, and sexism! I'm telling you! ... She's... she's... she's... she's a *turncoat*! That's what she is, mum. A *turncoat*! ... Mum! Why don't you ever say anything to her? Eh!? You must stop her!

P: I understand, darling, but you see...

D: (*continues*) ... "Chapter 8. Be Fruitful and Multiply. Reforming Capitalism." What's this got to do with anything? Ah? You see, mum... She's not that intelligent, I'm telling you! ... And then this: "Chapter 9. Weber's Protestant Ethics. What's there to protest about?" ... Ah? Mum!?

P: I understand, darling, but you see...

D: (*continues*) ... "Chapter 10. A Matter of Insults: Wanker, tosser, jerkoff, pickle tickler, prick, dick, dickhead, and fingerer." (*more quietly*) ... At least she didn't use the c-word... "Chapter 11. Horkheimer and Adorno on Sade's Juliette." ... Who the heck is this Juliette, mum, a new friend of hers? I bet she is a little sllll... oppy writer like herself! ... *Mum*!

Act Three

P: I understand, darling, but you see…

D: (*continues*) … "Chapter 12. Angela Carter's New Woman." … Who's that, ah? … "Chapter 13. For-profit Addiction or Addictionology?" More fancy words! *Madness*, mum! Madness! Ah!?

P: I understand, darling, but you see…

D: (*continues*) … "Chapter 14. Inside the Barrell. Diogenes is going solo," duh? … "Chapter 15. Constipated and In the Huff. The anal phase of Martin Luther. Chapter 16. Feminist Filljoys. Betty Dodson & Ellen Willis Be Blessed." … How can she write this stuff, mum. *How*? She'll end up using forbidden words!

P: I understand, darling, but you see…

D: And what is this, mum? (*reads from another small piece of paper*) Listen: "You can take a horse to the well, but you can't make it drink. You can take two horses to the well, but you can't make them drink. You can take three horses… and have a circus!" … What's this nonsense, ah? …

P: I understand, darling, but you see…

D: (*continues*) …"Your sick is my slick," "If you're smug and prissy, you want smut and pussy," "Cunts without cocks are empty, cocks without cunts are blind," "Towering neo-Victorians need evictions from their very old tower." Or, "You say it's sick? So do I!" … The insolence, mum! Though at least she isn't a man…

P: I understand, darling, but you see…

D: (*continues*) And this one, mum: "Buridan's ass is nothing compared to mine." … What is this nonsense? Ah? … And this endless talk of... rear ends, backsides, ... posteriors! What's that about? She is *sick*, mum, I'm telling you. Sick, sick, sick... *and* stupid! Sick and stupid!

P: I understand, darling, but you see...

D: I can't take it anymore! As if *I* weren't clever enough... She never listens to me! Never! She just laughs at me and walks away! Why does she treat me like that? And you don't say anything, mum! Never! Why do *you* treat me like that? Ah? ... Why do you *all* treat me like that, mum? Ah? ... Mum! It's just intolerable, mum! Intolerable! Eh!? Are you listening to me, mum!?

P: I understand, darling, but you see... I'M YOUR BLOODY FATHER!

Curtain.

LI – Tell 'Em All by Bedtime[286]

"Whe'e Mouse?," asked the little child.

"Mouse is...," tried to answer the mother, but she didn't complete the sentence. She didn't have any remaining strength. "Mouse," as the little child called her elder sister, had died of pneumonia four dark nights before that darker night. The mother had nothing left inside her grief-stricken spirit. She felt completely empty, gutted like a fish caught by a cruel angler—and not mercifully snuffed by a quick blow of the blade. She was drowning in the open air.

"Whe'e Mouse?," asked again the little child.

"Mouse is... not here," the mother replied.

"'Ayin'?," inquired the little child.

---

[286] Closure and closeness are open. If sad topics unnerve you, then skip this chapter altogether.

Act Three

"A....," went the mother, alarmed, but promptly grasped her child's meaning. "Yes, dear," she said. And so she started playing with her younger daughter, even if she felt like hanging both her daughter and herself in the small white bathroom, past the pale-green corridor. She had already made preparations to that end, right after discovering that her elder daughter would have never recovered from her illness.

The mother didn't know what they were doing. The little child did. They played. What the game was, it was a mystery to the mother. The little child knew it, however. The mother could only understand that it involved two potatoes, and that it had to take place on the kitchen floor and nowhere else. Only that particular floor would do, apparently.

Suddenly, as though out of nowhere, the little child started laughing. Gently at first, almost soundlessly; then slightly more audibly, gradually more and more so; hence almost violently, and finally in bursts and sputters of disorderly, unrestrained *joie de vivre*.

The mother looked at her little child. She listened to the child's laughter. Against all her expectations, and against her own conscious will, the mother started giggling, then guffawing, and eventually joined her little child into roaring, crying, and rolling together on the floor.

When they stopped, the mother embraced her little child and said to her: "I'm going to teach you a nice thing." And so she started reciting the few prayers that she still remembered from her own childhood. She prayed slowly, enunciating each word with the greatest care and clarity, and giving ample time to her younger and now sole daughter to make eager attempts at repeating those words after her. The words were new to the child, and difficult to repeat.

Somehow, Mouse seemed to be present in that cold kitchen, now —with the two of them, that is, and within her mother's heavy, sobbing, gasping heart: "*Are you there, Mouse?*"

LII – Looking for Something[288]

§1   Aristotle was surprised. His tasks had required less time than he expected. He was free to leave work. He left work. He went home. He expected his girlfriend to be there. He expected her to be waiting for him. He expected her to be happy to see him. They were happy together. They had been together for many years. They were going to get married. They planned to have children. He thought it natural to want to have children. He recalled Mary Poppins. He arrived. None of the three aforementioned expectations were met. His girlfriend was not there.

Aristotle was surprised. He thought about a probable alternative location. There could be several such locations. He considered them. He concluded that her girlfriend was likely to be at her most trusted girlfriend's place. He decided to go to hers. He wanted to surprise his girlfriend. He thought that doing so would be amusing. He liked seeing her laugh. He liked making her happy. He left his apartment. He walked for thirty-five minutes. The weather was bad. It rained. It was cold. He reached his destination. He buzzed the intercom. Nobody replied.

Aristotle was surprised. He buzzed again. Nobody replied. He looked at the intercom. The intercom was damaged. Green liquid oozed out of it. He checked the main entrance. It was open. He entered the building. He knew where his girlfriend's girlfriend lived. He walked upstairs. He got himself to the correct flat. The door was not shut. He heard noises. He became concerned. Robberies had taken place in that building. The neighbourhood had a bad reputation. He thought it wise to investigate. He entered. He peered. He listened. The noises grew louder.

---

[287] This fleuron is dedicated to Mouse's fictional yet fond memory.

[288] Good luck with that! Did you ask anyone for directions, or are you all alone?

Act Three

Aristotle was surprised. He was worried. He felt apprehensive. He approached the room whence the noises came. He looked inside. He saw his girlfriend. She was naked. She was on the bed. Her legs were spread wide open. A young man was penetrating her vagina. He was thrusting his penis inside and outside. He was doing that repeatedly. She was shaking. She was undulating. She was rocking. She was screaming. She was moaning. She was begging. She was asking for more. She was enjoying it. She loved it. Her facial expressions looked stupid. The penetrative process looked mechanical. The sight of it tore Aristotle's heart into pieces.

§2 Aristotle was surprised. He thought that his girlfriend was happy with him. He was happy with her. They had been together for a long time. He had always seen to her pleasure. He had never failed her. He had always done his duty. He had always made sure that she was more than satisfied. He had seen to her needs. He had been conscientious. He had been considerate. He had been caring. He had been kind. He had been affectionate. He had been attentive. He had been devoted. He had been loving. He had been betrayed. He had been betrayed.

Aristotle was surprised. He had been betrayed. He had been betrayed. He stood there awhile. The penetrative process still looked mechanical. Her facial expressions still looked stupid. She was still shaking. She was still undulating. She was still rocking. She was still screaming. She was still moaning. She was still begging. She was still asking for more. She was still enjoying it. She still loved it. The sight of it crushed the pieces of Aristotle's heart into dust.

Aristotle was surprised. He was startled. He was dismayed. He was disgusted. He was confounded. He was pained. He was hurt. He was bitter. He was jealous. He was enraged. He was furious. He was vengeful. He recalled *Othello*. But he valued her. He did not want to humiliate her. He loved her. He left without being heard. He walked around the building. He walked around the block. He walked around the city. He came back to his apartment three days later. He had not eaten. He had drunk water. He was sad. He did not greet his girlfriend. He grabbed few items from their bedroom. He left. He never returned.

§3 Aristotle was surprised. He had never thought before of suicide. Now he was thinking about it. He was doing so repeatedly. He was doing so mechanically. His facial expressions looked stupid. He recalled *Werther*. He recalled tragic films. He had watched a few of those in the recent past. He liked F.A.C. MacRunt's movies. They were unusual. They were profound. They were gripping. They were sad. They seemed close to real life. He now knew that they were so. He went to the pier. The sea was deep there. He filled his pockets with stones. He filled the inside of his clothes with bricks. He jumped into the water.

Aristotle was surprised. Because he woke up. He was lying on a beach. It was on the opposite side of the bay. He did not recall how he got there. He did not know why he was still alive. He was breathing. He could move. He could see the objects around him. He was not dead. There was a small cabin on the beach. He checked inside. The cabin was deserted. Three books, one net, one pot, one glass, and one silver cross were all the items that he found in the cabin. A brook ran nearby. The cabin had belonged to a hermit. Aristotle decided to become a hermit.

Aristotle was surprised. He thought it unnatural to live alone. He thought it unnatural not to have children. He changed his views. He realised that many paths of life are possible. He realised that many paths of life are natural. He himself had just taken a new path. He found it natural. He read the books. He meditated. He prayed. He caught fish. He boiled them. He ate them. He fetched water. He drank it. He slept. He repeated these actions for many years. He never did so mechanically. His facial expressions were not stupid. He was poor. He was content. His heart was never happier.

Act Three

LIII – Teller of the Flunkies[289]

One Act:
- *Young Anita B.A. Symonds, a barefoot child*
- *A ghost of a child, about the same age as Anita*

A very young Anita and a child's ghost converse—in a rather one-way manner, however.

Anita: (*annoyed*) I'm tired of you!

Ghost: (*inexpressive*) -

A: You follow me, *all* the time!

G: -

A: You never speak to me!

G: -

A: I don't even know your name!

G: -

A: You scare away my friends!

G: -

A: You never have tea with me!

---

[289] Don't be unduly afraid of friendly ghosts: They can lift the spirits.

G: -

A: You don't even leave me alone in the bathroom!

G: -

A: You are the first thing I see in the morning…

G: -

A: …and the last thing I see at night!

G: -

A: You don't tell me bedtime stories!

G: -

A: You never bring me presents!

G: -

A: You can't play any games!

G: -

A: You can't dance!

G: -

A: You can't sing!

G: -

A: You can't come up with funny stories!

Act Three

G: -

A: You can't come up with funny plays!

G: -

A: You can't act!

G: -

A: You can't make people laugh!

G: - (*the ghost turns towards the audience and makes a very silly face.*)

A: Now *you* go away!

G: -

A: Leave me alone!

G: -

A: I want to be with *my* friends!

G: -

A: Leave!

G: - (*The ghost leaves. Time elapses: Depending on the venue, between 20 and 60 seconds.*)

A: (*talking to herself*) My 'friends'... They *always* fight. They're *always* cruel. They *compete* all the time. Who's got the *most* chocolates? Who's got the *most* beautiful dress? Who's got the shini*est* shoes? Who got the *most* kisses from the prettiest boy?

Who got the *most* slaps from her mother? Who got the *most* slaps from her father? Who got the *most* slaps in total?

Anita looks sad. She pulls out a large multi-purpose Swiss-army pocket-knife and starts trimming her toenails. Time elapses (depending on the venue, between 20 and 120 seconds)

A: (*stops trimming, starts shouting*) Ghost! Come back! I'm sorry! *You* are my best friend!

The ghost comes back.

A: (*relieved*) Thank you! (*pause, goes back to trimming her toenails.*)

G: - 290

Curtain.

LIV – To Shout, To Shout, To Shout[291]

Zhang Juqian was in his office when he received a phone call. It was the worst phone call of his entire life. "Sir, there's been accident," it said, "please come to the corner between Jonas Passageway and Hobbes Alley. The police are already there." It was pretty clear who was involved in the accident. His beloved little rascal always went there to meet two of his best friends. They would go and play basketball at a nearby court. It wasn't a nice

---

[290] On a parallel ontological plane, the ghost kept wondering: 'Which eerie phantoms wrote these chapters?'

[291] How can there be worse? If sad topics unnerve you, then skip this chapter altogether.

Act Three

neighbourhood, but plenty of good people lived there. Good families. Families. Good.

Juqian took a cab. He never did it. He preferred buses. But he didn't own a motor. And he wanted to get *there* as quickly as possible. An ambulance was *there* already. Two or three police cars were *there* too. Juqian didn't stop to count them. The area had been cordoned off. A handful of passers-by were still loitering *there*, driven by morbid curiosity. Juqian signalled a policewoman with a tense yet solid bow of his head. She understood immediately who he was, and let him through. He saw his son, who was lying on the ground. Juqian almost fainted.

"A freak accident," said another policewoman, "I'm so sorry…" Juqian was already kneeling beside his silent, beloved little rascal—his one and only son. The ground was cold and hard. Juqian looked up and stared at the police officer, as if it was still possible to do something, or at least get an explanation, a means of consolation. She was pale. "That marble slab fell from the sky, literally…," she said, mournfully, "an abandoned apartment. We are trying to trace the last owner's name … these old buildings are falling apart. Crumbling… I'm so sorry."

"Can't he… ?," uttered Juqian, begging that very kind and obviously professional police lady for something which they both knew couldn't be done. The impossible is beyond the reach of any and every human being. Not even kind and professional police officers can reach it. "I'm so sorry," she repeated, "the doctor said that he's got very few minutes left, and that if we moved your son's injured body… so severely… he's just too severely…," and she didn't complete her sentence. There was no need for that. Juqian understood. He nodded, his heart crushed like his son's poor bones and poorer organs. The policewoman caught Juqian's sombre nod, and she indicated it by closing her eyes for a couple of seconds. No more words were exchanged.

Juqian stared back at his son's mangled, smashed, devastated body. Blood and guts were everywhere. The boy was still breathing, just barely, but less and less frequently. Overwhelmed by powerful grief and irrational guilt, Juqian started crying: "Why me? What did

I do? Why, why? ... My sweet boy ... My good, sweet boy!." Juqian took one of his son's scrawny hands between his own shaking hands. "My boy... My good, sweet boy...," and then Juqian started yelling in his mother tongue, which, after so many years in his adoptive country, he used exclusively at work—and which Juqian had never taught to his dear boy. The weeping teacher felt suddenly very remorseful about that. And so Juqian started sobbing even more bitterly.

Juqian heard a faint sound. His boy had opened his eyes. Those eyes were looking fixedly at Juqian. They were good, calm, sweet eyes from another world. His son barely moved his blood-stained, thin lips. He wanted to reassure his desperate father: "Daddy, no... I'll be an angel." Having said that, the boy died, quietly, in his father's trembling arms.

[292]

LV – Eleventh Day of March[293]

As recorded by the investigating commissioner:

"Our boss never came to the canteen with us. Never. Not once in all these years. She thought that her subordinates had to be kept at... a safe distance. Something like that... No mixing. No fraternising. 'I'm in charge and you're my minion,' that's the type of feeling you got from her. Very straightforward. 'It's good for business,' she used to say. Clear. Honest. Direct. No bullshit. 'That's me and that's you,' sort-of-thing... Teutonic... Efficient... Task-oriented!

"She would wait for everybody else to be done, and then she would eat and check her phone in peace and quiet. I didn't know her well, even if I've been working here for years. As I said, there wasn't

---

[292] This fleuron is dedicated to the memory of Juqian's child. He too, like Mouse, was innocent at heart.

[293] Mysteries are at work, daily. Miracles are at play, weekly. (**Punch**: You're adorable. **Judy**: So are you, love)

Act Three

any mixing. No fraternising. She liked it that way. And who are we, the workers, to complain about that? A wrong look, a bad word, a silly joke and... You know, you find yourself out on the street and have no, no bread for your kids. It can take just an instant!

"That day, I remember it... the 11th of this month... she just did the usual things. After we were done, she went down to eat all by herself and check her phone... We went back... There was a lot of stuff to do that day. What a day! The machinery was going hard, boom-boom-boom, and long, long hours... That way since morning: Boom-boom-boom! All day long. You couldn't hear much, you know? All that noise: Boom-boom-boom! That's why we wear ear defenders, you know? Or you go completely deaf after just two days that you've been working here!

"What I think... is that she chocked on that chicken bone they talked about, just like the boys who found her keep repeating. Bones... They've been so scared... You should have seen them when they came up screaming and telling us what they'd found. *Who* they'd found! Dead. ... Dead! ... Shock. Total shock. Shaking... That's what it was for them: A real shock. But you know, she was *alone* down there. Must have chocked on that bloody bone. Maybe gasped for air, asked for help... But she was alone. And all that noise... Alone. Dying... Nobody could hear her screams down there... She was alone. Everybody was back to work... Horrible.

"Some people around here say that she deserved it. 'Justice,' they say... Yes, *justice*. Poetic or Divine. You know, they say she was a heartless... bitch—I apologise for using this word, but that's what they call her... I mean, she was a hard woman. Hard. Really. The toughest boss I've had in my life. Bloody tough... *Cruel*, at times, you know... without any good reason. Just like that... Maybe 'cos she could... Sometimes, you, you can and so... You just give in... Don't all people have demons hiding in their souls? Give people the right circumstances, give their demons the right opportunities, and all sorts of mean... atavisms will come out... Scary.

"I mean, I dunno if it's true what they say, but they say that she once run a circus, of all places, and... Well, they say that she got fired because she was cruel to the animals. Cruel, yes. You know, *sadistic*. Real mean. Evil. Malicious. Like she had fun burning cigarettes on the zebras and cutting the elephants with a knife... At any rate, I don't know... I just don't know! Like, I've ever seen any bloody zebras! ... Zebras, ah! That'd be fun! Hamsters, maybe... No elephants or kangaroos, though ... Yes, I *had* a hamster—Plato, it was called—, I was seven, just a boy... I taught him a few tricks... He *was* clever, for a hamster. He's dead, now... Sad.

"You see, I've known her *here*. That's all. *Here*. Only *here*. All these years... Never been at the bloody circus in all my life! ... Never seen a zoo: Expensive. So, you can't trust the stuff people say, most of the time: You can't. It's bad... Bad! Like people who can't laugh anything off, let go of something, and nail themselves to some cross for ever and ever. Or people who think that they're always right. Or know no way to be tolerant. It's real bad... Well, better *not* do that. Keep your mouth shut, if you don't know what you're talking about. That's what I think. That's what I was taught in my family: If you don't know shit, just shut your mouth and don't make up shit, talk shit, be a shit, and be... Well, you get my point, I think... Shitty.

"You must understand... Gossip's a nasty thing. Real nasty. Gossip's bad. Bad. *So* bad! Gossip's... *cruel*, real cruel. My mum always said *that* about gossips and chatterboxes: That they're the *cruellest* people... And I listened to my mum, 'cos she had been around the block, seen the world, got to know people, their motives, the ways they act and feel... She was damn clever, good, and wise, my dear old mum! Always willing to forgive and help, she was. 'Like our dear Lord on the Cross,' my mum would say... And never a bad word about anyone, even if she saw and knew their faults, 'cos 'to know people you must look at sin in the face.' Gossips, instead... Other people don't realise how cruel gossips and chatterboxes are because it's not like you're going around with a big pickaxe murdering children, you see?

"But they *are* so! My dear old mum knew all that... Gossip's *worse* than a' that! Much worse. Worse than a bloody pickaxe! Even if you can't scream or jump when you see it. Even if it makes nobody bleed. It's... *crueller*. 'Cos, you see... It's subtler, it's hidden... It can hide behind a smile, a joke, or a bunch of people laughing. But it's actually like venom, or some horrible disease... Doesn't go away, you know, not even after you're dead. And *she*'s dead now. Dead! My old boss can't defend herself, if you say something nasty about her. That's *mean*. There's no compassion. It's low. It's really low. I don't think it's right. She's dead: She deserves some respect. Even if she was a hard woman, and a cruel boss. She was all that, for sure... But she was also a real *person*, wasn't she? She had a spark of God's love inside her, didn't she?

"And well, as far as her heart is concerned... Her heart... Good question, that one is...! Who knows? Do you? Does anyone? I mean... I'm no heart doctor... and I'm no bloody priest either. Even my mum wouldn't be able to tell you. Still... You know... I think she must have had one. *One. A* heart. A human heart. One that pumps blood, of course, but also one that feels, gets excited, loves, fears, and suffers. One that makes you feel you're tiny and insignificant, but also tells you you're like... the son of God Almighty, or something like that... Infinite. Capable of grasping all of our giant cosmos in just one idea or one emotion. Even if you're tiny-small. A speck of dust, but... *thinking*. A feeling, sensing speck of dust... Know what I mean?

"Maybe her heart *was* made out of stone. Like the fucking Nazis. Maybe wood. Like the Romans who hanged Our Lord on the cross. Maybe iron. Like good old Maggie. Maybe money. Like all those fuckers in the City or Wall Street: Bloody vultures who come to a war-torn country and strip it of all they've got left... You know, greedy scavengers like Michael Douglas or Leo DiCaprio! Or maybe her heart was made out of smelly stuff. Like Imelda Marcos, Priti Patel, or the circus' animals crapping all over the place... I don't know! But she must have had *a* heart, *one*, like everybody else, even if miniscule and hard as diamonds. What was inside it... Well, only God can see inside a person's heart... Do you even know what's inside *yours*?"

❦[294]

LVI – Dynamo[295]

One Act:
- *Alice C. Ponyrev (carrying a water bottle and ad-hoc tools)*
- *Hella B. Lutwidge (carrying transparent plastic bags and ad-hoc tools)*
- *A third person (chiefly in the backstage)*
- *A goat (other domestic or farm animals can do as well)*

Officers Ponyrev and Lutwidge are hard at work on the verge of a road, close to More Square.

Alice: (*friendly and fairly matter-of-fact all the time*) Would you believe it?

Hella: (*idem*) I know!

A: A kangaroo!

H: Yep. And it's not like we're in Australia!

A: Of all beasts…

H: … Poor beast.

A: Yeah. Poor animal! All the way up here from down under and…

H: Yep. Driven over by a yellow bus! Just like that.

---

[294] This fleuron is dedicated to the cruel boss' memory. For all her faults, she was still a human being.

[295] Down under's down under's down… There's brightness at the bottom.

A: And scattered all over the place! (*she sips water from her water bottle*)

H: That's the concertina effect... (*ironic*) More fun for us two!

A: Yeah! Think of going home and say: "Darling, I've had a grand old day! I've been scraping and scrubbing teaspoonfuls of expired kangaroo all over the road. How've you been? Any fun?"

H: (*smiling*) Well, you could use that one in one of your stories.

A: Aye, right. Because people care about real stories. Come on!

H: I know, I know... But there's something... you know, *moving*, about a splattered kangaroo. It makes you all soppy inside. Makes you think about the meaning of life.

A: (*serious*) ... Jumping from one tragedy to another, till you reach the final one...

H: Yeah. That's right. It's like a metaphor, an aaaa... (*trying to recall the word*) ...allegory of life!

A: (*ironic*) As long as it's not another aaaa...utobiography!

H: (*pause, very slightly irritated*) Why? Don't you like them?

A: No, I don't. There's no... *imagination*... They're like... the bare minimum.

H: What d'you mean, "*the bare minimum?*"

A: It's just... Writing only about the stuff *you think you know*. Never stretching *beyond*, never trying to *imagine* other lives, other paths, or playing with imagery and paths that you've fabricated, thrown together, and tinkered with... Or having fun with prototypes, symbols, personifications... You know, irony, *ideas*. That too is great, and fun. Fiction that's not 'reality.'

H: I see... You like imagination... Ideas... So you write about *fiction*, not *reality*...

A: That's what all decent novelists and dramatists have been doing since Homer's day. Why wasting time on... autobiographies, just 'cos that's the neighbourhood *you think you know*!

H: ... Interesting ... Not enough imagination, you say...

Shouts from backstage: "La duchesse de Pompierdur, la Marquise de la Pipe! Allons-y!"

H: (*surprised*) What was that?

A: (*calm*) A different play, (*reassuringly*) don't worry... Imagination... Really, don't worry.

H: (*a bit lost*) ... Ok, ok... if you say so... So, well... So, imagination, autobiographies...

A: Right! ... Also, in a sense, *all* works are autobiographic anyhow, including technical manuals.

H: (*puzzled*) What?

A: It's bloody old Kant, or Gestalt psychology...

H: In what sense?

A: In the sense that the universe orbits around the mind that studies it and looks at it!

Act Three

H: (*even more puzzled*) ... Explain, please. 'Cos you're making *no* sense at all now!

A: You see... (*stops suddenly*) Here's the other half! YES!

H: ... Half of what?

A: The library card! The one we found in the kangaroo's pouch! (*pause*) ... He's called *Socrates*.

H: (*glad*) Socrates? ...Ok. That's good... Now, see if you can find the rest of that income tax return form that... *Socrates* was carrying around as well! I've been looking for it everywhere...

A: Right... Well, as I was saying. *All* works, *all* books, are autobiographic, in a sense. Because any author, and every author, can *only*, and I repeat, *only* create what she creates by using *only* her own ideas, images... figments. Everything that an author can write about, whatever it is that she's writing about, is stuff that she's processed inside *her own* brain. Mental stuff...

H: ... Like what?

A: Gosh! What's *not* in there? *Everything*: Anticipations, beliefs, curiosities, desires, experiences, gut feelings, intimations, half-remembered jokes, memories, precise observations, questions, vestiges of very old studies, unforgotten umbrages, wild wonkeries... *Et cetera*!

H: That's quite a list!

A: As I said, *everything*'s in there. In the head. In the spirit. And that's all you can write about.

H: So, you mean... writers are always writing about themselves?

A: Yes and no... Not just *that*... Writing is closer to confections than confessions.

A voice is heard from backstage shouting this line from Puccini's La Bohème: *"Ecco i giocattoli di Parpignol! / Ecco i giocattoli di Parpignol!." Hella looks at Alice with a perplexed face, but doesn't say anything, and doesn't stop the ongoing conversation between them.*

H: ... So... You said... "*Confections*," right? Not "confessions" ... What d'you mean?

A: Well, what an author does is like... I mean... You throw all the ingredients into a shaker and mix them, and try and produce a cocktail. If the cocktail is any good, that's a different issue.

H: (*sarcastic*) Then all books should state, in the introduction: "Welcome to my little bar. I hope you'll enjoy the evening!," the way there are warnings about cancer on cigarette packs!

A: (*smiling*) Yes, I think they should! And they should add a warning about multiple authorship...

H: Ah? "*multiple authorship*"? I don't understand... (*ironic*) What have *you* been smoking?

A: (*serious*) Each and every author is a *plurality* of authors. Not only because, in their depths, all souls are... multiple, which is why one can laugh *at* as well as *with* some cruel comedian. But also and above all because nearly all authors come up with different narrators, characters, storylines, perspectives, colours. All based on stuff the authors have seen. That's actually the *fun* of writing: Imagining, seeing, feeling the world from different *angles*. Especially odd ones. Even cruel ones, at times.

Act Three

H: ...Sorry, but, you keep saying "seeing"... Then... What about science fiction, or fantasy. You know, funky stuff that nobody can have seen in reality? Like green monsters, you know?

A: It's *all* been *seen*! All of it! Under the author's silly pate! Inside the mind or soul... *Imagination,* you know? Then you blend all the bits and pieces, and try to do something with them. That's how it works, basically. I know it sounds strange, but it's like architects putting together mathematical abstractions and real stones to make a building out of them. Or tailors...

H: (*quietly*) ...Stitching together...

A: Yes! *Stitching*! And using the imagination... I mean... There's no worst form of poverty than having no imagination. Think of that: Being completely and utterly devoid of imagination!

H: (*ponders briefly*) Well, having no sense of humour is pretty tragic too. Or no self-irony... I recall an aunt who couldn't stand jokes about menstruations, especially if a man made them!

A: Fair point, no self-irony... (*pause, serious*) Still, having *no* imagination... It *scares* me!

H: ... It can't be good, I guess...

A: No, never! That's what makes people petty, narrow-minded, intolerant, cruel, nasty. It can be worse than ignorance. Much worse! It's why people start throwing around words like "truism," "bromide," "inappropriate," "inauthentic," or "this-ism" and "that-ism," making all sorts of illogical generalisations—which just mean that *those* people don't like what *they* have read or seen.

H: But why do they do that? I mean, they ruin their own game, don't they? ... Why doing it?

A: Mainly it's because they can't even begin to imagine what the world could look like from other perspectives, including yours. They have only one pair of shoes that fits them. Some people can't fathom how it is even possible to *imagine imagining* what the world could look like from other perspectives. You see... HEY! (*lifts a blob of something and inspects*) What's this?

H: (*intrigued*) ... I think it's a pancreas... No, wait. It's a kidney!

A: (*smiling*) Socrates' kidney! (*pause*) Left or right?

H: (*shrugs*) No clue! (*fetches the blob and stores it in a transparent plastic bag*) But, please, let's go back to your explanation. It's really interesting. You think that these negative people want you to just, like, *see* things from inside one tradition, one perspective, and only one, right?

A: Basically. Or the few perspectives that they're familiar with. It's probably the main reason why some people can't really *engage* with your material, and dismiss it as being "just like" someone else or something else that they've read a long time before and they vaguely recall...

H: Are these people... dumb? You know, just plain dumb?

A: Well, some of them are. What is it that they say in Italy? ... "The mother of idiots is always pregnant;" and that's a good one... But there are clever people who would simply and always want you to just preach and preach, like an apostle or a broken record. And repeat, you know, the party line—*their* party line! Squashing books and art into *one* person, *one* view. Squashing symbols into signs, polysemy into univocity... *1984*'s Newspeak, that's what they want!

H: Critics, you mean, right? ... These people?

Act Three

A: Yes, those for sure, but readers too… (*she sips water from her water bottle*)

H: Readers… Why? … I mean, how can readers be a problem?

A: Readers can be a real pain! Especially those who think that what *they*'ve understood—the few *bits* that *they*'ve been able to make some sense of—is both *right* and *all* that there is to it.

H: Like it's *tiny bits of tiny bits* that they're stitching, combining, and think it's *all* your work, eh?

A: Pretty much. Few, tiniest-tiny fragments, and they think they've got it all. Ah! The irony! Like when they obsess about one word out of 100,000!

H: (*reflecting*) I guess… Still, *you*, the author, have to stitch *all* the… *bits* together, right?

A: (*enthusiastic*) Yes, and you can use *a lot* of imagination doing that! *Play* with those… *bits*!

H: Totally unreal, then?

A: A good part of it. Most, actually. Nearly everything. Reality is just a minor part, a starting point.

H: So, there's *some* reality in it, right?

A: Much less than most people think. You know, *they* think that *they*'ve guessed this or that, but don't realise that *they*'re off track, or that *they*'re missing 99.9% of what the author meant…

The same voice from backstage shouts: "La duchesse de Pompierdur, la Marquise de la Pipe!"

H: (*less surprised*) … The other play?

A: Yes, precisely… *Imagination*: Hence yet another possible facet of the world… Don't worry!

H: Yeah, yes… I get it now. So, no reality, fantasy, imagination… "fiction," as you said…

A: Yep. Pretty much… And that's the fun: *Fiction*! Besides, realism's overrated! Screw that!

H: (*curious*) What d'you mean, "realism is overrated?"

A: (*serious*) Come on! Reality is… dull! Who would care reading about two police officers like us, for instance, scraping the remains of a dead kangaroo!? Cleaning up after the late jumper!?

H: (*serious, puzzling things together*) You've got a point there…

A: Or ordinary gangsters, nuns, talking bats, ex-cons, and run-of-the-mill porno stars!?

H: (*positive*) Yeah, yeah… I see what you mean.

A: Exactly, when you can have stories about, say, plumbers, bookkeepers, or periodontists!?

H: Right. Right… You're right… (*smiling*) Yeah. No doubt about that!

A: What would *you* rather read about: Plumbers, or one of the many superheroes we've got in our town, and currently looking for a job? Some silly-named porno star, or pa and ma having lazy sex in the morning? Or the two octogenarians who live upstairs a' your place 'n wake up frisky?

Act Three

H: (*declamatory*) Plumbers, lazy sex, and octogenarians, (*normal*) naturally! Something exotic, exciting! Obvious, no? I'm no different than other people, who fantasise about how it would be like to live and... die in all kinds of ways... Not those they're living, and will probably die.

A: Precisely my point... Not to mention the real distorters and effective co-authors...

H: (*puzzled*) What? "Co-authors"? ... Who are they?

A: Those who distort the story, fill the gaps, read between and behind the lines, coming up with all kinds of interpretations... All kinds of crazy shit *you* hadn't even thought about. That's fun too!

H: Oh? ... Ok, but... who are those?

A: The readers, my dear, the readers! (*she sips water from her water bottle*)

H: Ah? Again?

A: Think about it. It's like putting a mirror in front of them. You, the author, make the mirror... You take the sand and all the reagents you need... You also make a nice frame... There you have it. The mirror's ready. That's your story, novel, poem, film... Whatever!

H: Right...

A: ... And then you stick it front of the readers, the audience, the viewers, and so on.

H: Uh ... So what?

A: The readers will see *themselves*. Not *you*. Even if they are going to think that it's all about you, the world that you share with them, or both things. What they're seeing, though, is *themselves*.

A naked man with a fez on his head and a goat on the leash appear on stage, walking slowly from the right to the left, and only briefly interrupting the two main characters' conversation, which will then continue as though the man and the goat weren't there.

H: So... Readers read your stuff and... (*ah-ah Erlebnis*) see their own reflection and think it's yours?

A: Yes! *They* see *their* frustrations, hopes, dreams, memories, inhibited desires, old readings, raw nerves, the few things *they* recall from school, *their* dogmas, fears, the films *they*'ve watched...

H: (*more positive*) I see...

A: ...Reflected *in* yours and projected *as* yours...

H: Hm...

A: ... The readers may even get offended and mad at you for things you didn't say or didn't mean. And that's both funny and scary: They're seeing *themselves* and they think it's *you*!

H: (*a little more puzzled*) ... But, why's that? Why?

A: Because, like it happens with the author, everything that *they* are and have, exists in *their* souls, *their* minds, and *they*'re going to see it in the mirror, in one way or another, and think...

H: (*excitedly, with conviction*) ... That it's either you or the shared world that you're describing, right?

Act Three

A: Right! And the more fantastic is the story...

H: ...The more gaps they have to fill... And the more crazy interpretations they come up with?

A: (*satisfied*) Yes! Of course! That's it. And that's the trick, you know? Though some people never get past sheer knee-jerk reactions...

H: Clever... (*pause, cheeky*) And what's the trick to finish scraping the kangaroo off the road?

A: Hard work, my dear. Hard work! Elbow grease. Nothing else.

H: (*ironic*) There's nothing like an honest job well done...

A: (*playfully*) You've got it, sis!

H: ... Hey! ... (*glad*) The income tax form!

A: Wow! ... Great! That's very good... Let's...

H: (*interrupts, sombre*) Oh! ... Wait a minute... (*even more disappointed*) Would you believe it?

A: What's wrong?

H: This one belongs to a zebra. It's not the kangaroo's! ... (*upset, softly*) Bloody Socrates!

A: (*upset, loud*) Damnit! ... Bloody Socrates!

H: (*upset, softly*) Damn... Bloody Socrates!

Curtain.

LVII – In the Gage[296]

Dear Aristotle,

I received your letter from Lesbos. I am sorry for you and, to be frank with you, a little worried. I know far too well how life has been unkind to you, but I implore you not to despair, not to give up. Do not do anything foolish or unwarranted. Be patient and resilient. The best persons are always those who have suffered the most—the sage's heart is covered in scars! And keep studying: The sciences to change the world; the humanities to change your own self.[297]

As your former mentor, I feel compelled to share with you the following pearls of wisdom, which have taken me many decades to fully grasp and recognise *qua* primary truths about the world which we inhabit. Find them below as concise aphorisms, store them in a safe place inside your good soul, recover them whenever you need to reflect on the harshness and uncertainty of human existence, and let their profundity grow within you as time goes by.

One day, when you are about my age now, you will candidly and forcefully acknowledge to yourself their fundamental importance, probably after resisting it for many years. That too is part of the process. We are what we become; hence we mature by fighting with ourselves, more often than not. It is a hard fight. It is a long fight. But it is also a fight that can and will be won. Trust instinct, insight, intellect, and irony. Drink tea. Swim. Above all, have faith in yourself.

- *Pain saves, for it tells you where it hurts.*
- *What can't be cured can be excised.*

---

[296] Also known as "Life's a Challenge." And we are facing it.

[297] Change once stated: "My own ways aren't always the same."

Act Three

- *What kills you brings you before the gods. Be worthy of their respect.*
- *Should there be no gods, then there will be perpetual rest.*
- *Whatever good you do, somebody will always find you at fault for something.*
- *Don't mind other people's judgment, unless they are wise.*
- *No truly intelligent person will ever fail to appreciate your true intelligence.*
- *Illness can be cured, at times. Idiocy can never be reverted.*
- *Don't write books. There are already more than enough out there.*
- *If your teeth hurt, go and see a dentist.*

Yours truly, P.

⚓

LVIII – Back in N.B.C.[298]

§1 It is the year 2085. In New Baghdad City, two friends are running a shelter where they receive European refugees, who are fleeing a devastated continent where war, atomic radiation, barbarism, Covid-39, cavities, and poor hygienic standards have been causing countless tragic deaths for decades. Both friends have ancestors who, long before the catastrophic war with Russia erupted, had left their developing-yet-never-developed nations and sought fortune in the then-wealthy West. It seems almost ironic, but history's good and bad fortunes can sometimes swap places: *Sic transit gloria mundi.* The Popes of old had got that one right, at a minimum.

§ 2 "What did your great-grandfather do in Europe, do you know that?," asked Merab.

---

[298] There will be a place. (**Judy**: Why are we still searching? **Punch**: It shows gratitude.)

"No idea!," replied Mehmet, "yours?"

"… Neither," lamented Merab, "Eh!"

"It's a pity. But time…," hinted Mehmet.

"Yes, time erodes everything, and erases all memory!," stated Merab, poetically.

"Sand, grains of sand," added Mehmet, implicitly competing for lyrical acumen.

"And yet human wisdom is acquired by preserving memory, not damning it," Merab considered, with a tinge of melancholy colouring his gentle, manly, baritone voice.

"True," commented Mehmet, "but grains of sand *are* we nonetheless!"

"You are right, my friend… Still, *we* are here…," suggested Merab, enigmatically.

"And so?," queried Mehmet.

"So, that means that our ancestors *survived* in those remote lands. And they probably found *more* than just mere shelter and material aid, insofar as their line continued and reached all the way… down to the two of us," reasoned Merab.

"That's probably true," noted Mehmet, "and very plausible."

"Man, woman, foreign, national, black, white, young, old, believer, unbeliever… It never truly matters, for all we are is but humankind, and *all* we all are is human beings—all of us, all the time, all times!," commented Merab, who was prone to bouts of rhetorical grandeur.

"Common humanity, equality, our shared condition!," synthesised Mehmet.

"Photophobia isn't blindness," said Merab, "one home, not hundreds of pigeonholes!"

"Ah!," smiled favourably Mehmet, unsure about the exact meaning of that remark.

"Each one of us," insisted Merab, "a person: First of all, and above all!"

"… Persons," understood and underlined Mehmet, "to be respected, no matter what."

Act Three

"If those people, in those savage lands of the West, showed compassion to our ancestors, and in those very primitive times mind you, then how could *we* be any less generous..." uttered Merab, "... here, today, now, of all times and places?"

"You are right, my friend," nodded approvingly Mehmet, "goodness must endure."

"Yes," emphasised Merab, "goodness must endure."

LIX – The Bat Flies Down on Broadcasts[299]

One Act:
* *Prof. F.F.B. Benedict, wearing a tuxedo and a technicolour dreamcoat.*
* *A giant bat, wearing a duly-modified pseudo-silk kimono and a fez.*

A famous academic, and giant bat, is being interviewed by Prof. Benedict at the local theatre.

Professor F.F.B. Benedict: Dear Dr Bat, we are all very excited and most grateful. Thank you for being here with us tonight!

Bat: - (*opens the mouth, emits an inaudible sound for 5 seconds, and bows to the audience*)

PFFB: Thank you, thank you! ... (*smiling*) I can't imagine what it must be like for you...

B: - (*opens the mouth, emits an inaudible sound for 6 seconds*)

---

[299] Do not be afraid, please. (**Judy**: Why are we still conversing? **Punch**: It shows intelligence.)

PFFB: Yes, indeed! (*chuckles*) But you seem to be neither choleric nor phlegmatic! (*brief pause, serious*) As you know, the interview is going to be broadcast by the city's main radio services.

B: - (*opens the mouth, emits an inaudible sound for 7 seconds*)

PFFB: (*chuckling*) No, no! I wouldn't worry. Your accent will *not* be a problem!

B: - (*opens the mouth, emits an inaudible sound for 8 seconds*)

PFFB: I see. You're very kind. (*short pause*) Now, let's cut to the chase. You've been working primarily on 20th-century French existentialism, isn't it correct?

B: - (*opens the mouth, emits an inaudible sound for 9 seconds*)

PFFB: Interesting… Yes, there's always a received x and a different, real x… And so you have…

B: - (*opens the mouth, emits an inaudible sound for 10 seconds*)

PFFB: What about Sartre's take on the same subject: Are scientific minds in a state of denial, then?

B: - (*opens the mouth, emits an inaudible sound for 11 seconds*)

PFFB: But are educated people really capable of pondering issues long and hard, before passing any kind of judgment? Doesn't culture make us even cockier and more arrogant, in a way?

B: - (*opens the mouth, emits an inaudible sound for 12 seconds*)

PFFB: …"Positive nihilism is closet dogmatism,"… Would that apply also to Marcel's *homo viator*?

Act Three

B: - (*opens the mouth, emits an inaudible sound for 13 seconds*)

PFFB: Indeed... I see your point... Well, then, it wouldn't be inappropriate for me to ask you the crucial question... May I? I'm sure our audience is looking forward to hearing your answer...

B: - (*opens the mouth, emits an inaudible sound for 5 seconds*)

PFFB: Of course! (*chuckles*) Only open minds can entertain new ideas... (*serious*) Ok, here it comes: (*asks the question in a slow, serious, and declamatory tone*) What is the meaning of life?

B: - (*turns towards the audience, opens the mouth, emits an inaudible sound for 30 seconds*)

PFFB: (*ecstatic*) ... Oh my! ... I had never thought of that! ... YES! YOU'RE RIGHT!

B: - (*opens the mouth, emits an inaudible sound for 5 seconds*)

PFFB: Yes, yes, yes... It's true, TRUE! ... Thank you, thanks, thank you... THANK YOU, Dr Bat!

B: - (*opens the mouth, emits an inaudible sound for 2.5 seconds*)

PFFB: Please, ladies and gentlemen, a round of applause for our guest! Thank you, Dr Bat! Thank you!

B: - (*opens the mouth, emits an inaudible sound for 5 seconds, while bowing to the crowd*)

Curtain.

LX – For Dormant Friends[300]

§1 Despite being physically close to the ever-busy university campus, our town's cemetery is a dead place: Dead. I'm not trying to be funny. I wouldn't dare. Rather, I'm stating a fact: A sad fact. Apart from the beginning of November and a few Sundays, hardly anyone comes here to pay their respects to the people who lie buried in the ground. It's really sad. It's as if people have forgotten how to show any compassion, any love. Besides, propriety should always entail a touch of piety. Yet very few people seem to care about that today… Don't you think it's sad?

In any case, cemeteries should be… happy places. Yes, happy! Again, I am *not* joking. All those bodies, urns, coffins… All entombments are like… emergency capsules ejected into space from a flying spaceship—the cemetery, if you're following… Those capsules are destined to land into… onto… God, His embrace, His… *love*. Because God's love is *everywhere*. Space itself, vast and seemingly cold, is part of God's vast love, which created that space too—the universe, that is—and all of its rational, orderly, intelligible laws, as well as their occasional, miraculous loopholes and soul-saving clauses. Think of it: What a legislative marvel!

Should there be no God, as some educated but superficial people like to argue, then those capsules would still enjoy the peace of deep space, *forever*… Think of that too: Peace, rest, quiet… Isn't that… joyful, somehow? *Loving*? They call it "nirvana," in the East.

§2 Considerably less joyful, visibly unloving, and unceremoniously knee-deep in the dirt, Merab can be found digging in that same cemetery. Can you spot him? He's working. It's a filthy job alright. But it pays well, all things considered. He is actually

---

[300] Because we are all friends, when all sense is said and all good is done.
Punch: What's friendship? **Judy**: It's a sort of… life's vessel.

thinking of his old pal Abe. What an end! What a terrible end! Can't you recall what happened to Abraham Herrera?

Merab feels sorry for him. That man Abe may have been a very bad man, judging by the awful crimes that he had committed, but he was... a man, a person. And no man, no person, deserves to end up the way Abraham Herrera did. Who could be so heartless as to wish a man to be torched alive? A man who had already spent years in prison, mind you, going through God-knows-what, and expiating, atoning, while being punished for the terrible things that he had done. What a terrible way to end... Horrible. Inhumane. Cruel, actually. Even for a bad man.

In all probability, Merab is thinking of his old pal because, a few days before, two police officers had talked to Merab about some serious business of theirs. As they put it, there could be "some evidence that they might need," whatever that could be. Have you got any idea what that's about? I don't know any police officers in town and, even if I did, I can't really go around and ask them about their business, can I? Also, I don't entirely trust the force, to be honest.

Anyhow, the two police officers only told Merab that it was "evidence which might have been buried in one of the latest tombs" —hence his involvement. The two women didn't tell Merab what *exactly* they were looking for, nor where *exactly* he would have had to dig in that large, muddy cemetery. They just said that they would come back, "had *it* been necessary."

Probably, as Merab has by now concluded, *it* hadn't been necessary, whatever their serious business could be. And he is *happy* about it. Yes, happy. It doesn't take much, does it?

§3 A frequent visitor, Reverend Bowles, is preparing for a memorial, walking up and down the cemetery, while rehearsing a non-standard eulogy, apparently lost amidst some of the oldest tombstones. Many of them, regrettably, are in a very poor state: Abysmal, sometimes. What is worse, even some of the recent ones are already in a disheartening condition of pitiful disarray. I think it is deplorable. It's… cultural decline, chaos, dupery... Don't you find it deplorable?

The pious reverend thinks that the local nuns are actually right in arguing that the faithful ought to pray also and especially for *those* sorely-neglected brothers and sisters. He may be unconvinced by the theology behind the local nuns' argument, but he has found the practice that they promote to be truly respectful, loving, and deeply Christian. Such a practice, he believes, can make a person's heart develop the right feelings, foster the proper attitudes of the spirit, and stimulate the conscience in a constructive manner. "Prompting the soul," he calls it. Take death seriously, then, and your life will be less likely to be a farce, and end in tragedy.

Reverend Bowles and the nuns agree as well on the notion that children should be taught about Jesus and raised in the faith, whichever prayers, liturgy, and Christian tradition they may be exposed to. Without *any* of that, then the kids become adults who are quite simply incapable of making sense of, or even perceiving, their own spiritual feelings. Like kids who have never been taught any music or maths, who then try to fill those gaps in adulthood—it's cruelly impossible, most times. It's like having a cat that was never around people in the formative early years: She will always be scared and run away, or refuse to be picked up by a person.

Yet hardly anyone cares about what the reverend believes, or what the local nuns believe and practice. Clergymen and coenobites are seen as antiquated and creepy oddballs, these days; Muslim clerics as potential terrorists to boot. Don't *you* see them that way, for example? Ah, who is immune from prejudice?

As an involuntary confirmation of these people's suspected weirdness, the local nuns are the most assiduous visitors of our cemetery. They come every week, on routine Friday visits, plus a number of additional Sundays and other religious festivities, the precise calendar of which is probably known to them alone. And maybe some of you as well. I certainly don't know it. Naturally, they always come on the 2nd of November… Have you ever met them here?

Act Three

The nuns look like a platoon of hard-praying professionals, who conscientiously stop before the least well-tended and, let's be honest, most desolate tombs. Two Carmelite sisters, however, do regularly depart from the platoon, and go to pray on—and sometimes bring flowers to—two recent, better-kept graves. They can spend a long time there, meditating and praying. It is a still yet moving picture to contemplate, if you know what I mean: Still, but moving.

Those are the graves of the late F.A.C. MacRunt, a minor filmmaker that the world of cinema has already forgotten, and a very old general, who enjoyed a curious final spell in his life as the most devout and most passionate church-going parishioner of the local Catholic community. Some of you might have heard or known of him, or even know well who he was. He was reasonably famous around town. Ironically, he was a war hero, back in his day.

§4 Frequent are also the visits to the cemetery that are paid by the most illustrious member of our small city. I'm talking of none less than D.J. Trump, who some readers may remember as being the President of the United States. He comes to the churchyard every month and brings flowers to an empty grave. Yes, empty! ... That being the tomb in which, at some point in a hopefully distant future, he himself will have to be buried. By doing so, he is certainly showing a degree of foresight. He's being clever, in a way. Ah, how shrewd our politicians can be!

Right beside that empty grave, an old philosophy teacher has found his final resting place. Nobody comes to visit his tomb, except for a former student, a man called Aristotle, who shows up once or twice a year. Morose. Saturnine. Sullen. A miserable fellow, seen from afar. Long beard, long face... He isn't cheerier seen from close-up either, the poor bloke! Still, he shows up for his old teacher. *That* must count for something. Don't you agree?

Far more frequent are, instead, the total visits put together over the decades by a centenarian, one of the very few who live in our noteworthy little city, if not the only one. The centenarian brings the most beautiful flowers and the most burning tears to two old graves. Very old. Very, very, very old. Clean, well-kept, those two old tombs have been some of the nicest in our cemetery for very many years. Decades, in fact.[301] That is, as far as any tomb can be said to be "nice." But I confide in your charitable interpretation of my poorly-chosen words. Can you be charitable and forgive my errors?

The centenarian looks like a scrawny tortoise, if I can be candid about it, and walks in an almost ludicrous manner. Yet again, his wrinkled face expresses a sentiment of genuine grief that has hardly been seen before on our planet, or will ever be seen after he's gone. Perhaps some of you have witnessed it, and know what I mean. It can be like staring into the abyss. It's so dark, and bleak, in there. Like an empty blackness, but sad…. It's difficult to explain.

Every so often, a former student accompanies that sorry old man and stands nobly beside his venerable teacher, in respectful, mournful silence. They both look very sad. No happiness there, on those faces, in those eyes, in their aching hearts… An outright shame, right?

§5   An eccentric character, who is known in our town as a former clown as well as a retired logician, comes once or twice a year to the local cemetery in order to pay his respects to the grave of a late colleague, fellow logician, and very close friend of his. He brings no flowers for his old, deceased, unbreathing pal. Just some… *tobacco*. Think of that! He then smokes most of it himself in his long pipe, and scatters the rest on the burial mound… like dark confetti.

I don't know whether or not smoking is banned in other cemeteries around the world, but I wouldn't mind if such a regulation were introduced as a very strict bylaw applying to our local graveyard. Wouldn't you agree? The stench itself is already despicable. But the very act of smoking in a cemetery! There's something so… wrong about it. Disrespectful. Profoundly disrespectful. Would you stand and say your prayers at the grave of a friend or relative of yours, and smoke? Or have someone else

---

[301] This is a joke, not reality. No such letters were ever written nor sent in the reader's world: Only in this philosophical satire's one. Please read the opening disclaimer.

Act Three

smoking right beside you? Come on! What a reprehensible nonsense! Don't you find it reprehensible? I think it's a real disgrace... Isn't it? I know that without freedom of expression all other freedoms are moot, but there must be limits, or not?

§6 Three more persons can only be seen here two or three times a year. Not many times, I must admit, but at least they've been fairly consistent visitors over the years. They are Miss Monica Symonds, her devoted and distinguished partner, Mr Gavin S. Fonda, and a cheeky-wee-monkey of a wild, carefree teenager jumping about all over the place—as if the cemetery were his playground... Incredible! Leaping about like that! Well, anyhow... Where was I?

Ah! Yes, ... Miss Symonds is... was... a local celebrity, let's say... and, together with her partner, they perform an oddly analogous ceremony when visiting the tomb of a priest, who died *ages* ago. No, they don't smoke. They don't do that. Rather, twice or thrice a year, they come to pray and... well, pour a glug of whisky on the dead priest's grave... Yes, *whisky*! Not water, whether it's blessed or not, if you believe in that kind of... tradition. Why they do that, it's still a mystery. At least, it is a mystery to *me*. Whether or not that is acceptable... I have my doubts. What do *you* think? I find it quaint, to say the least. I mean, whisky on a tomb!

At the same time, it is not difficult to understand why the three of them visit another tomb, which is situated quite far to the west of to the long-dead clergyman's one in our cemetery's beautiful, geometrical layout. A really beautiful layout, I should say... That other one being the grave belonging to one of Miss Well... Symonds' sisters, Michelle, who died in her early 40s while giving birth to a boy, who has, luckily, survived unscathed the... tragic event. Thank God for that! ... But that poor mother... What a sad, cruel fate she had!

It's all so awful, at times, but birth itself can be a capital sentence... Even today, in spite of all the medical knowledge, hospitals, nurses, physicians... It's like you can't defeat death and suffering, no matter what humankind concocts and creates. In any case, it was a horrible tragedy, and all the people and newspapers in our town talked about it for months. Months! Until, that is, a fresher horrible tragedy occurred to someone else… But I'm quite sure that you are familiar with Michelle Symonds' heart-wrenching death, not to mention her earlier… tragedies. So, I don't have to belabour it here. Let me know if you want me to do it, ok?

§7 Seldom, very seldom, have other characters known to the reader ever showed up at the local cemetery. For instance, a grey-haired man called Mehmet, but known in town as 'Duck,' would occasionally bring some cheap flowers to his old friend 'Tinder.' Mehmet killed Tinder, unintentionally, while sparring on the canvas… Maybe two or three times over the past ten years…. Not much… And the flowers, well… But people can only do what they they can do. Can you be charitable and forgive their errors?

Oh? … The canvas? Yes, the canvas… Horrific! What a sporting accident! If you can call boxing a sport. Would you call it a sport? I'm not sure it qualifies. Boxing is notorious for being a dangerous form of entertainment and physical activity. Don't you think they should ban it? And rugby too. And American football. And wrestling… And all those collisions in football… You know, the brain injuries and the Alzheimer that results from them? Dreadful!

…And have you ever seen a ballerina's feet and ankles? Dreadful too. Really dreadful. The way they torture those poor little girls! Stretch that, twist that, jump here, hop there… Torture, I'm telling you! Someone should write a long exposé about such an unseen cruelty.

§8 Few more in total number have been the actual times when the most esteemed thespian of our community, Mr H.S. Racket, has come and visited his beloved wife's tomb, over which he has been witnessed spending up to two hours—yes, two hours—crying like a baby. Two hours! Two whole hours! It's almost like going to the movies… Can you believe it?

Some uncharitable fellow-citizens claim that his prolonged acts of grief are nothing but a shameful travesty, a pathetic theatrical performance. I have no reason to be so cynical and… cruel. And I

Act Three

am sure that you support me on this point. What you might ignore, though, is that Mrs Racket, Stella, lost her life in a domestic accident. Horribly, she died electrocuted while using a metal knife and trying to hook a slice of whole-grain bread out of a defective toaster.

Professor Emeritus F.F. Benedict has also been seen visiting Stella's grave, and he too has been observed crying—also like a baby—though for considerably shorter lengths of time than Mr Racket. Why such visits and acts of deep grief have been the case, nobody knows. Professors are peculiar people. So, maybe, that's all there is to it. However, if you do know anything else about this outré crying-like-a-baby professorial affair, please contact me. I've been interested in these matters since an old professor said to me, many years ago: "I was holding my newborn baby in my arms. There it was. It didn't have a name yet. We hadn't chosen one. 'Another person condemned to suffer and die,' I thought. At the same time, I knew that it was the right thing to do, especially as far as that tiny, defenceless person was concerned." Also, can you recall who said: "We are not shooting enough professors..."? I really can't, right now.

§9 Everybody knows very well Dora and Anita Symonds, who come to the cemetery only once a year, generally in November, and pray for their sister Michelle, as well as their deceased father and mother, who lie buried together, in the same tomb, after dying on the same day at St. Stephen's. It's a rare love story that was meant to continue in the afterlife. Romantic... Poetic.

Dora Symonds still lives in her parents' ancestral home, together with one quiet old cat and three noisy cockatoos. She is currently between jobs. Her brilliant career as the top manager of a fast-growing private-investment firm specialised in creating and supervising ethical funds for transitioning oil- and tobacco conglomerates was cut short by a rather shameful and bizarre incident. It was an unsettling incident, involving the police force and the local courts of justice. As the records show, Ms Symonds had been sending hundreds of anonymous death threats to Phyllis

Chesler and Camille Paglia, among others, for many years... decades, in fact. They even say that she had plans to kidnap some Finnish professor of media studies!

...But *Anita*, well, *she* is happily married! She's the proud mother of *four* healthy and beautiful daughters—you don't mind me mentioning the fact that they're beautiful, do you? I don't want to sound... superficial, or sexist, you know? Anyway, the daughters are called... the eldest is Susanna, just like Anita's mother; and then there are Nadine, Catharine and... what's that one? The youngest one... Ah! She's Corrinne, yes! That's the name! ... Anita works as an endodontist and is one of the wealthiest citizens in our pretty little city, as well as the entire surrounding region. Her husband, an exodontist of foreign origin, is her subordinate. The two of them, on weekends, organise well-attended séances in their cottage by the lake.

§10 Everybody in town can also easily recognise Iris Arctović, a dignified, stylish, radiant, and still-attractive old widow, who visits her... husband's burial place once a year. (You don't mind me mentioning the fact that she is still attractive at her age, do you? It's something about which people talk openly in our, I guess, provincial, but well-meaning and caring community. We notice and admire beauty, that's all!) She always brings a bunch of chrysanthemums to decorate the tomb, and spends many mournful minutes reflecting in respectful silence and, yes, praying... God alone knows for what or whom she's praying, that woman... Poor widow!

After her second husband's sudden death, news has spread around our pretty town concerning the despicable conduct of her... awful husband. That poor woman... Poor widow!

Professionally, it was discovered that her late husband stole ideas from dead theologians, philosophers, writers, and mystics, gave them technical-sounding fancy new names, polled a few powerless undergraduate students of his, and then published articles claiming that he had come up with a totally novel concept in experimental psychology. The sort of intellectual dishonesty displayed by Erving Goffman, who kept stealing aplenty from Kenneth Burke for many

Act Three

years, or Kuhn and Hayek, who were busy robbing their best ideas from Michael Polanyi and never acknowledged their debt... Privately, her second husband's conduct was even more... loathsome... But, well, I am sure that you have already heard of it. Poor widow!

Many right-thinking members of our community think that she should have *no* reason whatsoever to show up here. Would you ever pay your respects to a deceased, violent, cruel partner? Her behaviour is... inappropriate, in a way. Almost indecorous, if not indecent... They say that it's irresponsible, that it furthers violence, that it could damage other women, that it reinforces patriarchal oppression... They say that there can and should be no personal passion, religious clemency or fond early memory capable of justifying her... perplexing visits... These right-thinking members of our community repeat these comments again and again. I've even heard a retired bus driver doing just that this morning, at a bar of all places, while having her breakfast... Black coffee or black tea, and a sausage roll, I believe it was... Poor widow!

Then again, here she is, Mrs Arctović, in our cemetery. Perhaps, that too is love, which can be found in the least likely places, beyond all rational criteria, and in shapes and forms that defy all expectations, measures, principles, preferences, standards, conditions... Love is strong, love is powerful... Somehow, not even death can win over love, because love never dies... Didn't they write a song about that? Or is it a short story in some silly book that I've read?[302]

---

[302] Read books, please, read! Whatever they may be! Even old telephone directories!

Final Considerations[303] For Two Puppets[304]

Punch: Is this really… the end?
Judy: Yes, it is, dear.
Punch: Oh… What a pity!
Judy: Don't worry, love; I shall think of something else.
Punch: Is that why you've got some stuff sticking out of your nose?
Judy: Have I? Hm, that's strange... Let me check…°

° *Final considerations[305] for two nostrils:*

Left nostril: Is this really… the end?
Right nostril: Yes, it is, love.
Left nostril: Oh… What a pity!
Right nostril: Don't worry, dear; I shall think of something else.
Left nostril: Is that why you've got two hairs sticking out of you?
Right nostril: Have I? Hm, that's strange... Let me check…°°

---

[303] One consideration says to another: "Everything returns, yet it is never the same as before."

[304] Readers affected by pupaphobia or unnerved by puppets may wish to skip this chapter.

[305] Two considerations enter the present page: They are holding hands.

Act Three

°° *Final considerations*[306] *for two hairs:*

Hair #1: Is this really... the end?
Hair #2: Yes, it is, dear.
Hair #1: Oh... What a pity!
Hair #2: Don't worry, love; I shall think of something else.
Hair #1: Is that why you've got some follicle stuck on you?
Hair #2: Have I? Hm, that's strange... Let me check...°°°

°°° *Final considerations*[307] *for two follicles:*

Lymph node #1: Is this really... the end?
Lymph node #2: Yes, it is, love.
Lymph node #1: Oh... What a pity!
Lymph node #2: Don't worry, dear; I shall think of something else.
Lymph node #1: Is that why you've got vessels attached to you?
Lymph node #2: Have I? Hm, that's strange... Let me check...°°°°

°°°° *Ad libitum.*[308]

N.B.
A Joint Neutralization Team (JNT) was dispatched by the Bureau for Orderly Syntax & Semantics (BOSS) and the Western Institute for Moral & Political Sobriety (WIMPS), in order to assassinate the author of this book and its publishers. Travelling at night, the secret agents got distracted by the starry heavens above and fell into a well. Because of that, the brave agents were unable to carry out their duty.

---

[306] One consideration looks amiably at another, which smiles in return.

[307] One consideration asks another: "Can you hear the music?"
"Yes," the latter consideration replies.
"Listen well," the former insists.
"Why?" the latter queries.
"Because it's all there is," the former consideration explains, humming away.

[308] Couney's *Infantoriums* were a source of amusement, and much-needed survival.

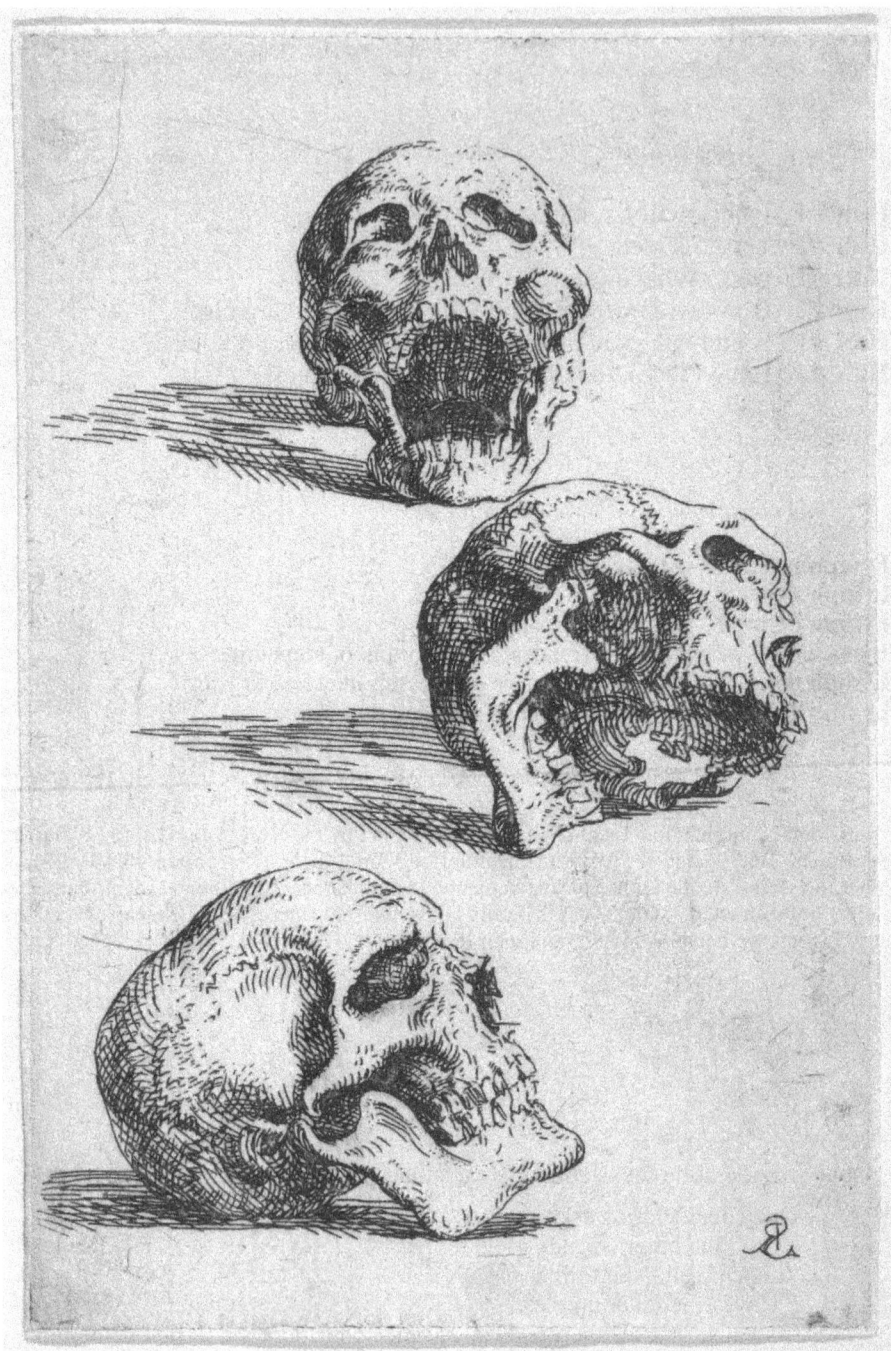

Salvator Rosa, *Three human skulls, study for "Democritus in Meditation"* (1662)
New York (United States), MET 53.509.5.
CC0 — Wikimedia Commons — Public Domain.